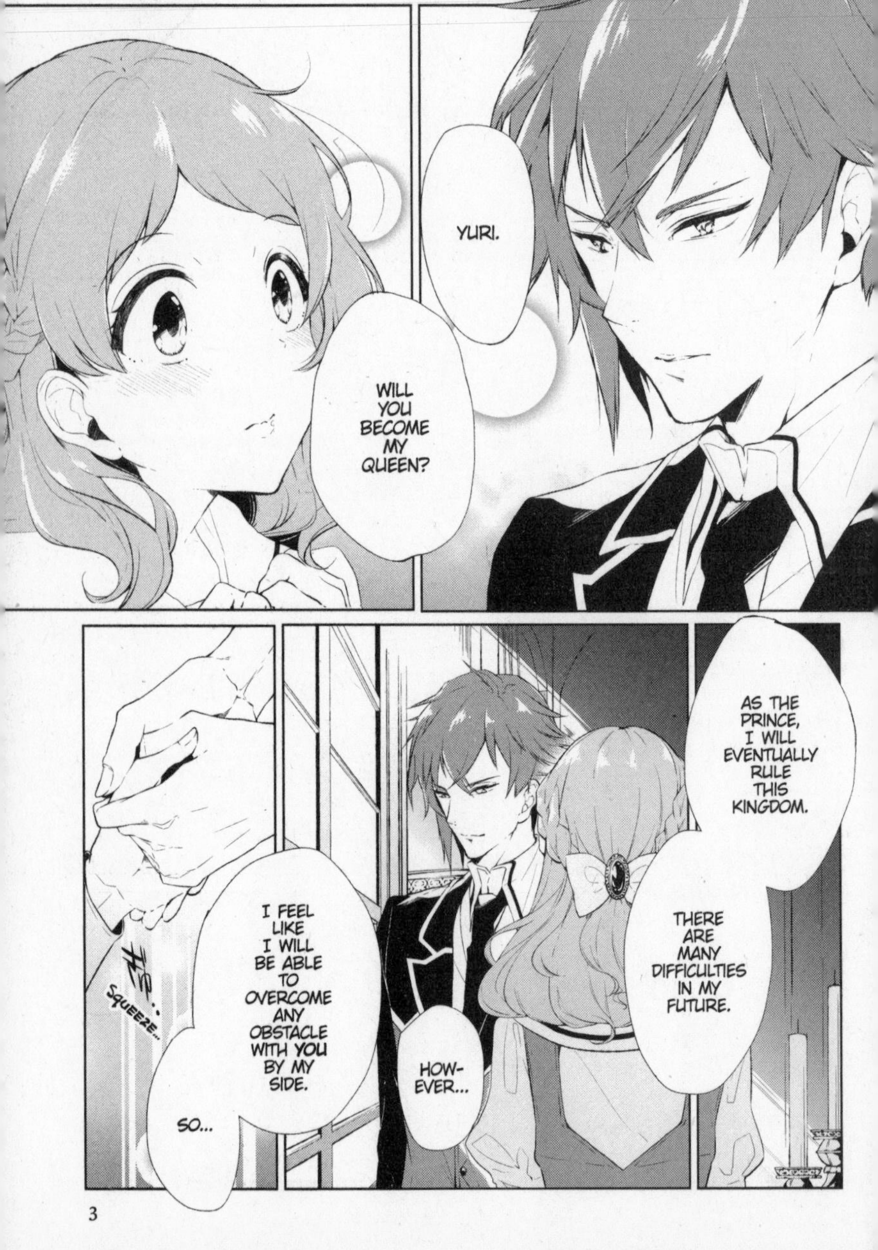
YURI.
WILL YOU BECOME MY QUEEN?
AS THE PRINCE, I WILL EVENTUALLY RULE THIS KINGDOM.
THERE ARE MANY DIFFICULTIES IN MY FUTURE.
HOW-EVER...
I FEEL LIKE I WILL BE ABLE TO OVERCOME ANY OBSTACLE WITH YOU BY MY SIDE.
SO...
Squeeze...

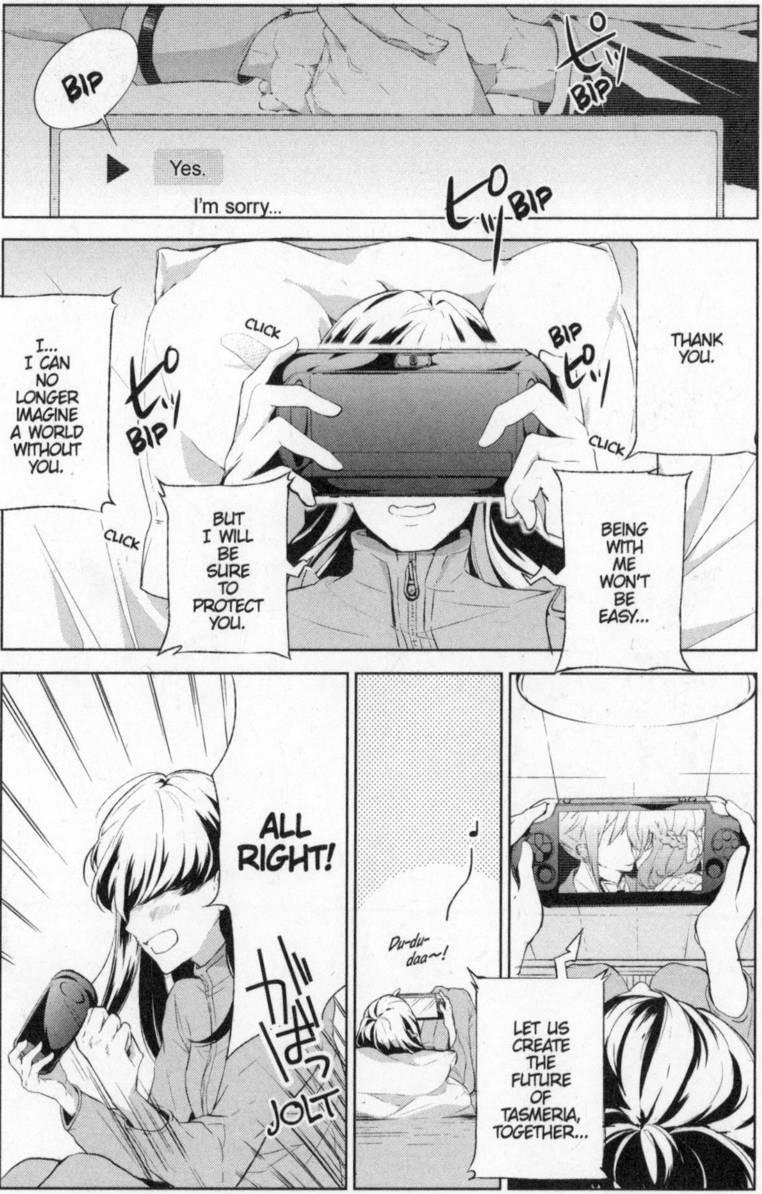
ピッ
BIP
BIP
Yes.
I'm sorry...
ピッ
BIP
THANK YOU.
BIP
ピッ
CLICK
CLICK
BEING WITH ME WON'T BE EASY...
BUT I WILL BE SURE TO PROTECT YOU.
I... I CAN NO LONGER IMAGINE A WORLD WITHOUT YOU.
ピッ
BIP
CLICK
LET US CREATE THE FUTURE OF TASMERIA, TOGETHER...
Du-du-daa~!
ALL RIGHT!
がばっ
JOLT

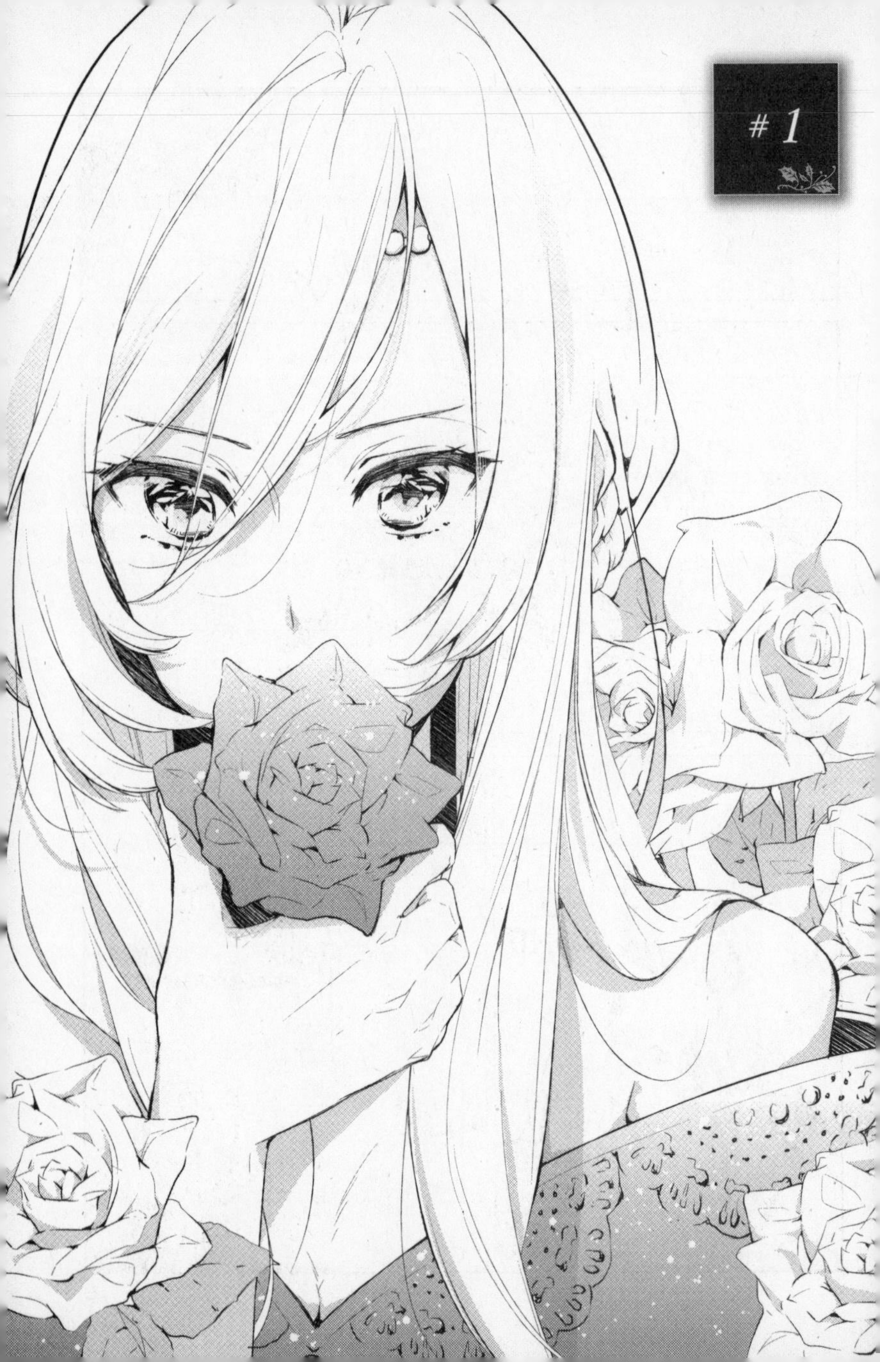

1

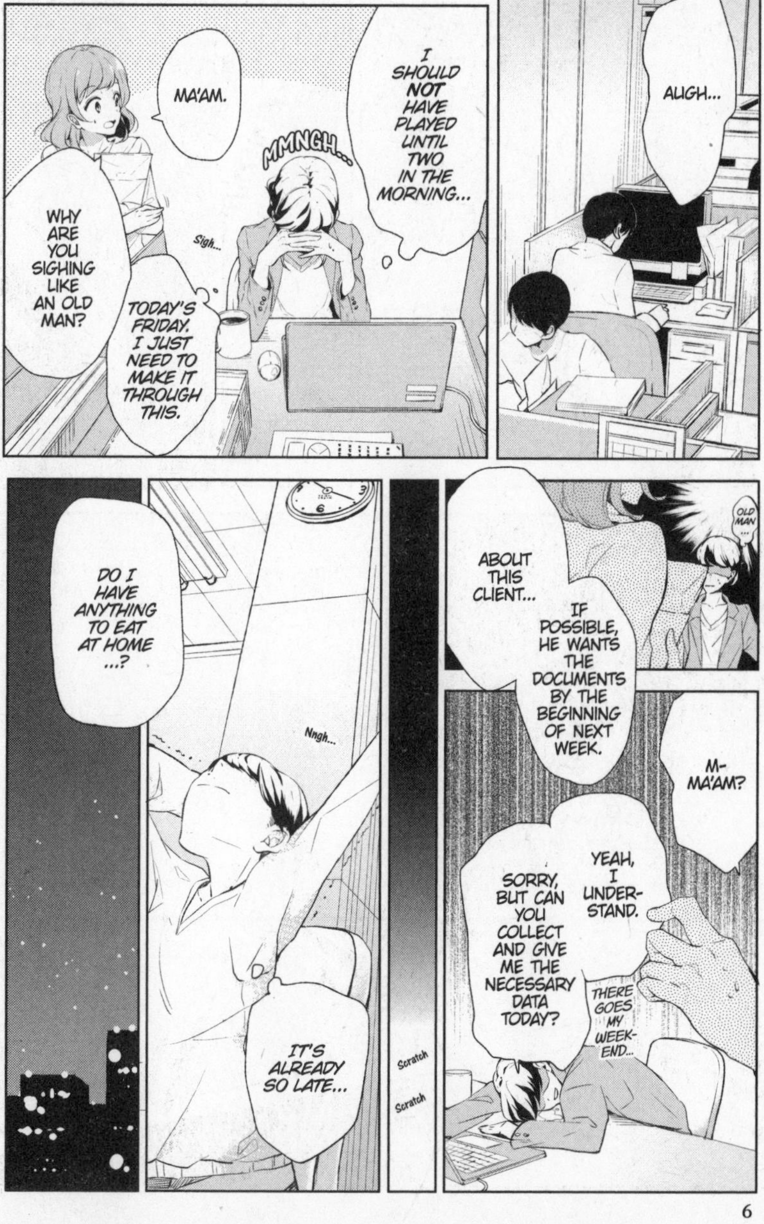
AUGH...
I SHOULD NOT HAVE PLAYED UNTIL TWO IN THE MORNING...
MMNGH...
Sigh...
TODAY'S FRIDAY. I JUST NEED TO MAKE IT THROUGH THIS.
MA'AM.
WHY ARE YOU SIGHING LIKE AN OLD MAN?
OLD MAN...
ABOUT THIS CLIENT...
IF POSSIBLE, HE WANTS THE DOCUMENTS BY THE BEGINNING OF NEXT WEEK.
M- MA'AM?
YEAH, I UNDER-STAND.
SORRY, BUT CAN YOU COLLECT AND GIVE ME THE NECESSARY DATA TODAY?
THERE GOES MY WEEK-END...
Scratch
Scratch
Nngh...
IT'S ALREADY SO LATE...
DO I HAVE ANYTHING TO EAT AT HOME ...?

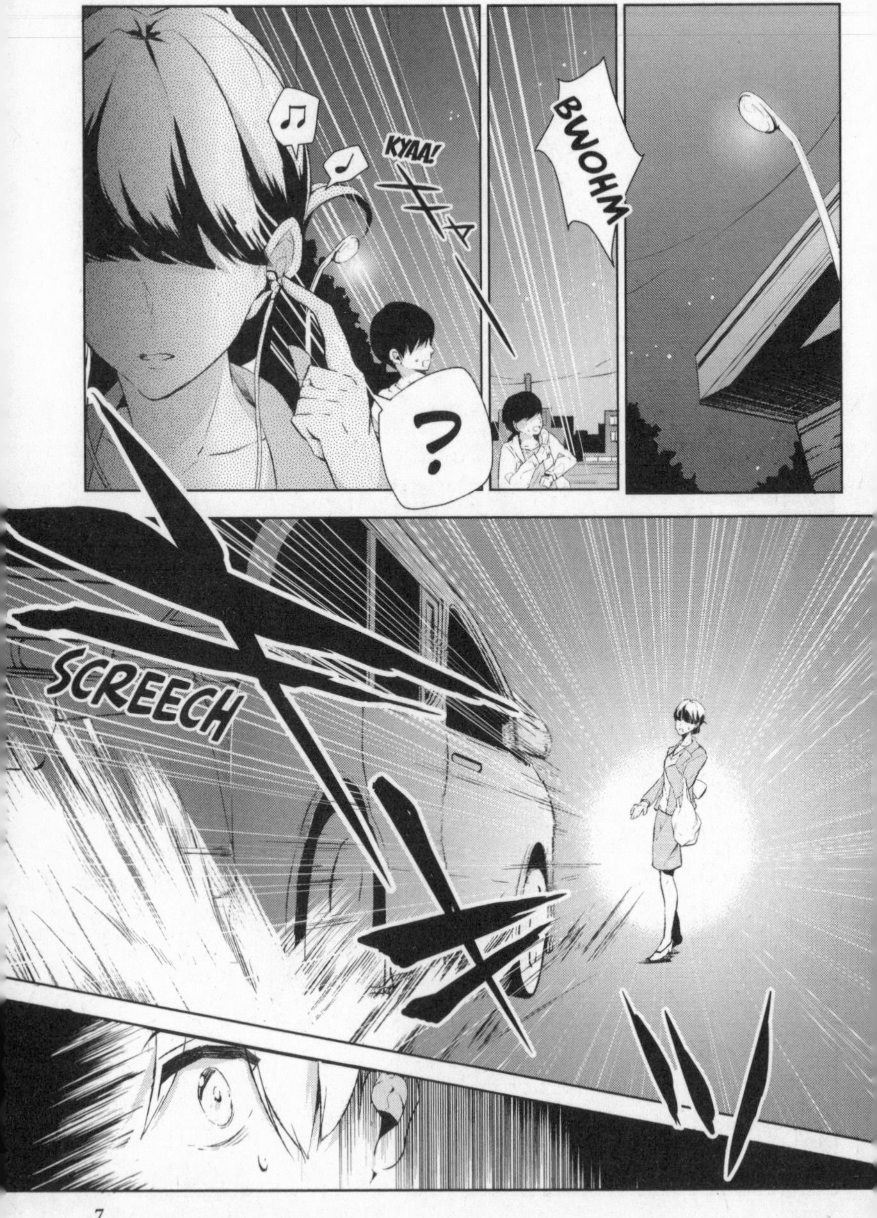
BWOHM
♫
♪
KYAA!
?
SCREECH

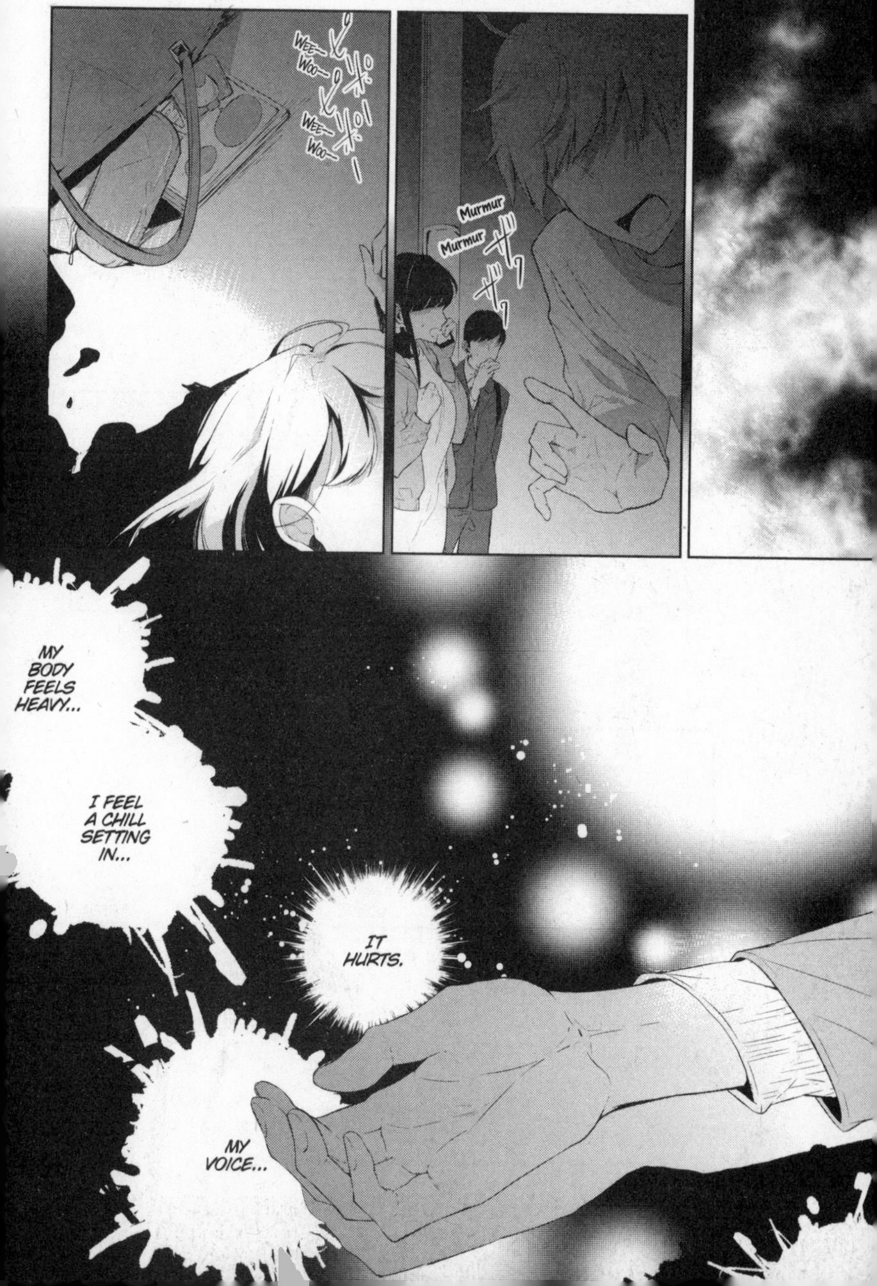
Murmur
Murmur
WEE-
WOO-
WEE-
WOO-
MY BODY FEELS HEAVY...
I FEEL A CHILL SETTING IN...
IT HURTS.
MY VOICE...

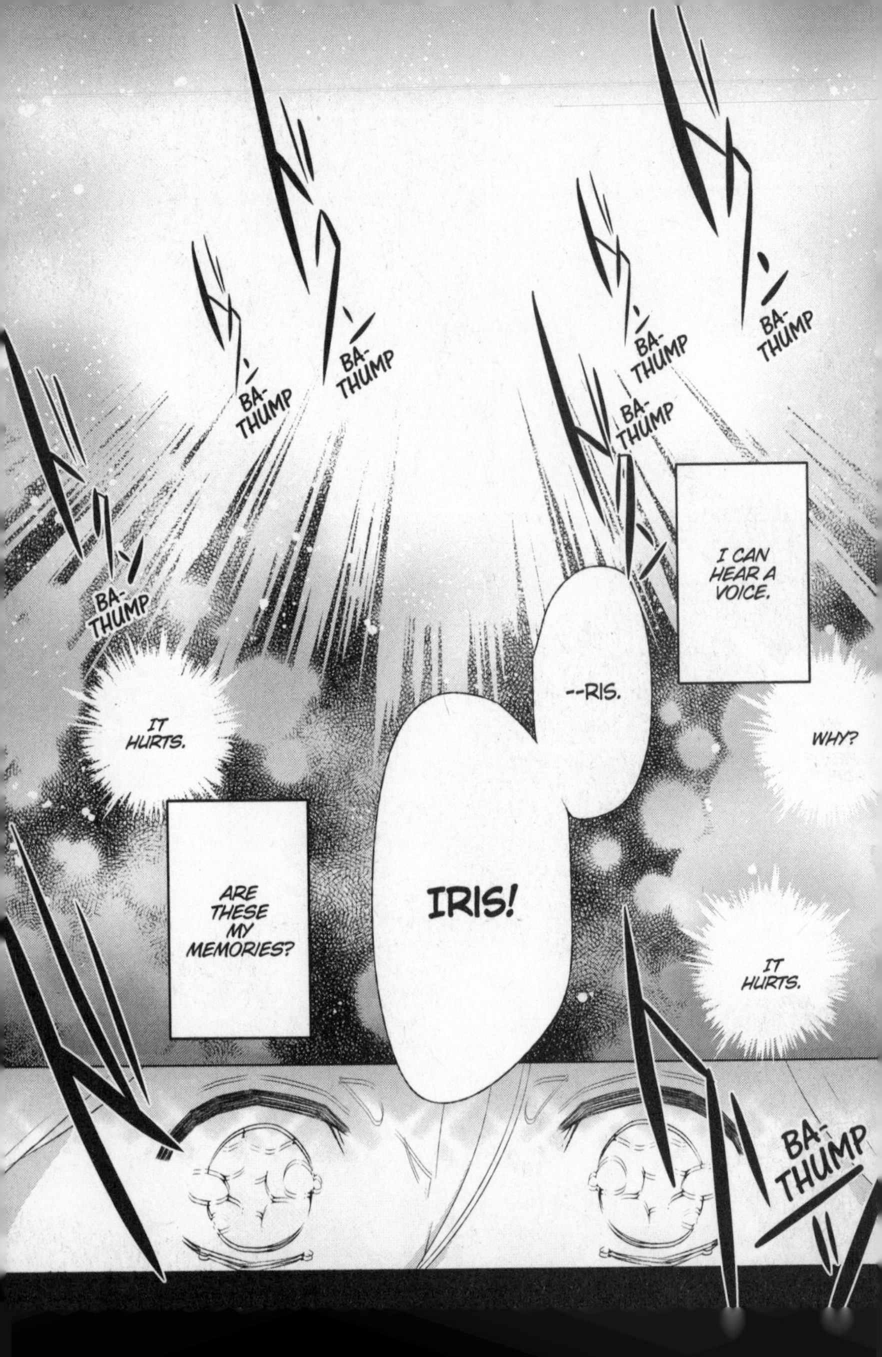
BA-THUMP
BA-THUMP
BA-THUMP
BA-THUMP
BA-THUMP
BA-THUMP
I CAN HEAR A VOICE.
--RIS.
WHY?
IT HURTS.
IRIS!
IT HURTS.
ARE THESE MY MEMORIES?
BA-THUMP

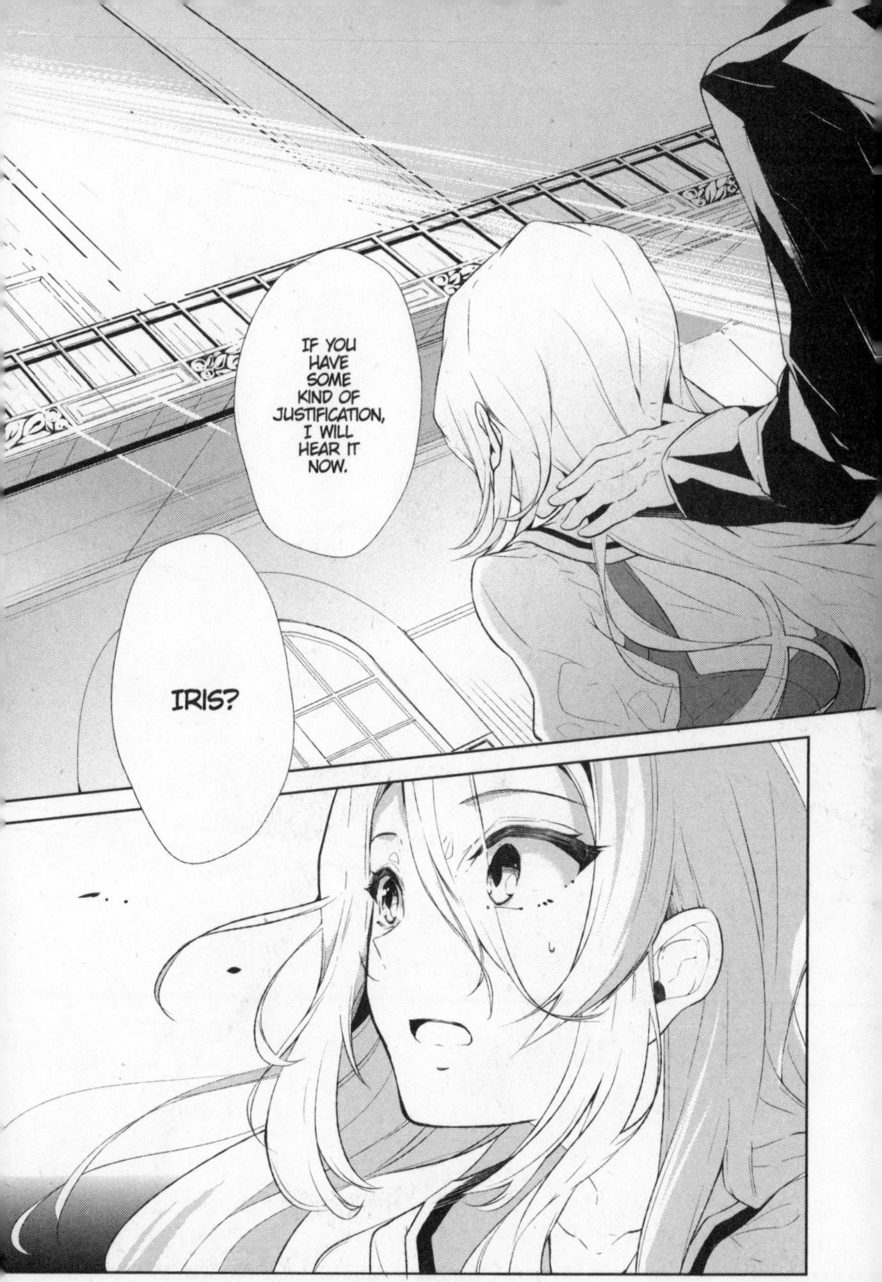
IF YOU HAVE SOME KIND OF JUSTIFICATION, I WILL HEAR IT NOW.
IRIS?
...

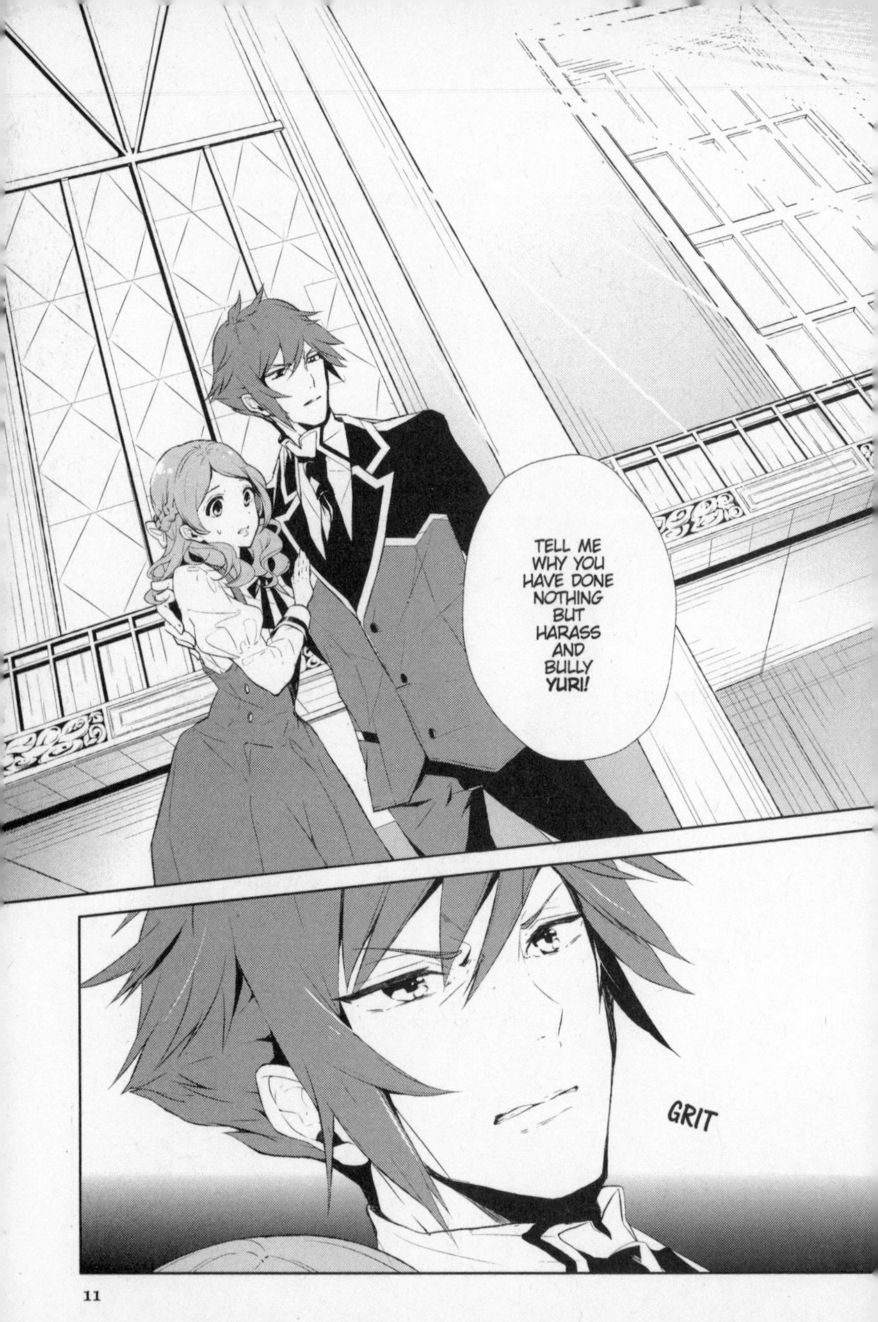
TELL ME WHY YOU HAVE DONE NOTHING BUT HARASS AND BULLY YURI!
GRIT

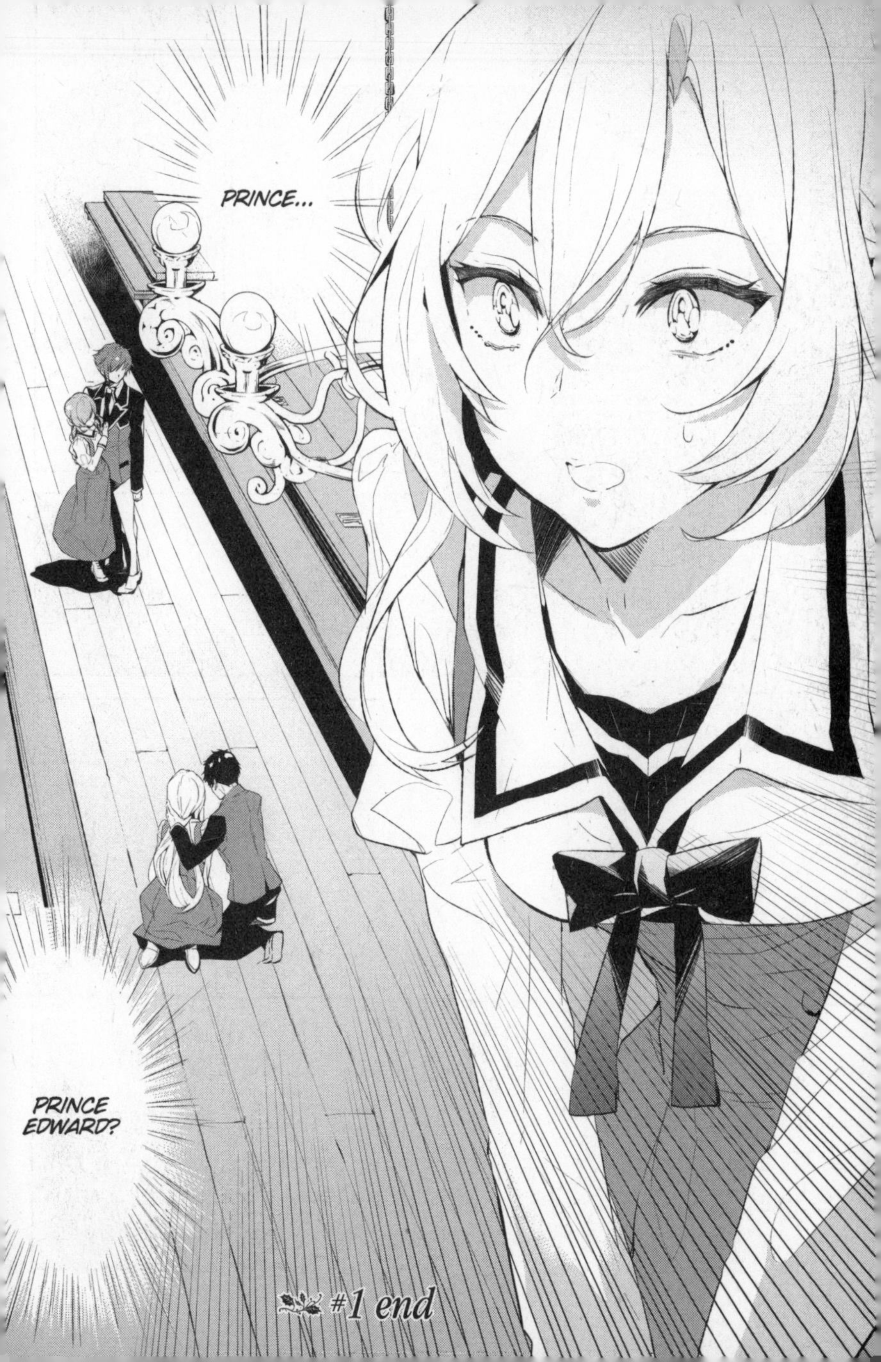
PRINCE...
PRINCE EDWARD?
#1 end

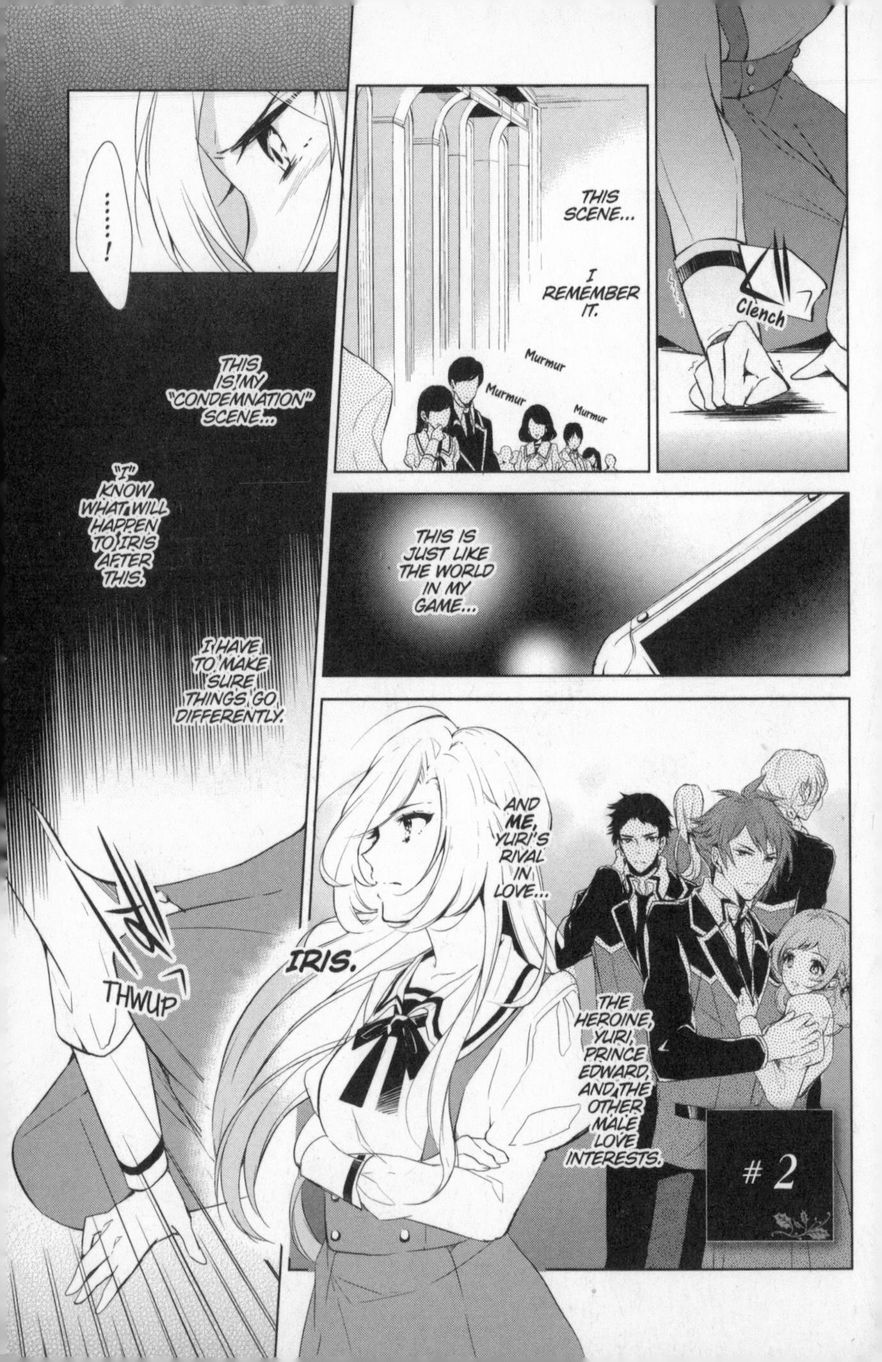

Clench
THIS SCENE...
I REMEMBER IT.
Murmur
Murmur
Murmur
......!
THIS IS JUST LIKE THE WORLD IN MY GAME...
THE HEROINE, YURI, PRINCE EDWARD, AND THE OTHER MALE LOVE INTERESTS.
AND ME, YURI'S RIVAL IN LOVE...
THIS IS MY "CONDEMNATION" SCENE...
"I" KNOW WHAT WILL HAPPEN TO IRIS AFTER THIS.
I HAVE TO MAKE SURE THINGS GO DIFFERENTLY.
THWUP
IRIS.
2

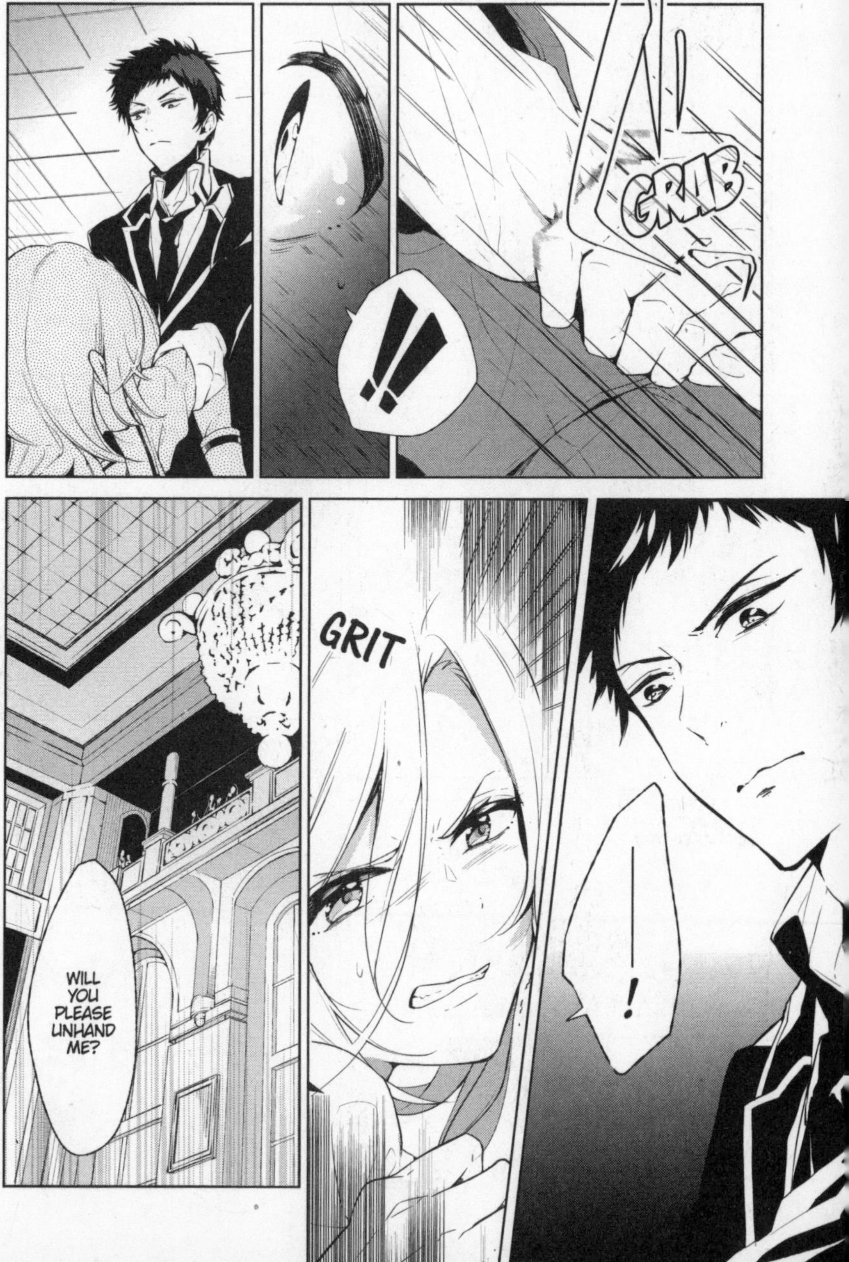
GRAB
!!
!
GRIT
WILL YOU PLEASE UNHAND ME?

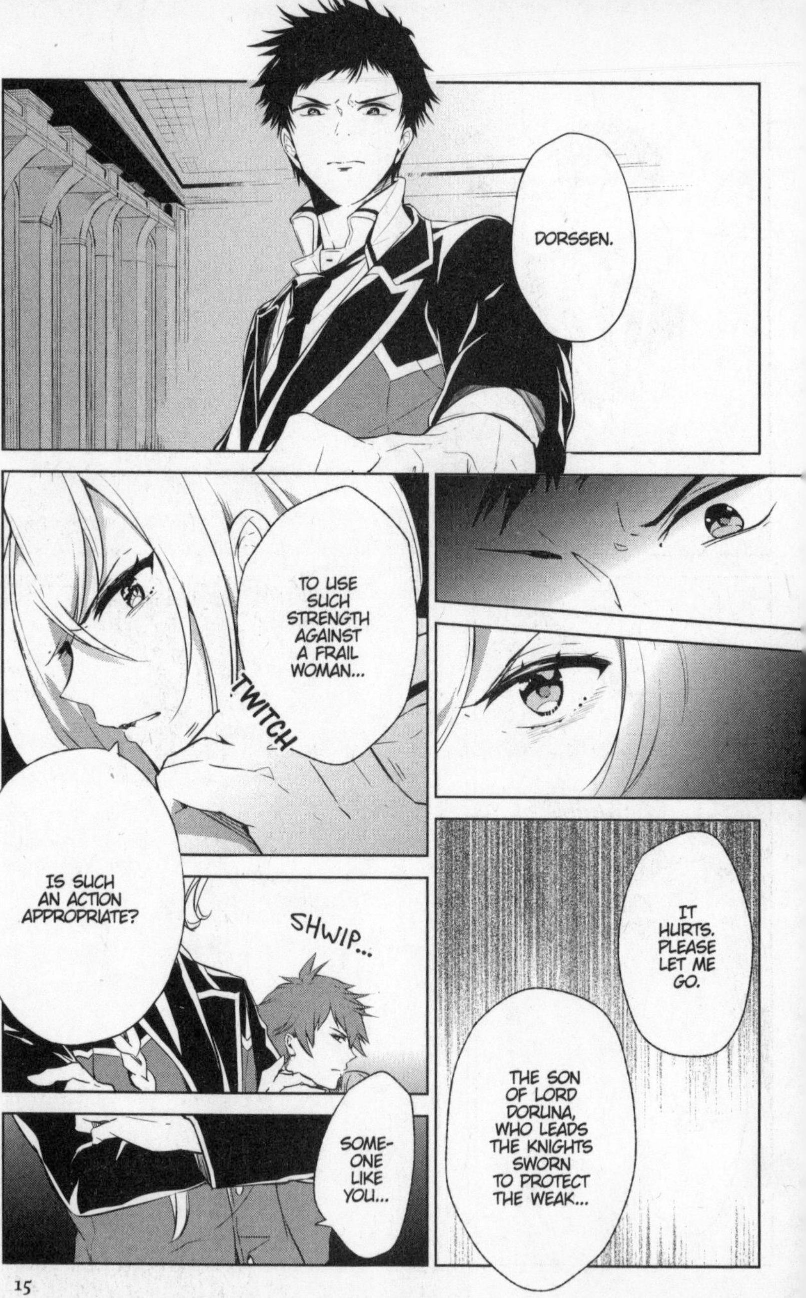
DORSSEN.
TO USE SUCH STRENGTH AGAINST A FRAIL WOMAN...
TWITCH
IT HURTS. PLEASE LET ME GO.
THE SON OF LORD DORUNA, WHO LEADS THE KNIGHTS SWORN TO PROTECT THE WEAK...
IS SUCH AN ACTION APPROPRIATE?
SHWIP...
SOME-ONE LIKE YOU...

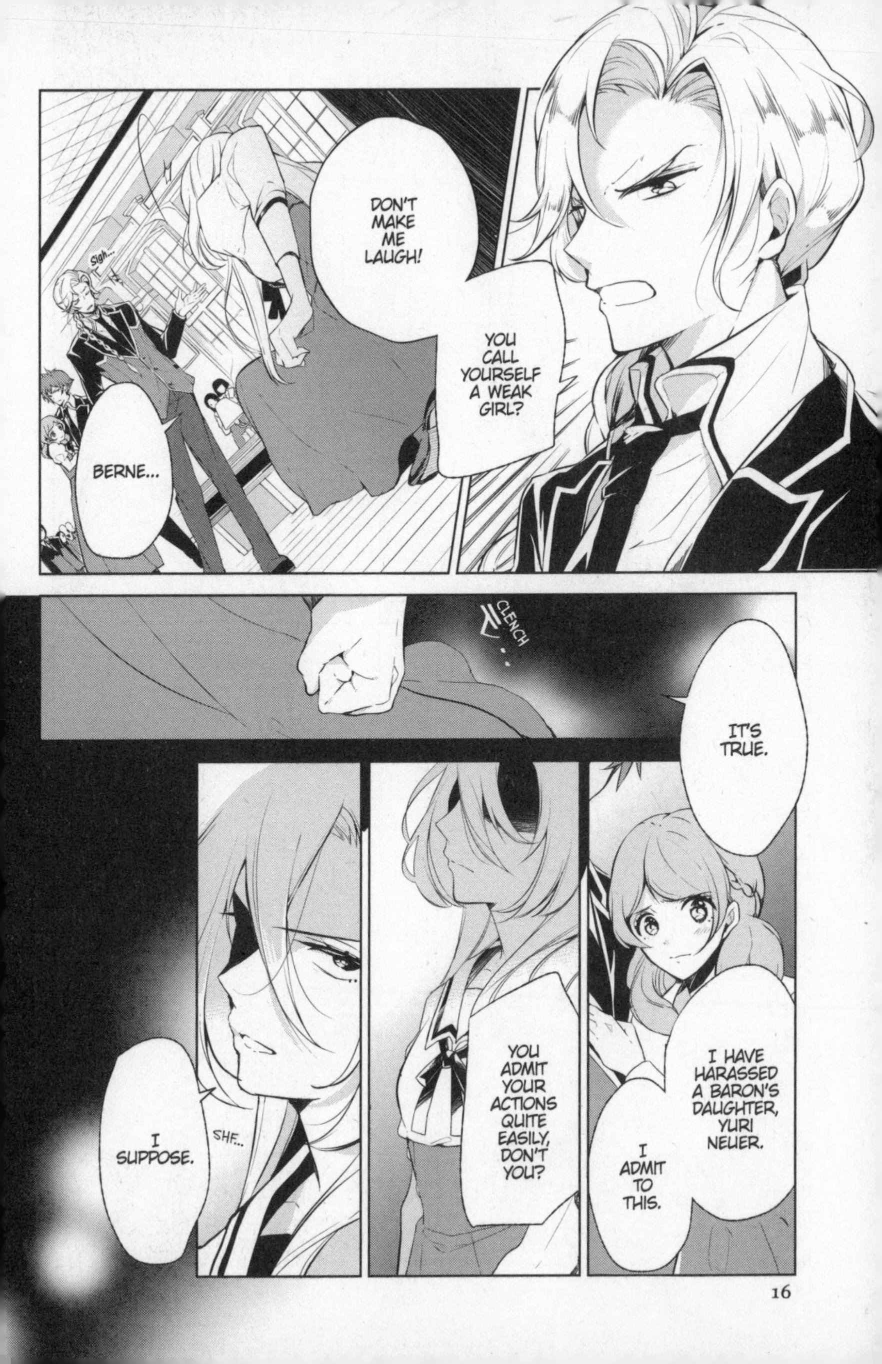
DON'T MAKE ME LAUGH!
YOU CALL YOURSELF A WEAK GIRL?
Sigh...
BERNE...
CLENCH
IT'S TRUE.
I HAVE HARASSED A BARON'S DAUGHTER, YURI NEUER.
I ADMIT TO THIS.
YOU ADMIT YOUR ACTIONS QUITE EASILY, DON'T YOU?
SHF...
I SUPPOSE.

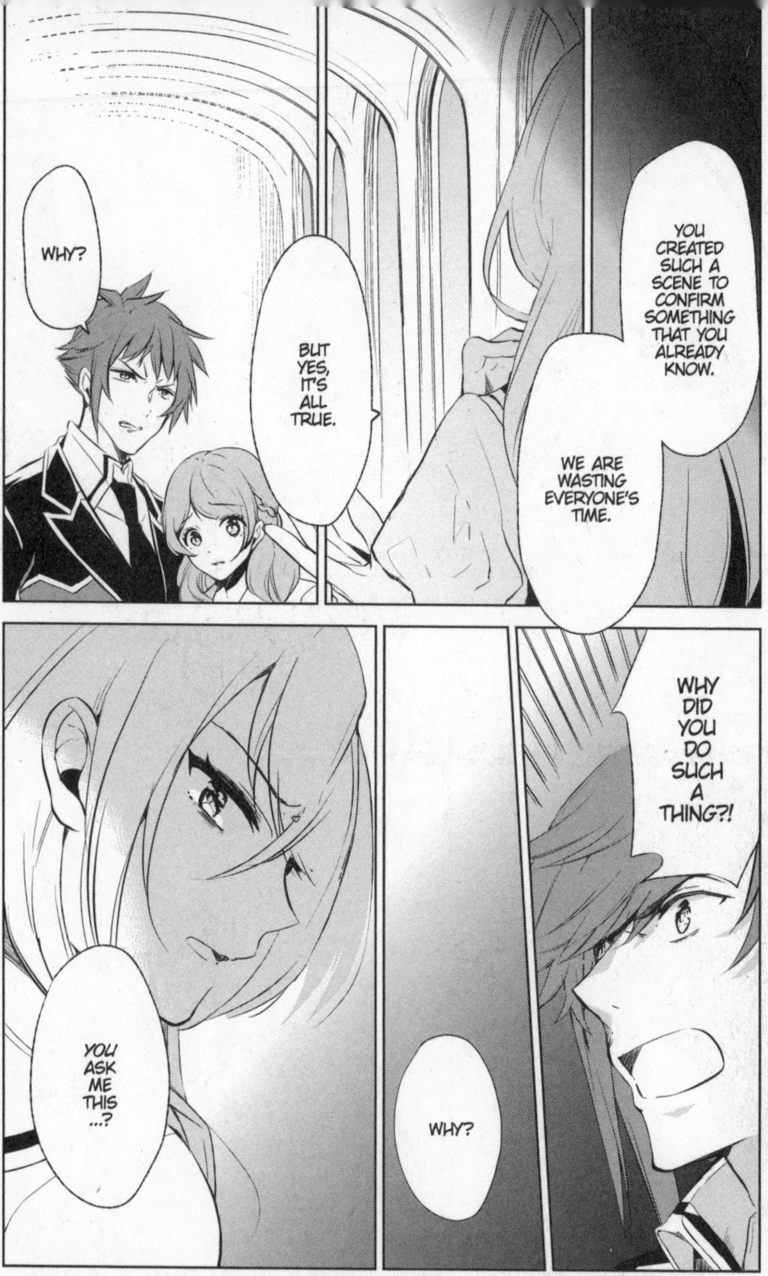
YOU CREATED SUCH A SCENE TO CONFIRM SOMETHING THAT YOU ALREADY KNOW.
WE ARE WASTING EVERYONE'S TIME.
BUT YES, IT'S ALL TRUE.
WHY?
WHY DID YOU DO SUCH A THING?!
WHY?
YOU ASK ME THIS ...?

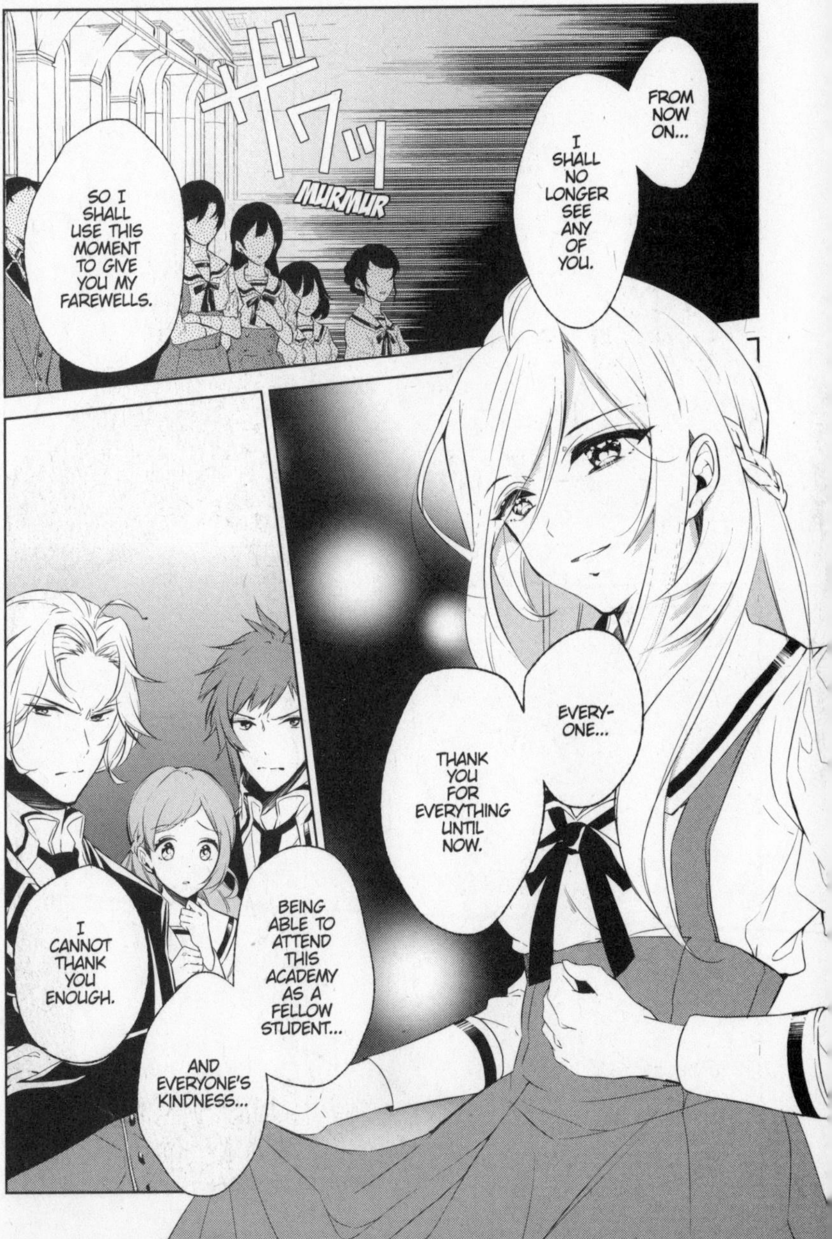
FROM NOW ON...
I SHALL NO LONGER SEE ANY OF YOU.
ザワッ
MURMUR
SO I SHALL USE THIS MOMENT TO GIVE YOU MY FAREWELLS.
EVERY-ONE...
THANK YOU FOR EVERYTHING UNTIL NOW.
BEING ABLE TO ATTEND THIS ACADEMY AS A FELLOW STUDENT...
AND EVERYONE'S KINDNESS...
I CANNOT THANK YOU ENOUGH.

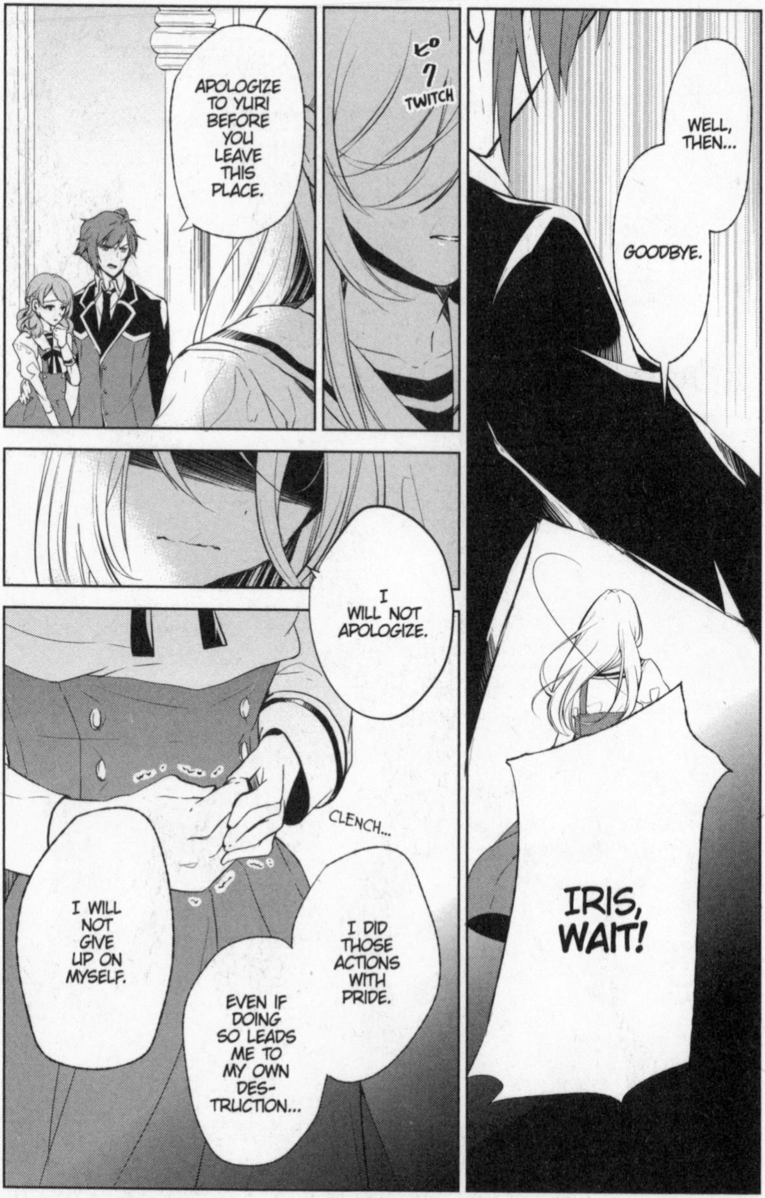
WELL, THEN...
GOODBYE.
IRIS, WAIT!
ピク
TWITCH
APOLOGIZE TO YURI BEFORE YOU LEAVE THIS PLACE.
I WILL NOT APOLOGIZE.
CLENCH...
I DID THOSE ACTIONS WITH PRIDE.
I WILL NOT GIVE UP ON MYSELF.
EVEN IF DOING SO LEADS ME TO MY OWN DES-TRUCTION...

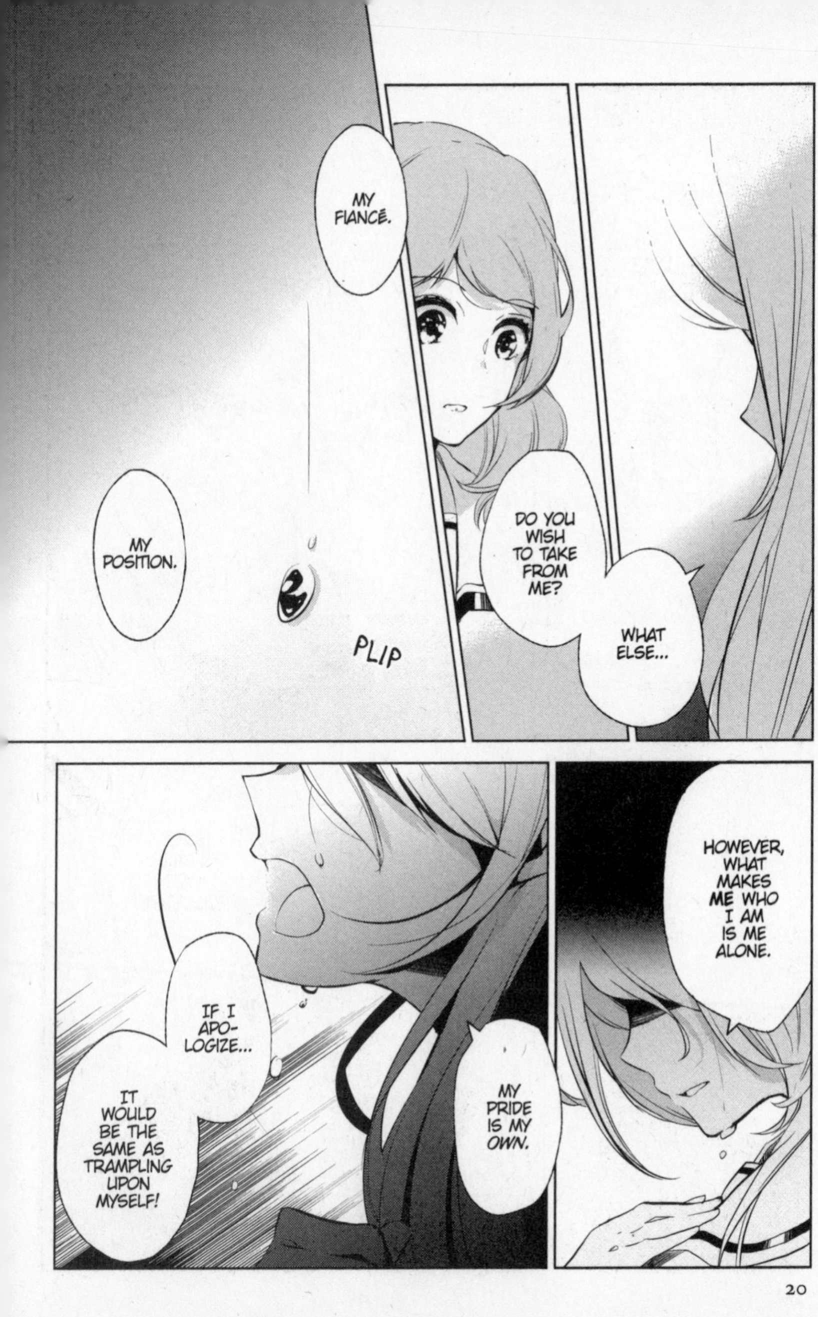
WHAT ELSE...
DO YOU WISH TO TAKE FROM ME?
MY FIANCÉ.
MY POSITION.
PLIP
HOWEVER, WHAT MAKES ME WHO I AM IS ME ALONE.
MY PRIDE IS MY OWN.
IF I APOLOGIZE...
IT WOULD BE THE SAME AS TRAMPLING UPON MYSELF!

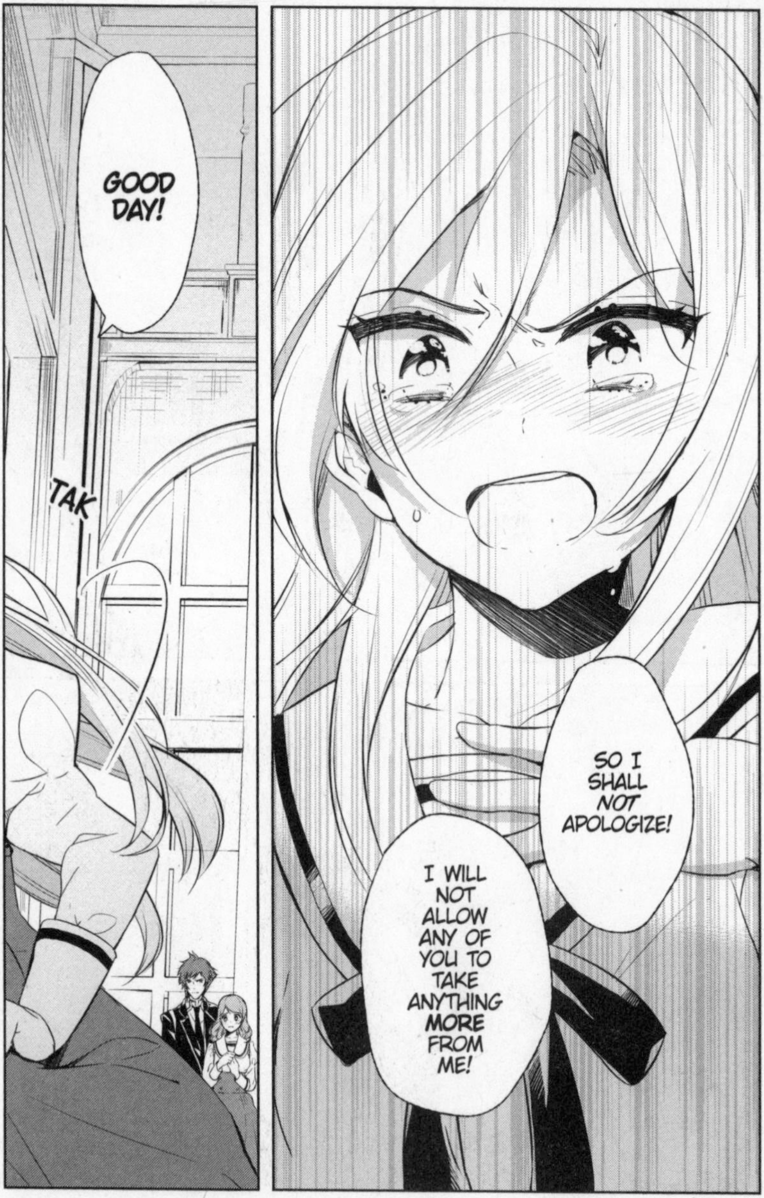
SO I SHALL NOT APOLOGIZE!
I WILL NOT ALLOW ANY OF YOU TO TAKE ANYTHING MORE FROM ME!
GOOD DAY!
TAK

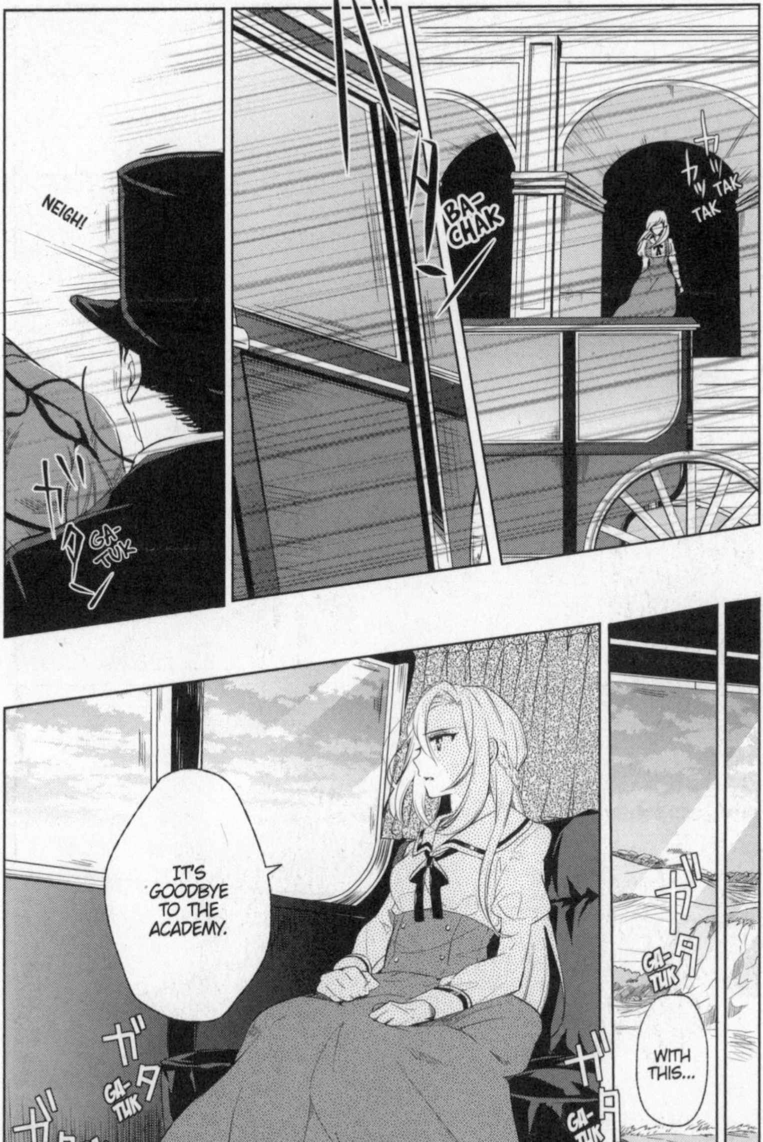
TAK TAK
BA-CHAK
NEIGH!
GA-TUK
GA-TUK
WITH THIS...
GA-TUK
IT'S GOODBYE TO THE ACADEMY.
GA-TUK
GA-TUK

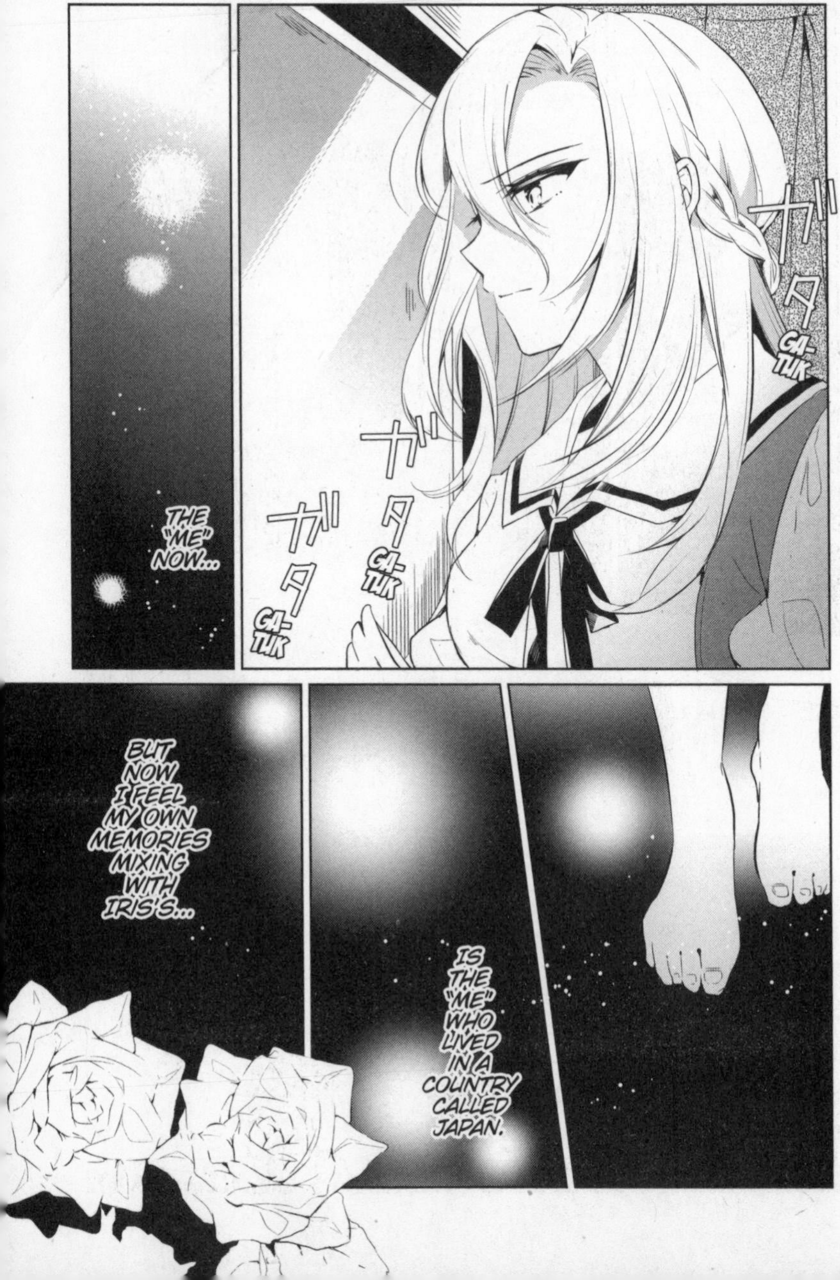

ガタ
GA-TUK
ガタ
GA-TUK
ガタ
GA-TUK
THE "ME" NOW...
IS THE "ME" WHO LIVED IN A COUNTRY CALLED JAPAN.
BUT NOW I FEEL MY OWN MEMORIES MIXING WITH IRIS'S...

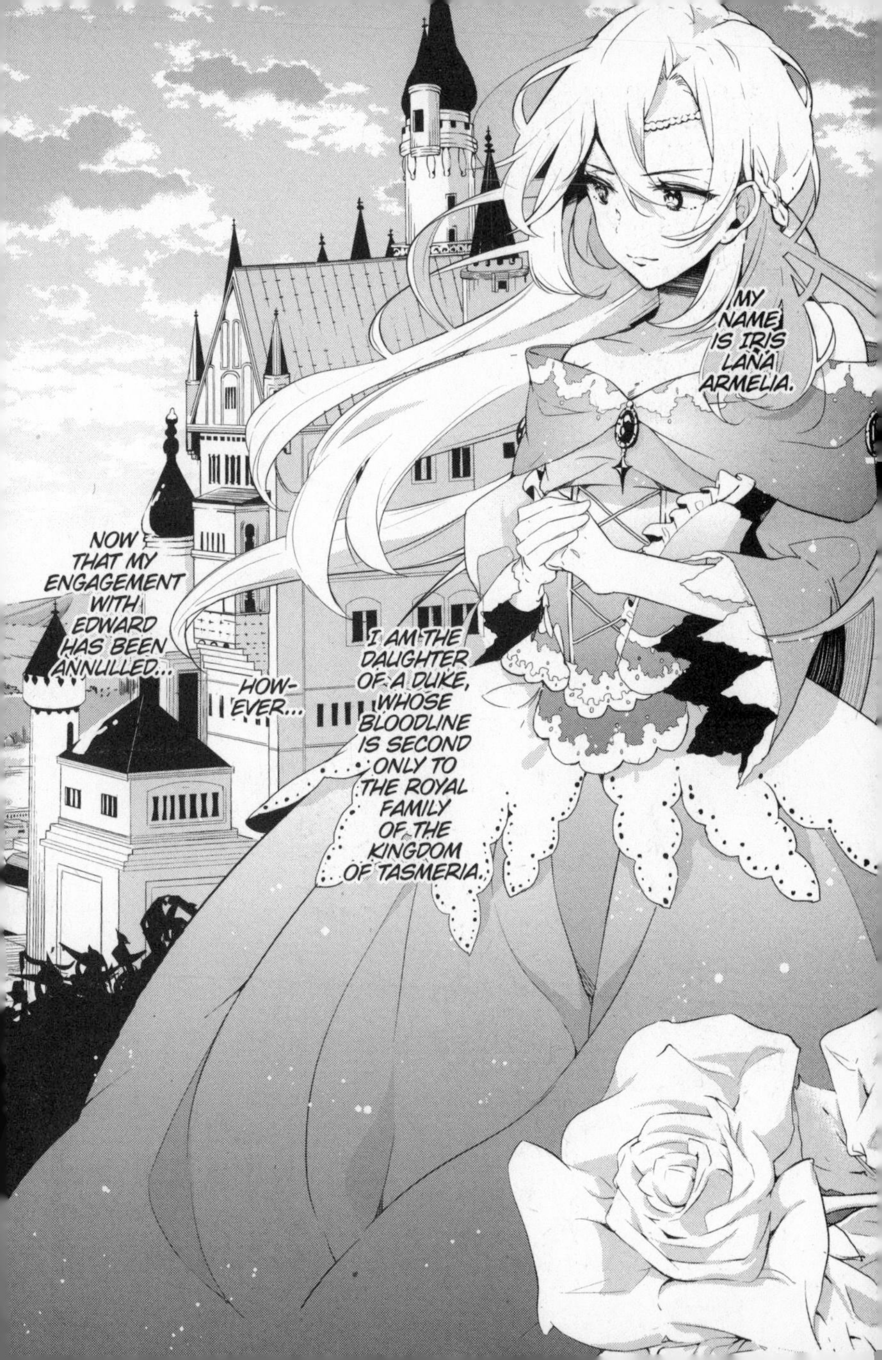
MY NAME IS IRIS LANA ARMELIA.
I AM THE DAUGHTER OF A DUKE, WHOSE BLOODLINE IS SECOND ONLY TO THE ROYAL FAMILY OF THE KINGDOM OF TASMERIA.
HOW-EVER...
NOW THAT MY ENGAGEMENT WITH EDWARD HAS BEEN ANNULLED...

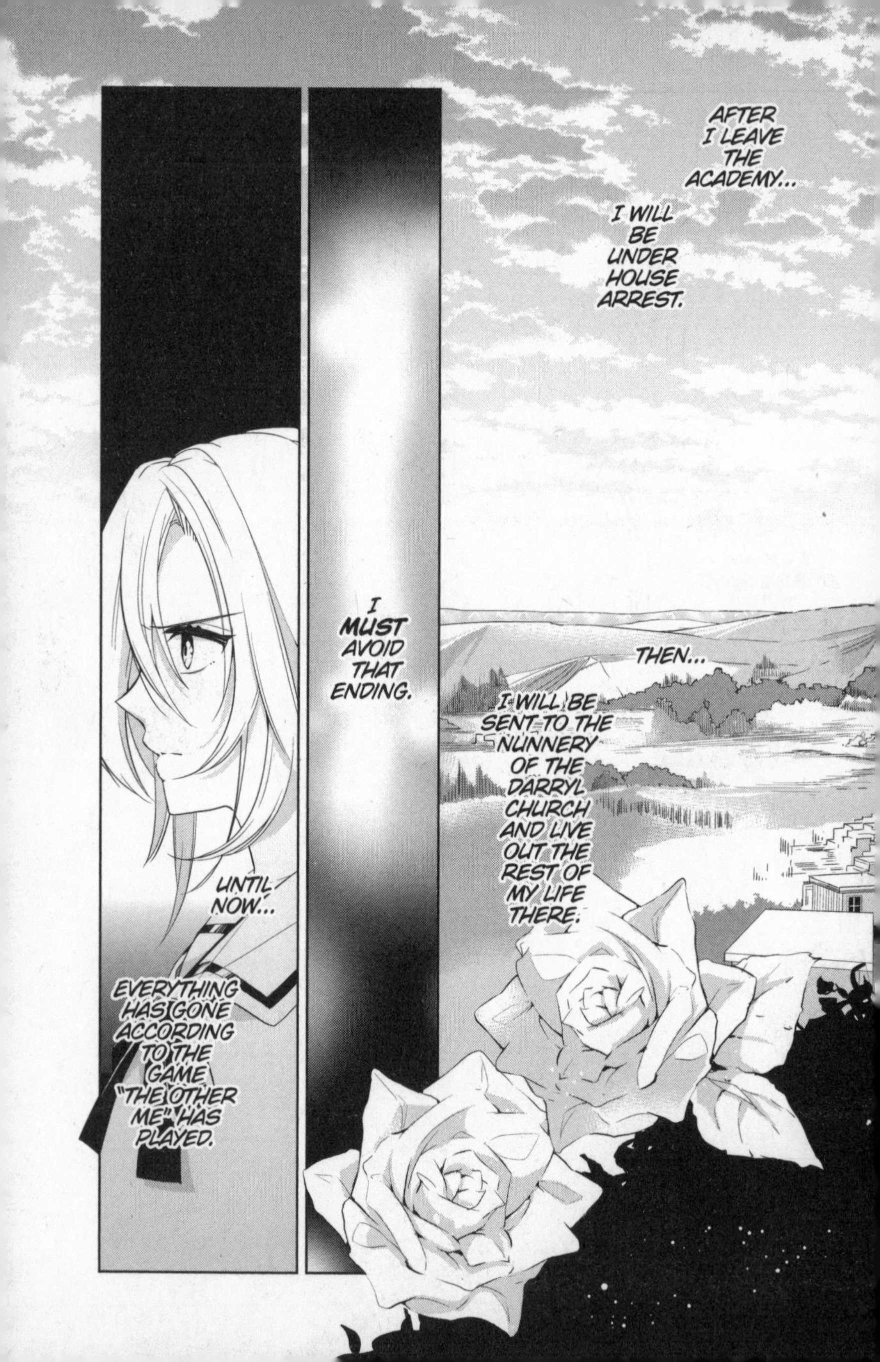
AFTER I LEAVE THE ACADEMY...
I WILL BE UNDER HOUSE ARREST.
THEN...
I WILL BE SENT TO THE NUNNERY OF THE DARRYL CHURCH AND LIVE OUT THE REST OF MY LIFE THERE.
I MUST AVOID THAT ENDING.
UNTIL NOW...
EVERYTHING HAS GONE ACCORDING TO THE GAME "THE OTHER ME" HAS PLAYED.

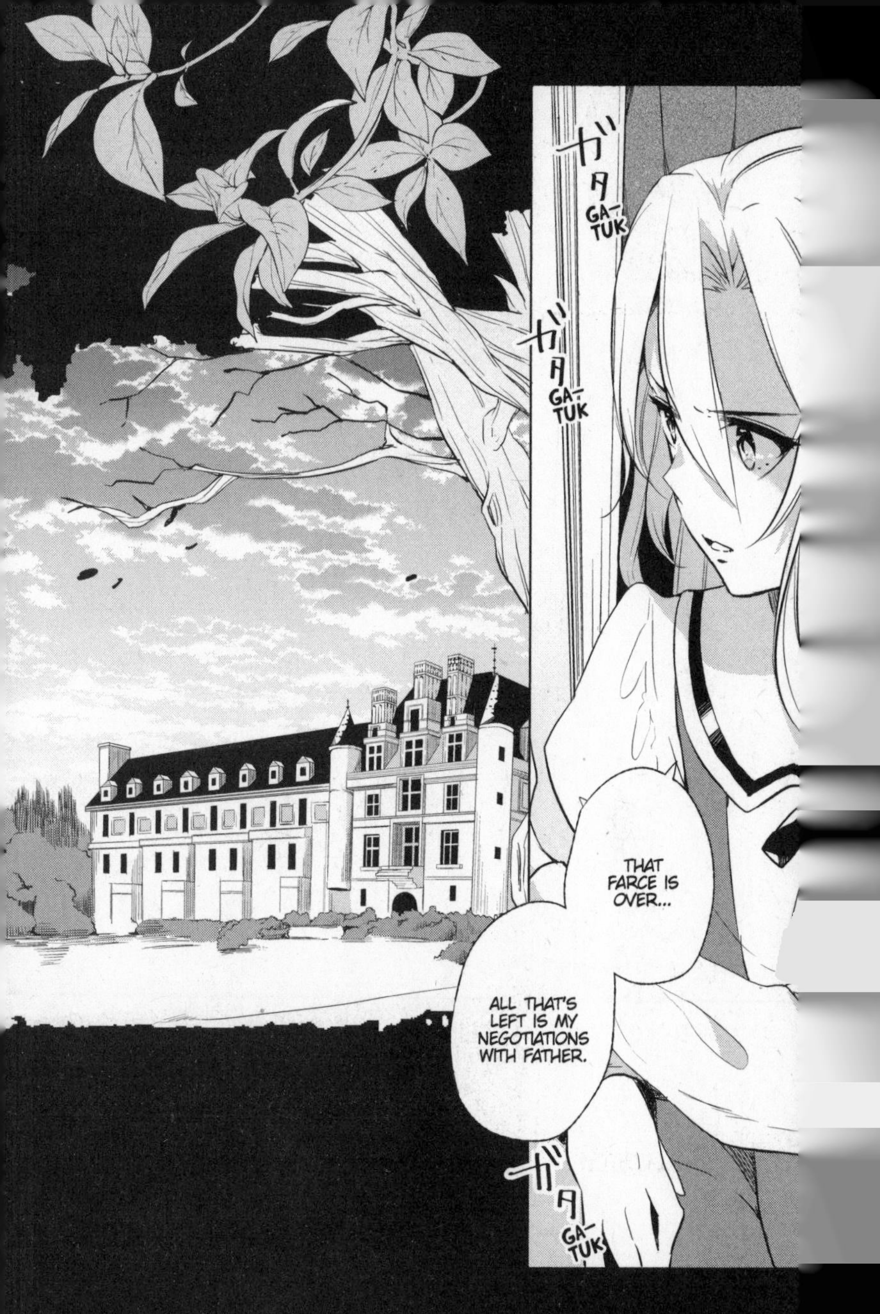

ガタ GA-TUK
ガタ GA-TUK
THAT FARCE IS OVER...
ALL THAT'S LEFT IS MY NEGOTIATIONS WITH FATHER.
ガタ GA-TUK

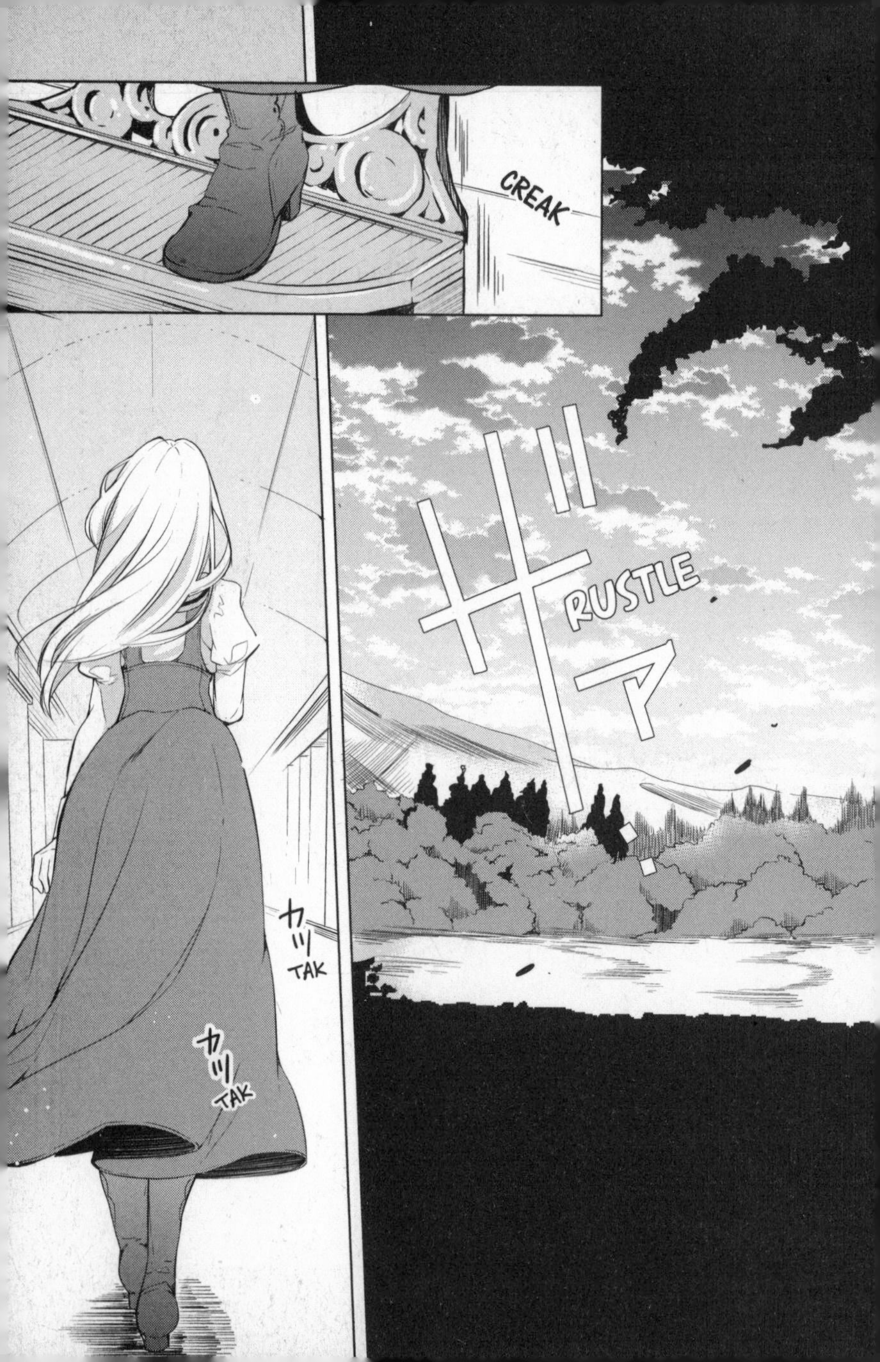
CREAK
ザァ
RUSTLE
カツ
TAK
カツ
TAK

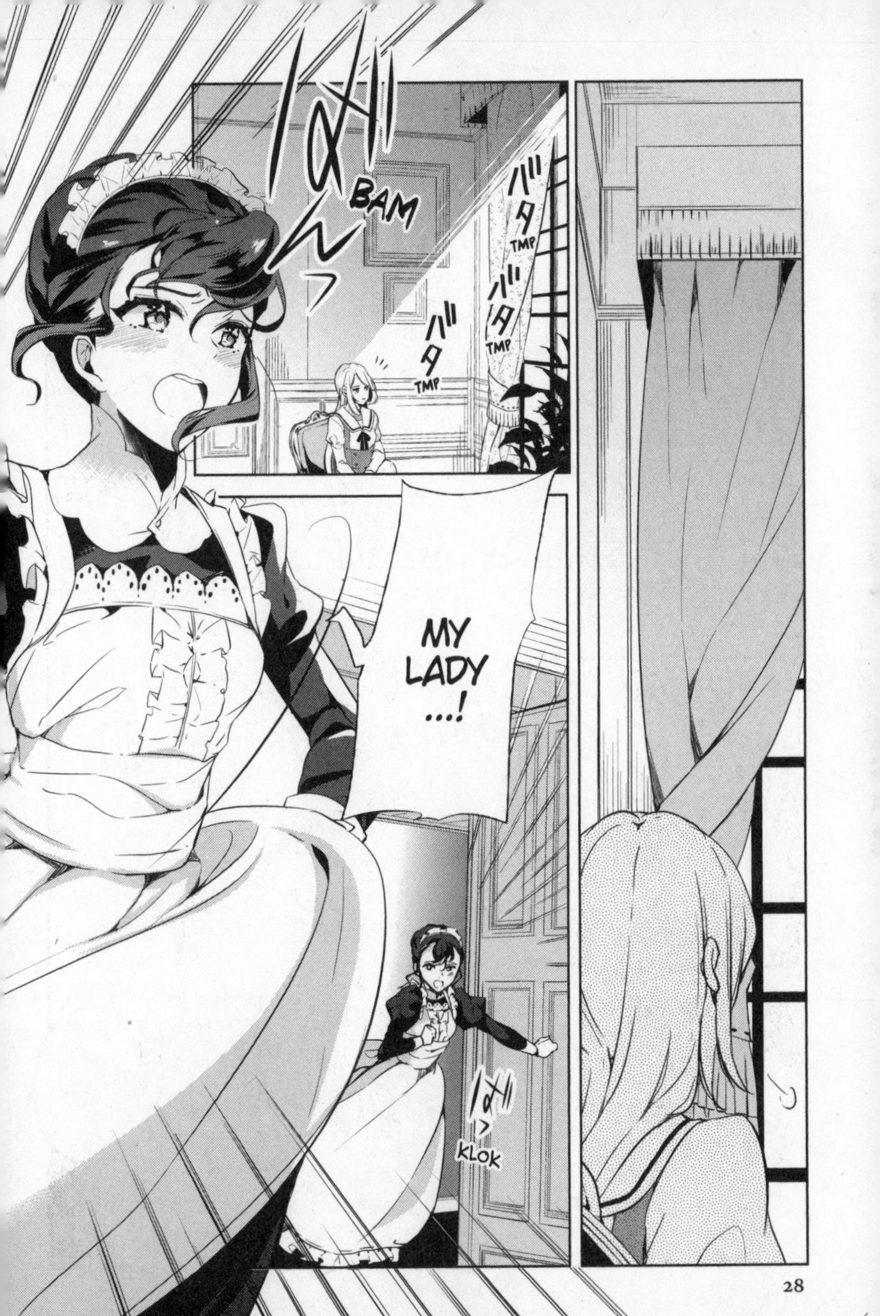
ばん
BAM
バタ
TMP
バタ
TMP
バタ
TMP
MY LADY ...!
ぱ
KLOK

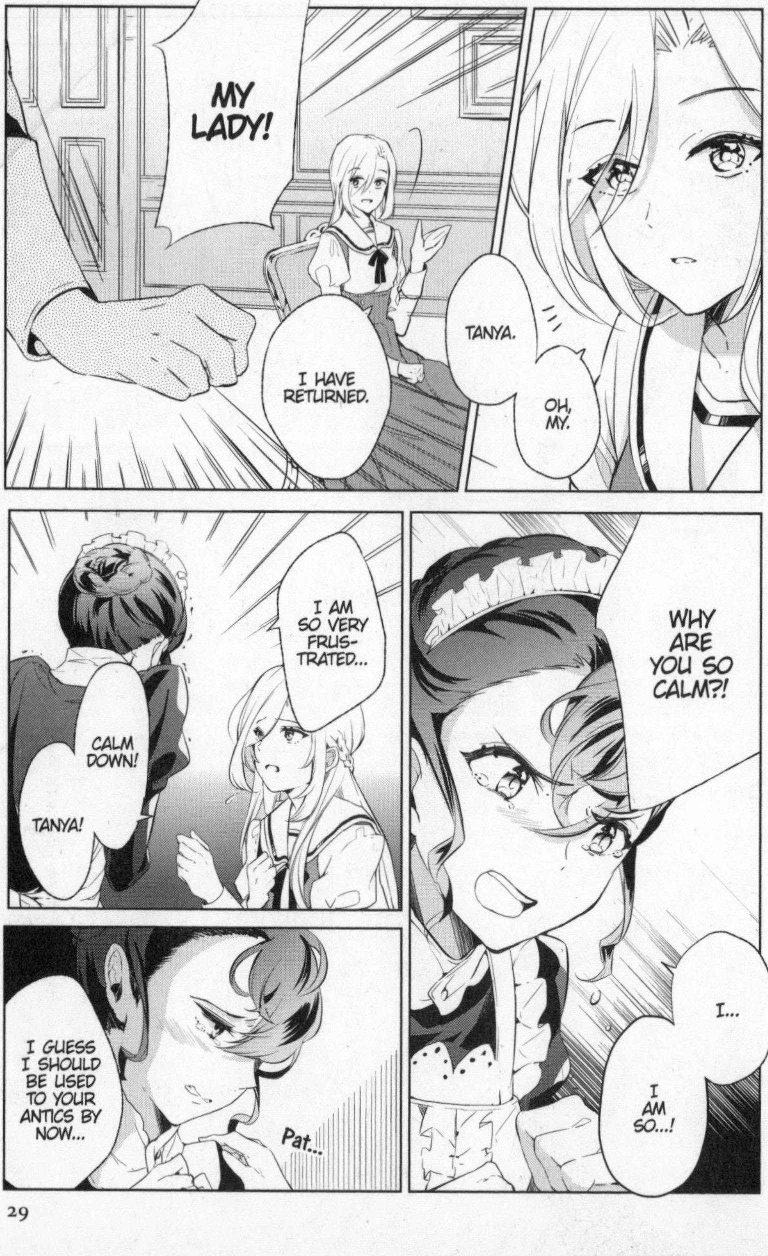

TANYA.
OH, MY.
MY LADY!
I HAVE RETURNED.
WHY ARE YOU SO CALM?!
I...
I AM SO...!
I AM SO VERY FRUS-TRATED...
CALM DOWN!
TANYA!
I GUESS I SHOULD BE USED TO YOUR ANTICS BY NOW...
Pat...

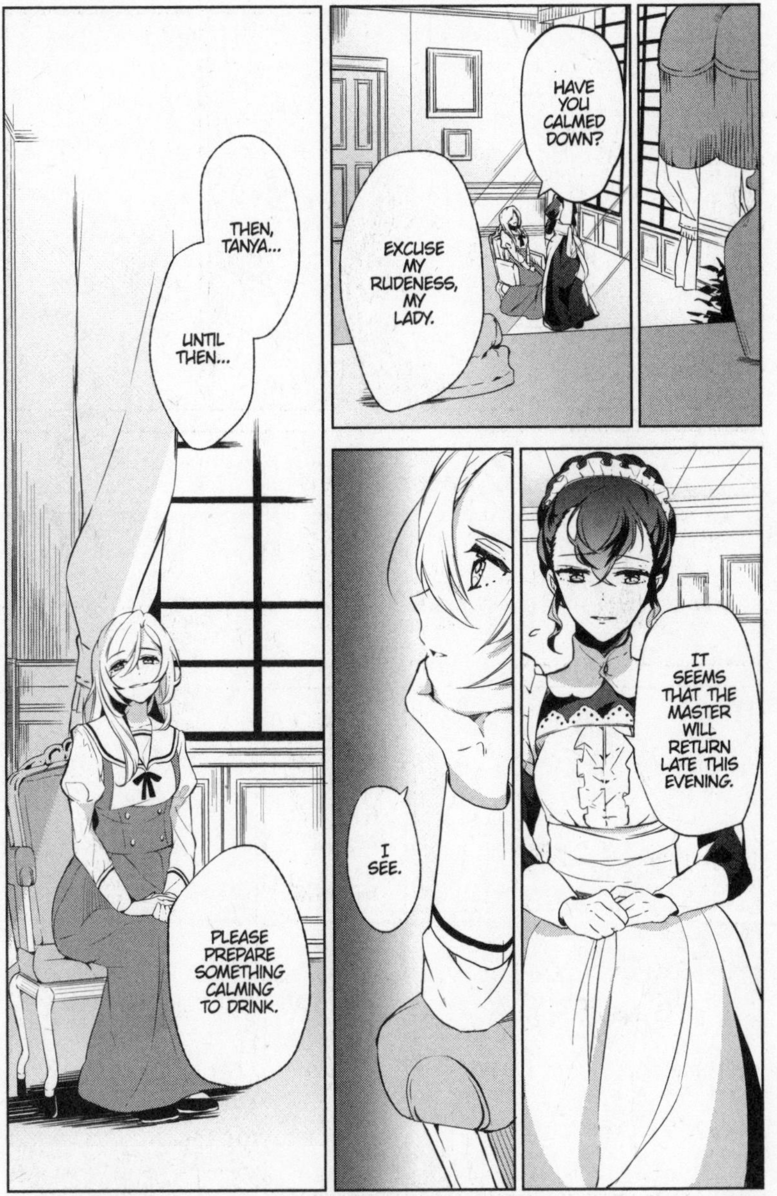
HAVE YOU CALMED DOWN?
EXCUSE MY RUDENESS, MY LADY.
IT SEEMS THAT THE MASTER WILL RETURN LATE THIS EVENING.
I SEE.
THEN, TANYA...
UNTIL THEN...
PLEASE PREPARE SOMETHING CALMING TO DRINK.

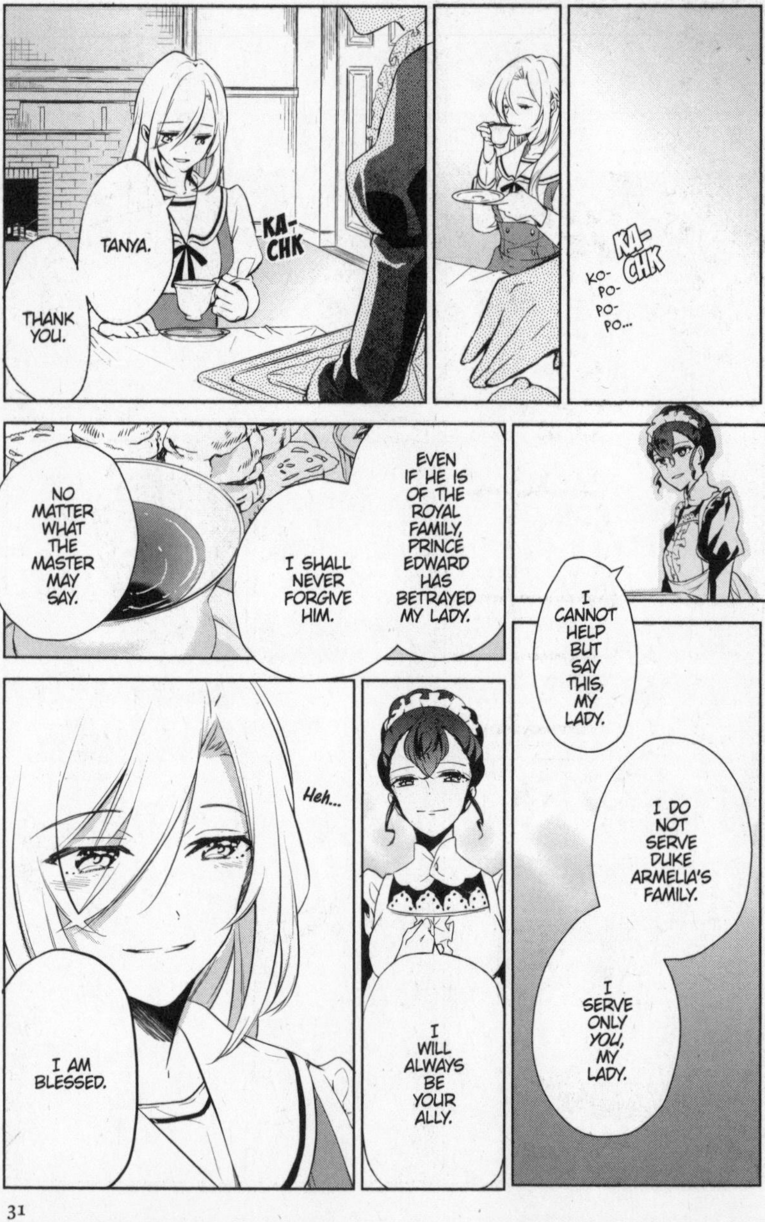
KA-CHK
KO-PO-PO-PO...
KA-CHK
TANYA.
THANK YOU.
I CANNOT HELP BUT SAY THIS, MY LADY.
EVEN IF HE IS OF THE ROYAL FAMILY, PRINCE EDWARD HAS BETRAYED MY LADY.
I SHALL NEVER FORGIVE HIM.
NO MATTER WHAT THE MASTER MAY SAY.
I DO NOT SERVE DUKE ARMELIA'S FAMILY.
I SERVE ONLY *YOU*, MY LADY.
I WILL ALWAYS BE YOUR ALLY.
Heh...
I AM BLESSED.

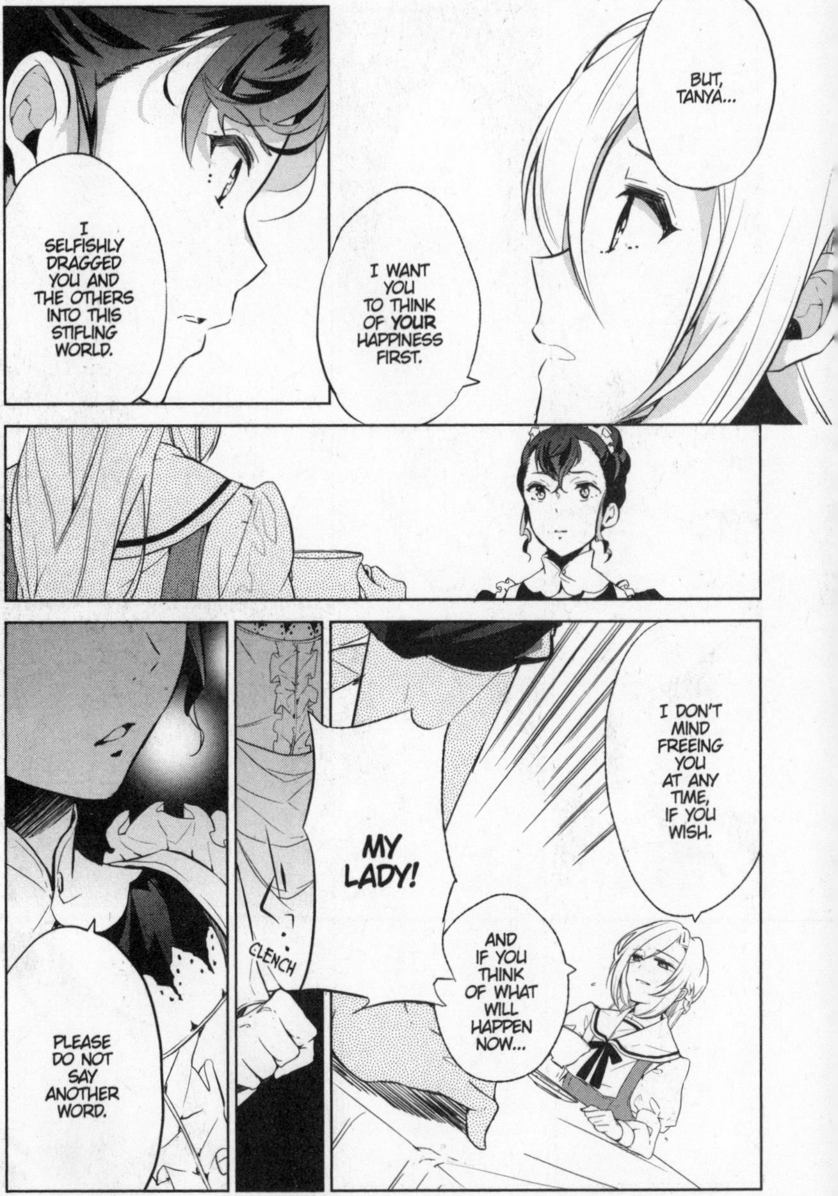
BUT, TANYA...
I WANT YOU TO THINK OF YOUR HAPPINESS FIRST.
I SELFISHLY DRAGGED YOU AND THE OTHERS INTO THIS STIFLING WORLD.
I DON'T MIND FREEING YOU AT ANY TIME, IF YOU WISH.
AND IF YOU THINK OF WHAT WILL HAPPEN NOW...
MY LADY!
CLENCH
PLEASE DO NOT SAY ANOTHER WORD.

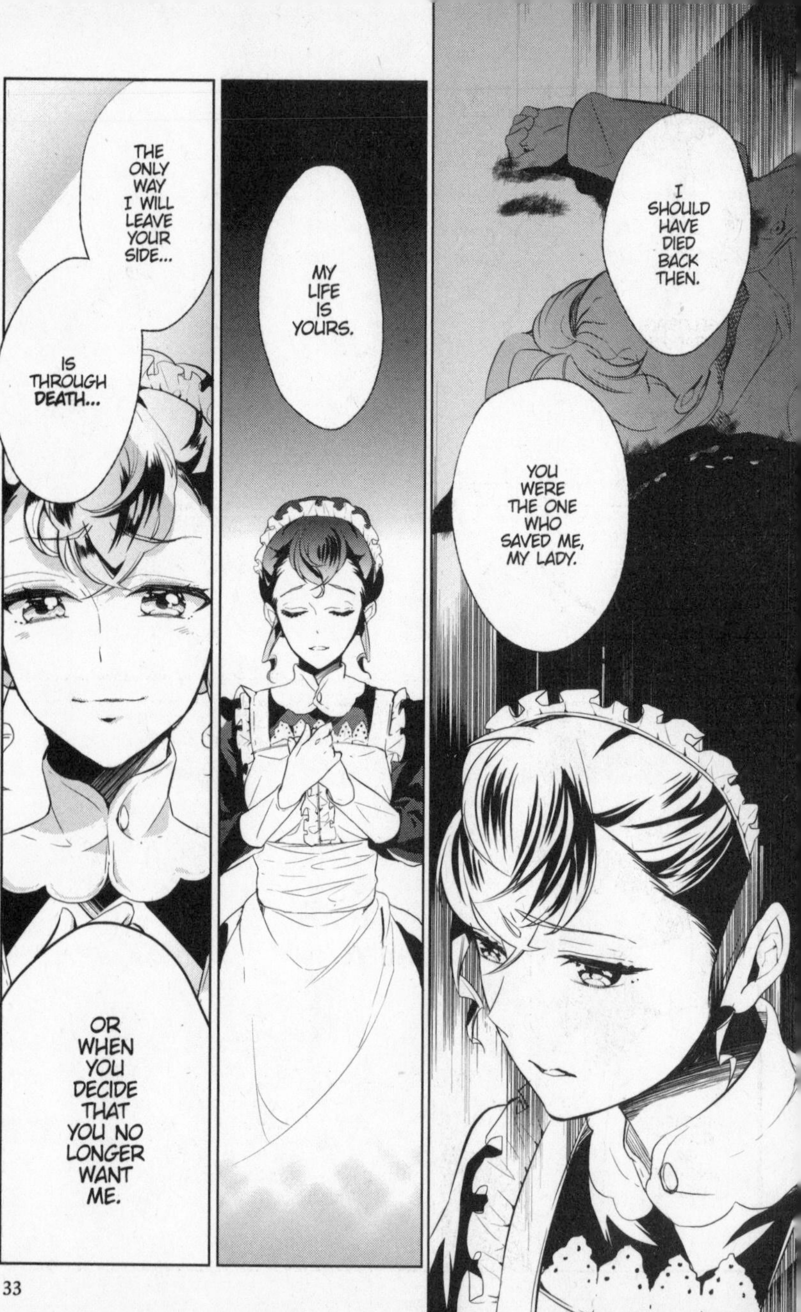
I SHOULD HAVE DIED BACK THEN.
YOU WERE THE ONE WHO SAVED ME, MY LADY.
MY LIFE IS YOURS.
THE ONLY WAY I WILL LEAVE YOUR SIDE...
IS THROUGH DEATH...
OR WHEN YOU DECIDE THAT YOU NO LONGER WANT ME.

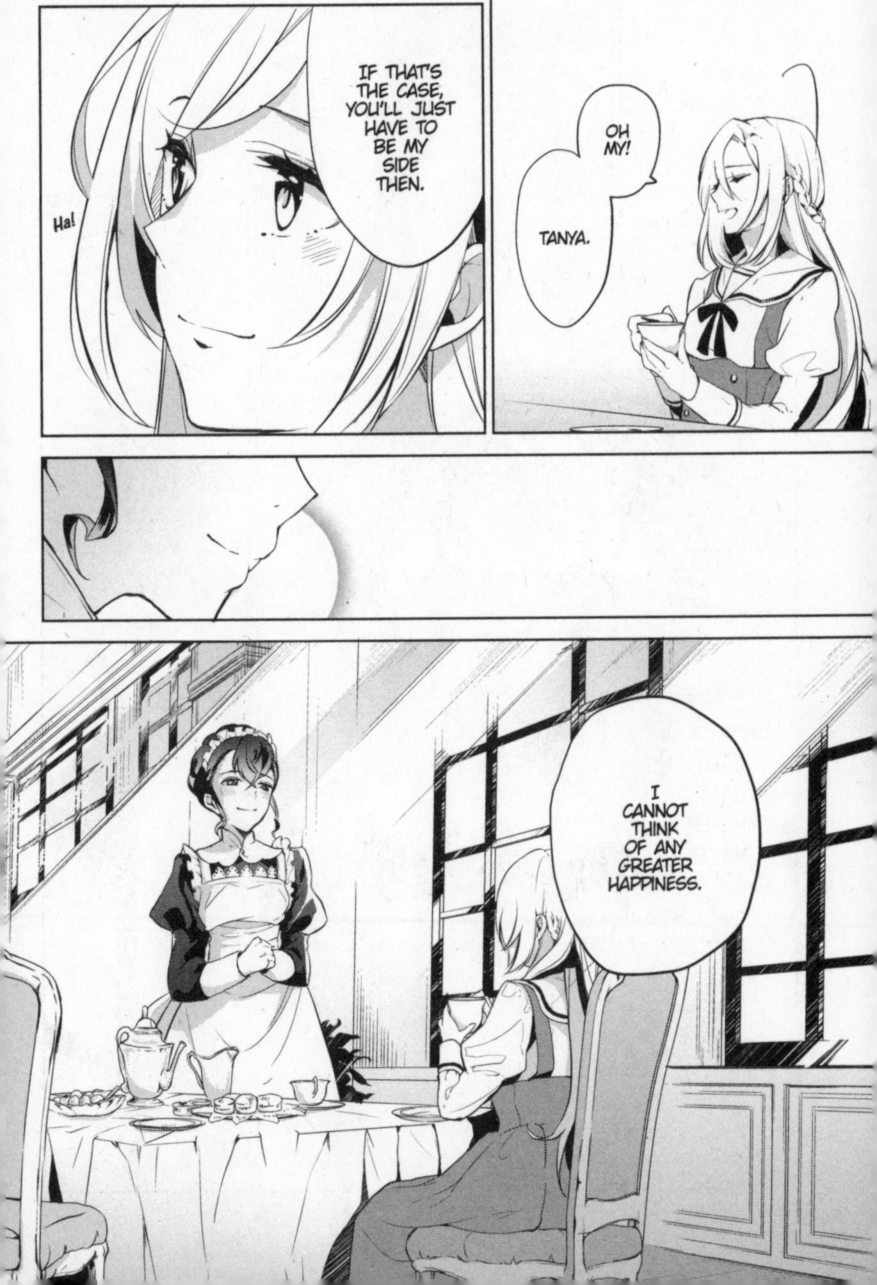
OH MY!
TANYA.
IF THAT'S THE CASE, YOU'LL JUST HAVE TO BE MY SIDE THEN.
Ha!
I CANNOT THINK OF ANY GREATER HAPPINESS.

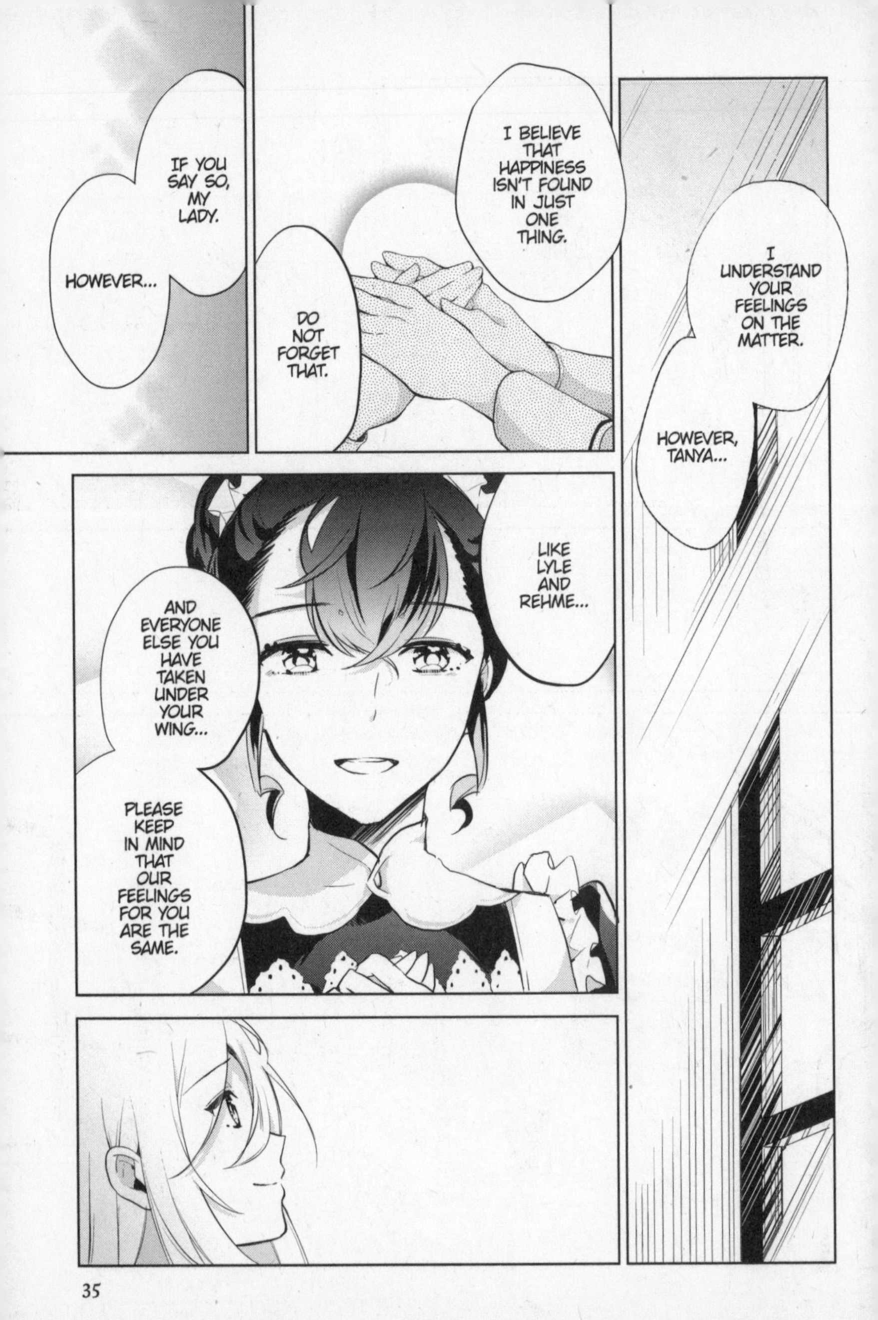
I BELIEVE THAT HAPPINESS ISN'T FOUND IN JUST ONE THING.
DO NOT FORGET THAT.
IF YOU SAY SO, MY LADY.
HOWEVER...
I UNDERSTAND YOUR FEELINGS ON THE MATTER.
HOWEVER, TANYA...
LIKE LYLE AND REHME...
AND EVERYONE ELSE YOU HAVE TAKEN UNDER YOUR WING...
PLEASE KEEP IN MIND THAT OUR FEELINGS FOR YOU ARE THE SAME.

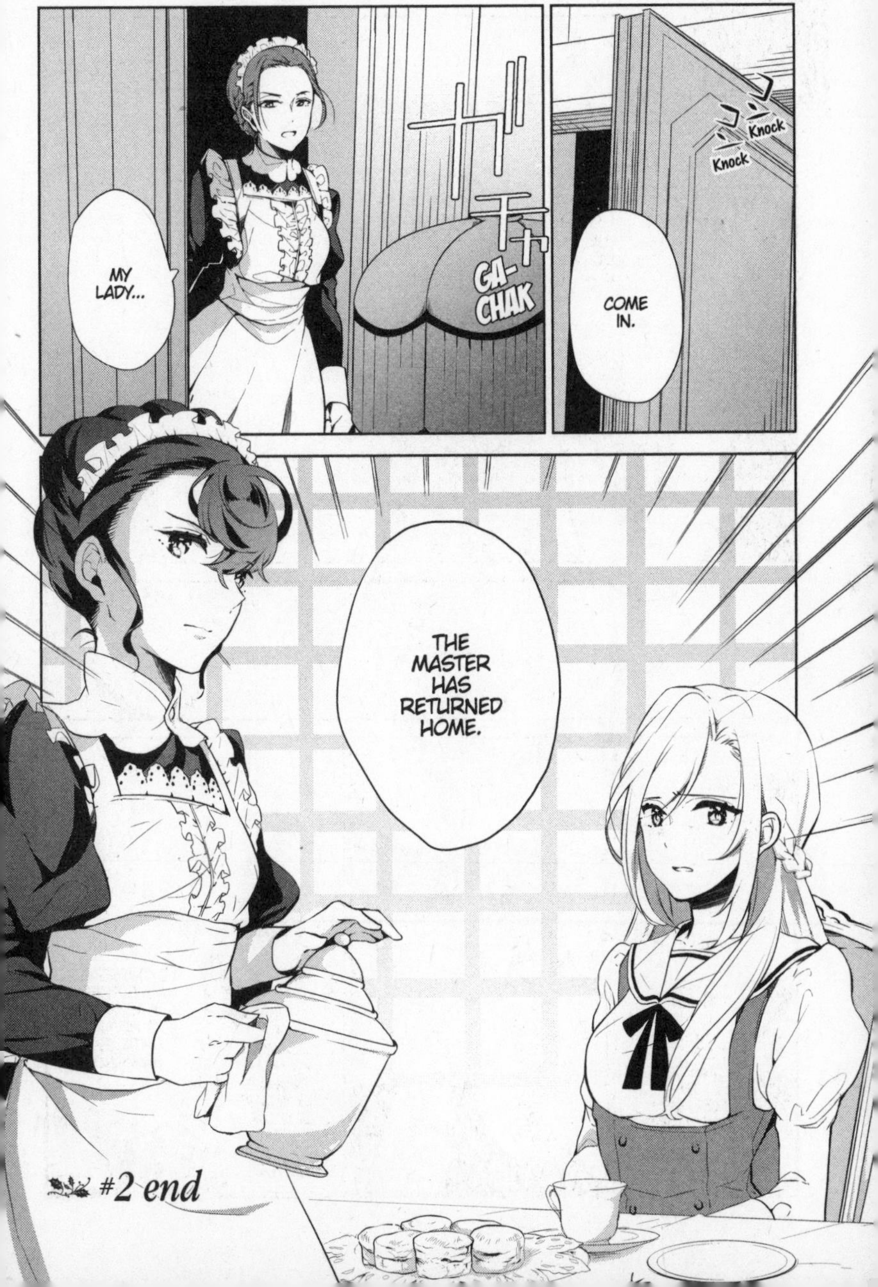
Knock
Knock
COME IN.
GA-CHAK
MY LADY...
THE MASTER HAS RETURNED HOME.
#2 end

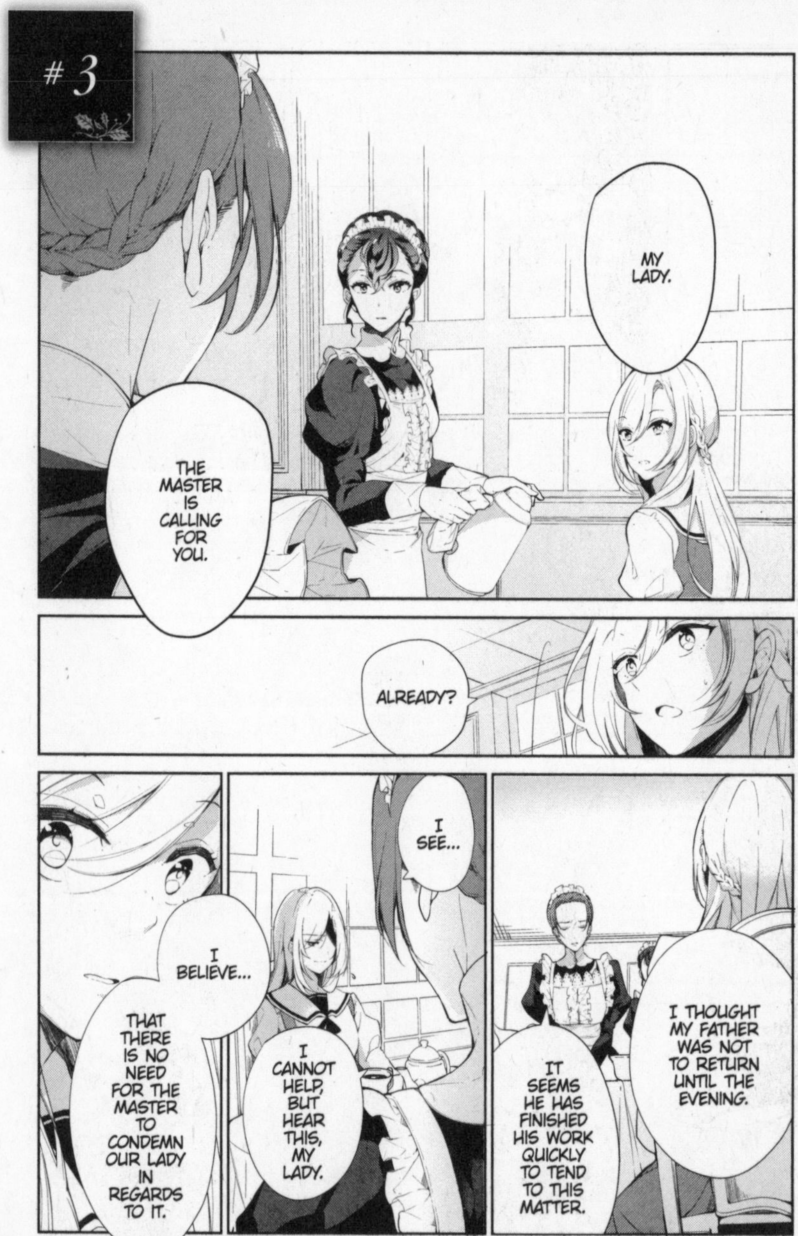

3
MY LADY.
THE MASTER IS CALLING FOR YOU.
ALREADY?
I THOUGHT MY FATHER WAS NOT TO RETURN UNTIL THE EVENING.
IT SEEMS HE HAS FINISHED HIS WORK QUICKLY TO TEND TO THIS MATTER.
I SEE...
I CANNOT HELP, BUT HEAR THIS, MY LADY.
I BELIEVE...
THAT THERE IS NO NEED FOR THE MASTER TO CONDEMN OUR LADY IN REGARDS TO IT.

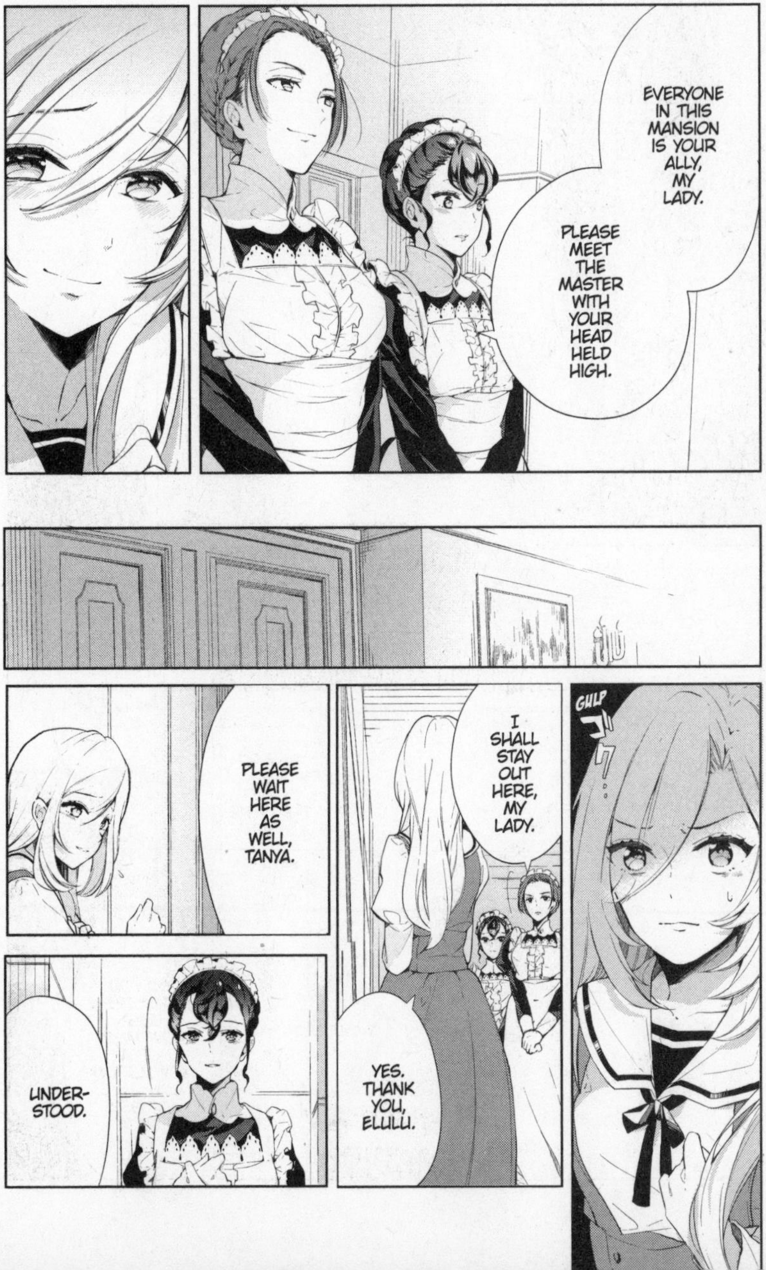
EVERYONE IN THIS MANSION IS YOUR ALLY, MY LADY.
PLEASE MEET THE MASTER WITH YOUR HEAD HELD HIGH.
GULP
ゴク…
I SHALL STAY OUT HERE, MY LADY.
PLEASE WAIT HERE AS WELL, TANYA.
YES. THANK YOU, ELULU.
UNDER-STOOD.

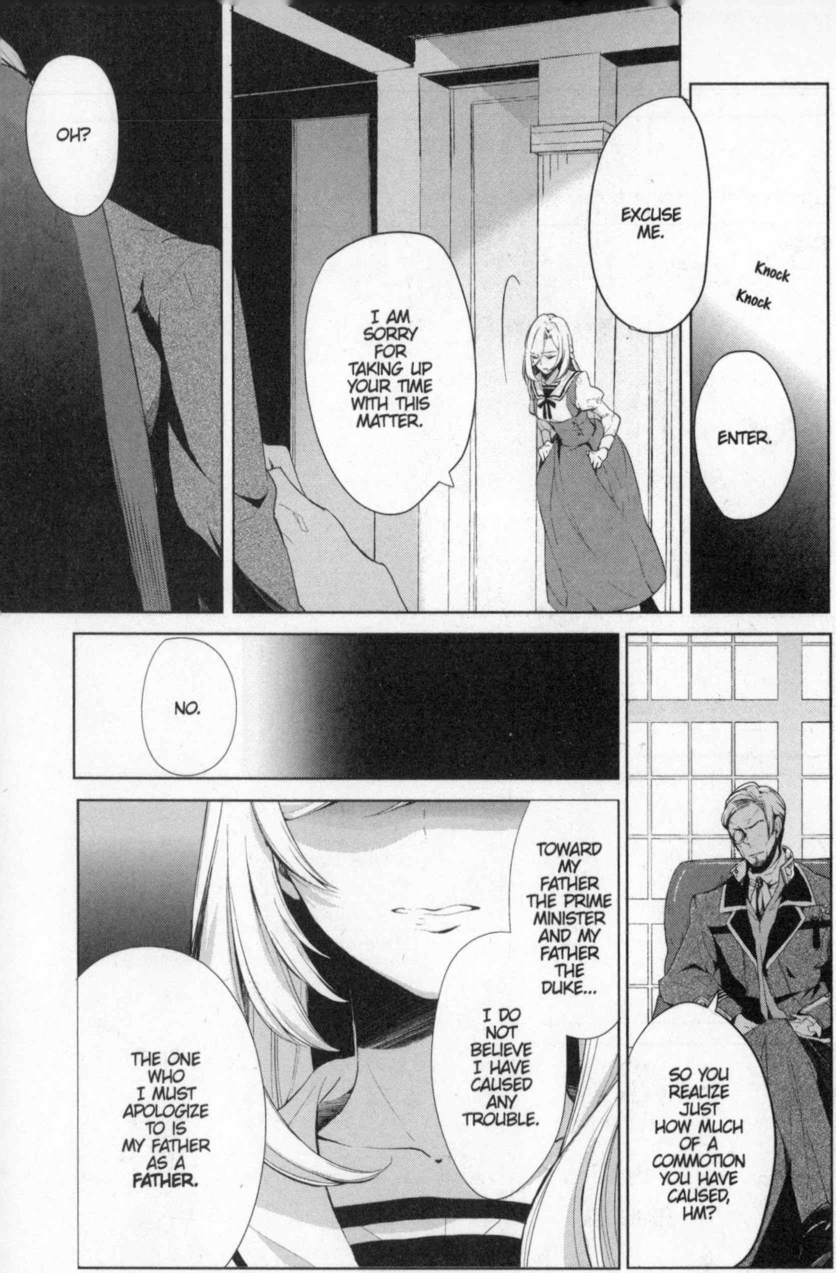
Knock
Knock
ENTER.
EXCUSE ME.
I AM SORRY FOR TAKING UP YOUR TIME WITH THIS MATTER.
OH?
SO YOU REALIZE JUST HOW MUCH OF A COMMOTION YOU HAVE CAUSED, HM?
NO.
TOWARD MY FATHER THE PRIME MINISTER AND MY FATHER THE DUKE...
I DO NOT BELIEVE I HAVE CAUSED ANY TROUBLE.
THE ONE WHO I MUST APOLOGIZE TO IS MY FATHER AS A FATHER.

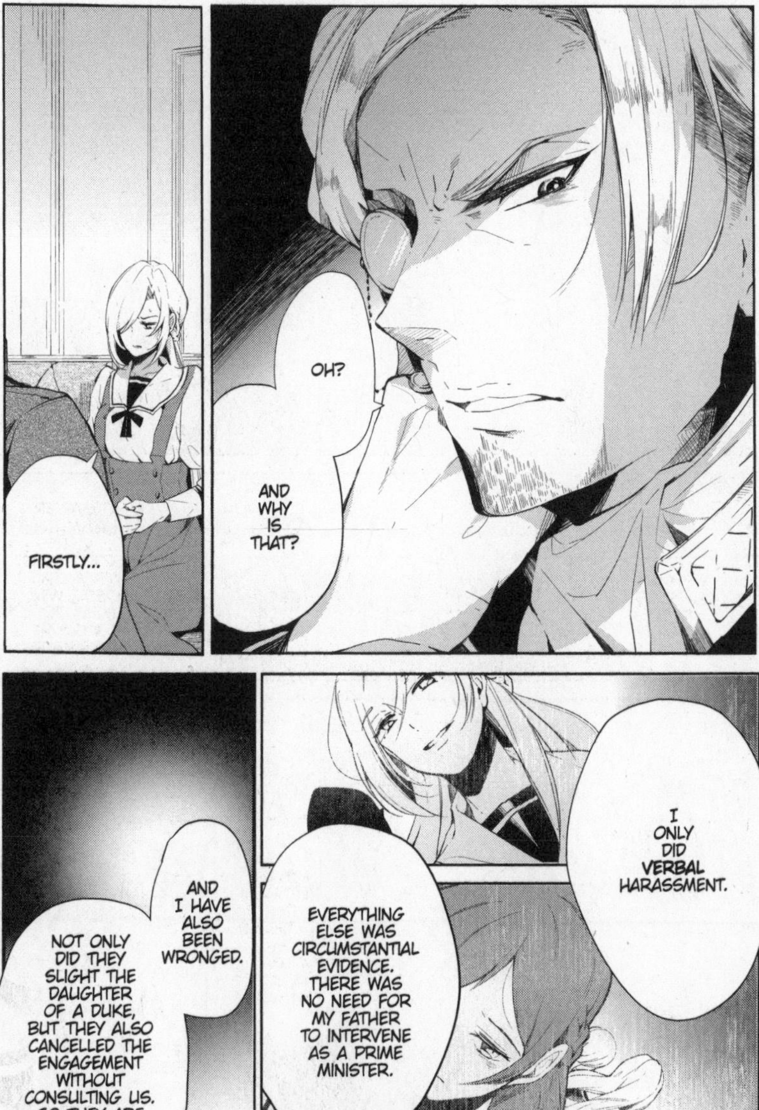
OH?
AND WHY IS THAT?
FIRSTLY...
I ONLY DID VERBAL HARASSMENT.
EVERYTHING ELSE WAS CIRCUMSTANTIAL EVIDENCE. THERE WAS NO NEED FOR MY FATHER TO INTERVENE AS A PRIME MINISTER.
AND I HAVE ALSO BEEN WRONGED.
NOT ONLY DID THEY SLIGHT THE DAUGHTER OF A DUKE, BUT THEY ALSO CANCELLED THE ENGAGEMENT WITHOUT CONSULTING US. SO THEY ARE HARDLY BLAMELESS HERE.

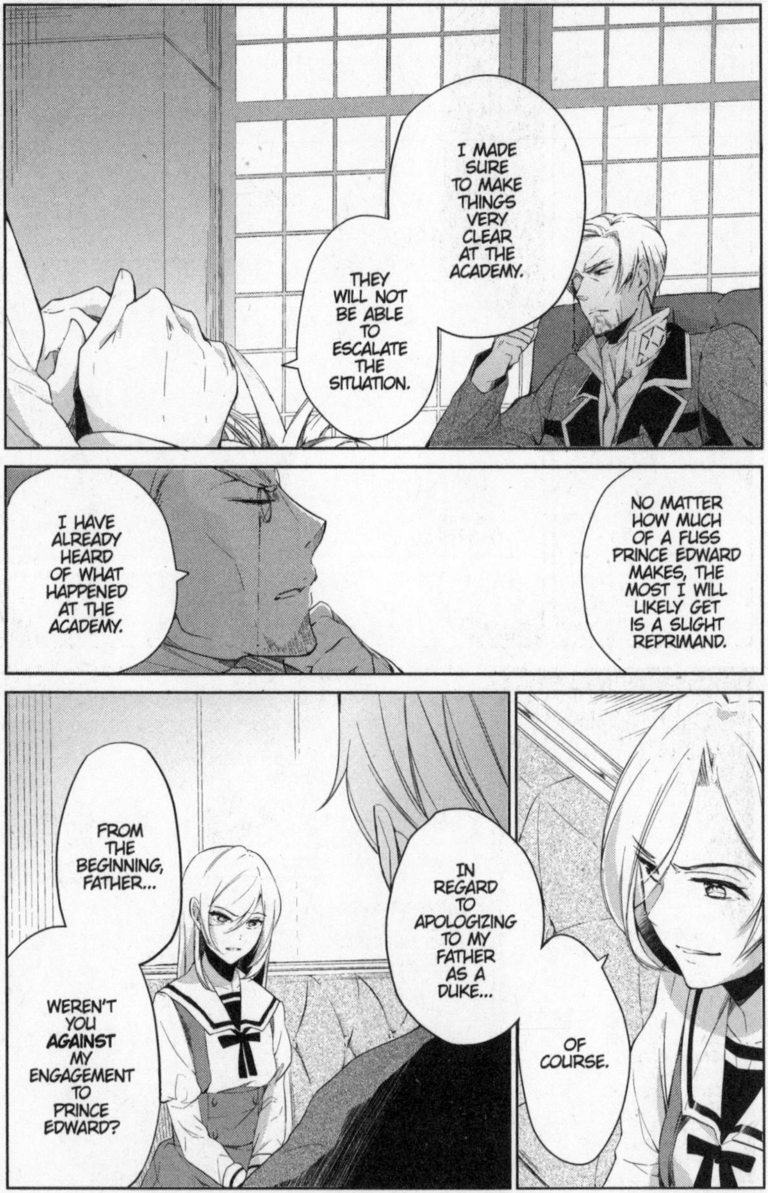
I MADE SURE TO MAKE THINGS VERY CLEAR AT THE ACADEMY.
THEY WILL NOT BE ABLE TO ESCALATE THE SITUATION.
NO MATTER HOW MUCH OF A FUSS PRINCE EDWARD MAKES, THE MOST I WILL LIKELY GET IS A SLIGHT REPRIMAND.
I HAVE ALREADY HEARD OF WHAT HAPPENED AT THE ACADEMY.
IN REGARD TO APOLOGIZING TO MY FATHER AS A DUKE...
OF COURSE.
FROM THE BEGINNING, FATHER...
WEREN'T YOU **AGAINST** MY ENGAGEMENT TO PRINCE EDWARD?

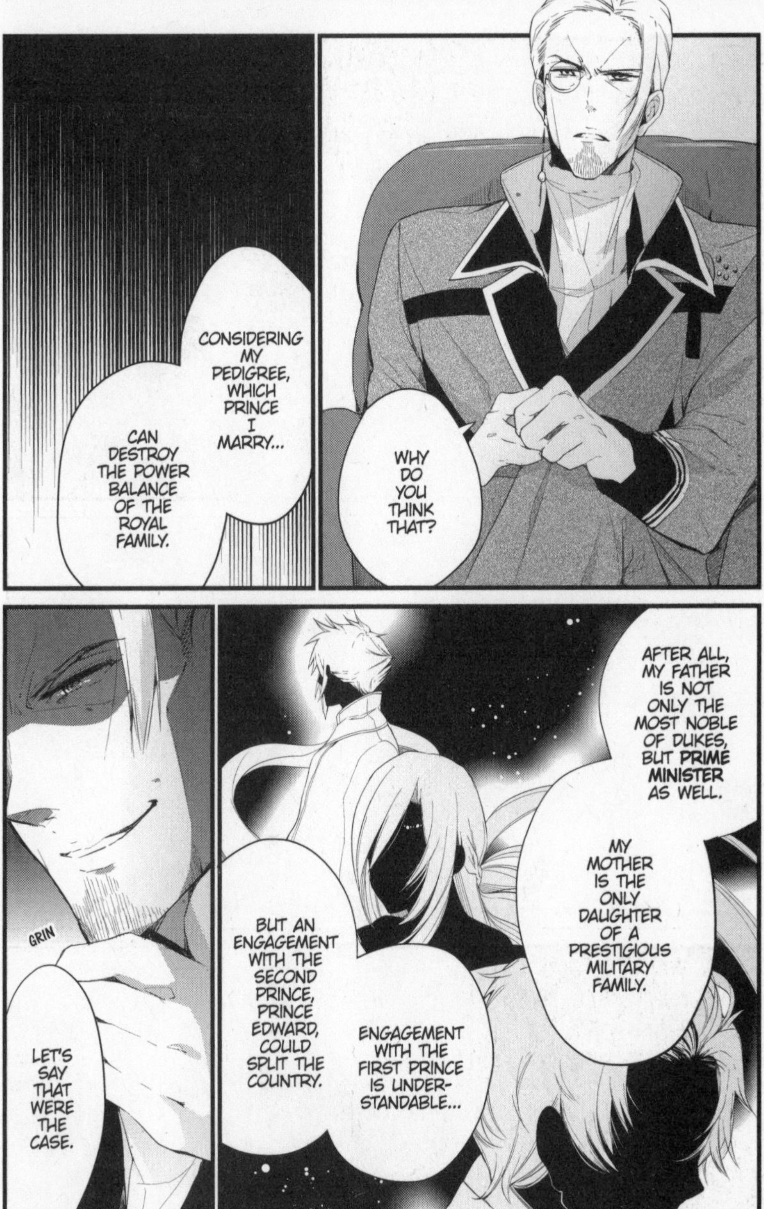
WHY DO YOU THINK THAT?
CONSIDERING MY PEDIGREE, WHICH PRINCE I MARRY...
CAN DESTROY THE POWER BALANCE OF THE ROYAL FAMILY.
AFTER ALL, MY FATHER IS NOT ONLY THE MOST NOBLE OF DUKES, BUT **PRIME MINISTER** AS WELL.
MY MOTHER IS THE ONLY DAUGHTER OF A PRESTIGIOUS MILITARY FAMILY.
ENGAGEMENT WITH THE FIRST PRINCE IS UNDER-STANDABLE...
BUT AN ENGAGEMENT WITH THE SECOND PRINCE, PRINCE EDWARD, COULD SPLIT THE COUNTRY.
GRIN
LET'S SAY THAT WERE THE CASE.

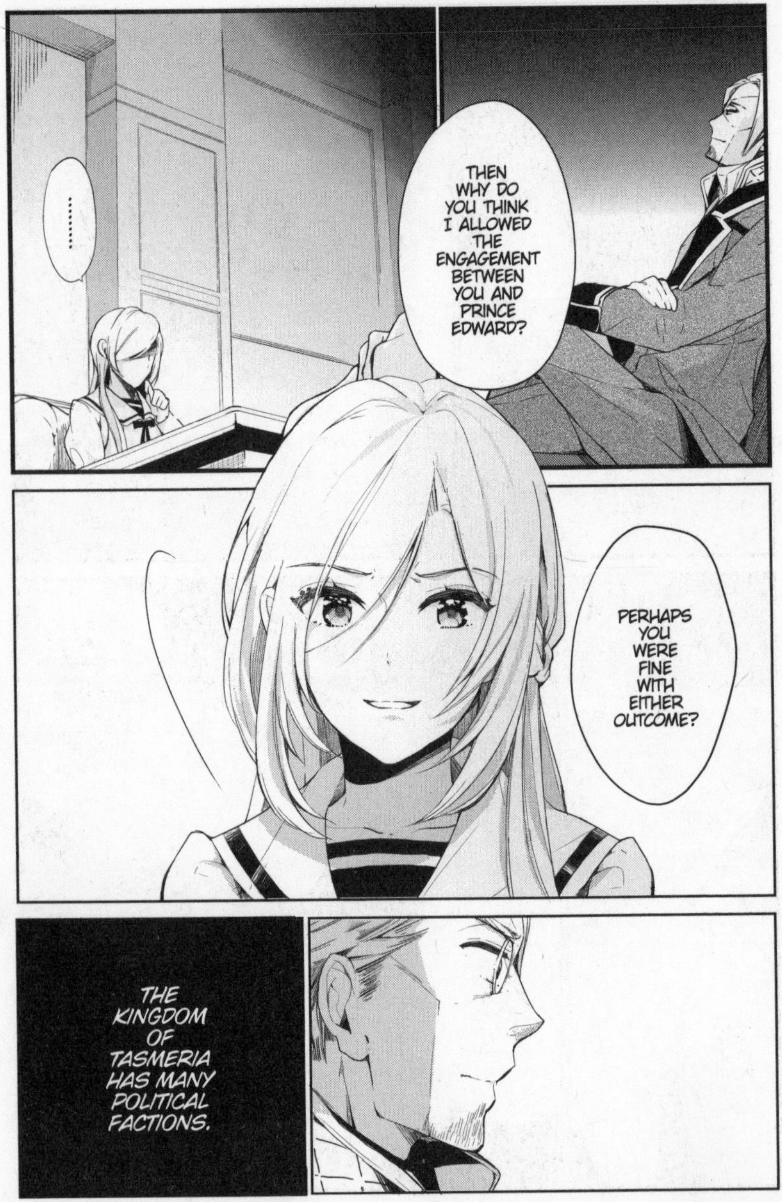
THEN WHY DO YOU THINK I ALLOWED THE ENGAGEMENT BETWEEN YOU AND PRINCE EDWARD?
......
PERHAPS YOU WERE FINE WITH EITHER OUTCOME?
THE KINGDOM OF TASMERIA HAS MANY POLITICAL FACTIONS.

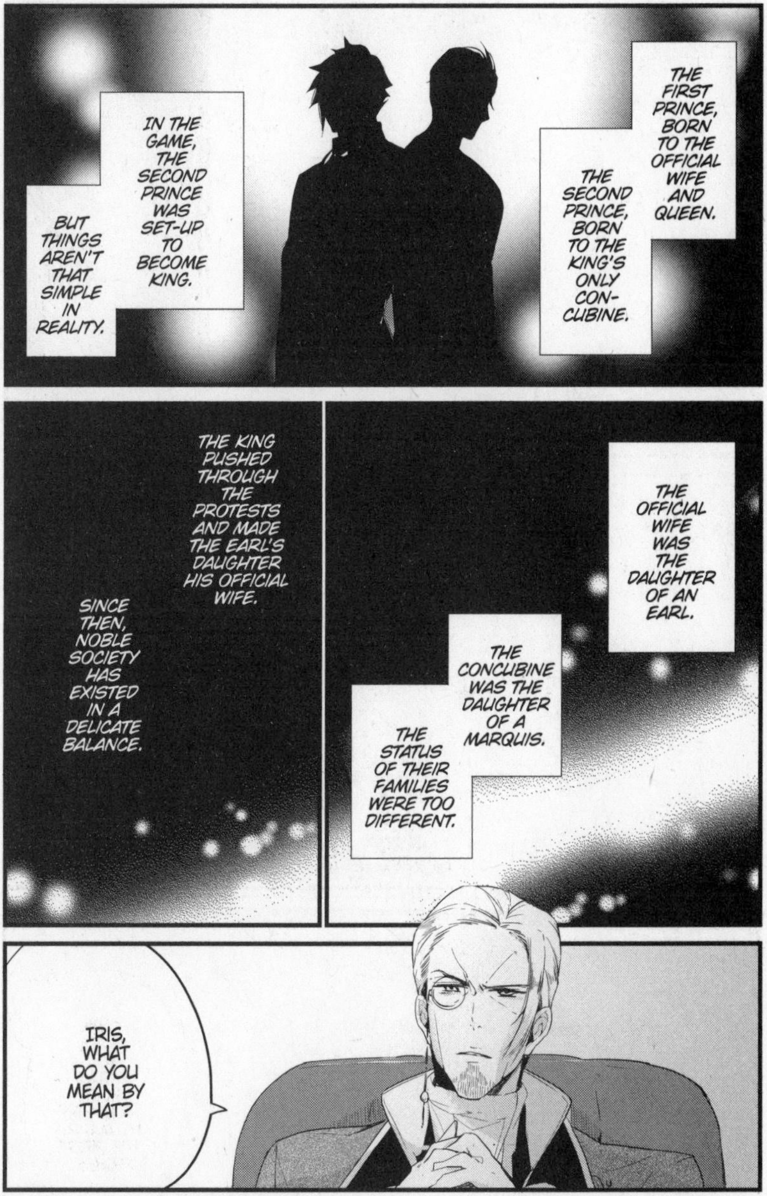
THE FIRST PRINCE, BORN TO THE OFFICIAL WIFE AND QUEEN.
THE SECOND PRINCE, BORN TO THE KING'S ONLY CON-CUBINE.
IN THE GAME, THE SECOND PRINCE WAS SET-UP TO BECOME KING.
BUT THINGS AREN'T THAT SIMPLE IN REALITY.
THE OFFICIAL WIFE WAS THE DAUGHTER OF AN EARL.
THE CONCUBINE WAS THE DAUGHTER OF A MARQUIS.
THE STATUS OF THEIR FAMILIES WERE TOO DIFFERENT.
THE KING PUSHED THROUGH THE PROTESTS AND MADE THE EARL'S DAUGHTER HIS OFFICIAL WIFE.
SINCE THEN, NOBLE SOCIETY HAS EXISTED IN A DELICATE BALANCE.
IRIS, WHAT DO YOU MEAN BY THAT?

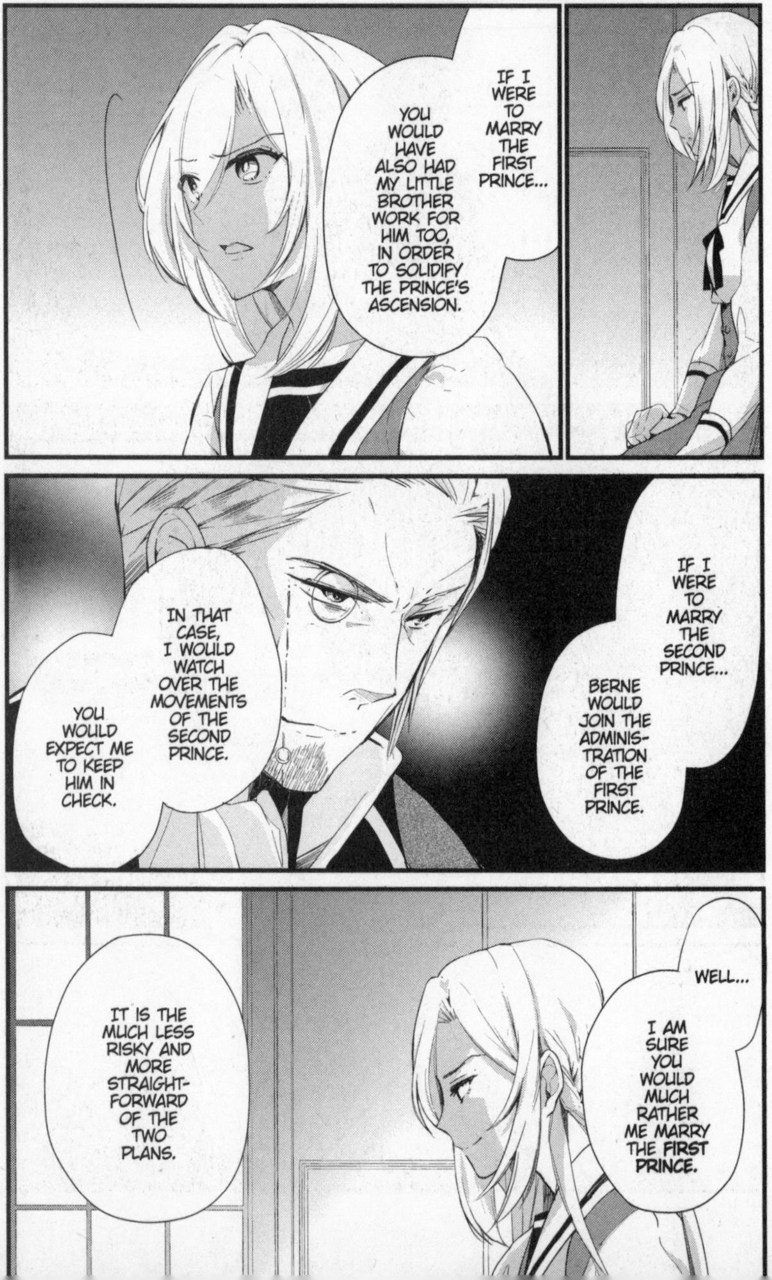
IF I WERE TO MARRY THE FIRST PRINCE...
YOU WOULD HAVE ALSO HAD MY LITTLE BROTHER WORK FOR HIM TOO, IN ORDER TO SOLIDIFY THE PRINCE'S ASCENSION.
IF I WERE TO MARRY THE SECOND PRINCE...
BERNE WOULD JOIN THE ADMINIS-TRATION OF THE FIRST PRINCE.
IN THAT CASE, I WOULD WATCH OVER THE MOVEMENTS OF THE SECOND PRINCE.
YOU WOULD EXPECT ME TO KEEP HIM IN CHECK.
WELL...
I AM SURE YOU WOULD MUCH RATHER ME MARRY THE FIRST PRINCE.
IT IS THE MUCH LESS RISKY AND MORE STRAIGHT-FORWARD OF THE TWO PLANS.

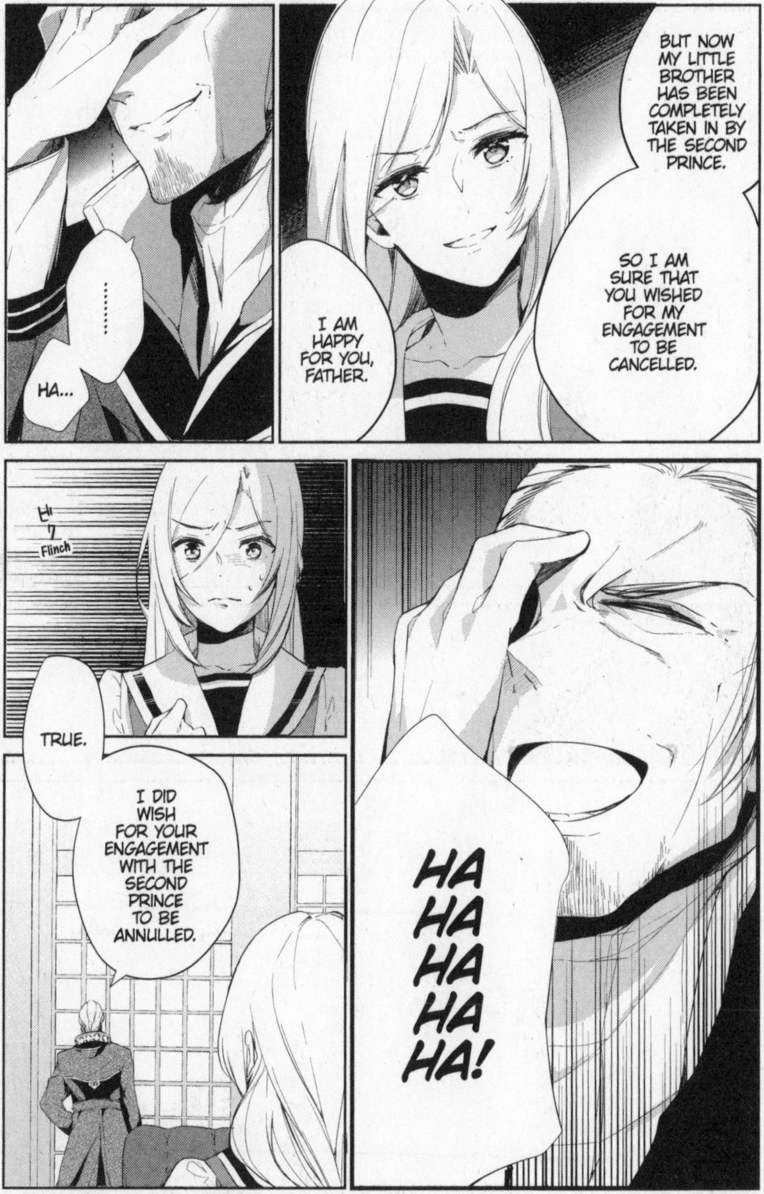

BUT NOW MY LITTLE BROTHER HAS BEEN COMPLETELY TAKEN IN BY THE SECOND PRINCE.
SO I AM SURE THAT YOU WISHED FOR MY ENGAGEMENT TO BE CANCELLED.
I AM HAPPY FOR YOU, FATHER.
......
HA...
HA HA HA HA HA!
ビク
Flinch
TRUE.
I DID WISH FOR YOUR ENGAGEMENT WITH THE SECOND PRINCE TO BE ANNULLED.

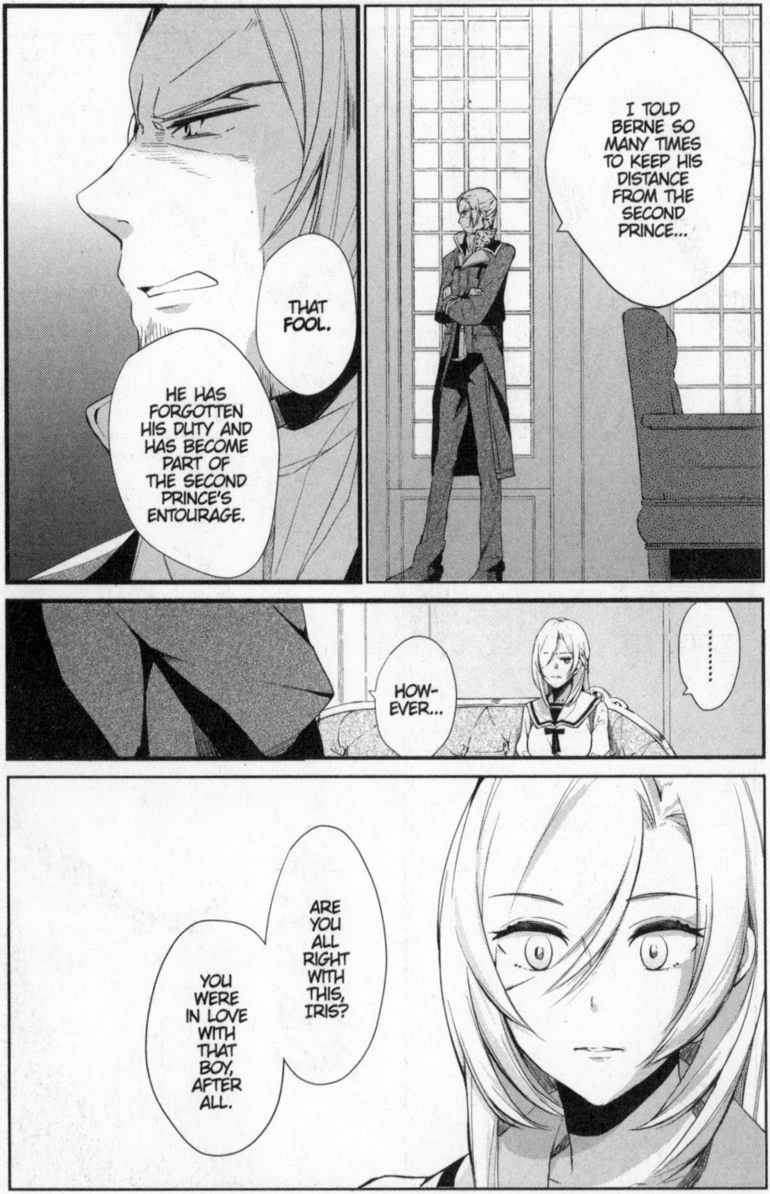
I TOLD BERNE SO MANY TIMES TO KEEP HIS DISTANCE FROM THE SECOND PRINCE...
THAT FOOL.
HE HAS FORGOTTEN HIS DUTY AND HAS BECOME PART OF THE SECOND PRINCE'S ENTOURAGE.
......
HOW-EVER...
ARE YOU ALL RIGHT WITH THIS, IRIS?
YOU WERE IN LOVE WITH THAT BOY, AFTER ALL.

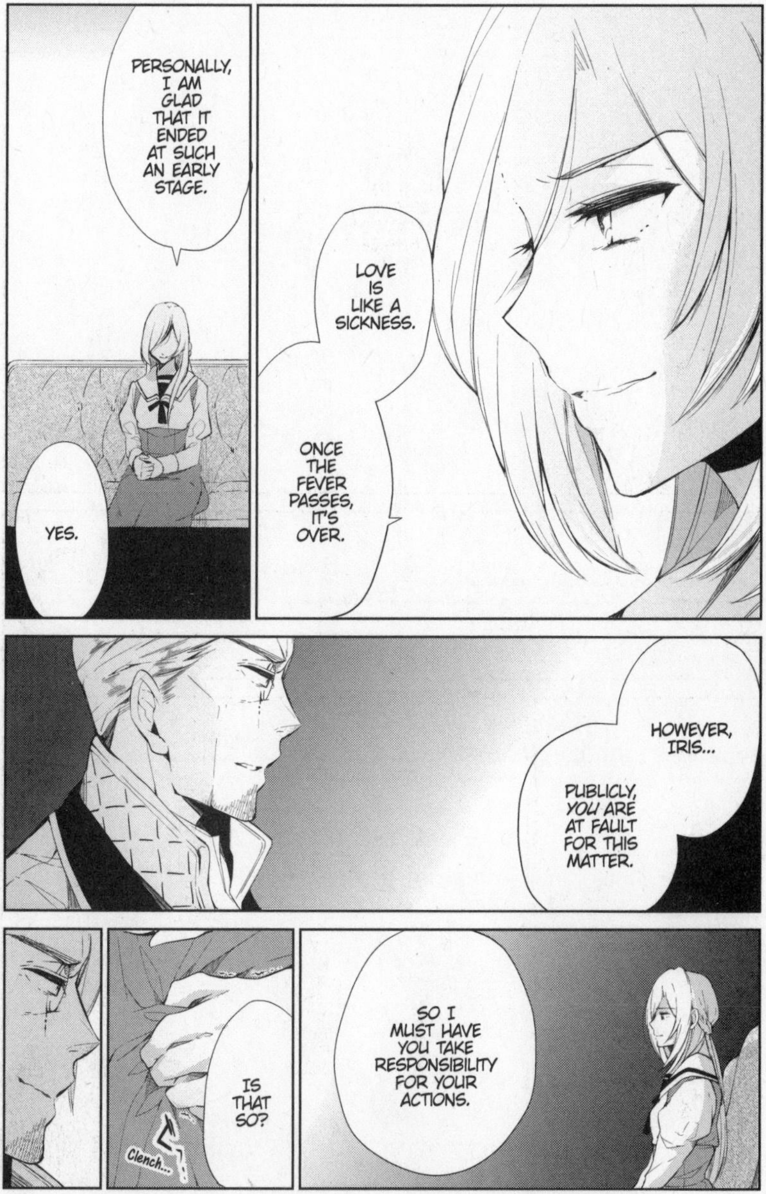
LOVE IS LIKE A SICKNESS.
ONCE THE FEVER PASSES, IT'S OVER.
PERSONALLY, I AM GLAD THAT IT ENDED AT SUCH AN EARLY STAGE.
YES.
HOWEVER, IRIS...
PUBLICLY, *YOU* ARE AT FAULT FOR THIS MATTER.
SO I MUST HAVE YOU TAKE RESPONSIBILITY FOR YOUR ACTIONS.
IS THAT SO?
Clench...

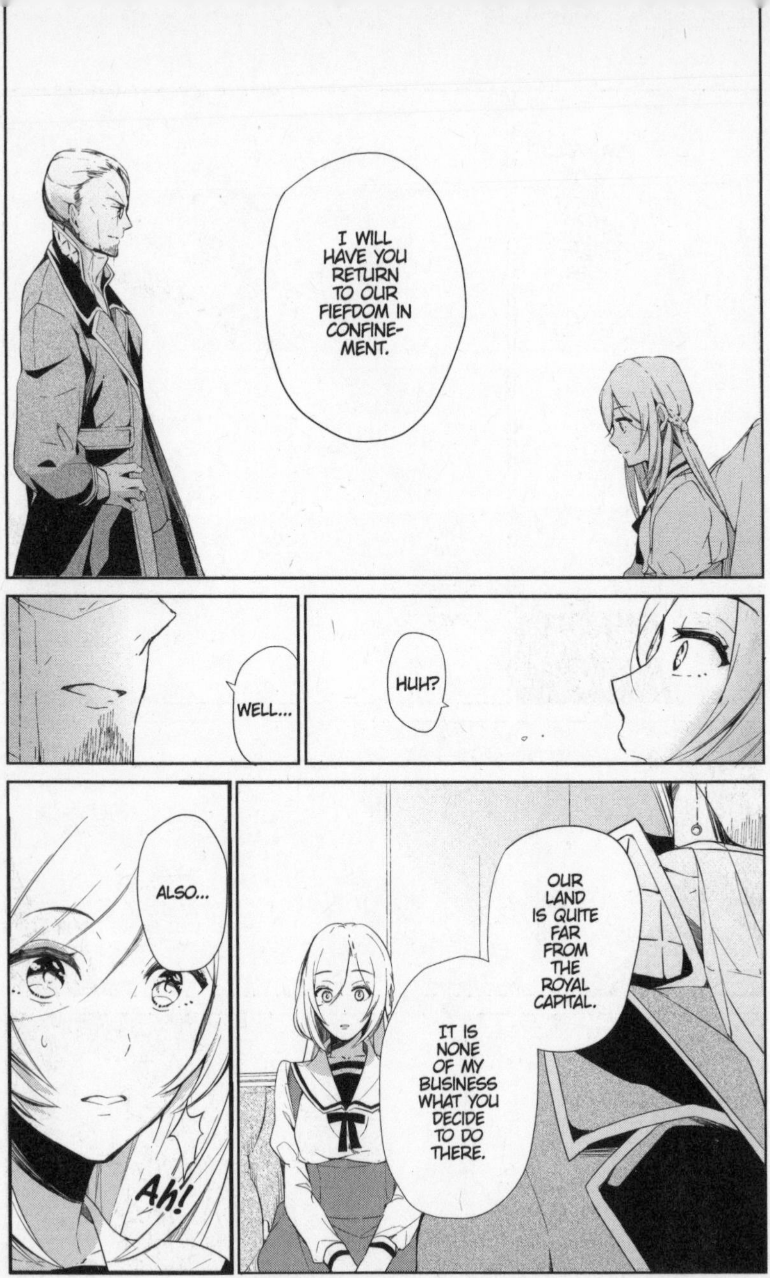
I WILL HAVE YOU RETURN TO OUR FIEFDOM IN CONFINEMENT.
HUH?
WELL...
OUR LAND IS QUITE FAR FROM THE ROYAL CAPITAL.
IT IS NONE OF MY BUSINESS WHAT YOU DECIDE TO DO THERE.
ALSO...
Ah!

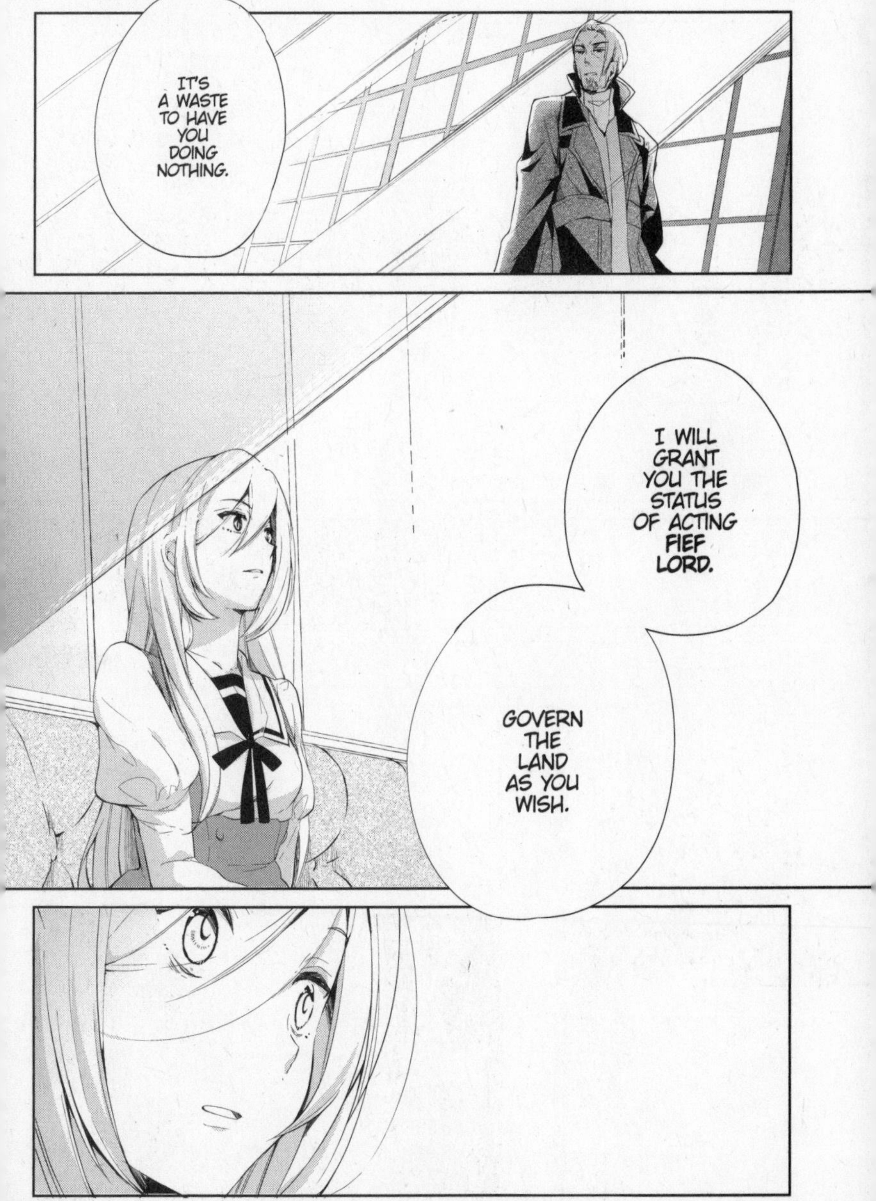
IT'S A WASTE TO HAVE YOU DOING NOTHING.
I WILL GRANT YOU THE STATUS OF ACTING FIEF LORD.
GOVERN THE LAND AS YOU WISH.

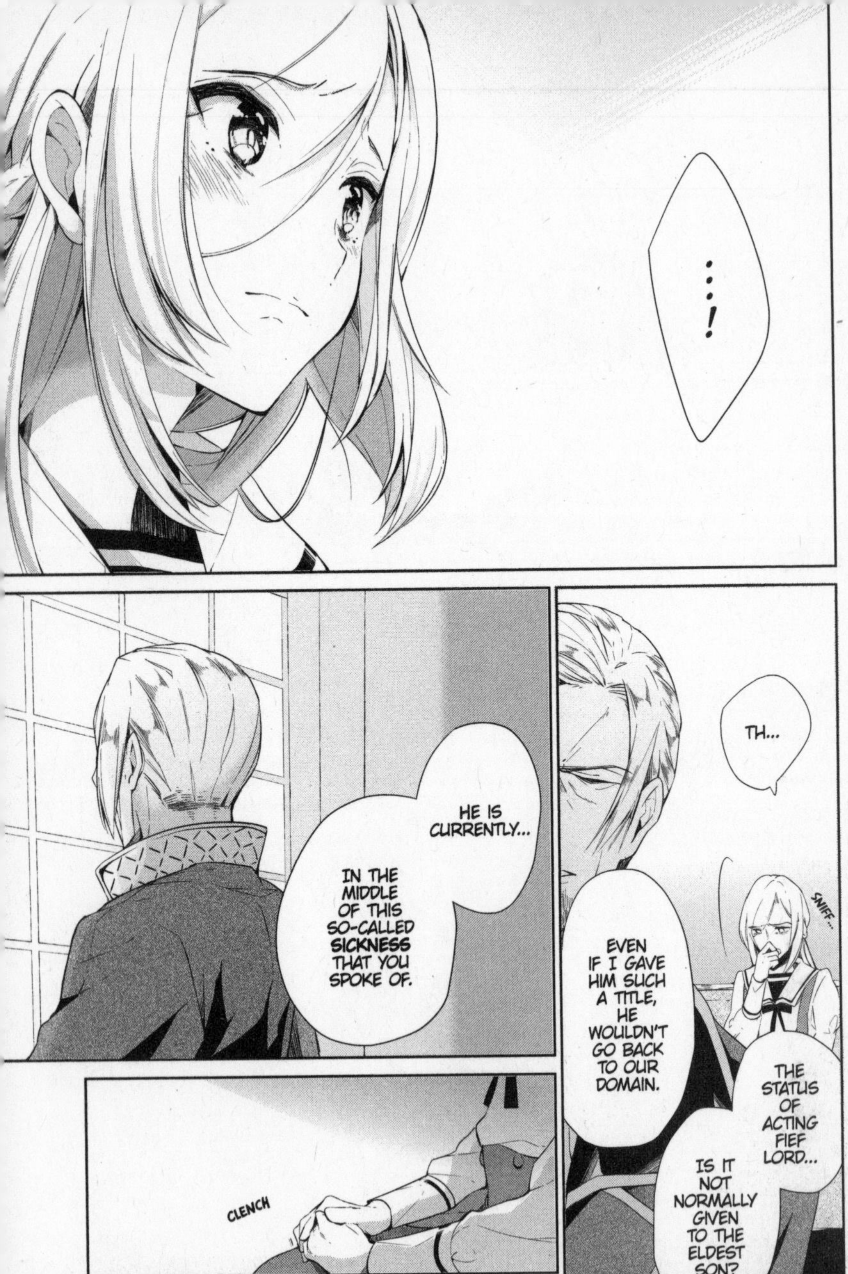
...!
TH...
SNIFF...
THE STATUS OF ACTING FIEF LORD...
IS IT NOT NORMALLY GIVEN TO THE ELDEST SON?
EVEN IF I GAVE HIM SUCH A TITLE, HE WOULDN'T GO BACK TO OUR DOMAIN.
HE IS CURRENTLY...
IN THE MIDDLE OF THIS SO-CALLED SICKNESS THAT YOU SPOKE OF.
CLENCH

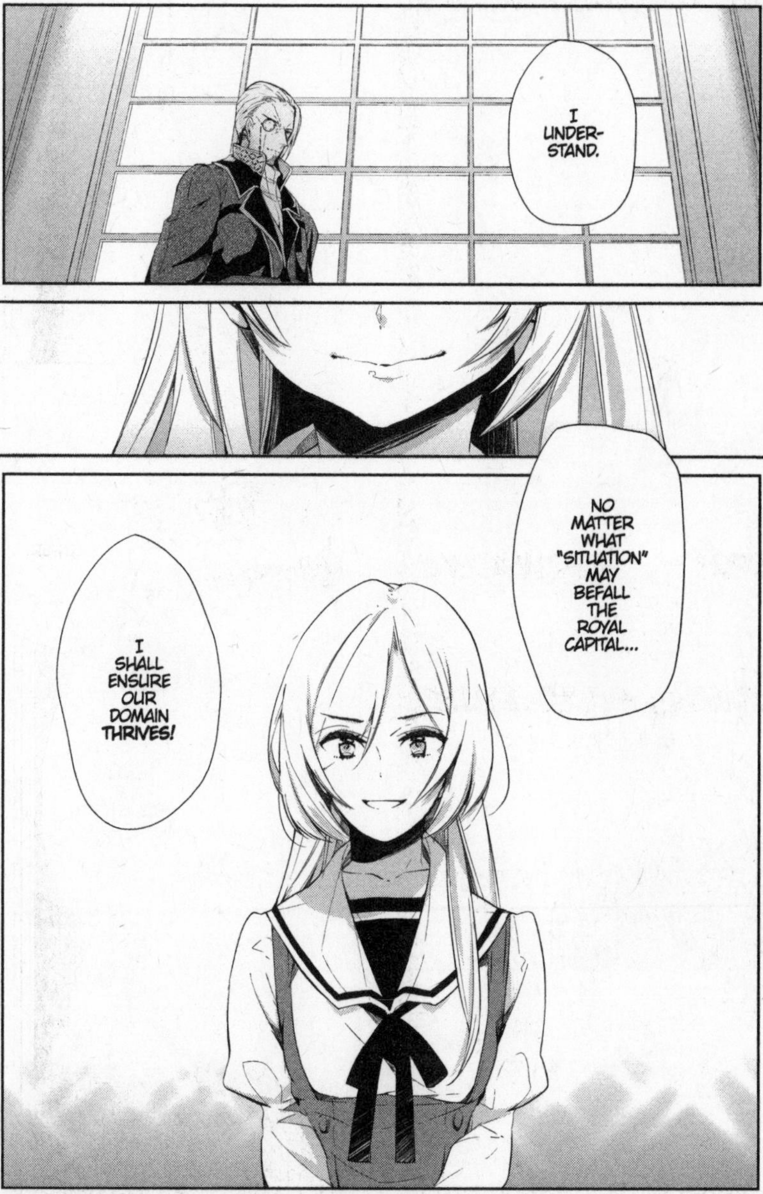
I UNDER-STAND.
NO MATTER WHAT "SITUATION" MAY BEFALL THE ROYAL CAPITAL...
I SHALL ENSURE OUR DOMAIN THRIVES!

#3 end

4

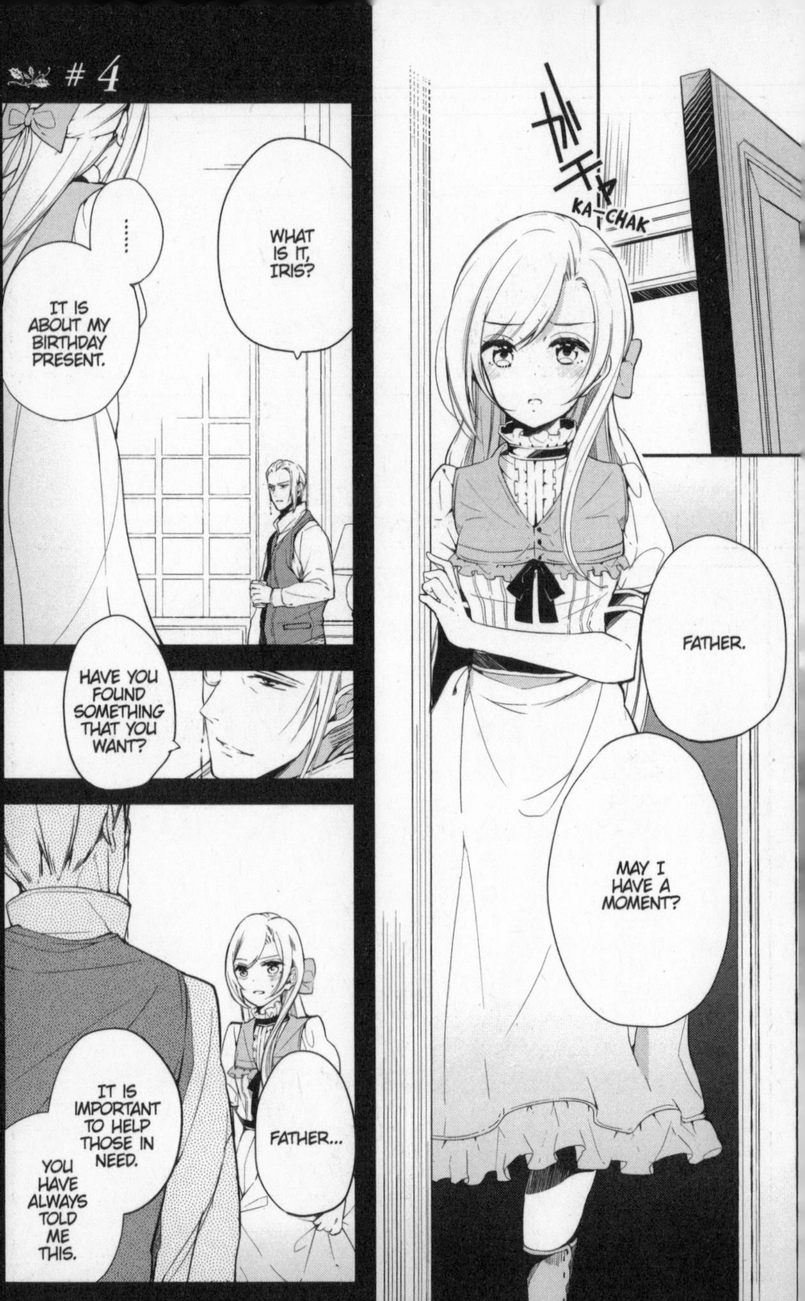
ガチャ
KA-CHAK
FATHER.
MAY I HAVE A MOMENT?
WHAT IS IT, IRIS?
......
IT IS ABOUT MY BIRTHDAY PRESENT.
HAVE YOU FOUND SOMETHING THAT YOU WANT?
FATHER...
IT IS IMPORTANT TO HELP THOSE IN NEED.
YOU HAVE ALWAYS TOLD ME THIS.

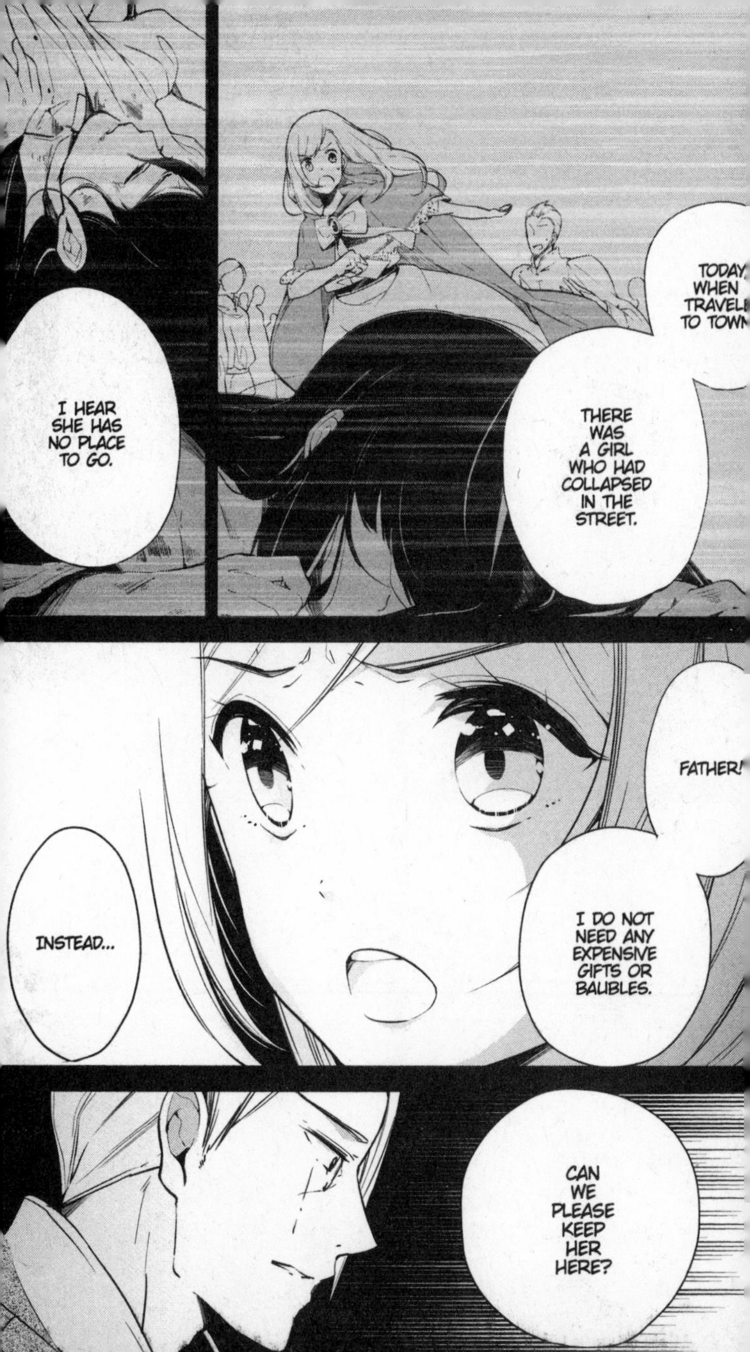
TODAY, WHEN TRAVELE TO TOWN
THERE WAS A GIRL WHO HAD COLLAPSED IN THE STREET.
I HEAR SHE HAS NO PLACE TO GO.
FATHER!
I DO NOT NEED ANY EXPENSIVE GIFTS OR BAUBLES.
INSTEAD...
CAN WE PLEASE KEEP HER HERE?

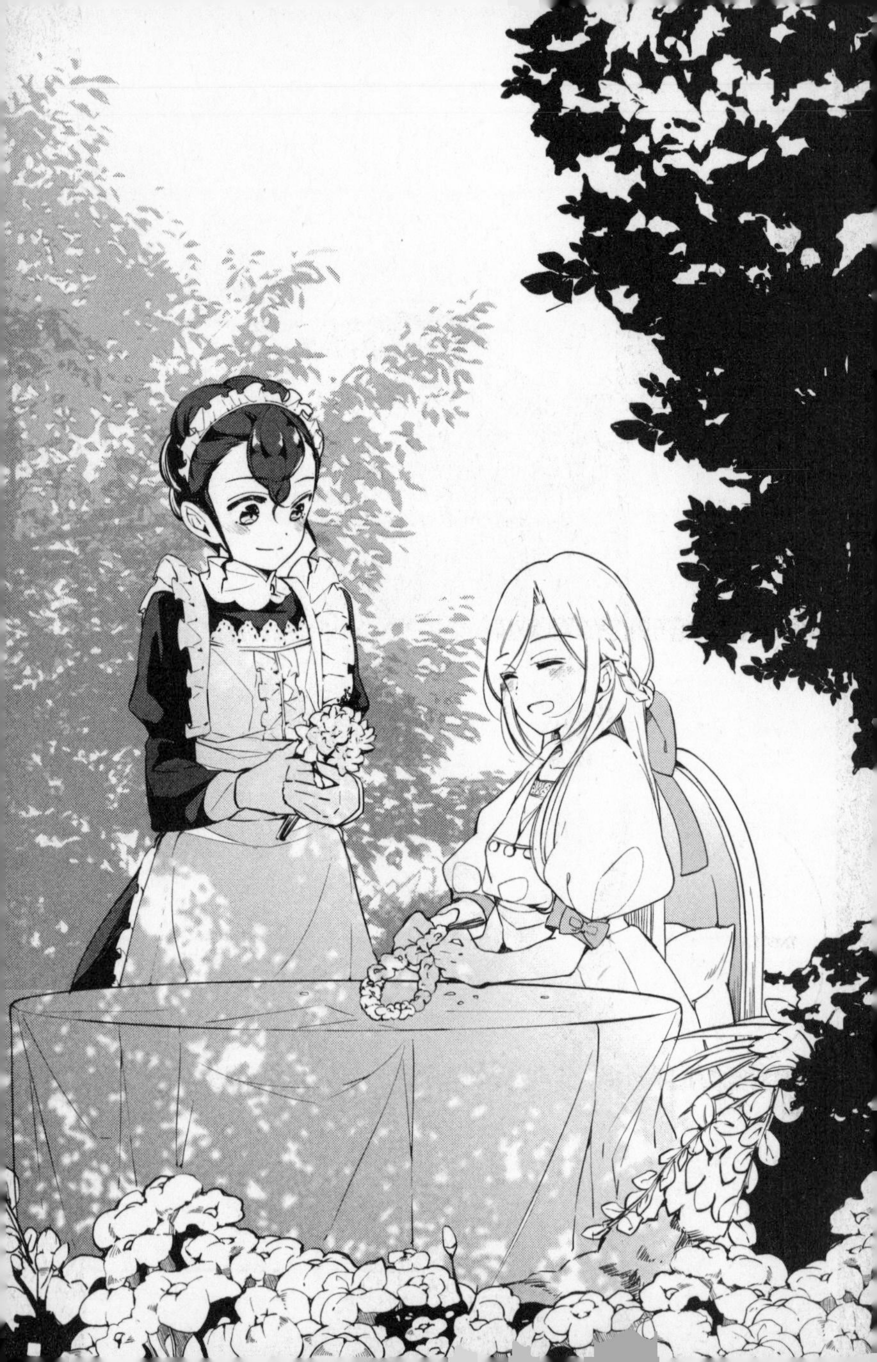

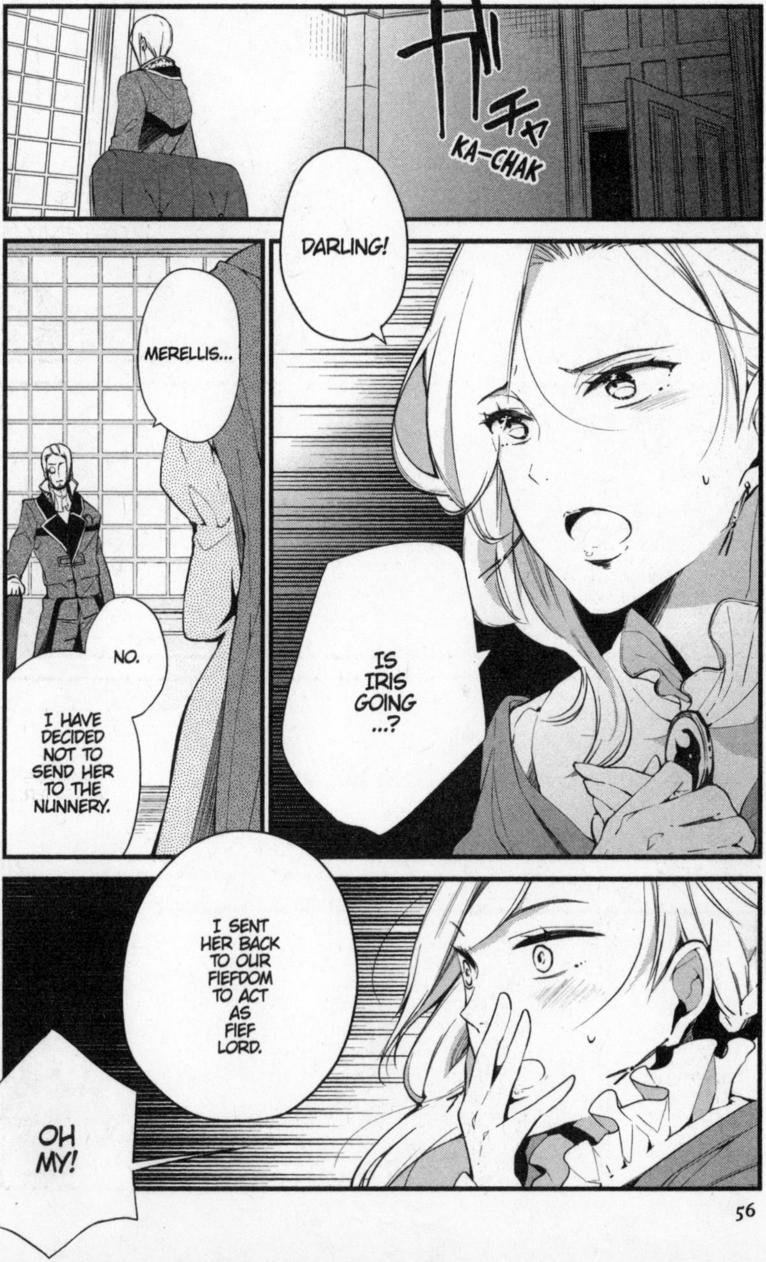
ガチャ
KA-CHAK
DARLING!
IS IRIS GOING ...?
MERELLIS...
NO.
I HAVE DECIDED NOT TO SEND HER TO THE NUNNERY.
I SENT HER BACK TO OUR FIEFDOM TO ACT AS FIEF LORD.
OH MY!

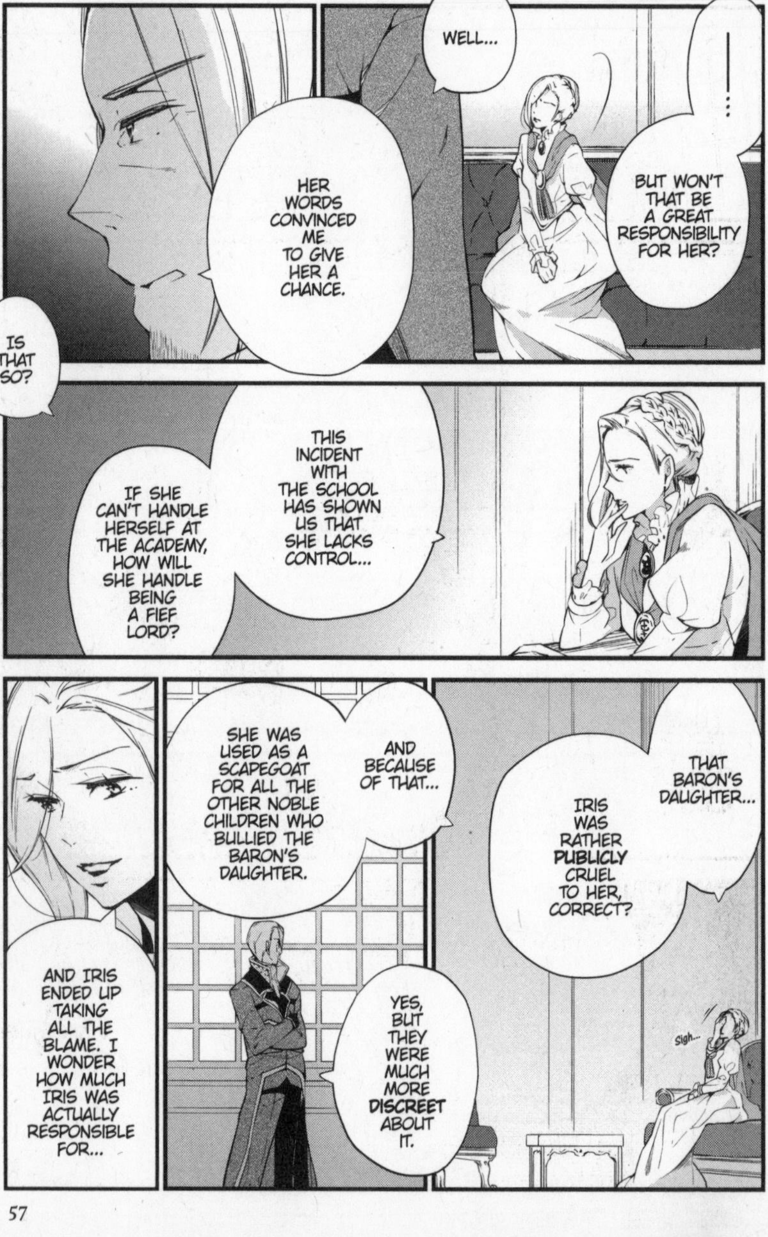
……!
BUT WON'T THAT BE A GREAT RESPONSIBILITY FOR HER?
WELL...
HER WORDS CONVINCED ME TO GIVE HER A CHANCE.
IS THAT SO?
THIS INCIDENT WITH THE SCHOOL HAS SHOWN US THAT SHE LACKS CONTROL...
IF SHE CAN'T HANDLE HERSELF AT THE ACADEMY, HOW WILL SHE HANDLE BEING A FIEF LORD?
THAT BARON'S DAUGHTER...
IRIS WAS RATHER **PUBLICLY** CRUEL TO HER, CORRECT?
Sigh...
YES, BUT THEY WERE MUCH MORE **DISCREET** ABOUT IT.
AND BECAUSE OF THAT...
SHE WAS USED AS A SCAPEGOAT FOR ALL THE OTHER NOBLE CHILDREN WHO BULLIED THE BARON'S DAUGHTER.
AND IRIS ENDED UP TAKING ALL THE BLAME. I WONDER HOW MUCH IRIS WAS ACTUALLY RESPONSIBLE FOR...

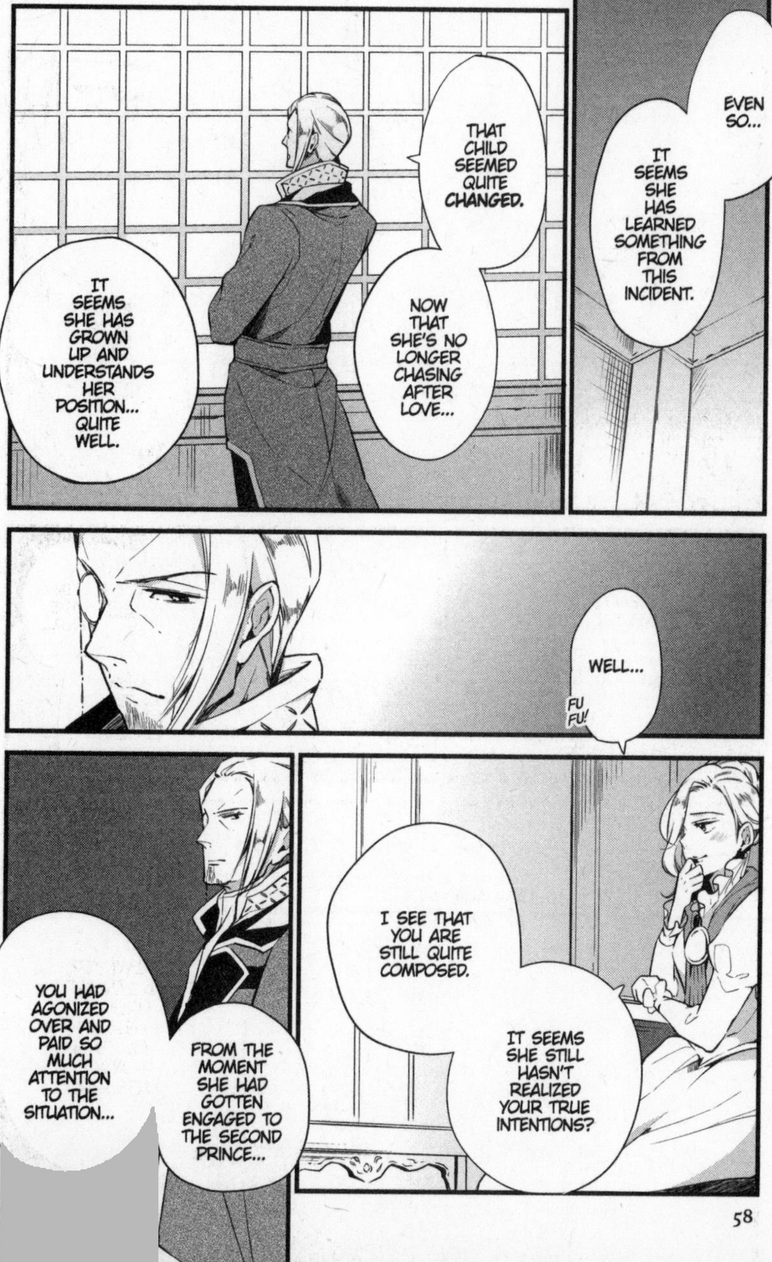
EVEN SO...
IT SEEMS SHE HAS LEARNED SOMETHING FROM THIS INCIDENT.
THAT CHILD SEEMED QUITE CHANGED.
NOW THAT SHE'S NO LONGER CHASING AFTER LOVE...
IT SEEMS SHE HAS GROWN UP AND UNDERSTANDS HER POSITION... QUITE WELL.
WELL...
FU FU!
I SEE THAT YOU ARE STILL QUITE COMPOSED.
IT SEEMS SHE STILL HASN'T REALIZED YOUR TRUE INTENTIONS?
YOU HAD AGONIZED OVER AND PAID SO MUCH ATTENTION TO THE SITUATION...
FROM THE MOMENT SHE HAD GOTTEN ENGAGED TO THE SECOND PRINCE...

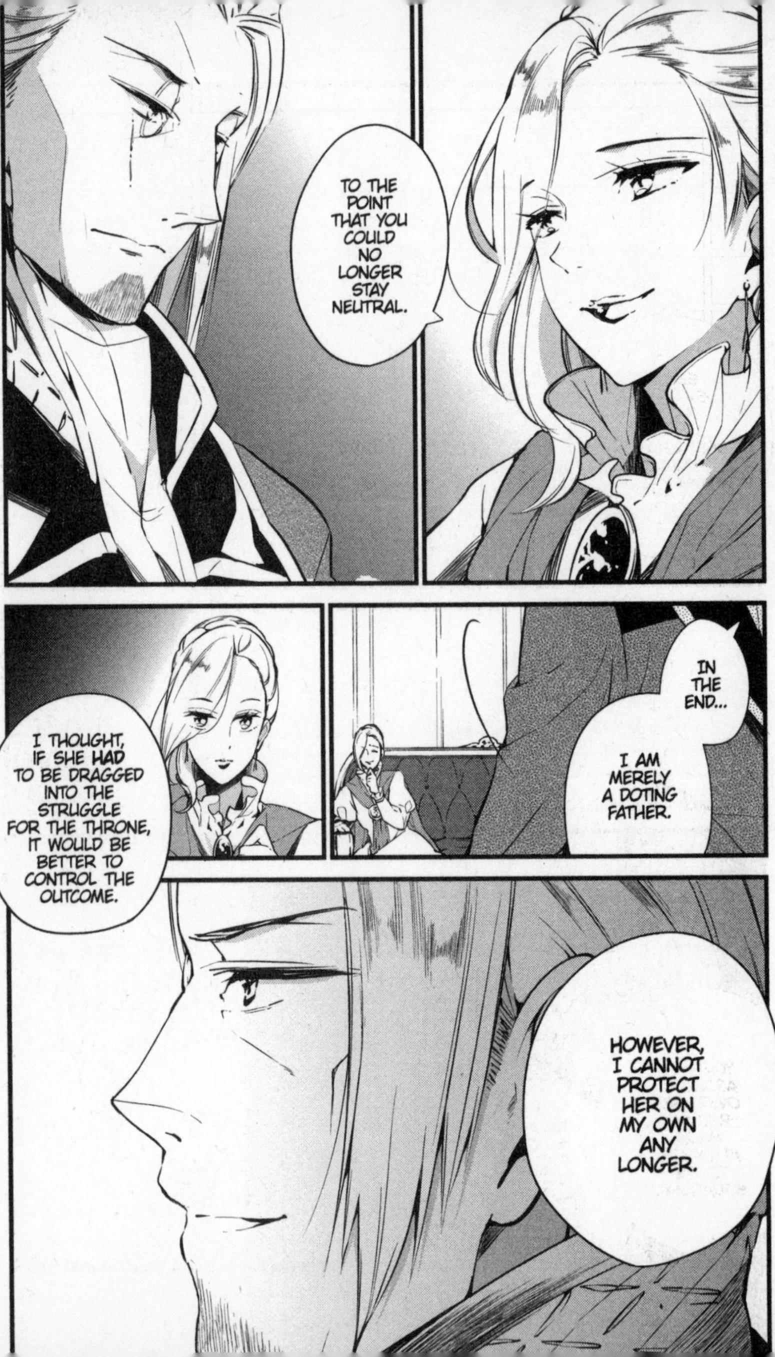
TO THE POINT THAT YOU COULD NO LONGER STAY NEUTRAL.
IN THE END...
I AM MERELY A DOTING FATHER.
I THOUGHT, IF SHE HAD TO BE DRAGGED INTO THE STRUGGLE FOR THE THRONE, IT WOULD BE BETTER TO CONTROL THE OUTCOME.
HOWEVER, I CANNOT PROTECT HER ON MY OWN ANY LONGER.

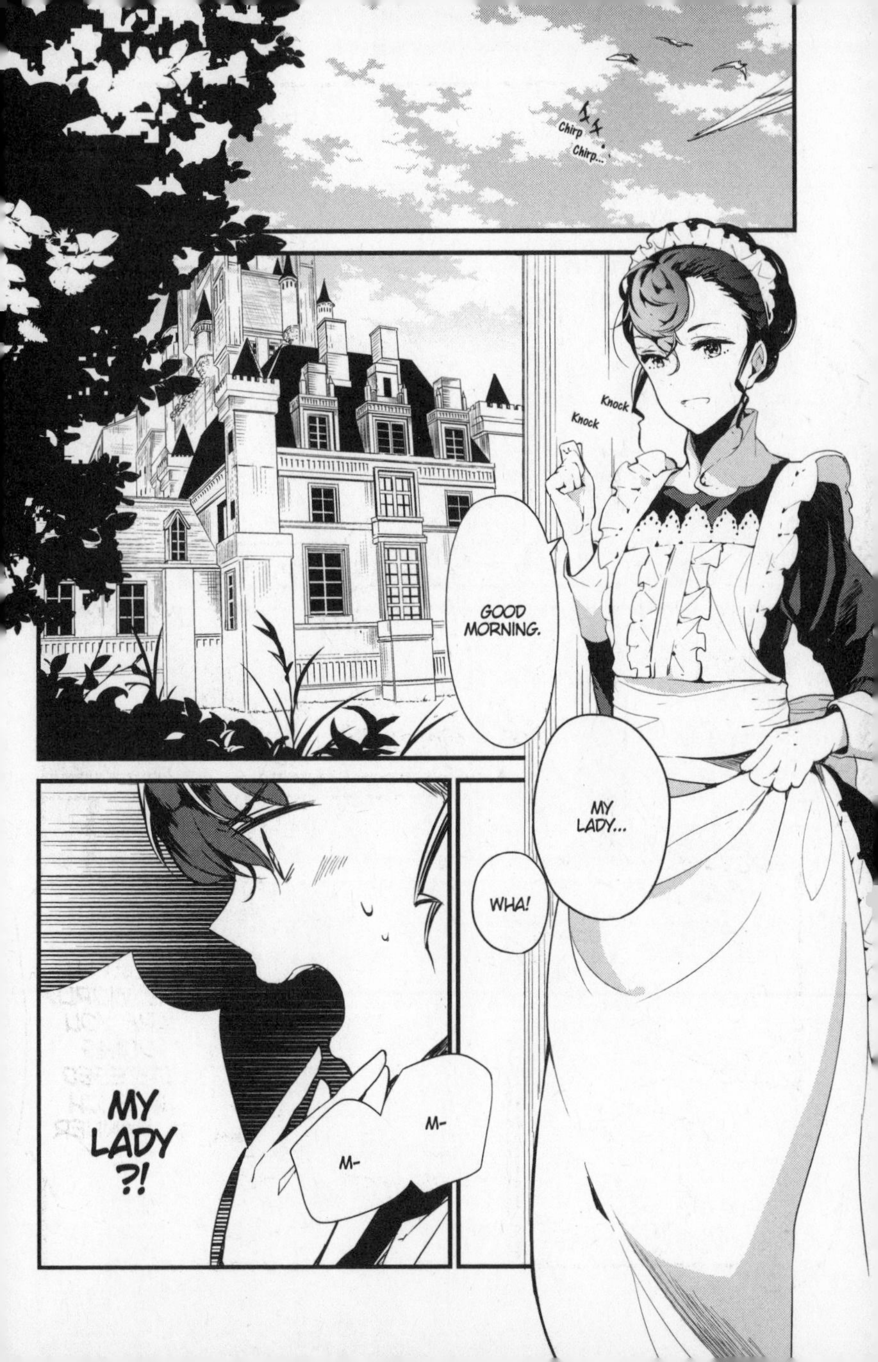
Chirp
Chirp...
Knock
Knock
GOOD MORNING.
MY LADY...
WHA!
M-
M-
MY LADY ?!

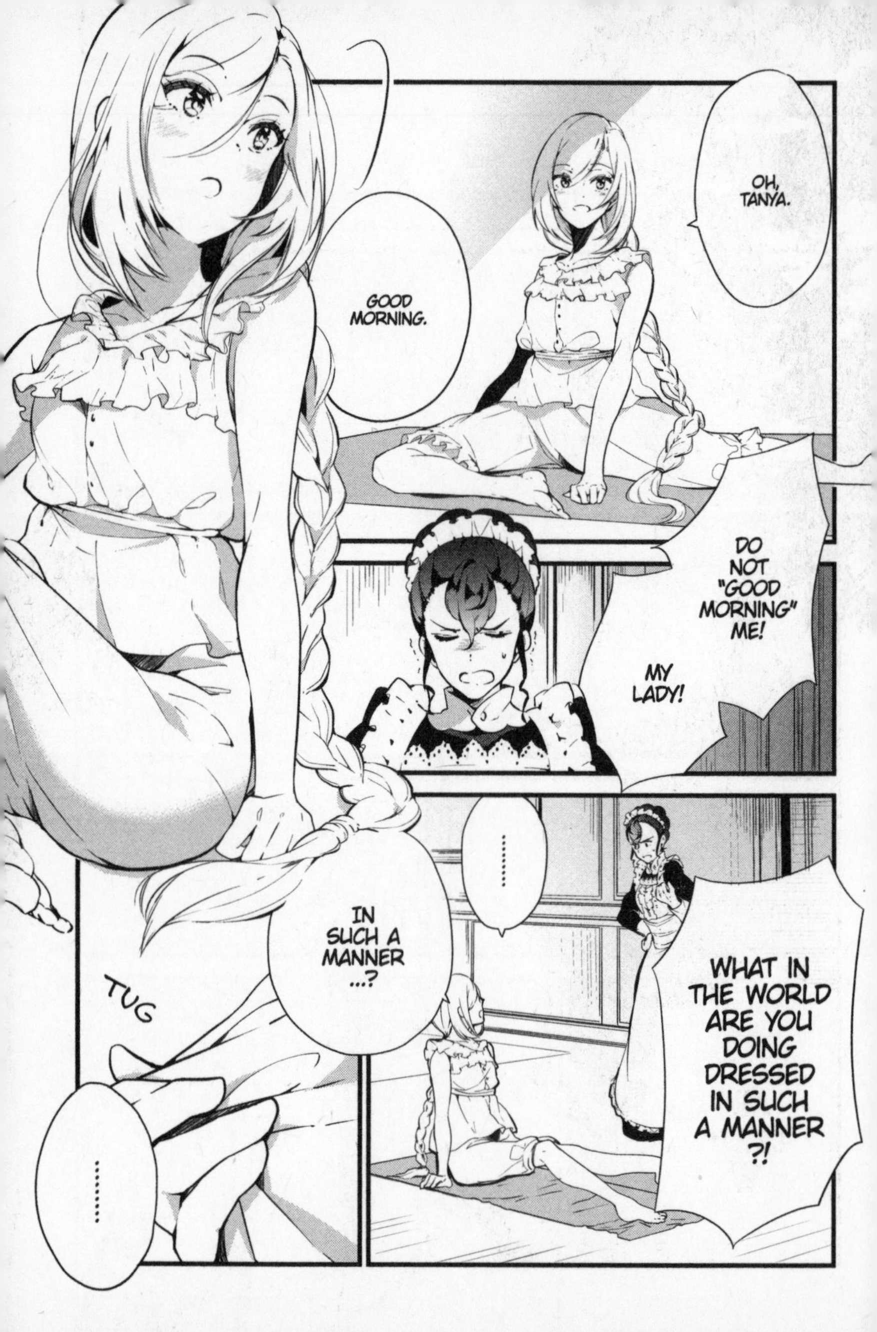
OH, TANYA.
GOOD MORNING.
DO NOT "GOOD MORNING" ME!
MY LADY!
WHAT IN THE WORLD ARE YOU DOING DRESSED IN SUCH A MANNER?!
......
IN SUCH A MANNER...?
TUG
....

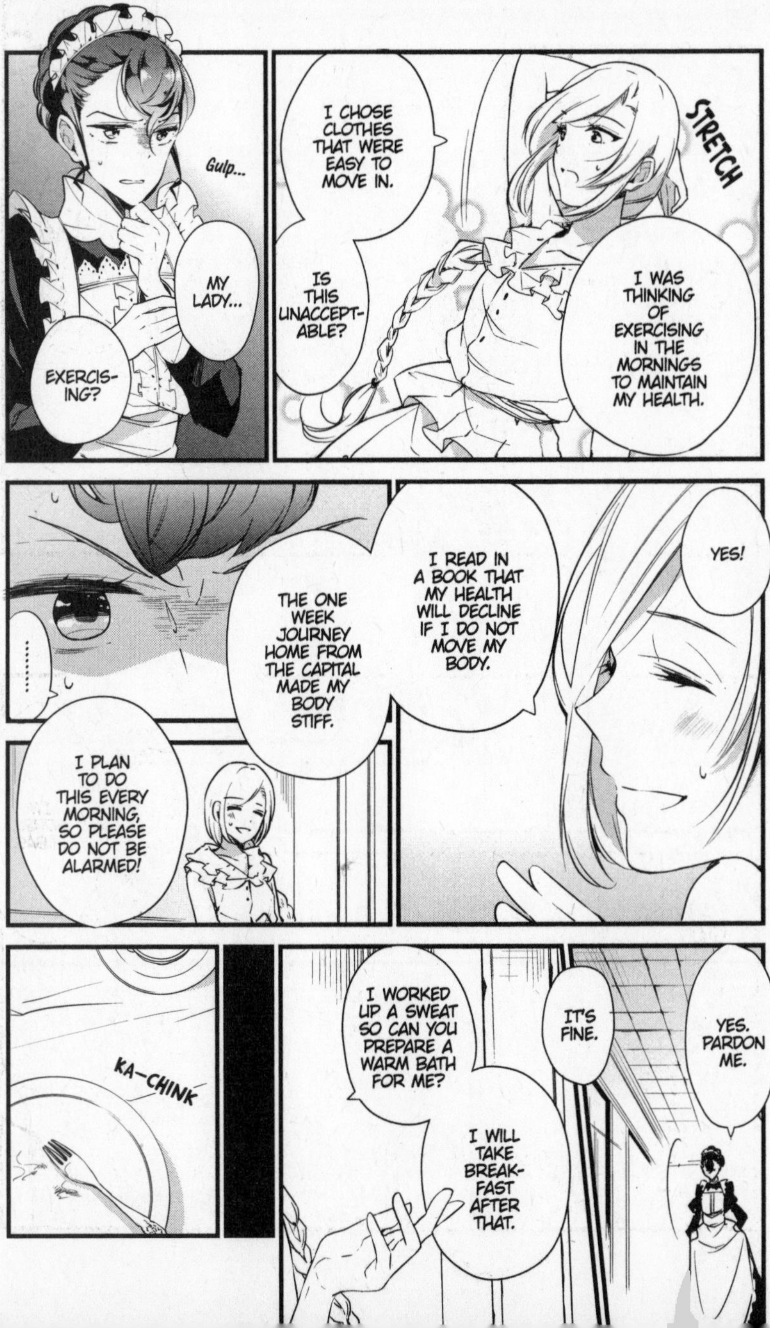

STRETCH
I CHOSE CLOTHES THAT WERE EASY TO MOVE IN.
IS THIS UNACCEPTABLE?
I WAS THINKING OF EXERCISING IN THE MORNINGS TO MAINTAIN MY HEALTH.
Gulp...
MY LADY...
EXERCISING?
YES!
I READ IN A BOOK THAT MY HEALTH WILL DECLINE IF I DO NOT MOVE MY BODY.
THE ONE WEEK JOURNEY HOME FROM THE CAPITAL MADE MY BODY STIFF.
......
I PLAN TO DO THIS EVERY MORNING, SO PLEASE DO NOT BE ALARMED!
YES. PARDON ME.
IT'S FINE.
I WORKED UP A SWEAT SO CAN YOU PREPARE A WARM BATH FOR ME?
I WILL TAKE BREAKFAST AFTER THAT.
KA-CHINK

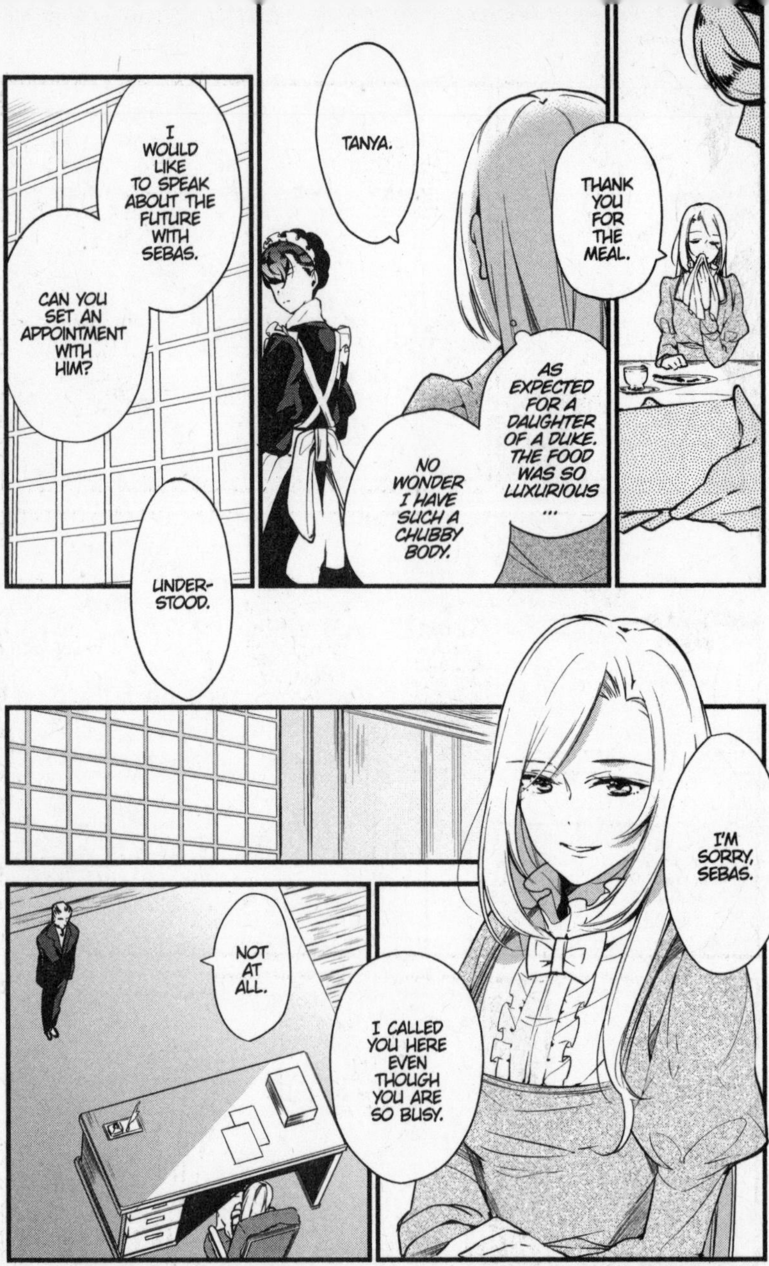
THANK YOU FOR THE MEAL.
AS EXPECTED FOR A DAUGHTER OF A DUKE. THE FOOD WAS SO LUXURIOUS ...
NO WONDER I HAVE SUCH A CHUBBY BODY.
TANYA.
I WOULD LIKE TO SPEAK ABOUT THE FUTURE WITH SEBAS.
CAN YOU SET AN APPOINTMENT WITH HIM?
UNDER-STOOD.
I'M SORRY, SEBAS.
I CALLED YOU HERE EVEN THOUGH YOU ARE SO BUSY.
NOT AT ALL.

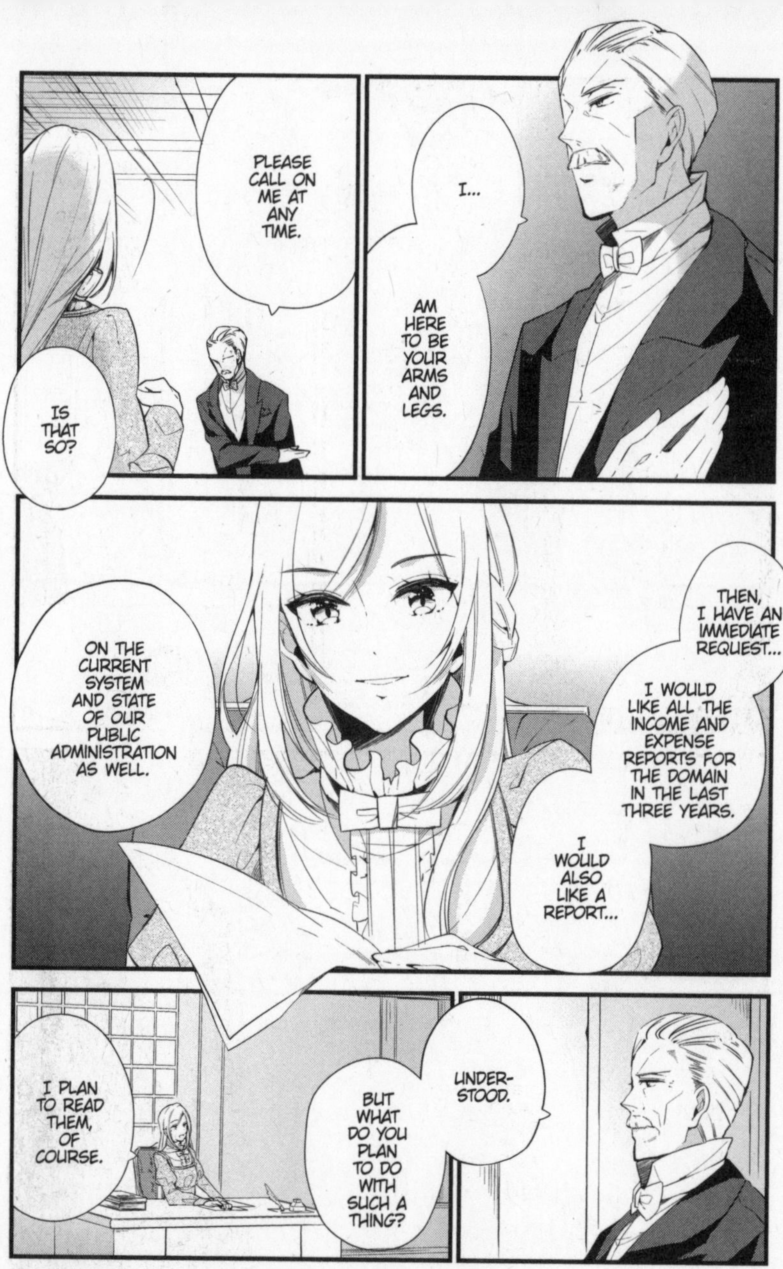
I...
AM HERE TO BE YOUR ARMS AND LEGS.
PLEASE CALL ON ME AT ANY TIME.
IS THAT SO?
THEN, I HAVE AN IMMEDIATE REQUEST...
I WOULD LIKE ALL THE INCOME AND EXPENSE REPORTS FOR THE DOMAIN IN THE LAST THREE YEARS.
I WOULD ALSO LIKE A REPORT...
ON THE CURRENT SYSTEM AND STATE OF OUR PUBLIC ADMINISTRATION AS WELL.
UNDER-STOOD.
BUT WHAT DO YOU PLAN TO DO WITH SUCH A THING?
I PLAN TO READ THEM, OF COURSE.

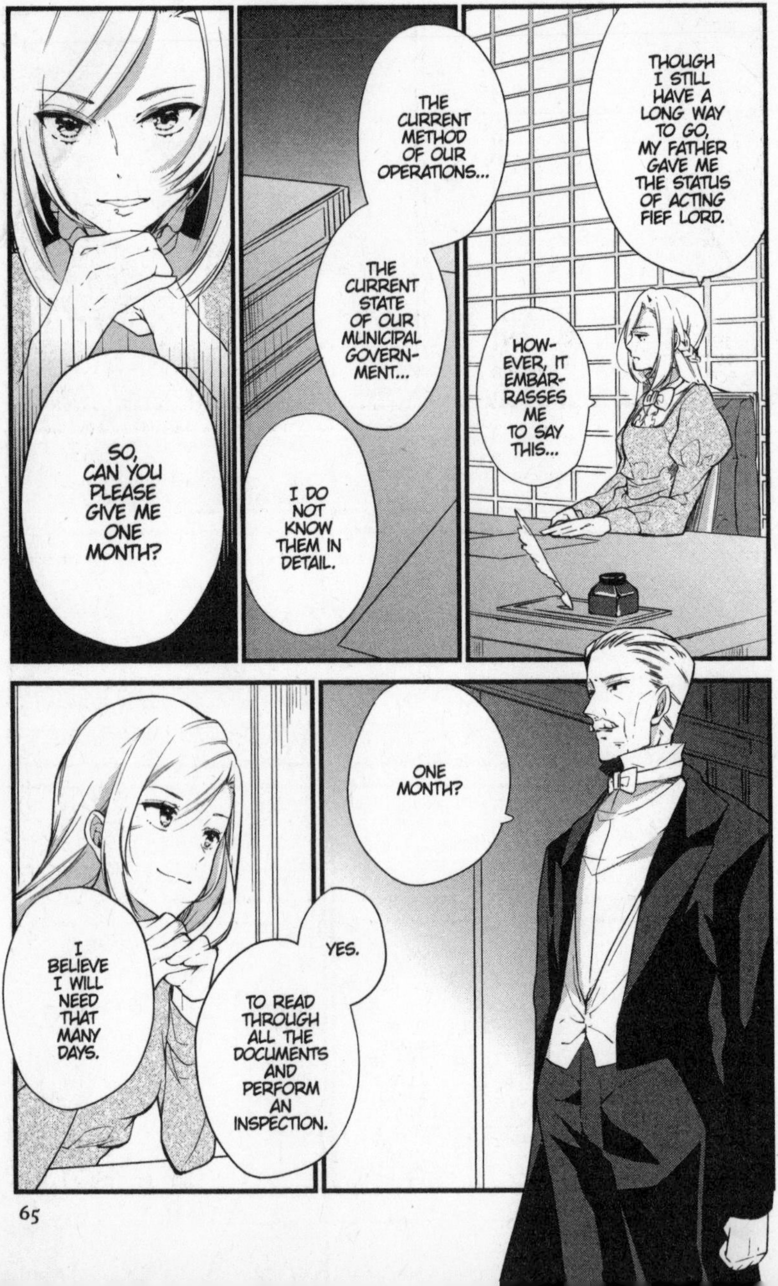
THOUGH I STILL HAVE A LONG WAY TO GO, MY FATHER GAVE ME THE STATUS OF ACTING FIEF LORD.
HOW-EVER, IT EMBAR-RASSES ME TO SAY THIS...
THE CURRENT METHOD OF OUR OPERATIONS...
THE CURRENT STATE OF OUR MUNICIPAL GOVERN-MENT...
I DO NOT KNOW THEM IN DETAIL.
SO, CAN YOU PLEASE GIVE ME ONE MONTH?
ONE MONTH?
YES.
TO READ THROUGH ALL THE DOCUMENTS AND PERFORM AN INSPECTION.
I BELIEVE I WILL NEED THAT MANY DAYS.

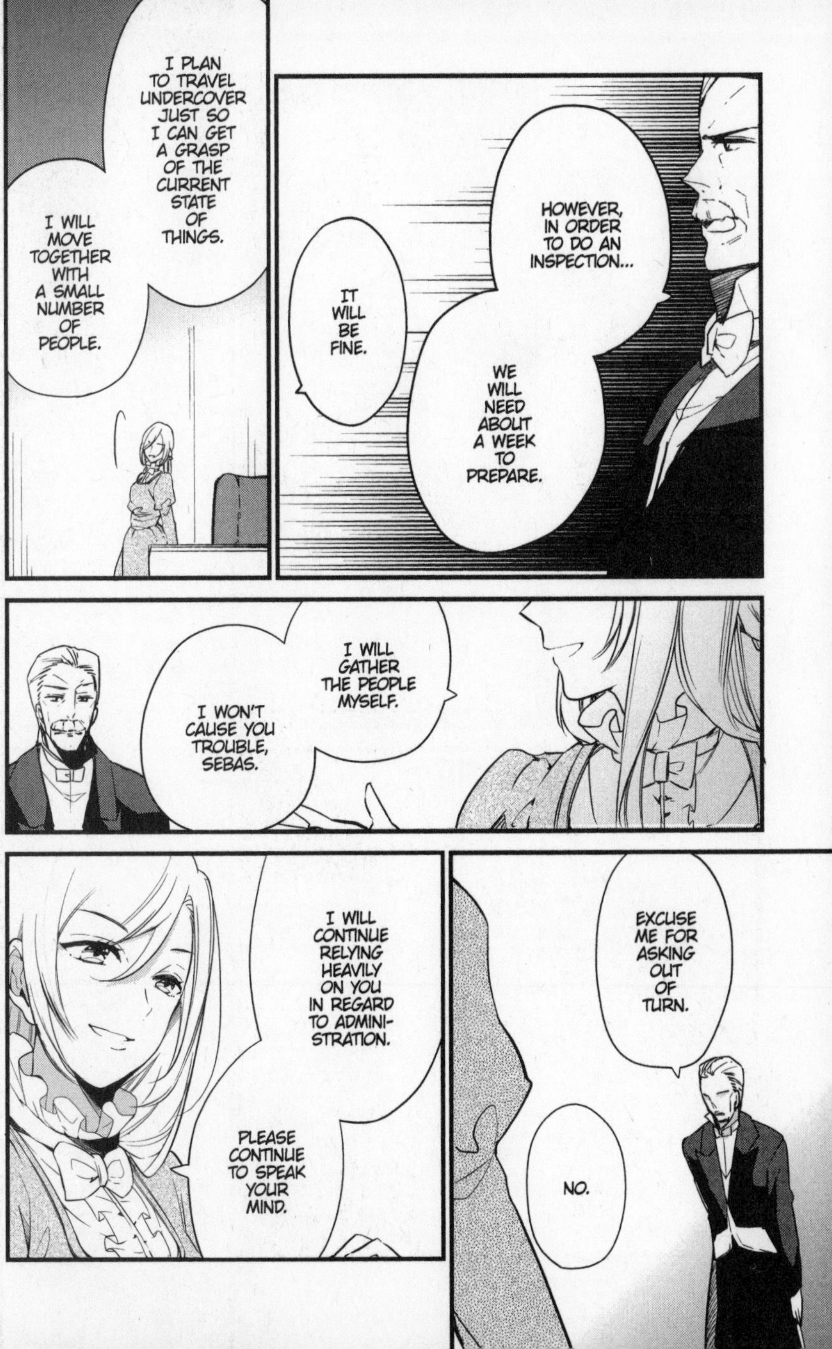
HOWEVER, IN ORDER TO DO AN INSPECTION...
WE WILL NEED ABOUT A WEEK TO PREPARE.
IT WILL BE FINE.
I PLAN TO TRAVEL UNDERCOVER JUST SO I CAN GET A GRASP OF THE CURRENT STATE OF THINGS.
I WILL MOVE TOGETHER WITH A SMALL NUMBER OF PEOPLE.
I WILL GATHER THE PEOPLE MYSELF.
I WON'T CAUSE YOU TROUBLE, SEBAS.
EXCUSE ME FOR ASKING OUT OF TURN.
NO.
I WILL CONTINUE RELYING HEAVILY ON YOU IN REGARD TO ADMINI-STRATION.
PLEASE CONTINUE TO SPEAK YOUR MIND.

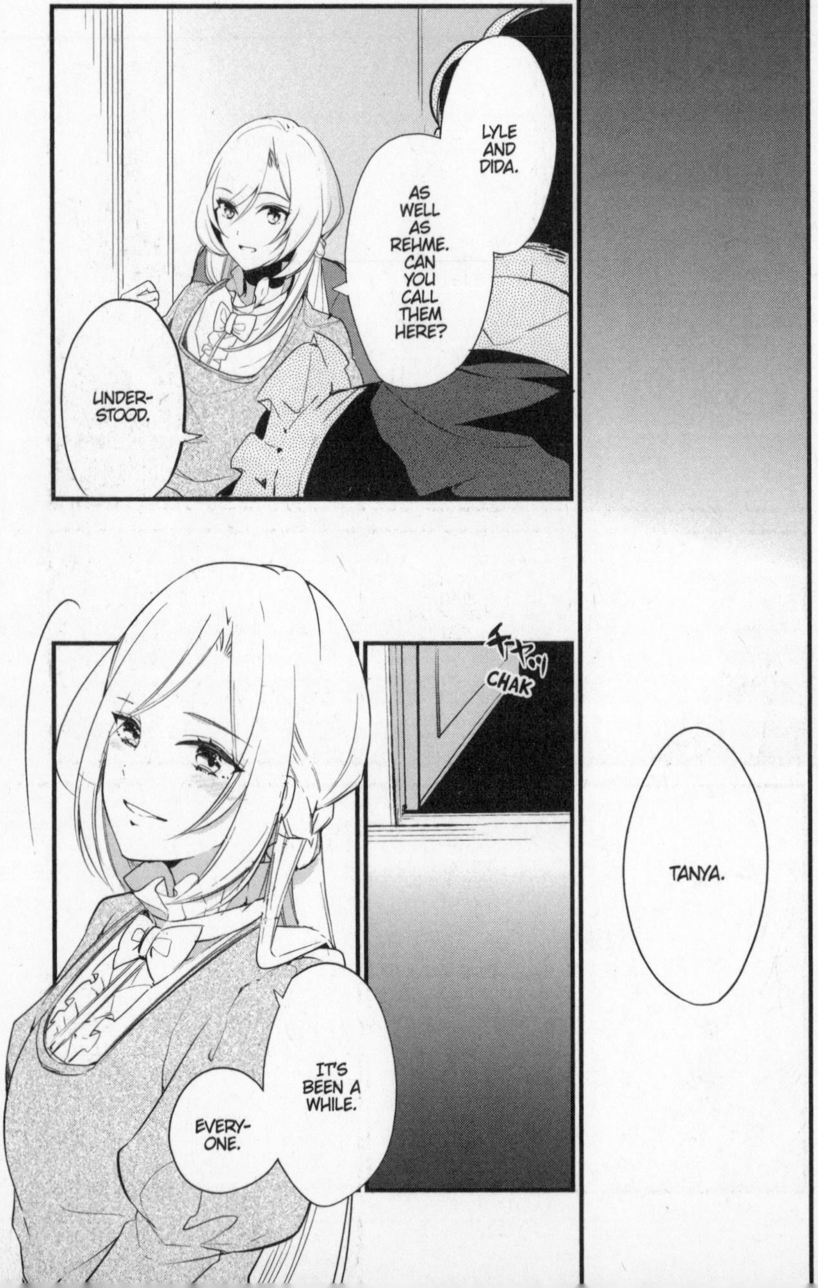
TANYA.
LYLE AND DIDA.
AS WELL AS REHME. CAN YOU CALL THEM HERE?
UNDER-STOOD.
CHAK
IT'S BEEN A WHILE.
EVERY-ONE.

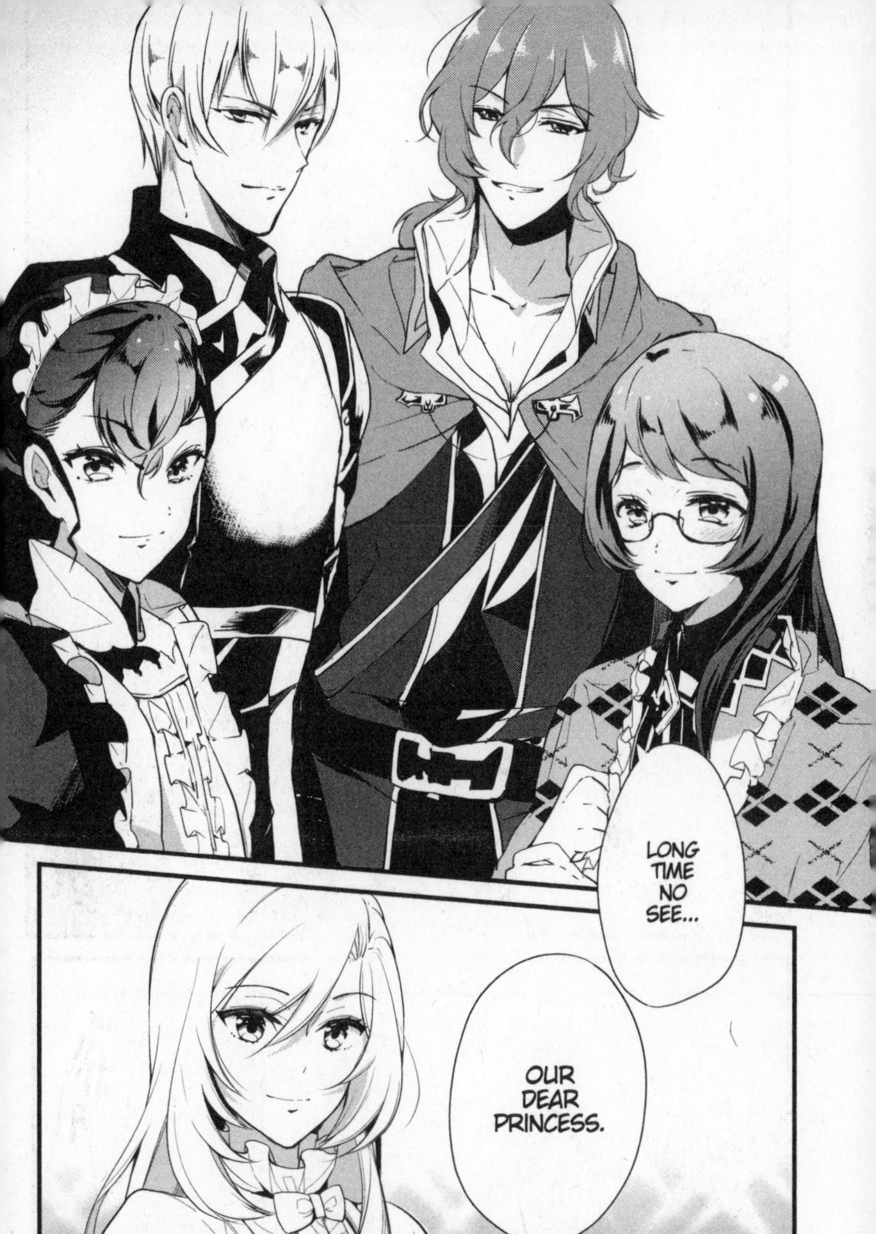
LONG TIME NO SEE...
OUR DEAR PRINCESS.

#4 end

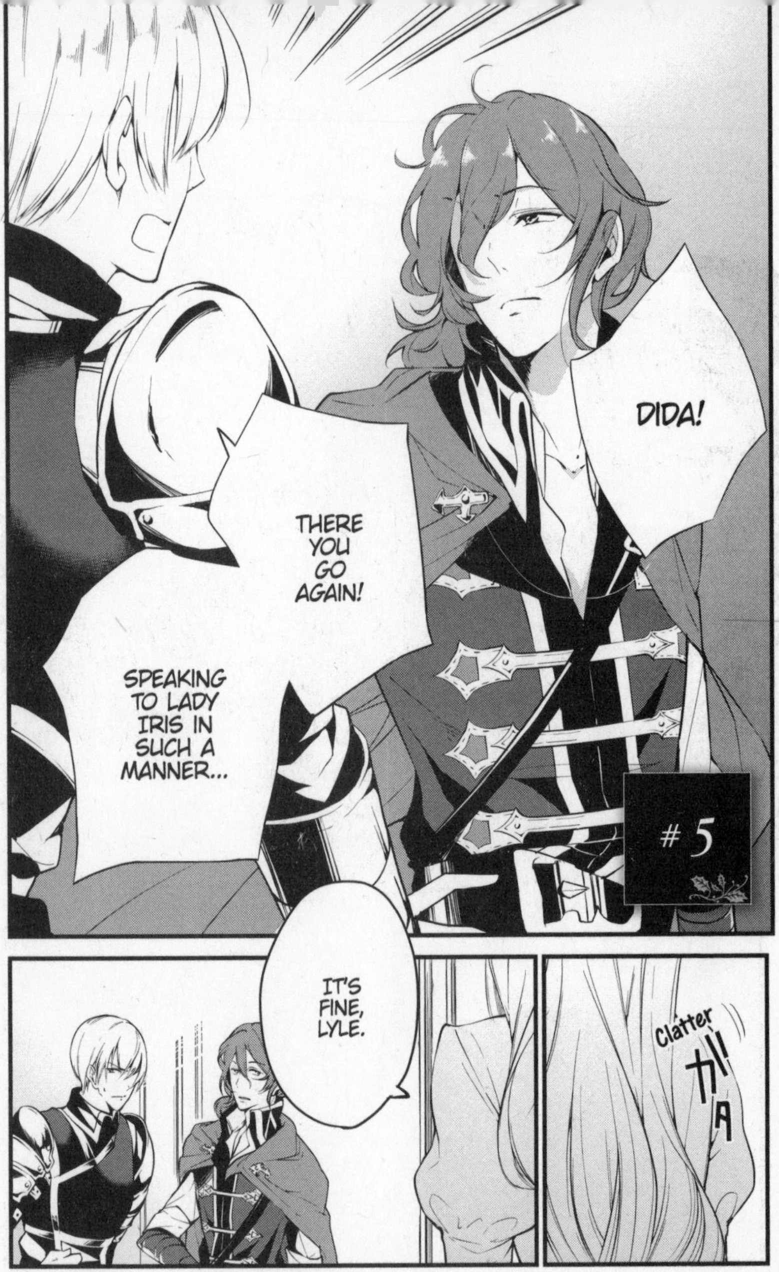
DIDA!
THERE YOU GO AGAIN!
SPEAKING TO LADY IRIS IN SUCH A MANNER...
5
Clatter
IT'S FINE, LYLE.

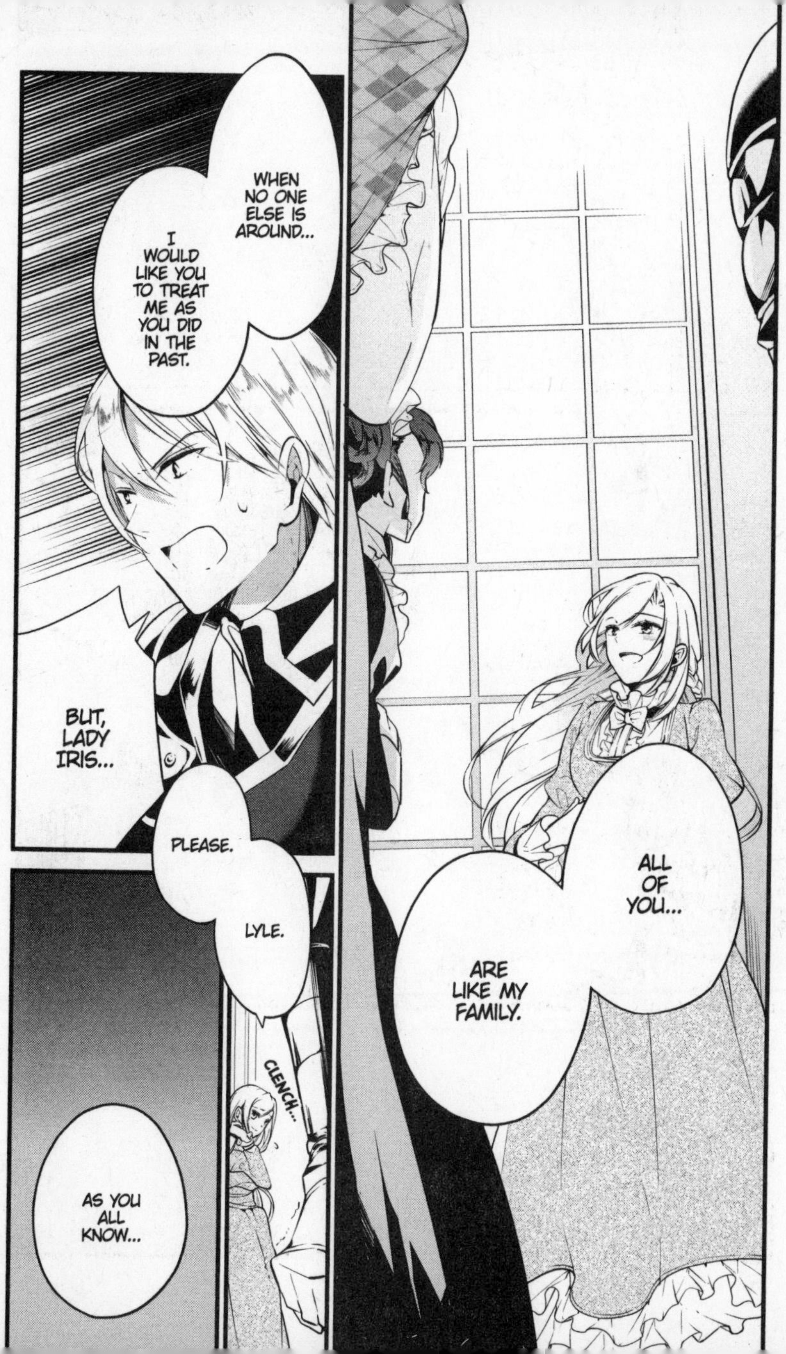
ALL OF YOU...
ARE LIKE MY FAMILY.
WHEN NO ONE ELSE IS AROUND...
I WOULD LIKE YOU TO TREAT ME AS YOU DID IN THE PAST.
BUT, LADY IRIS...
PLEASE.
LYLE.
CLENCH...
AS YOU ALL KNOW...

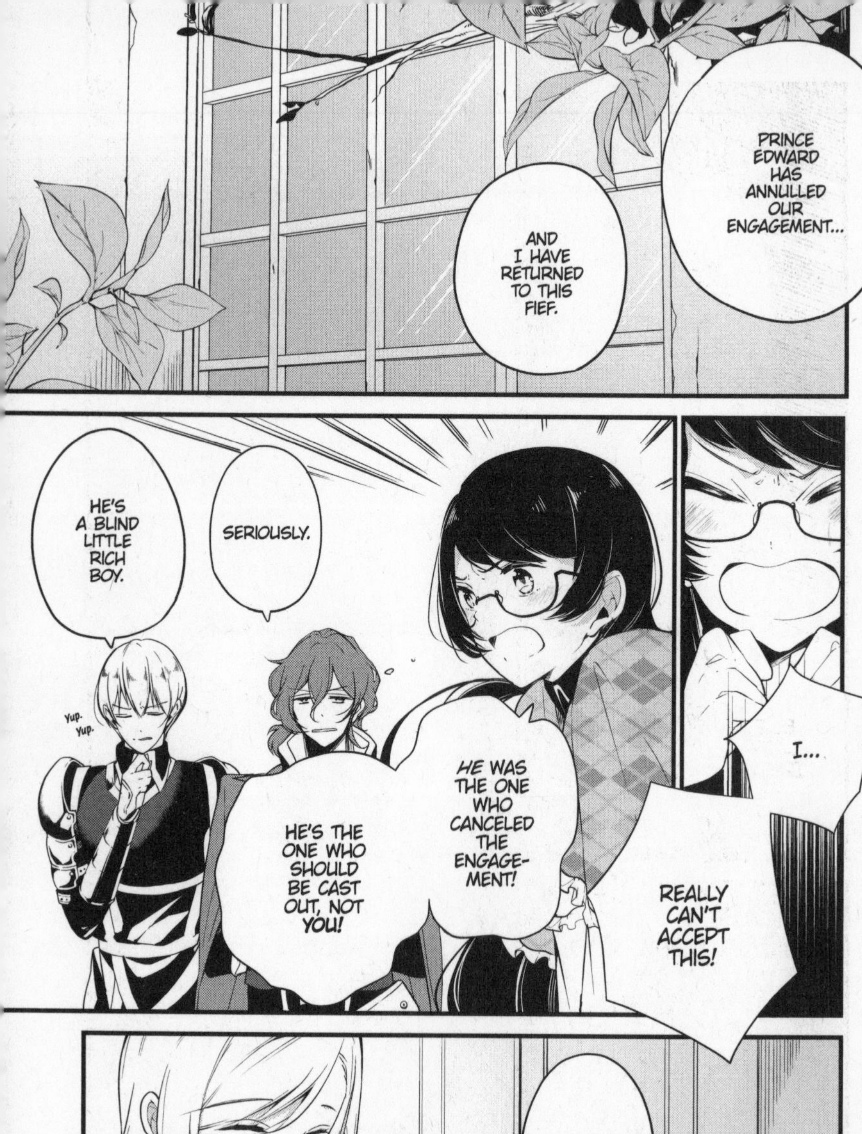
PRINCE EDWARD HAS ANNULLED OUR ENGAGEMENT...
AND I HAVE RETURNED TO THIS FIEF.
I...
REALLY CAN'T ACCEPT THIS!
HE WAS THE ONE WHO CANCELED THE ENGAGE-MENT!
HE'S THE ONE WHO SHOULD BE CAST OUT, NOT *YOU*!
SERIOUSLY.
HE'S A BLIND LITTLE RICH BOY.
Yup. Yup.
THANK YOU.
Hee hee!

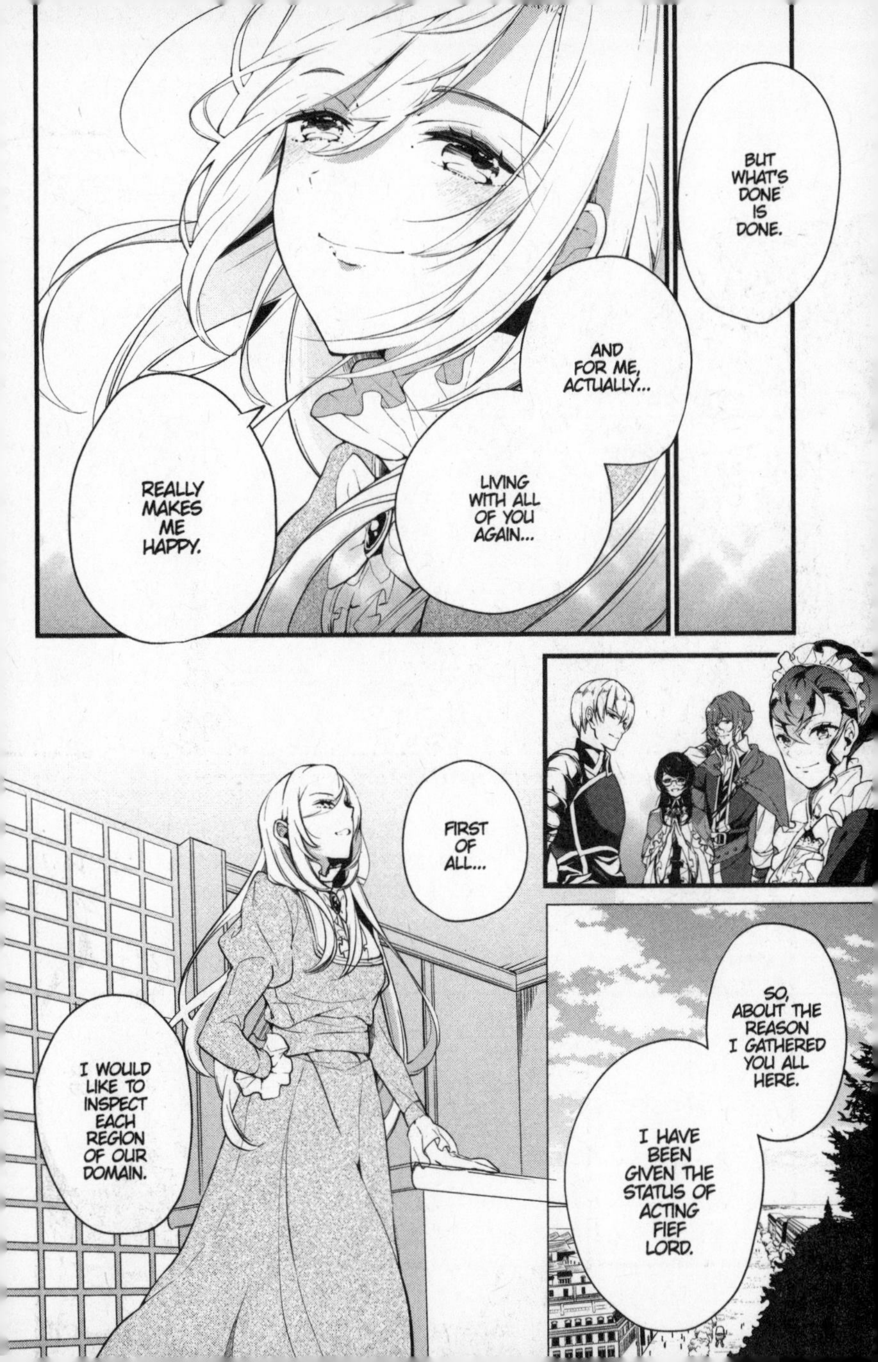
BUT WHAT'S DONE IS DONE.
AND FOR ME, ACTUALLY...
LIVING WITH ALL OF YOU AGAIN...
REALLY MAKES ME HAPPY.
SO, ABOUT THE REASON I GATHERED YOU ALL HERE.
I HAVE BEEN GIVEN THE STATUS OF ACTING FIEF LORD.
FIRST OF ALL...
I WOULD LIKE TO INSPECT EACH REGION OF OUR DOMAIN.

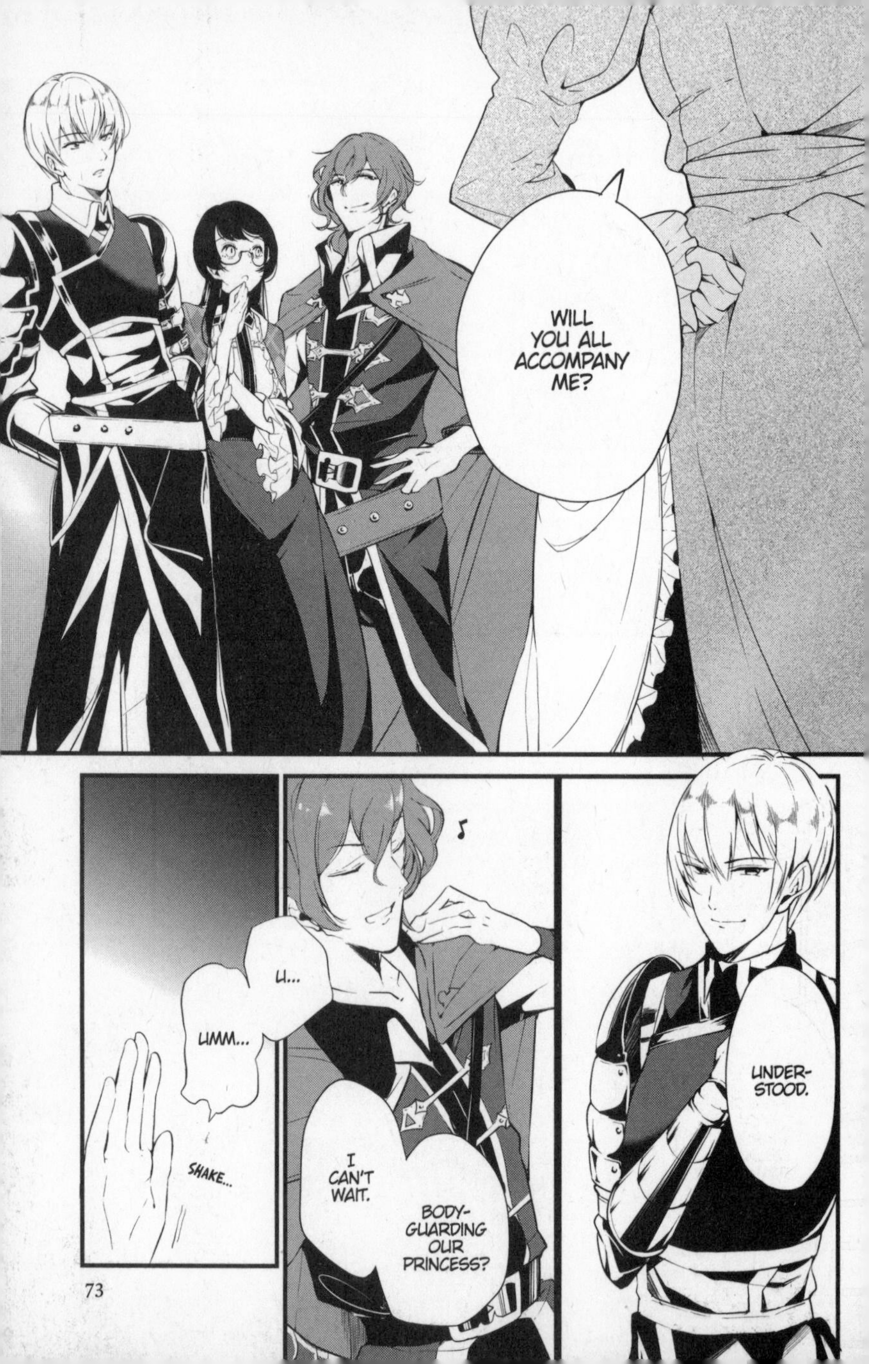
WILL YOU ALL ACCOMPANY ME?
UNDER-STOOD.
I CAN'T WAIT.
BODY-GUARDING OUR PRINCESS?
U...
UMM...
SHAKE...

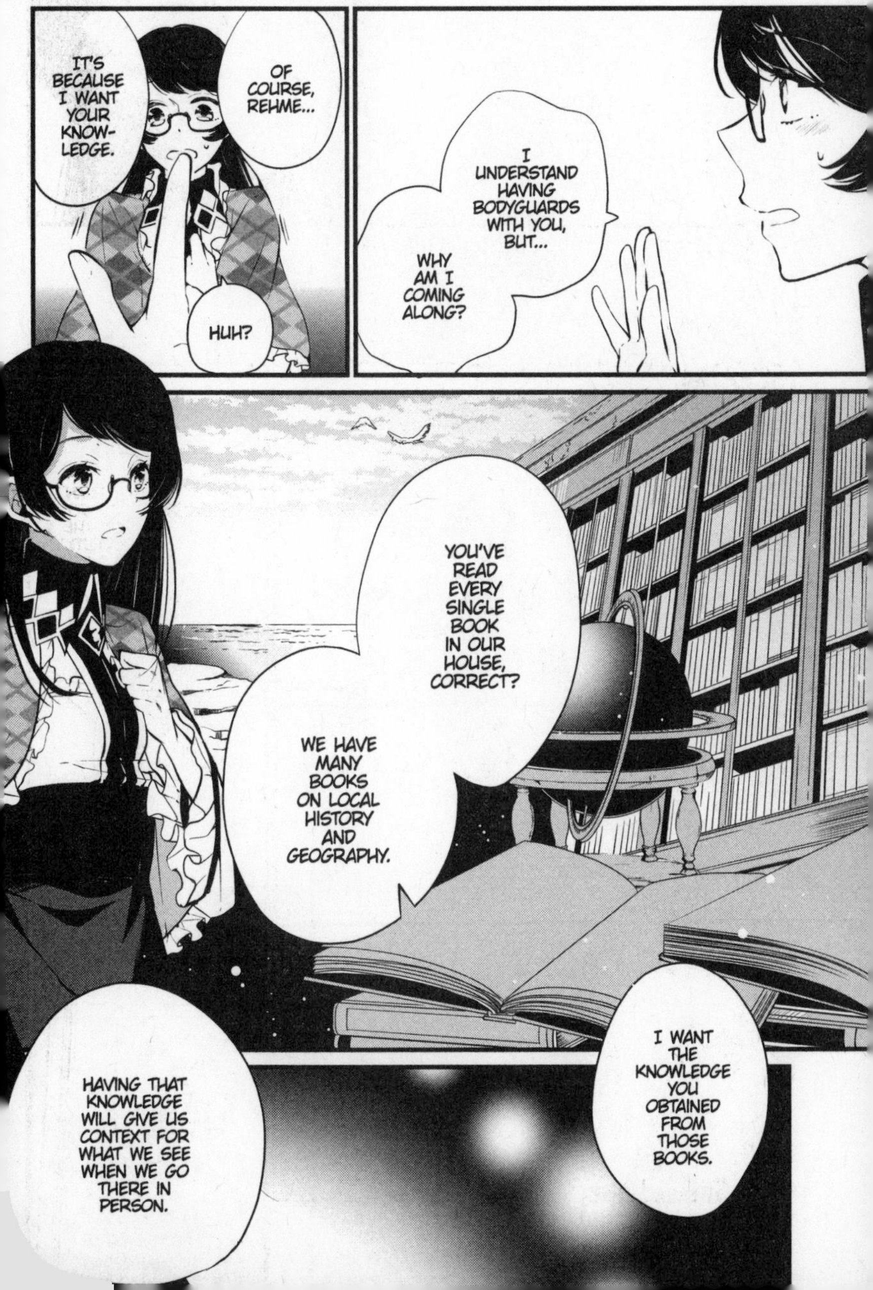
I UNDERSTAND HAVING BODYGUARDS WITH YOU, BUT...
WHY AM I COMING ALONG?
OF COURSE, REHME...
IT'S BECAUSE I WANT YOUR KNOW-LEDGE.
HUH?
YOU'VE READ EVERY SINGLE BOOK IN OUR HOUSE, CORRECT?
WE HAVE MANY BOOKS ON LOCAL HISTORY AND GEOGRAPHY.
I WANT THE KNOWLEDGE YOU OBTAINED FROM THOSE BOOKS.
HAVING THAT KNOWLEDGE WILL GIVE US CONTEXT FOR WHAT WE SEE WHEN WE GO THERE IN PERSON.

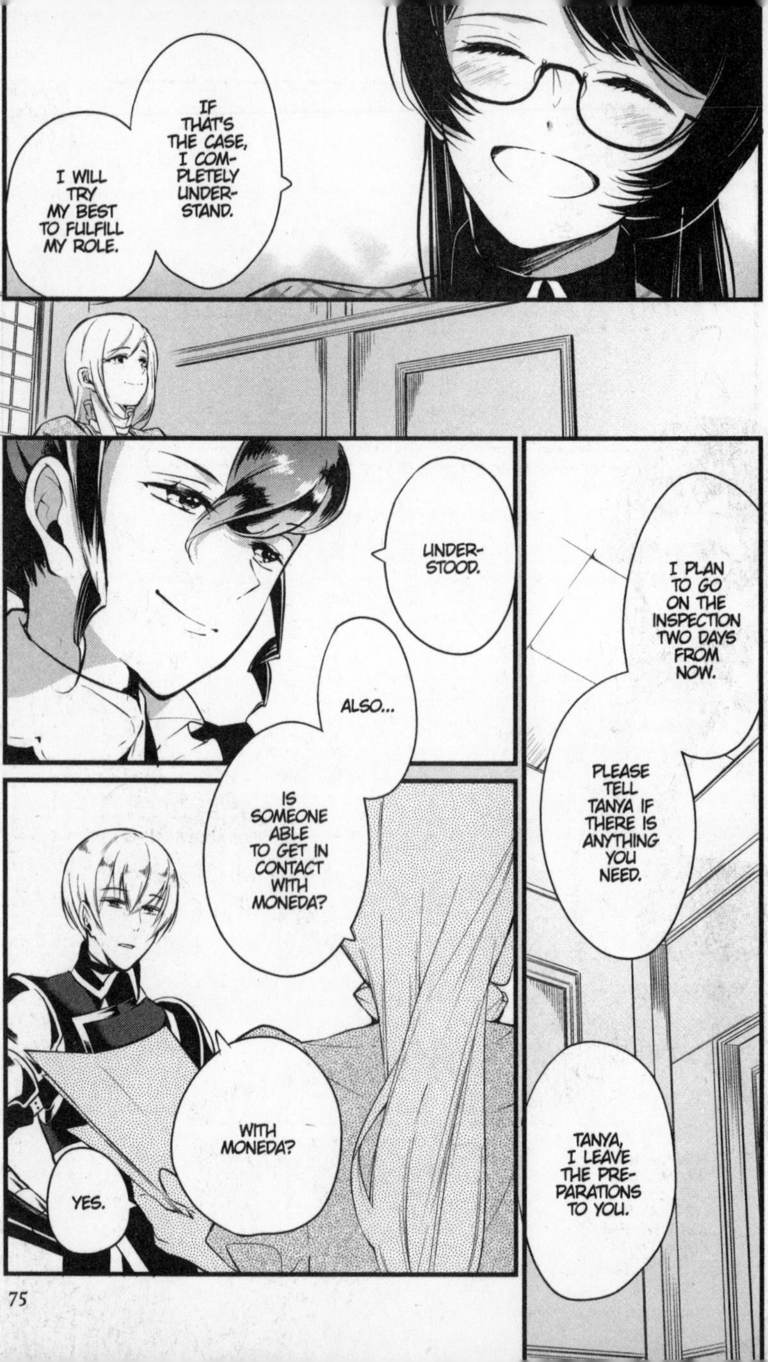
IF THAT'S THE CASE, I COMPLETELY UNDERSTAND.
I WILL TRY MY BEST TO FULFILL MY ROLE.
I PLAN TO GO ON THE INSPECTION TWO DAYS FROM NOW.
PLEASE TELL TANYA IF THERE IS ANYTHING YOU NEED.
TANYA, I LEAVE THE PREPARATIONS TO YOU.
UNDERSTOOD.
ALSO...
IS SOMEONE ABLE TO GET IN CONTACT WITH MONEDA?
WITH MONEDA?
YES.

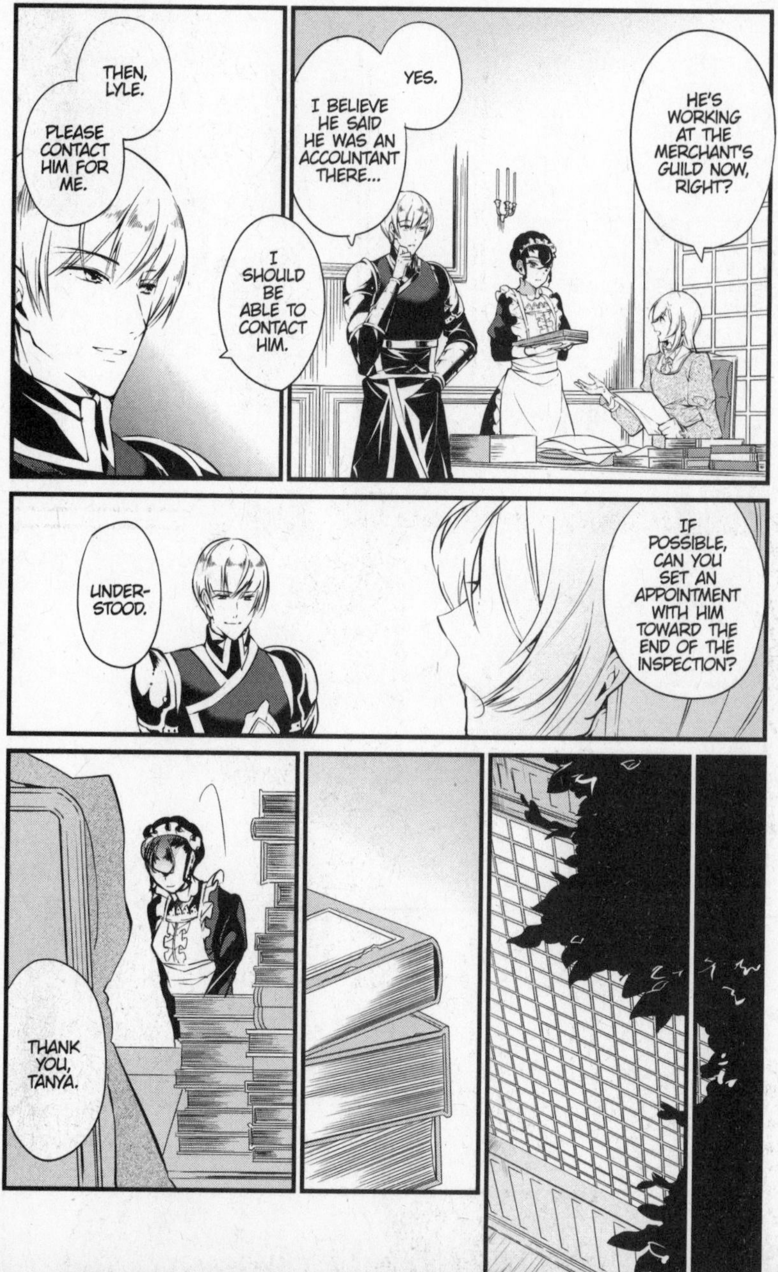
HE'S WORKING AT THE MERCHANT'S GUILD NOW, RIGHT?
YES.
I BELIEVE HE SAID HE WAS AN ACCOUNTANT THERE...
I SHOULD BE ABLE TO CONTACT HIM.
THEN, LYLE.
PLEASE CONTACT HIM FOR ME.
IF POSSIBLE, CAN YOU SET AN APPOINTMENT WITH HIM TOWARD THE END OF THE INSPECTION?
UNDER-STOOD.
THANK YOU, TANYA.

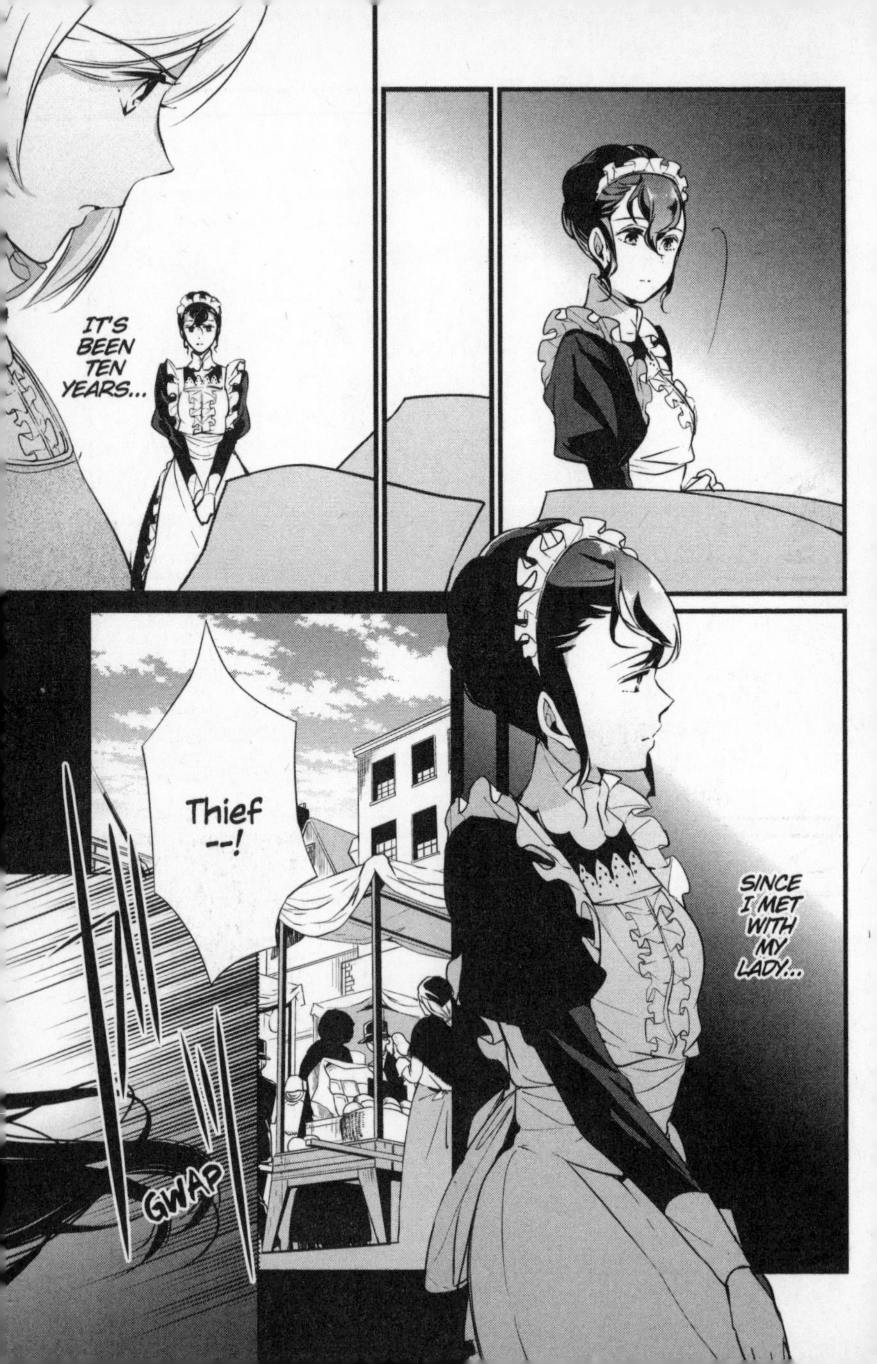
IT'S BEEN TEN YEARS...
SINCE I MET WITH MY LADY...
Thief --!
GWAP

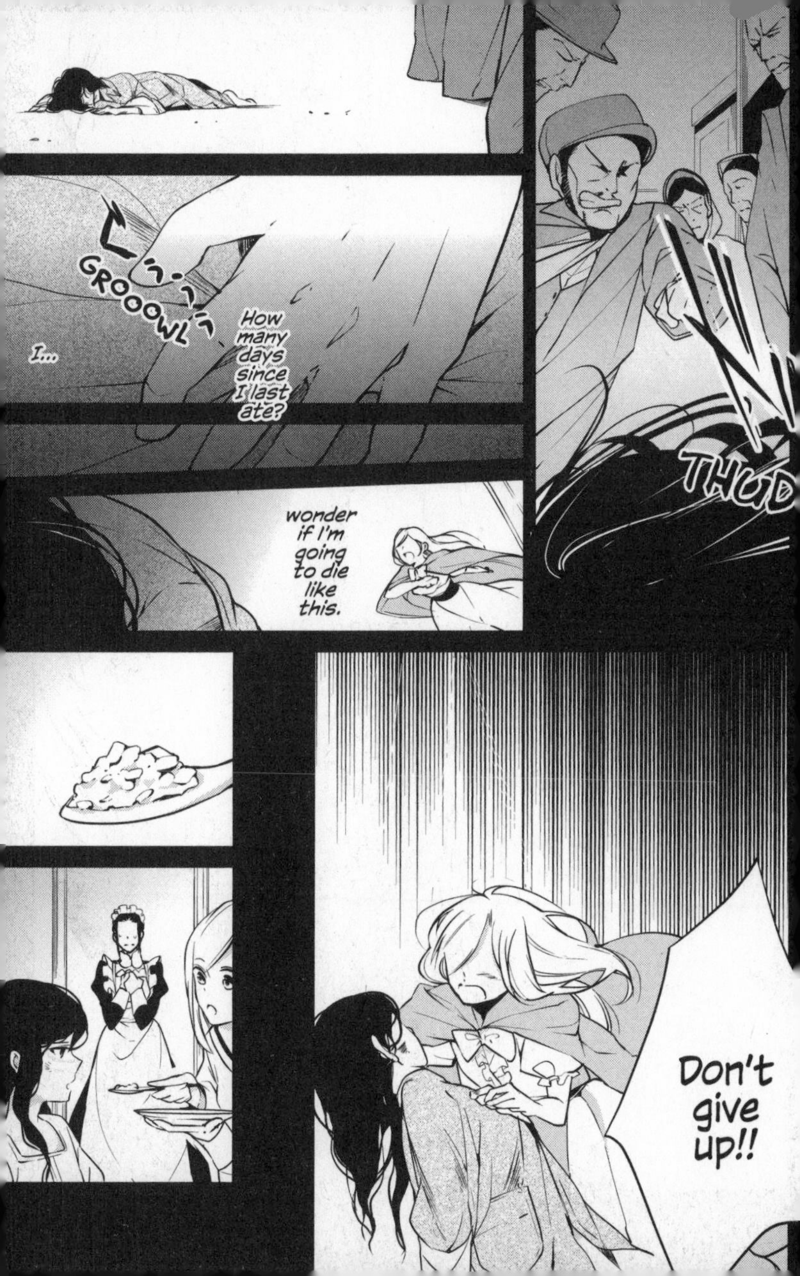
THUD
...
GROOOWL
How many days since I last ate?
I...
wonder if I'm going to die like this.
Don't give up!!

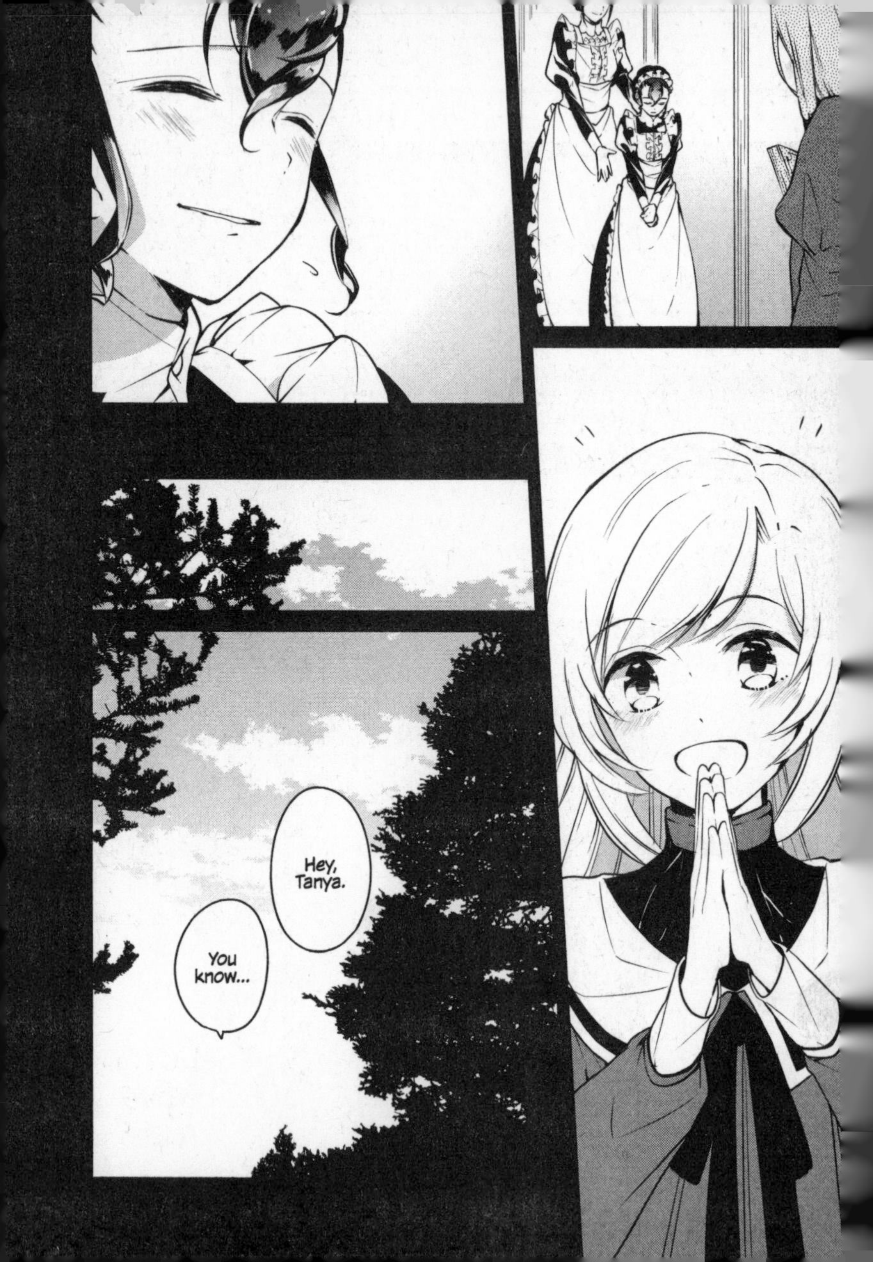
Hey, Tanya.
You know...

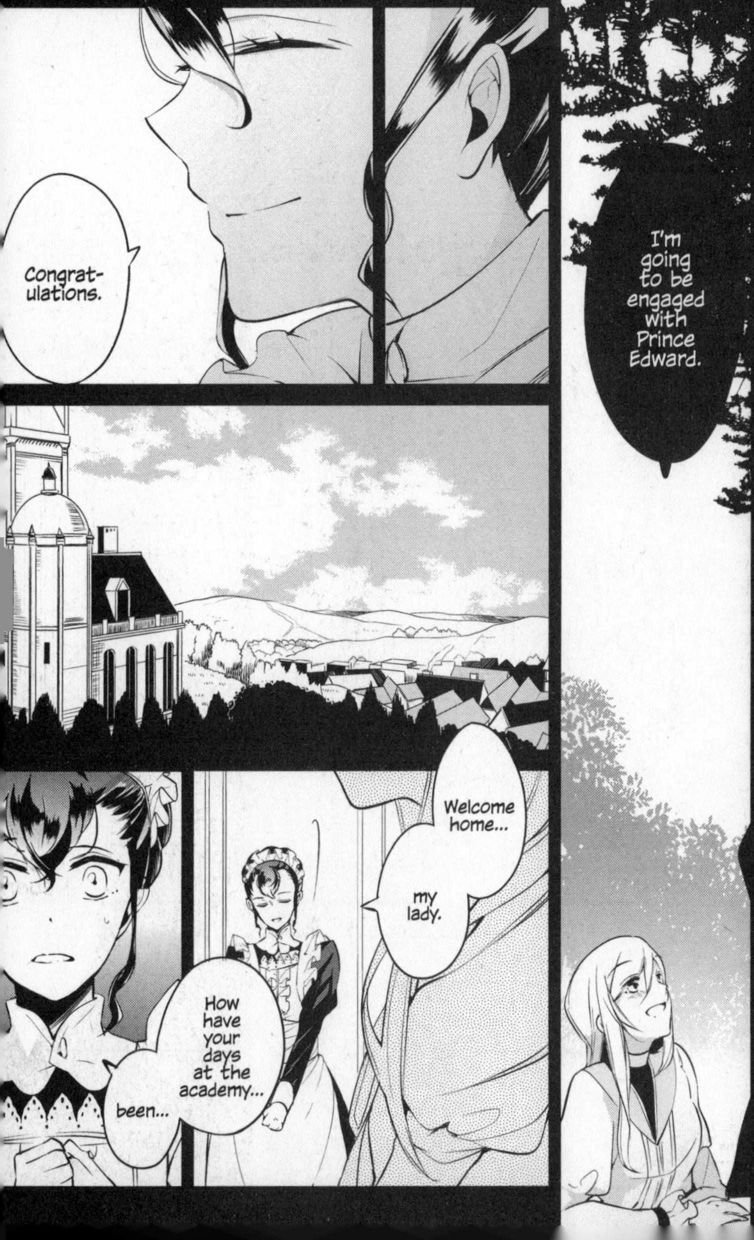
I'm going to be engaged with Prince Edward.
Congrat-ulations.
Welcome home...
my lady.
How have your days at the academy...
been...

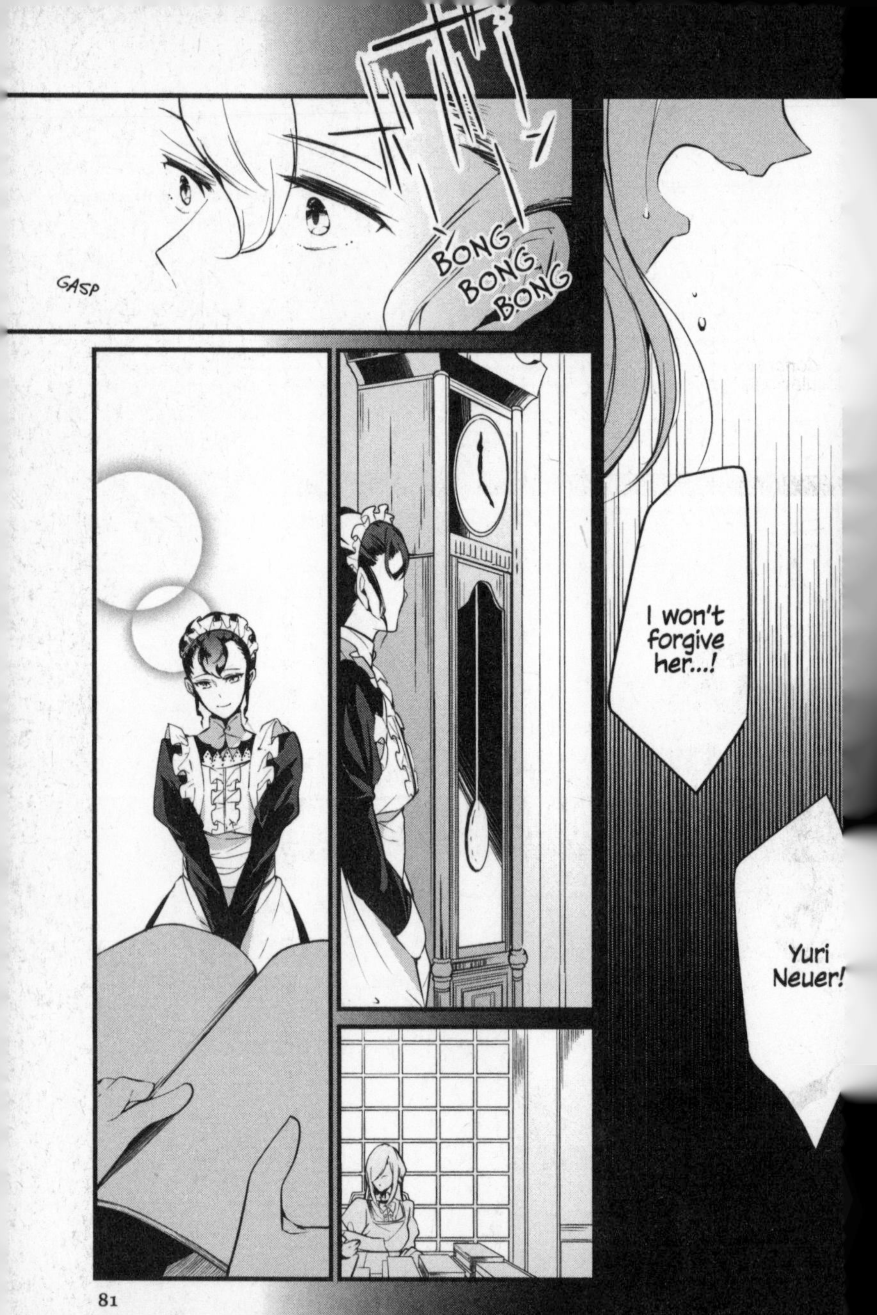
I won't forgive her...!
Yuri Neuer!
BONG BONG BONG
GASP

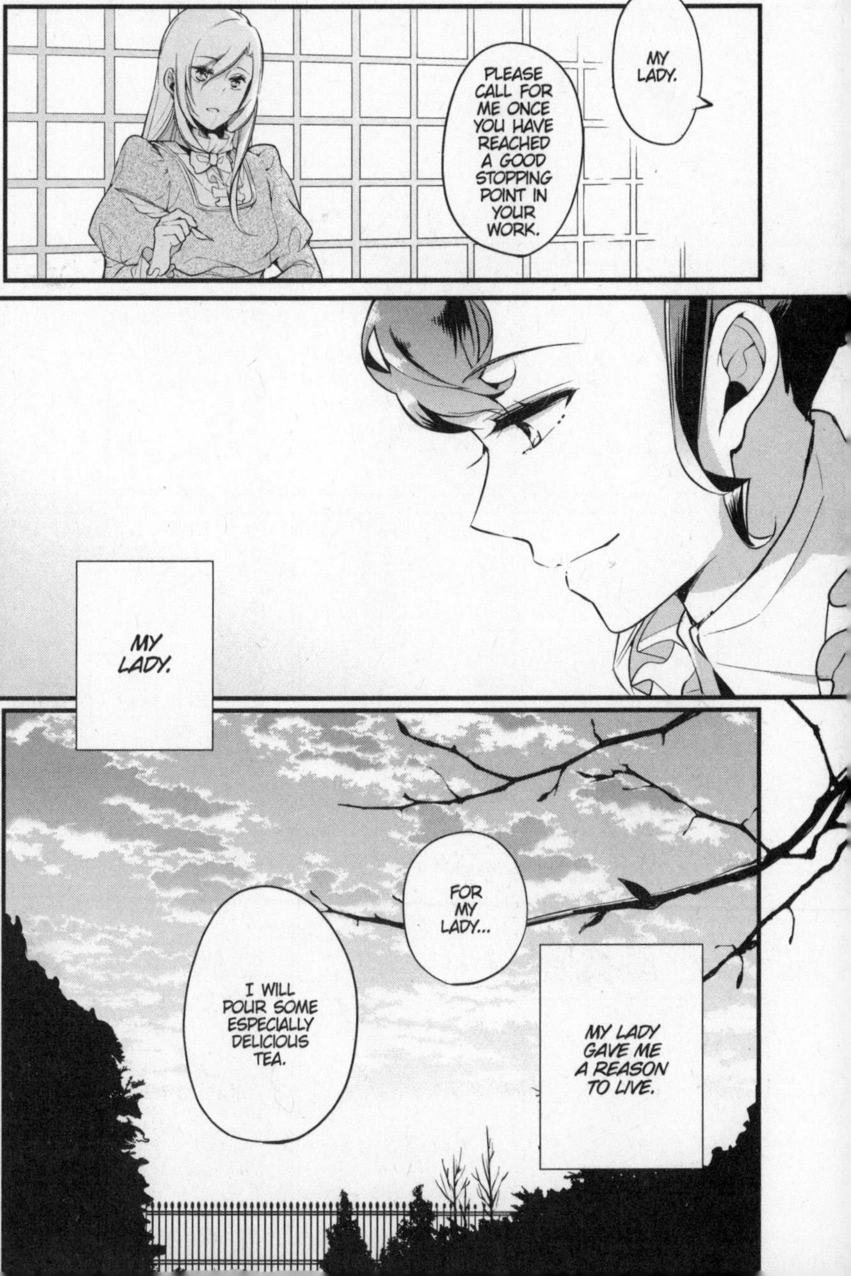
MY LADY.
PLEASE CALL FOR ME ONCE YOU HAVE REACHED A GOOD STOPPING POINT IN YOUR WORK.
MY LADY.
MY LADY GAVE ME A REASON TO LIVE.
FOR MY LADY...
I WILL POUR SOME ESPECIALLY DELICIOUS TEA.

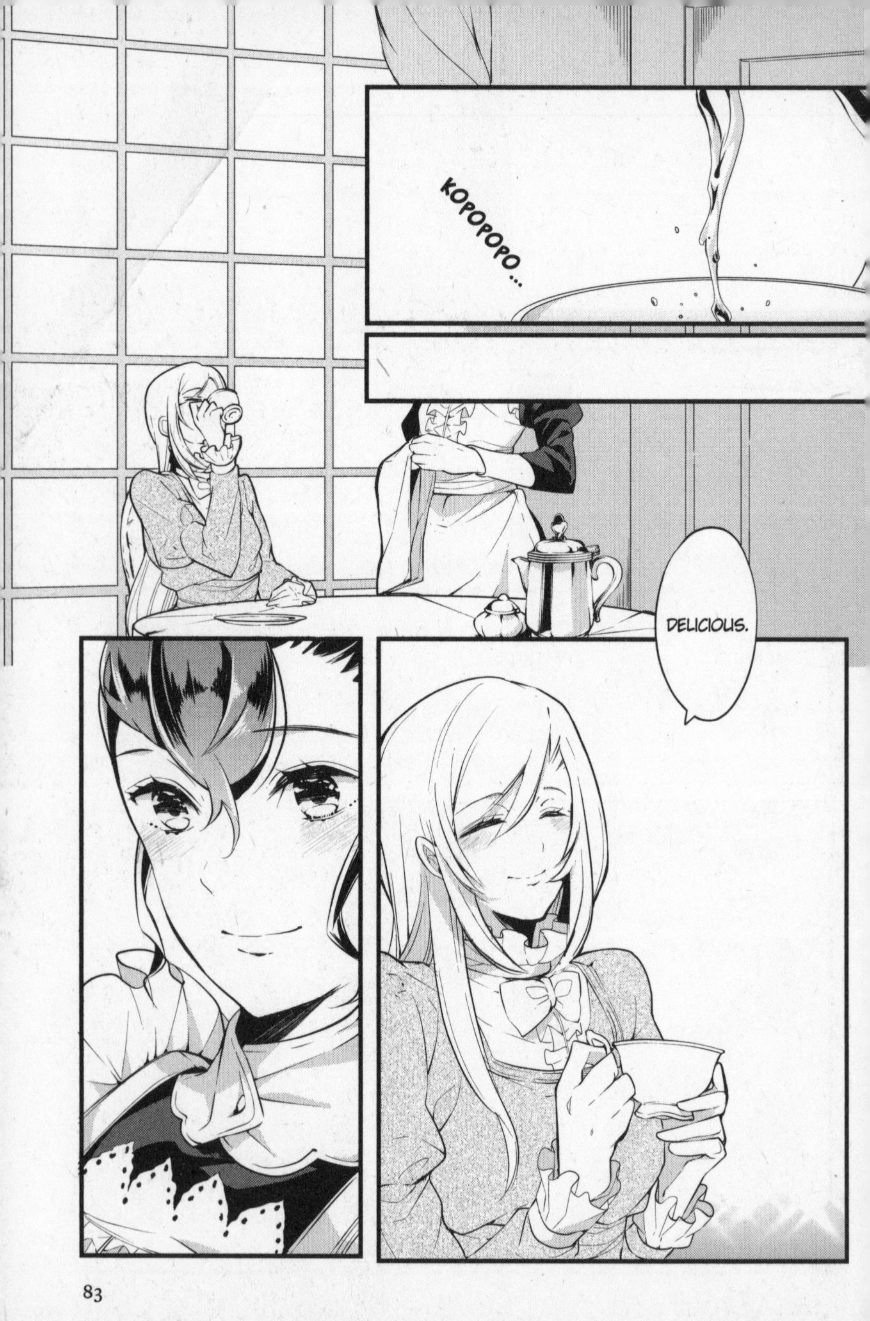
KOPOPOPO...
DELICIOUS.

THAT'S WHY, THIS TIME...
PA-TUNK
THANK GOODNESS HER SMILE HAS RE-TURNED.
I WILL PROTECT...
MY LADY.
I SHOULD PREPARE AN HERB TEA FOR HER EYES NEXT TIME...

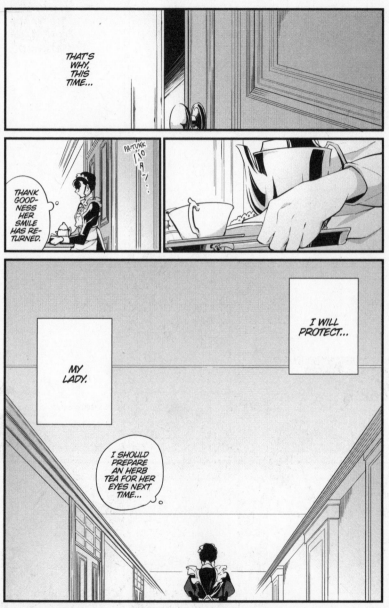

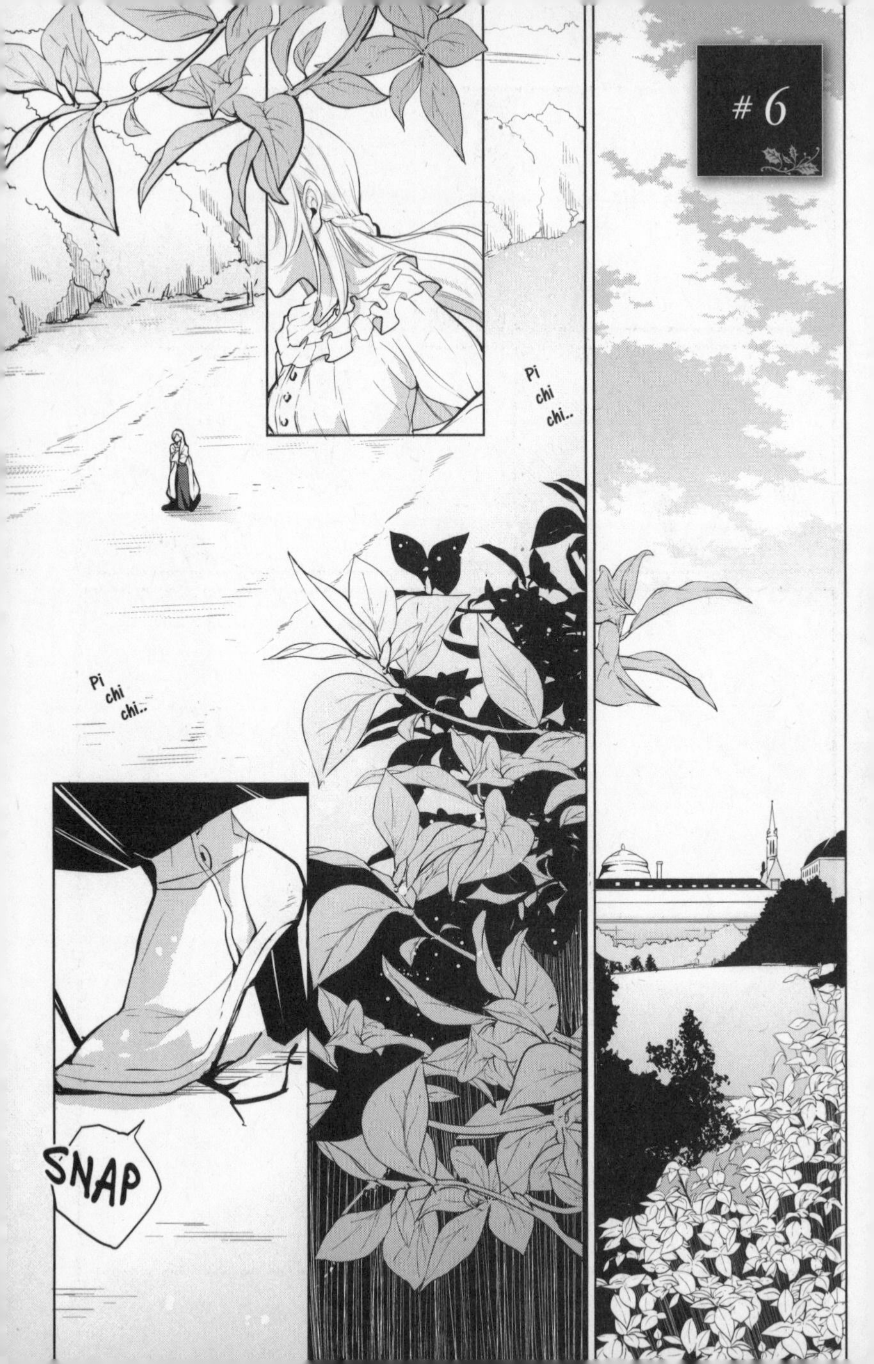

6
Pi chi chi..
Pi chi chi..
SNAP

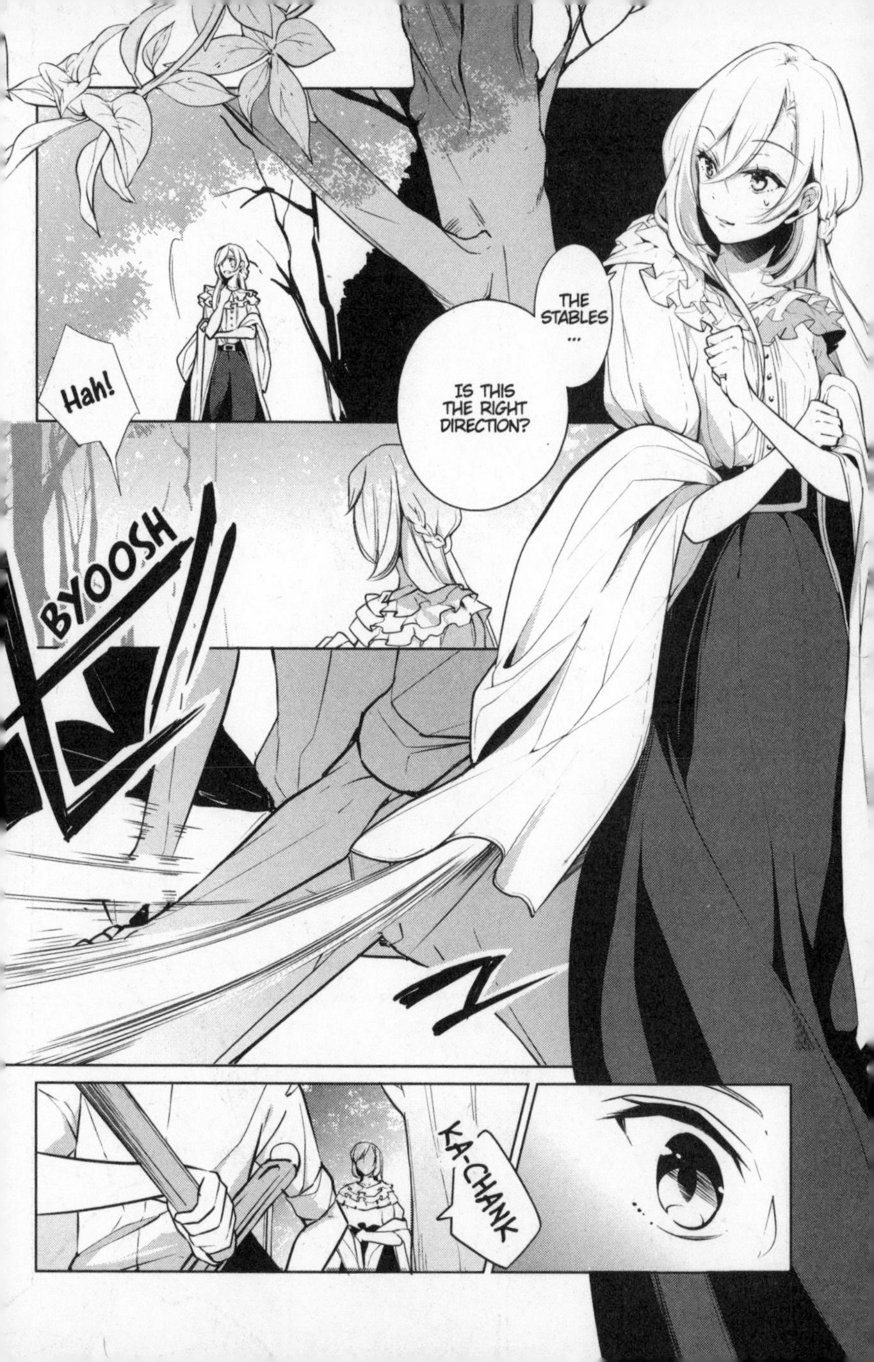
THE STABLES ...
IS THIS THE RIGHT DIRECTION?
Hah!
BYOOSH
KA-CHANK

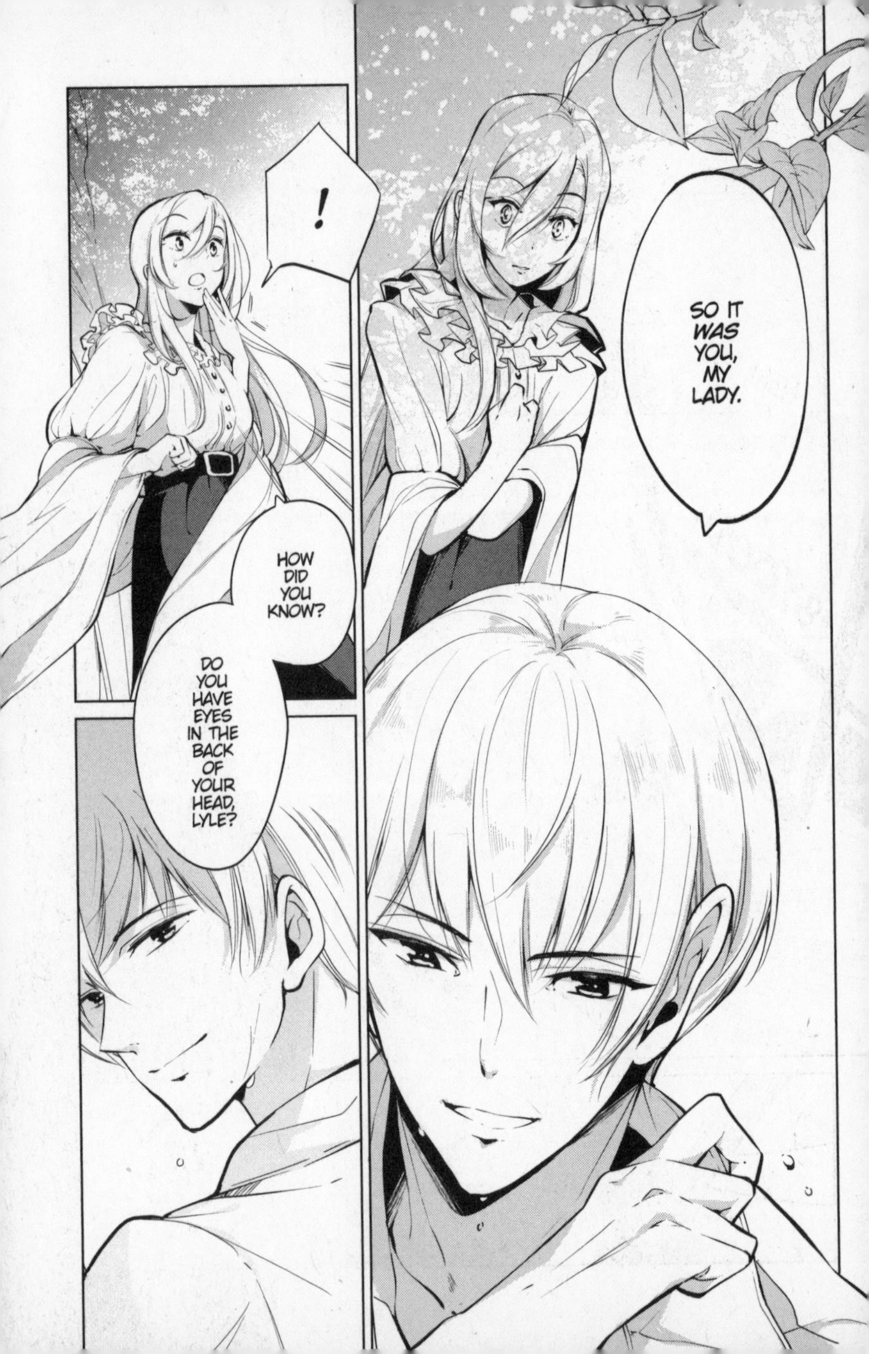
SO IT WAS YOU, MY LADY.
!
HOW DID YOU KNOW?
DO YOU HAVE EYES IN THE BACK OF YOUR HEAD, LYLE?

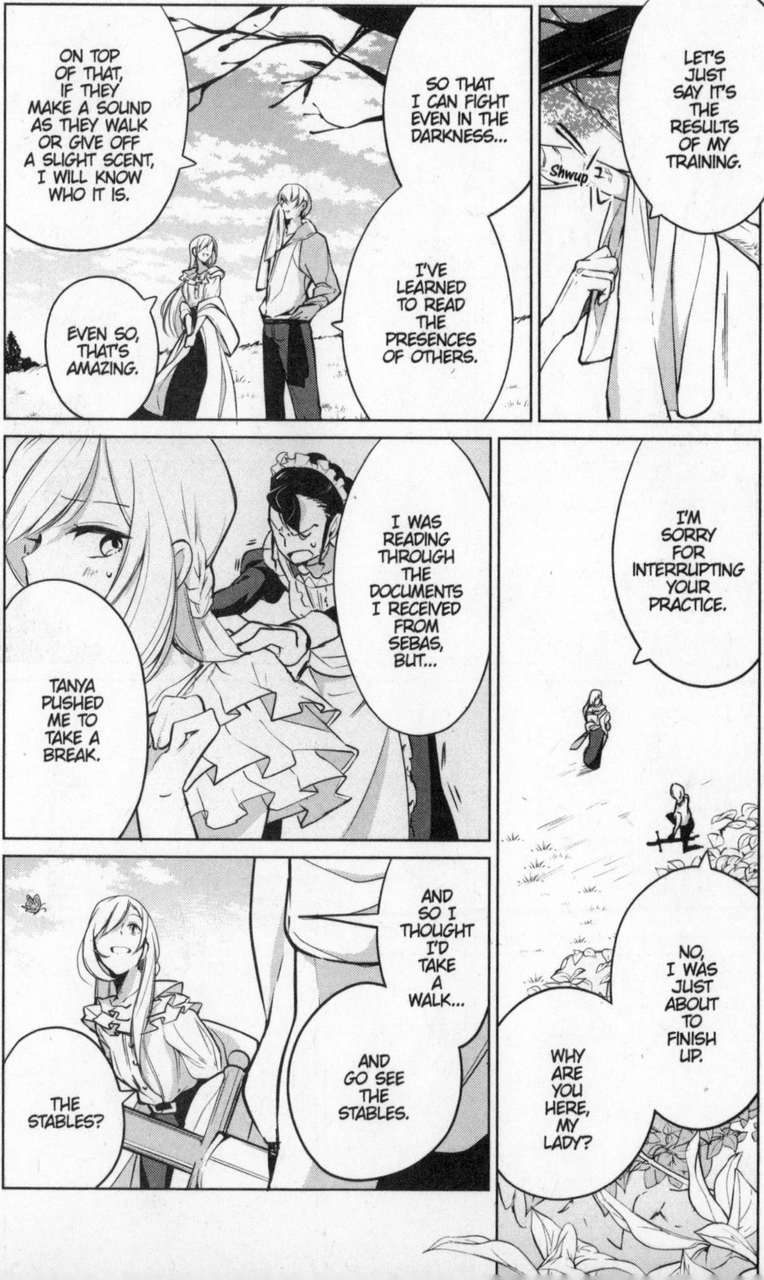

LET'S JUST SAY IT'S THE RESULTS OF MY TRAINING.
Shwup
SO THAT I CAN FIGHT EVEN IN THE DARKNESS...
I'VE LEARNED TO READ THE PRESENCES OF OTHERS.
ON TOP OF THAT, IF THEY MAKE A SOUND AS THEY WALK OR GIVE OFF A SLIGHT SCENT, I WILL KNOW WHO IT IS.
EVEN SO, THAT'S AMAZING.
I'M SORRY FOR INTERRUPTING YOUR PRACTICE.
NO, I WAS JUST ABOUT TO FINISH UP.
WHY ARE YOU HERE, MY LADY?
I WAS READING THROUGH THE DOCUMENTS I RECEIVED FROM SEBAS, BUT...
TANYA PUSHED ME TO TAKE A BREAK.
AND SO I THOUGHT I'D TAKE A WALK...
AND GO SEE THE STABLES.
THE STABLES?

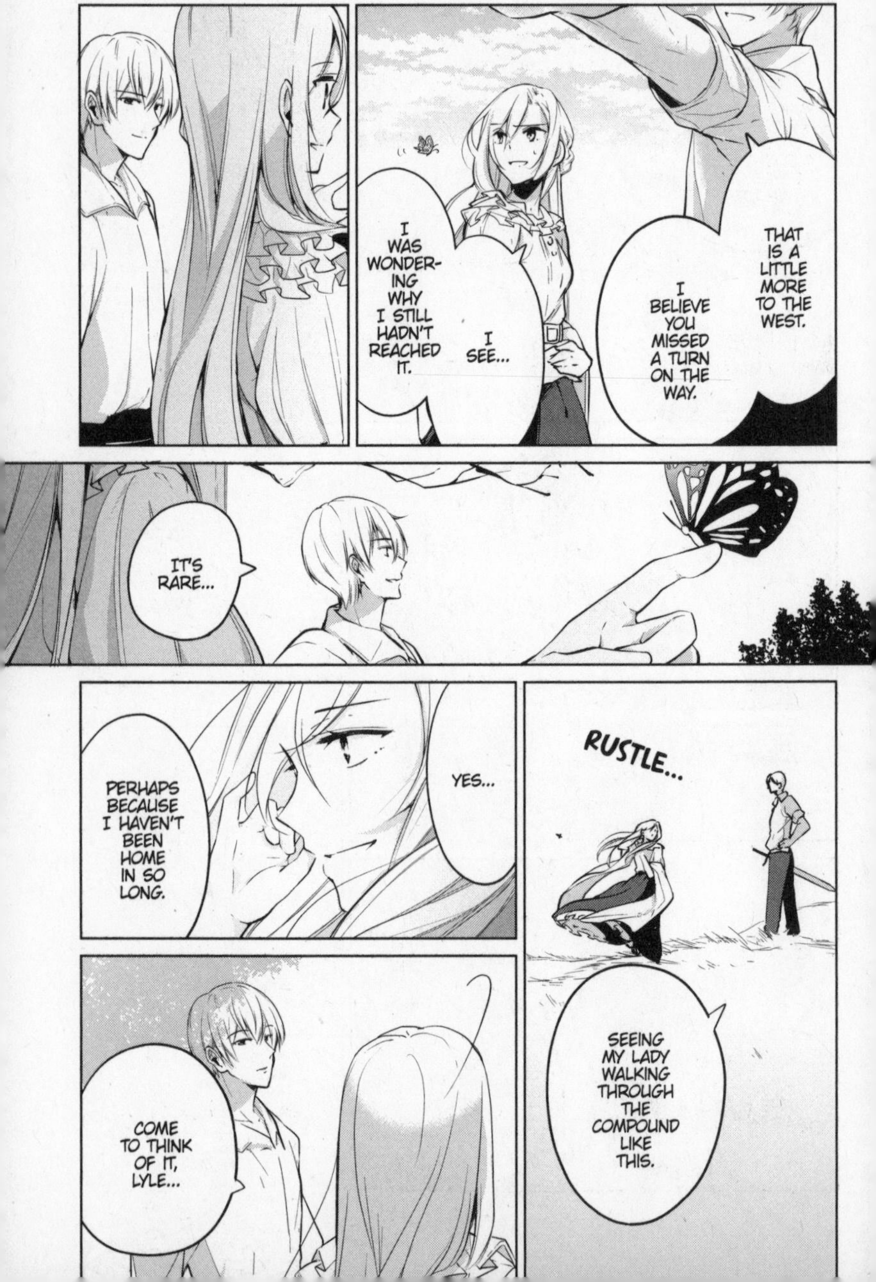
THAT IS A LITTLE MORE TO THE WEST.
I BELIEVE YOU MISSED A TURN ON THE WAY.
I SEE...
I WAS WONDERING WHY I STILL HADN'T REACHED IT.
IT'S RARE...
RUSTLE...
SEEING MY LADY WALKING THROUGH THE COMPOUND LIKE THIS.
YES...
PERHAPS BECAUSE I HAVEN'T BEEN HOME IN SO LONG.
COME TO THINK OF IT, LYLE...

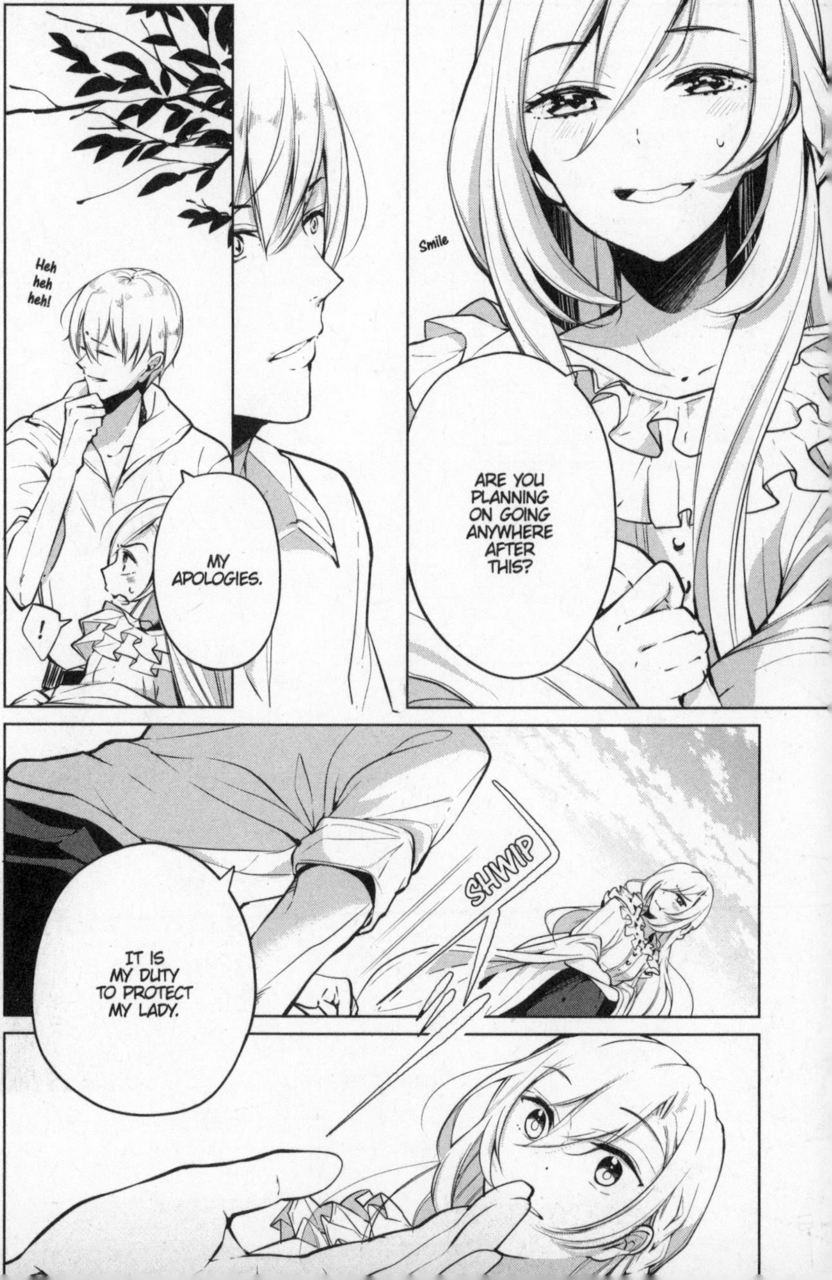
Smile
ARE YOU PLANNING ON GOING ANYWHERE AFTER THIS?
Heh heh heh!
MY APOLOGIES.
!
SHWIP
IT IS MY DUTY TO PROTECT MY LADY.

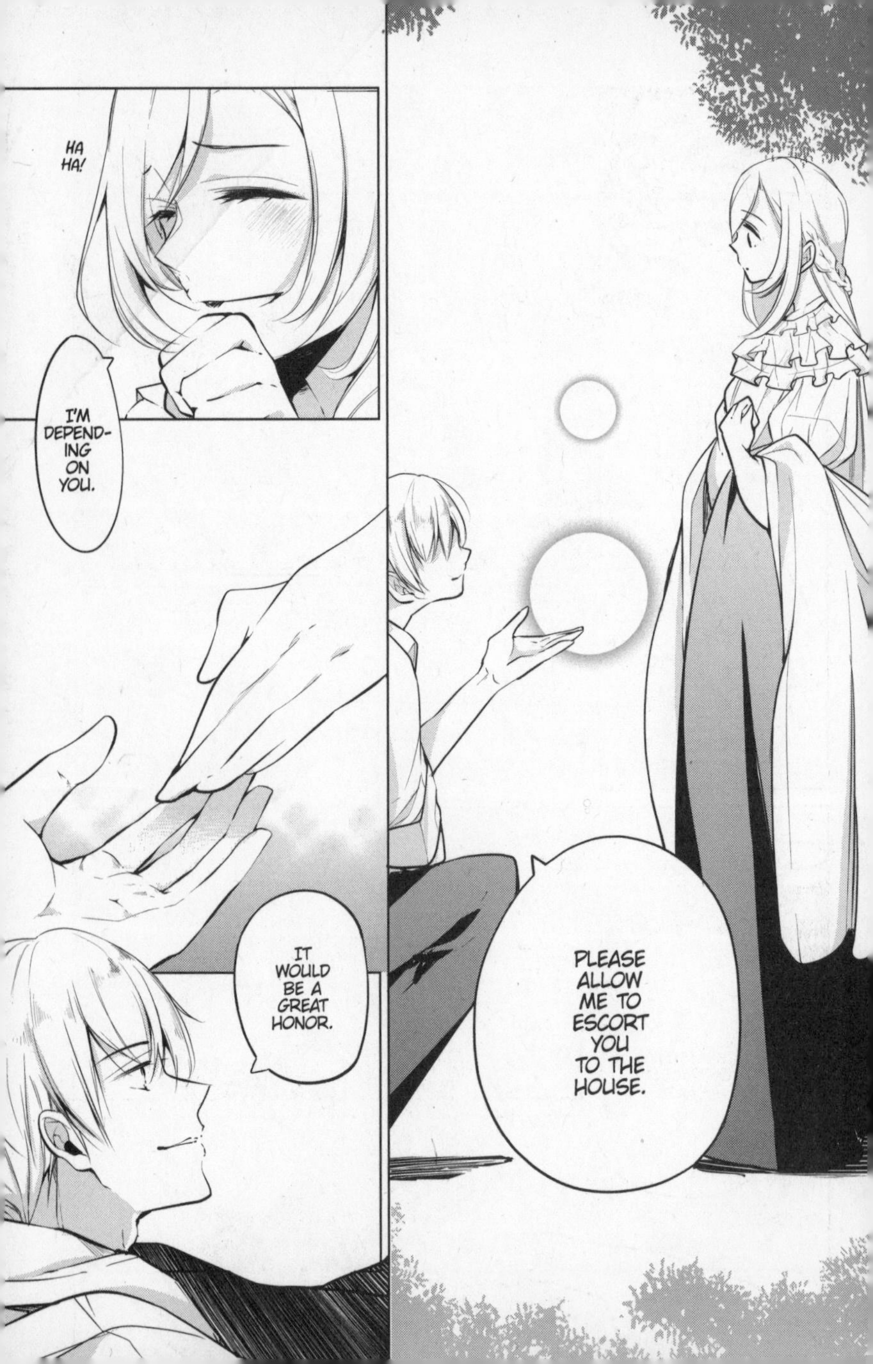
PLEASE ALLOW ME TO ESCORT YOU TO THE HOUSE.
HA HA!
I'M DEPEND-ING ON YOU.
IT WOULD BE A GREAT HONOR.

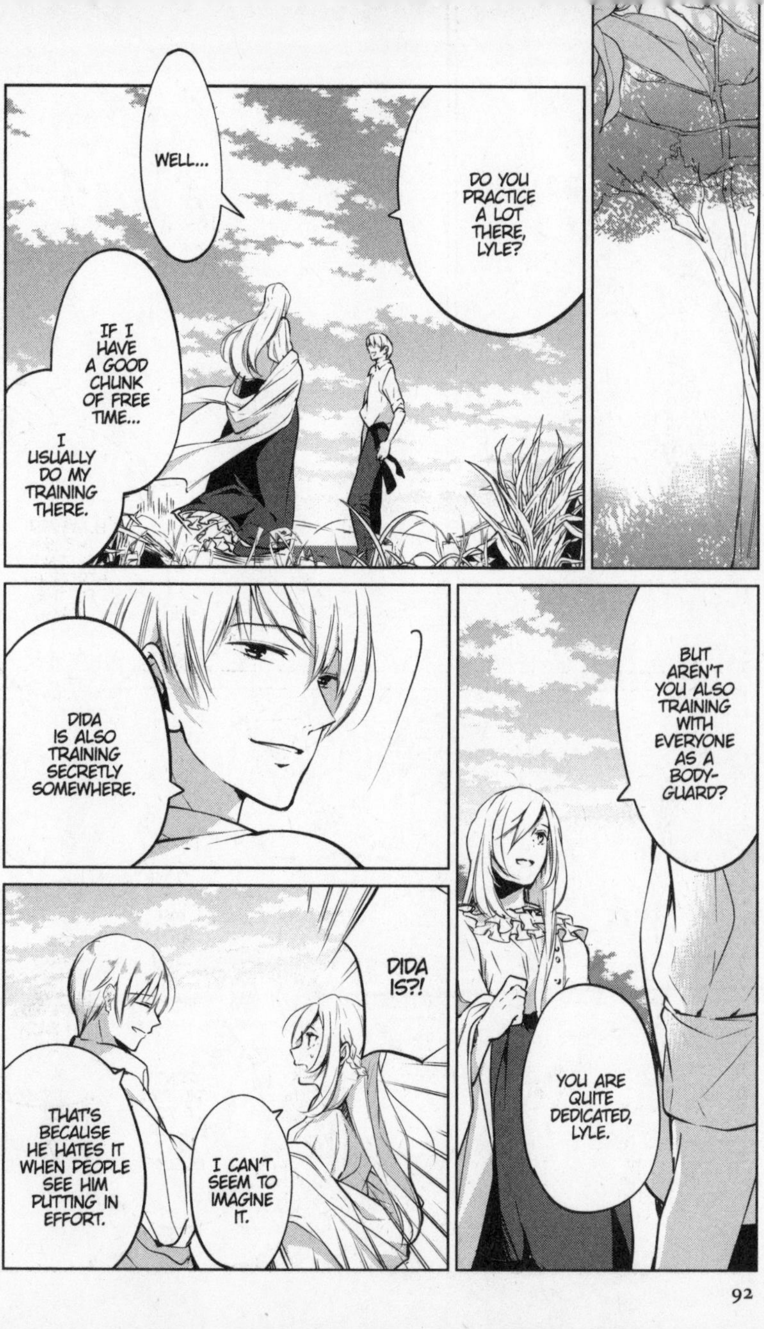
DO YOU PRACTICE A LOT THERE, LYLE?
WELL...
IF I HAVE A GOOD CHUNK OF FREE TIME...
I USUALLY DO MY TRAINING THERE.
BUT AREN'T YOU ALSO TRAINING WITH EVERYONE AS A BODY-GUARD?
YOU ARE QUITE DEDICATED, LYLE.
DIDA IS ALSO TRAINING SECRETLY SOMEWHERE.
DIDA IS?!
I CAN'T SEEM TO IMAGINE IT.
THAT'S BECAUSE HE HATES IT WHEN PEOPLE SEE HIM PUTTING IN EFFORT.

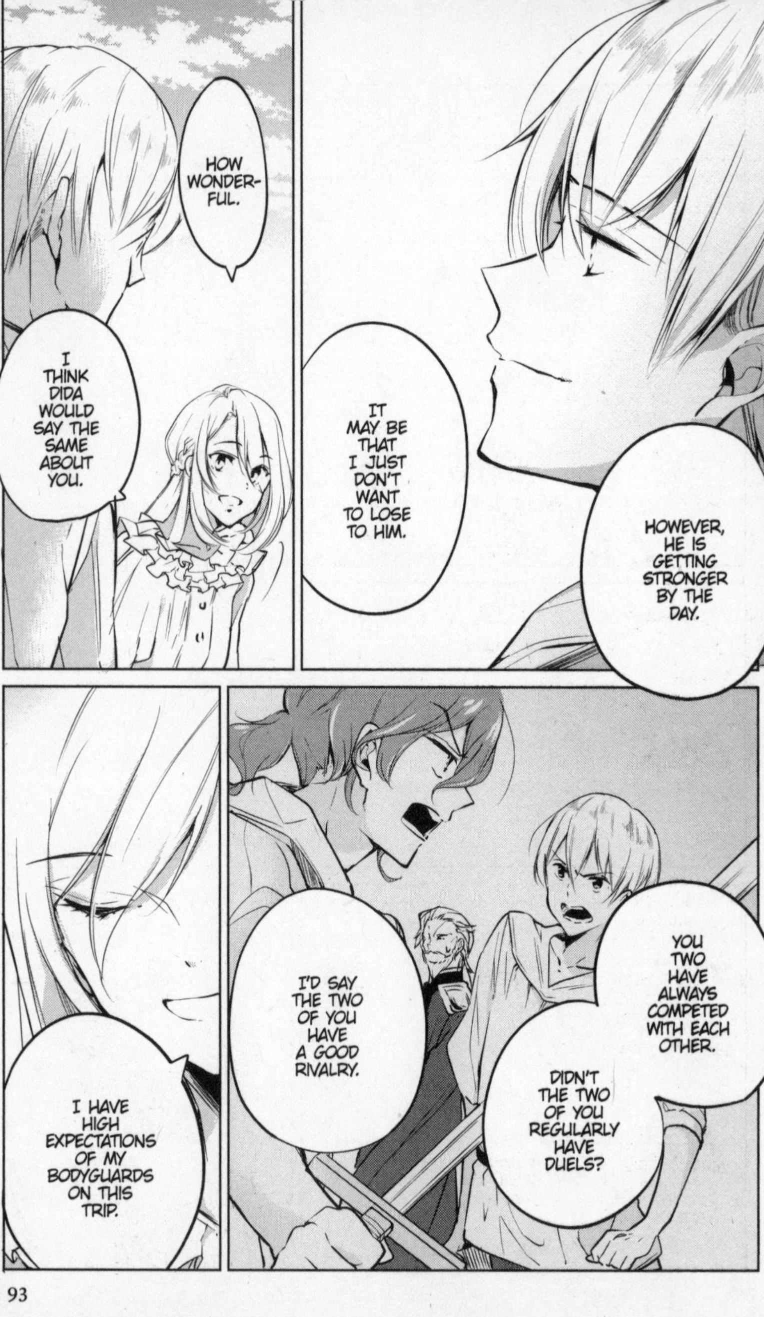
HOWEVER, HE IS GETTING STRONGER BY THE DAY.
IT MAY BE THAT I JUST DON'T WANT TO LOSE TO HIM.
HOW WONDER-FUL.
I THINK DIDA WOULD SAY THE SAME ABOUT YOU.
YOU TWO HAVE ALWAYS COMPETED WITH EACH OTHER.
DIDN'T THE TWO OF YOU REGULARLY HAVE DUELS?
I'D SAY THE TWO OF YOU HAVE A GOOD RIVALRY.
I HAVE HIGH EXPECTATIONS OF MY BODYGUARDS ON THIS TRIP.

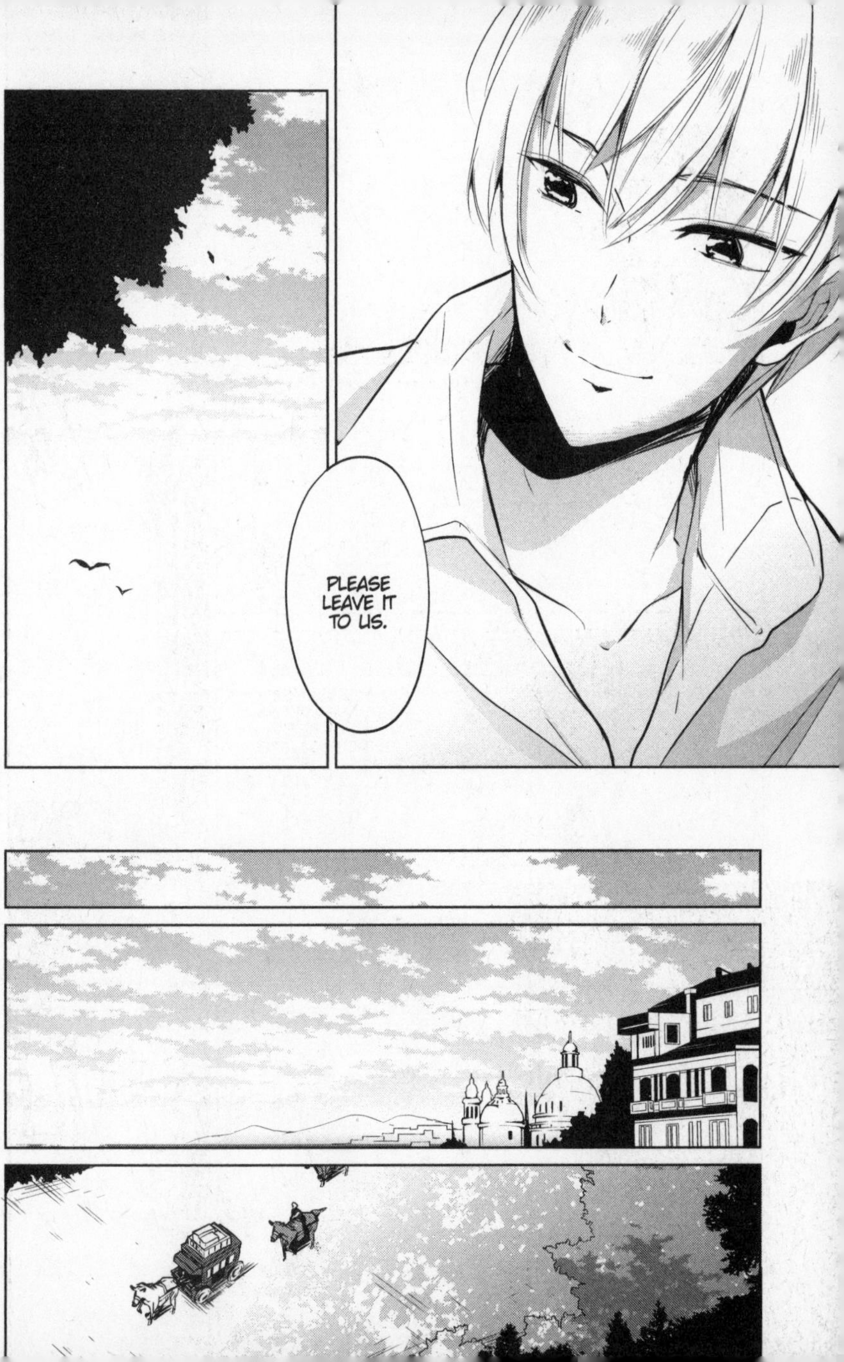
PLEASE LEAVE IT TO US.

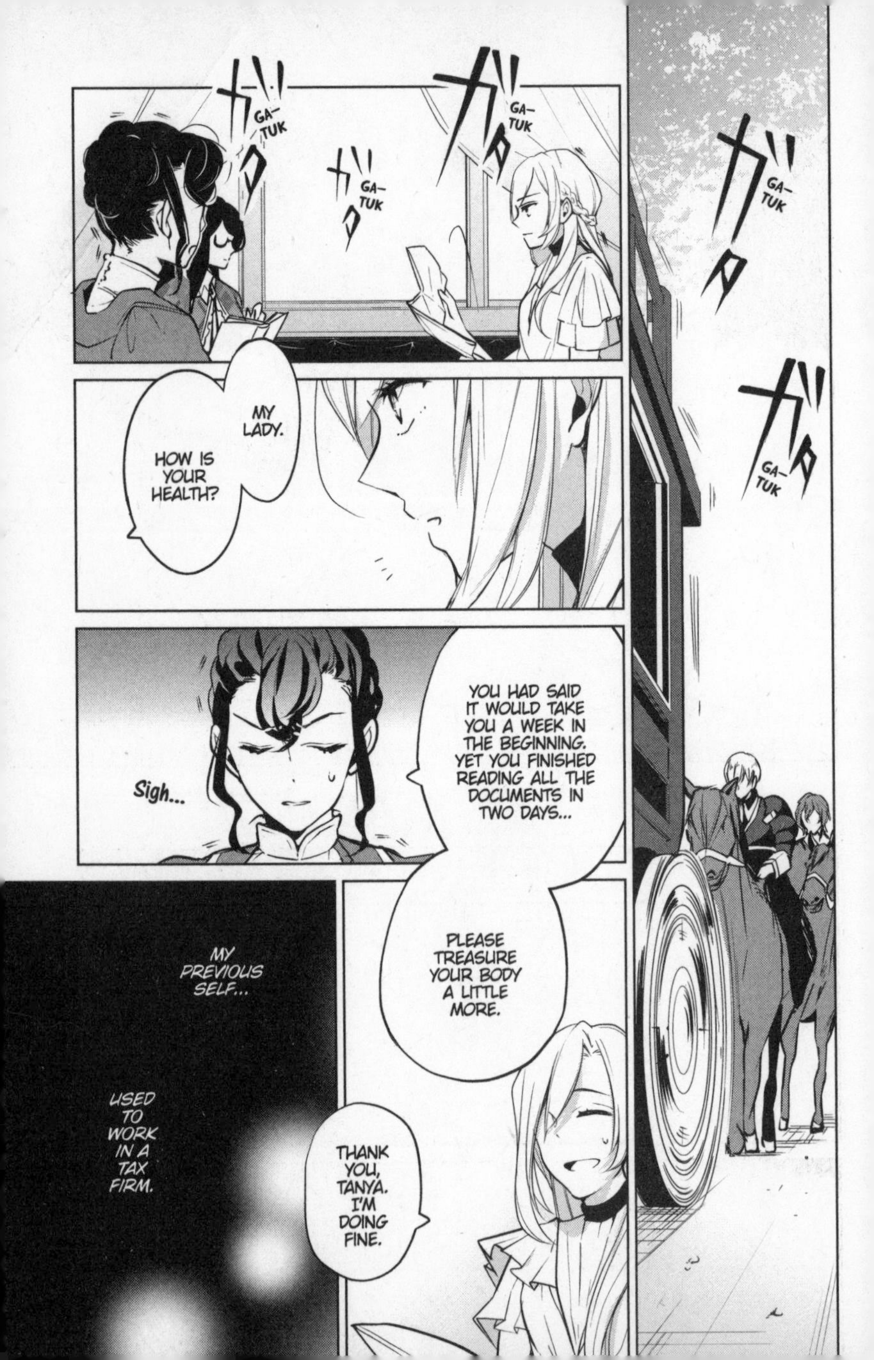
ガタ
GA-TUK
ガタ
GA-TUK
ガタ
GA-TUK
ガタ
GA-TUK
ガタ
GA-TUK
MY LADY.
HOW IS YOUR HEALTH?
YOU HAD SAID IT WOULD TAKE YOU A WEEK IN THE BEGINNING. YET YOU FINISHED READING ALL THE DOCUMENTS IN TWO DAYS...
Sigh...
PLEASE TREASURE YOUR BODY A LITTLE MORE.
THANK YOU, TANYA. I'M DOING FINE.
MY PREVIOUS SELF...
USED TO WORK IN A TAX FIRM.

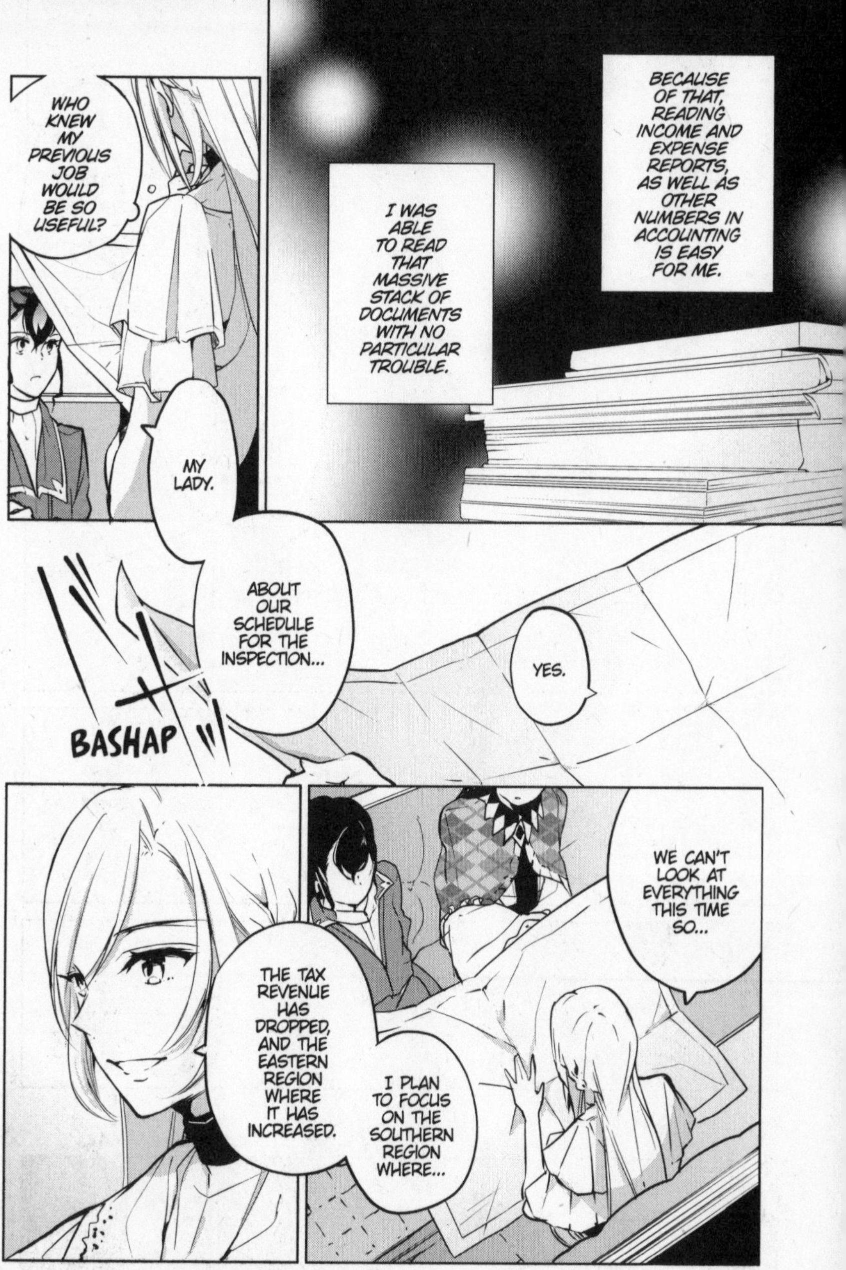
BECAUSE OF THAT, READING INCOME AND EXPENSE REPORTS, AS WELL AS OTHER NUMBERS IN ACCOUNTING IS EASY FOR ME.
I WAS ABLE TO READ THAT MASSIVE STACK OF DOCUMENTS WITH NO PARTICULAR TROUBLE.
WHO KNEW MY PREVIOUS JOB WOULD BE SO USEFUL?
MY LADY.
ABOUT OUR SCHEDULE FOR THE INSPECTION...
YES.
BASHAP
WE CAN'T LOOK AT EVERYTHING THIS TIME SO...
I PLAN TO FOCUS ON THE SOUTHERN REGION WHERE...
THE TAX REVENUE HAS DROPPED, AND THE EASTERN REGION WHERE IT HAS INCREASED.

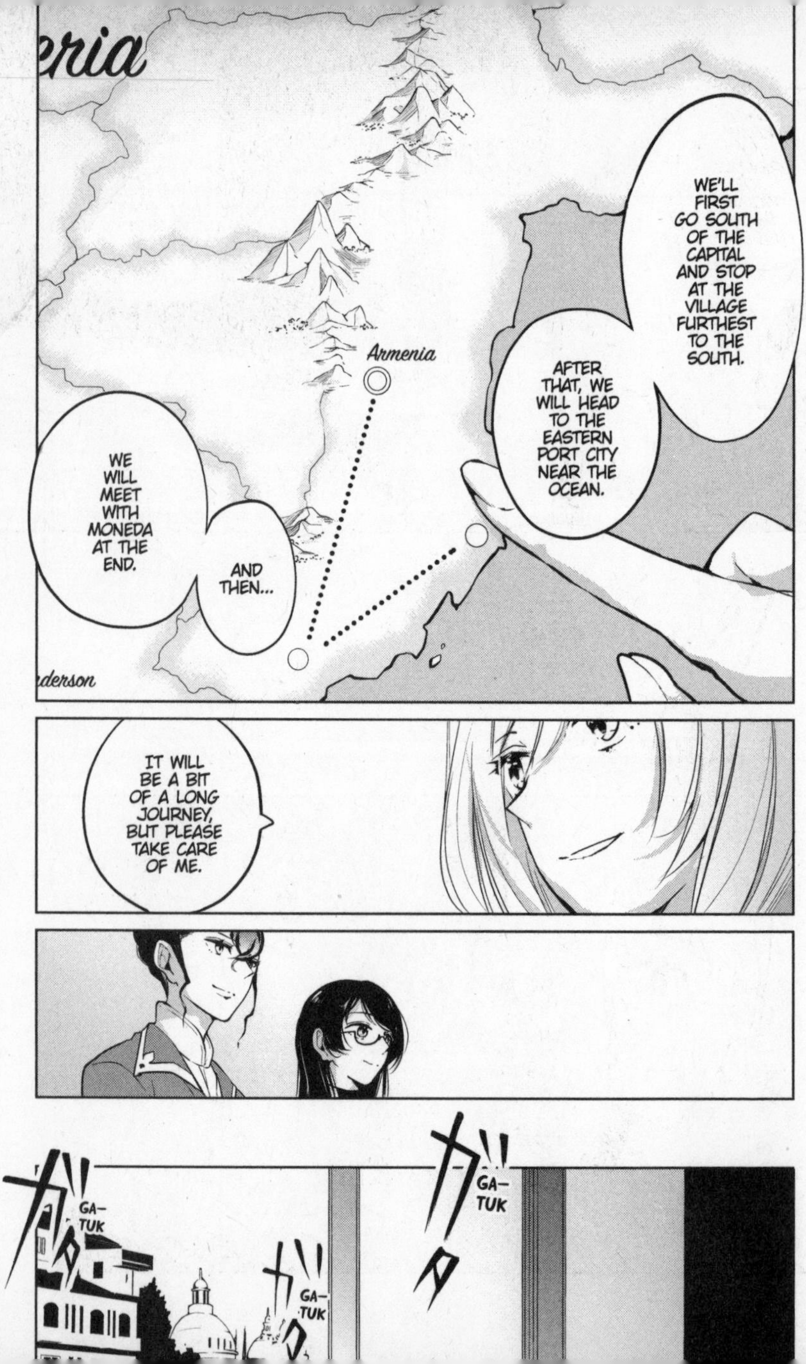
Armenia
WE'LL FIRST GO SOUTH OF THE CAPITAL AND STOP AT THE VILLAGE FURTHEST TO THE SOUTH.
AFTER THAT, WE WILL HEAD TO THE EASTERN PORT CITY NEAR THE OCEAN.
AND THEN...
WE WILL MEET WITH MONEDA AT THE END.
IT WILL BE A BIT OF A LONG JOURNEY, BUT PLEASE TAKE CARE OF ME.
GA-TUK
GA-TUK
GA-TUK

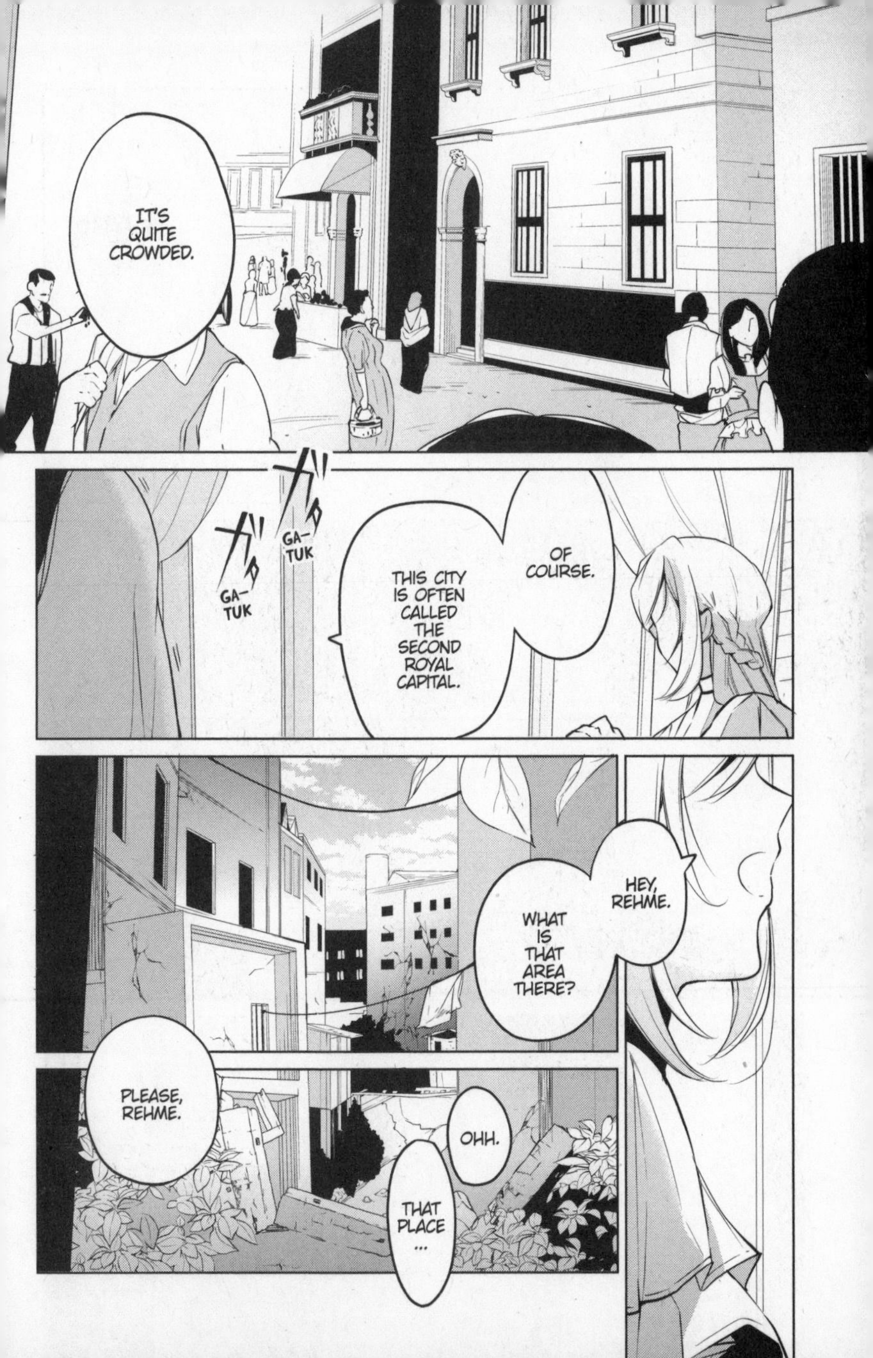
IT'S QUITE CROWDED.
OF COURSE.
THIS CITY IS OFTEN CALLED THE SECOND ROYAL CAPITAL.
GA-TUK
GA-TUK
HEY, REHME.
WHAT IS THAT AREA THERE?
OHH.
THAT PLACE...
PLEASE, REHME.

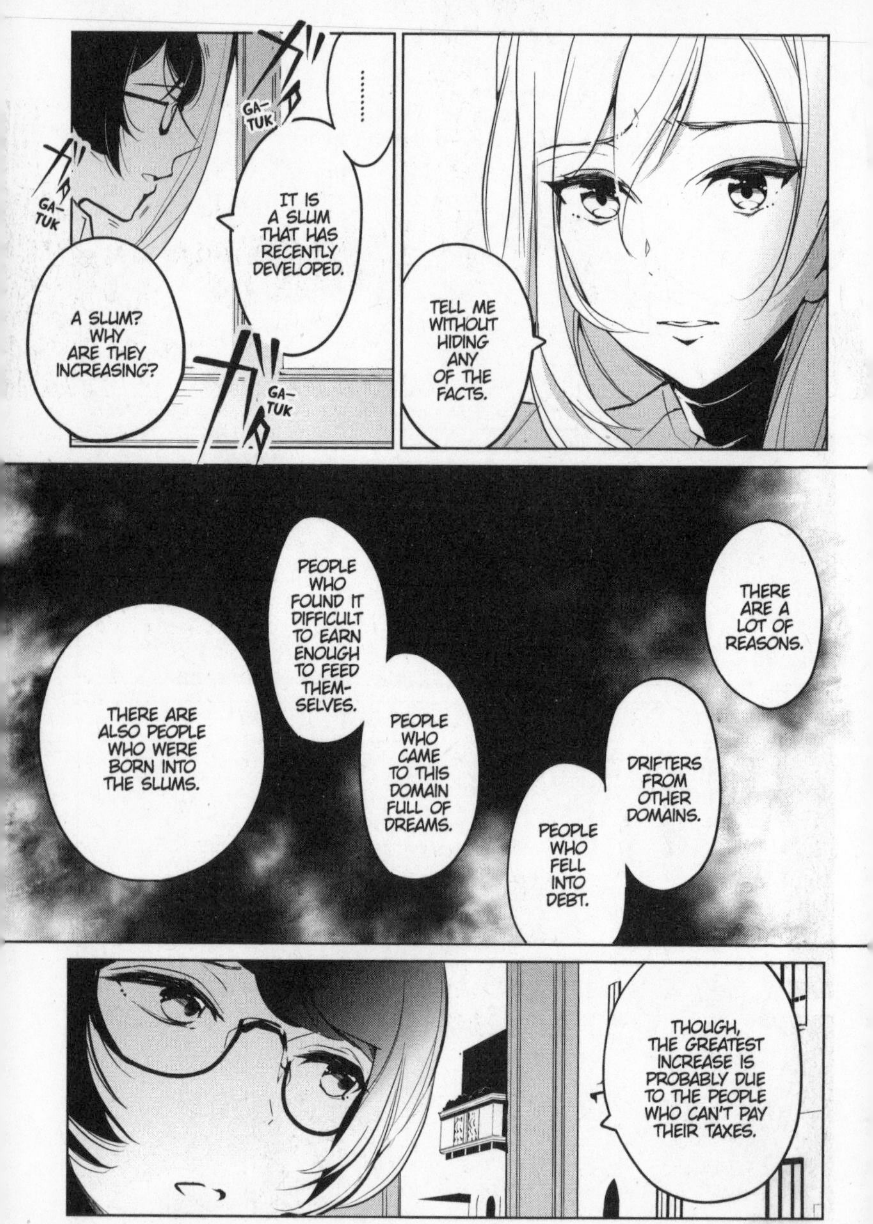
TELL ME WITHOUT HIDING ANY OF THE FACTS.
......
GA-TUK
IT IS A SLUM THAT HAS RECENTLY DEVELOPED.
GA-TUK
GA-TUK
A SLUM? WHY ARE THEY INCREASING?
THERE ARE A LOT OF REASONS.
DRIFTERS FROM OTHER DOMAINS.
PEOPLE WHO FELL INTO DEBT.
PEOPLE WHO FOUND IT DIFFICULT TO EARN ENOUGH TO FEED THEM-SELVES.
PEOPLE WHO CAME TO THIS DOMAIN FULL OF DREAMS.
THERE ARE ALSO PEOPLE WHO WERE BORN INTO THE SLUMS.
THOUGH, THE GREATEST INCREASE IS PROBABLY DUE TO THE PEOPLE WHO CAN'T PAY THEIR TAXES.

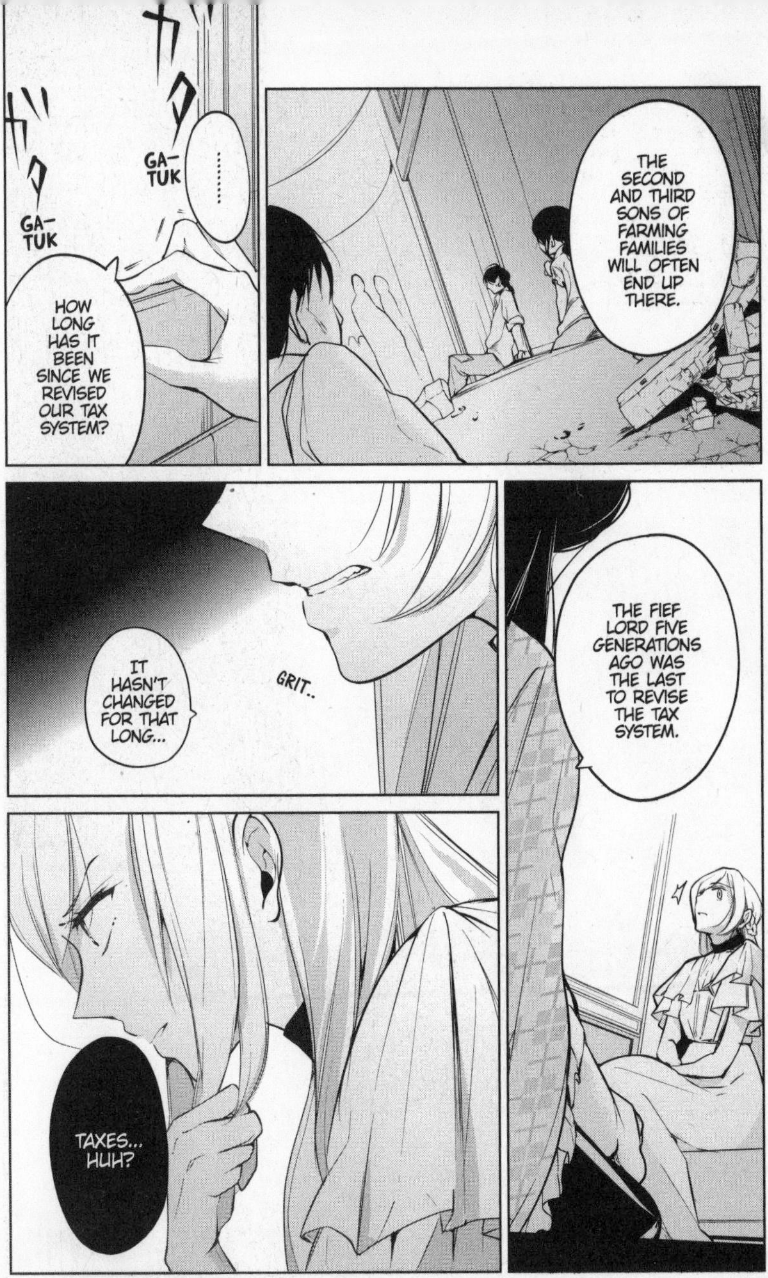
THE SECOND AND THIRD SONS OF FARMING FAMILIES WILL OFTEN END UP THERE.
GA-TUK
......
GA-TUK
HOW LONG HAS IT BEEN SINCE WE REVISED OUR TAX SYSTEM?
THE FIEF LORD FIVE GENERATIONS AGO WAS THE LAST TO REVISE THE TAX SYSTEM.
GRIT..
IT HASN'T CHANGED FOR THAT LONG...
TAXES... HUH?

#6 end

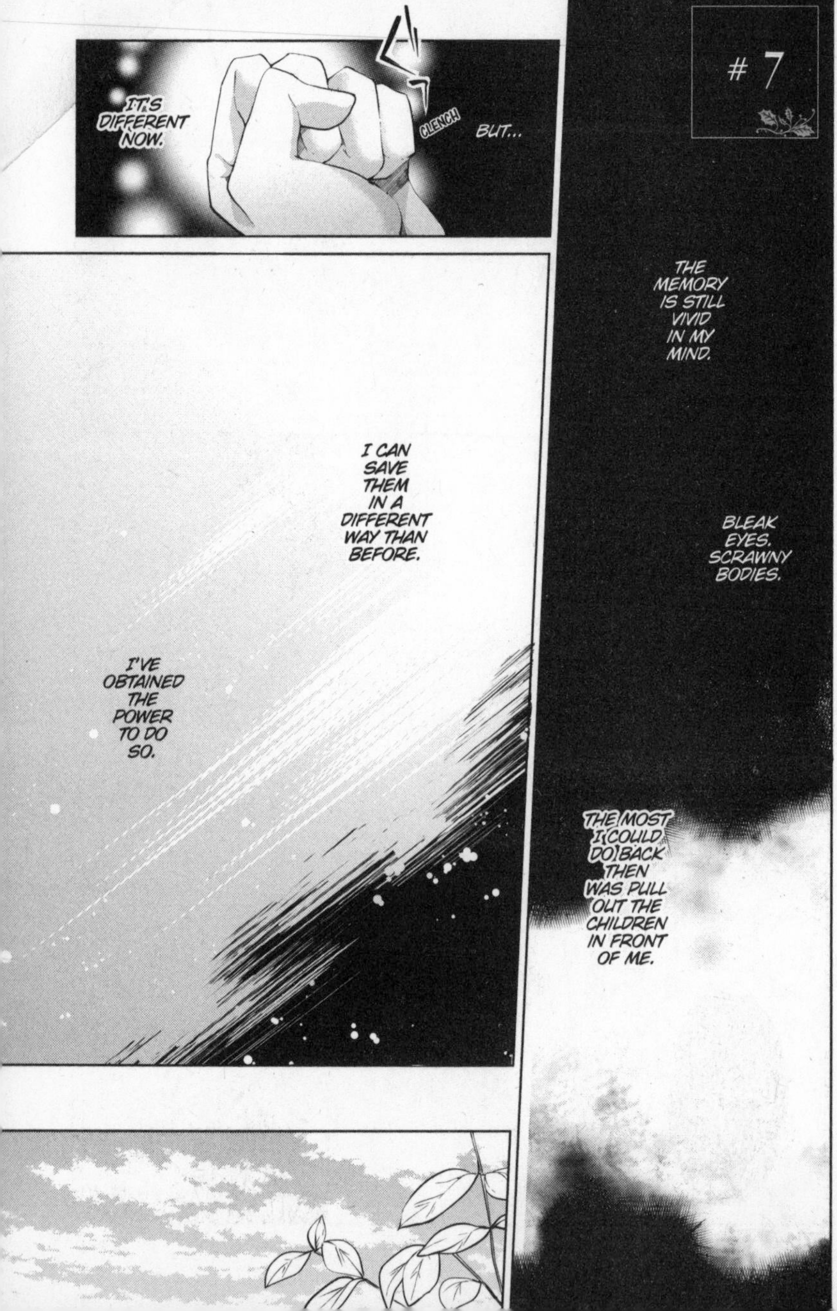

7
THE MEMORY IS STILL VIVID IN MY MIND.
BLEAK EYES. SCRAWNY BODIES.
THE MOST I COULD DO BACK THEN WAS PULL OUT THE CHILDREN IN FRONT OF ME.
BUT...
CLENCH
IT'S DIFFERENT NOW.
I CAN SAVE THEM IN A DIFFERENT WAY THAN BEFORE.
I'VE OBTAINED THE POWER TO DO SO.

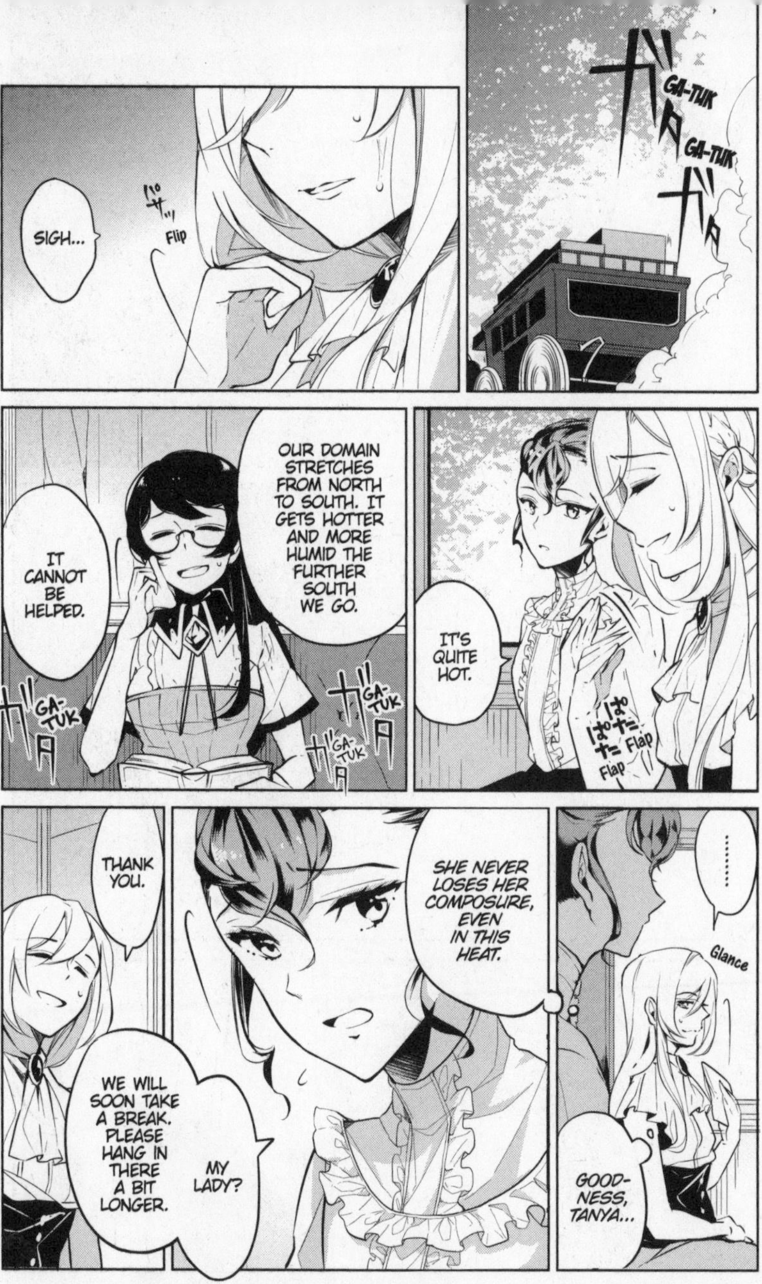
GA-TUK
GA-TUK
SIGH...
Flip
IT'S QUITE HOT.
Flap
Flap
OUR DOMAIN STRETCHES FROM NORTH TO SOUTH. IT GETS HOTTER AND MORE HUMID THE FURTHER SOUTH WE GO.
IT CANNOT BE HELPED.
GA-TUK
GA-TUK
GA-TUK
......
Glance
GOODNESS, TANYA...
SHE NEVER LOSES HER COMPOSURE, EVEN IN THIS HEAT.
THANK YOU.
WE WILL SOON TAKE A BREAK. PLEASE HANG IN THERE A BIT LONGER. MY LADY?

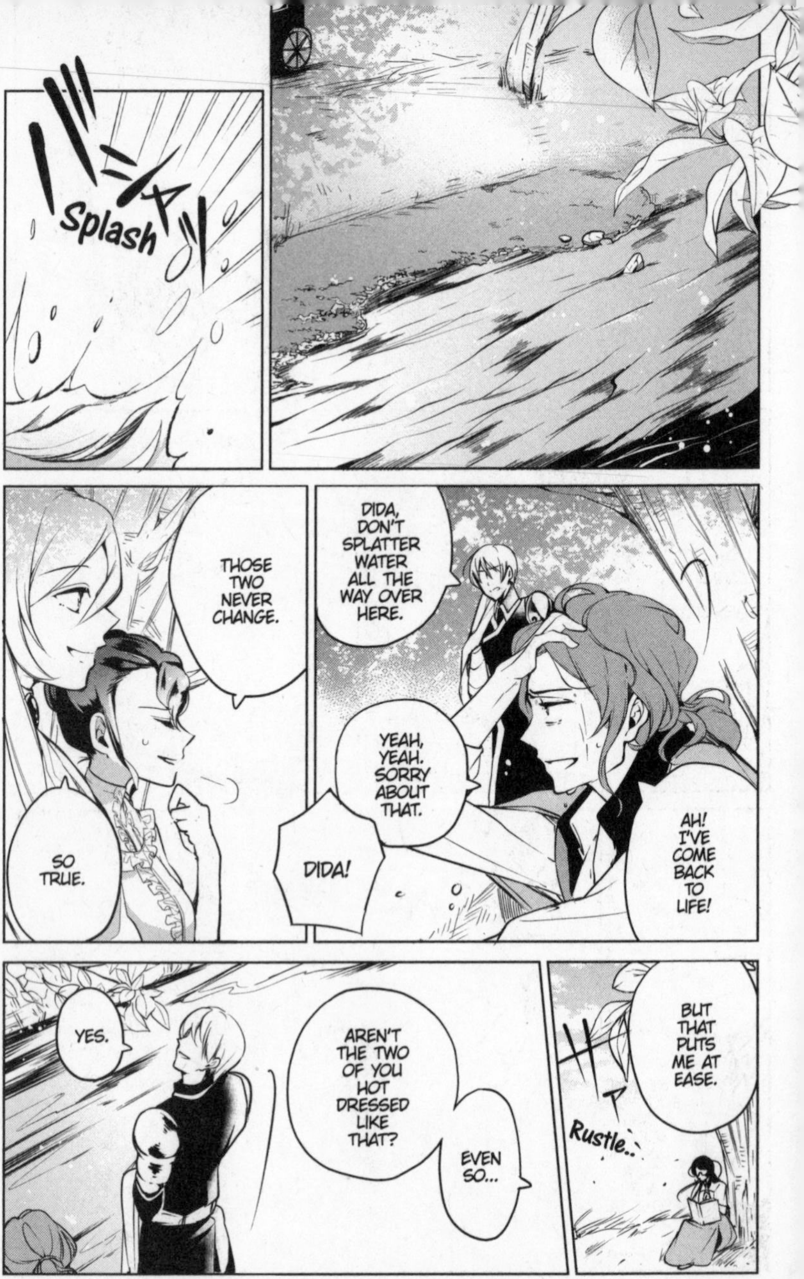
Splash
DIDA, DON'T SPLATTER WATER ALL THE WAY OVER HERE.
AH! I'VE COME BACK TO LIFE!
YEAH, YEAH. SORRY ABOUT THAT.
DIDA!
THOSE TWO NEVER CHANGE.
SO TRUE.
BUT THAT PUTS ME AT EASE.
Rustle...
EVEN SO...
AREN'T THE TWO OF YOU HOT DRESSED LIKE THAT?
YES.

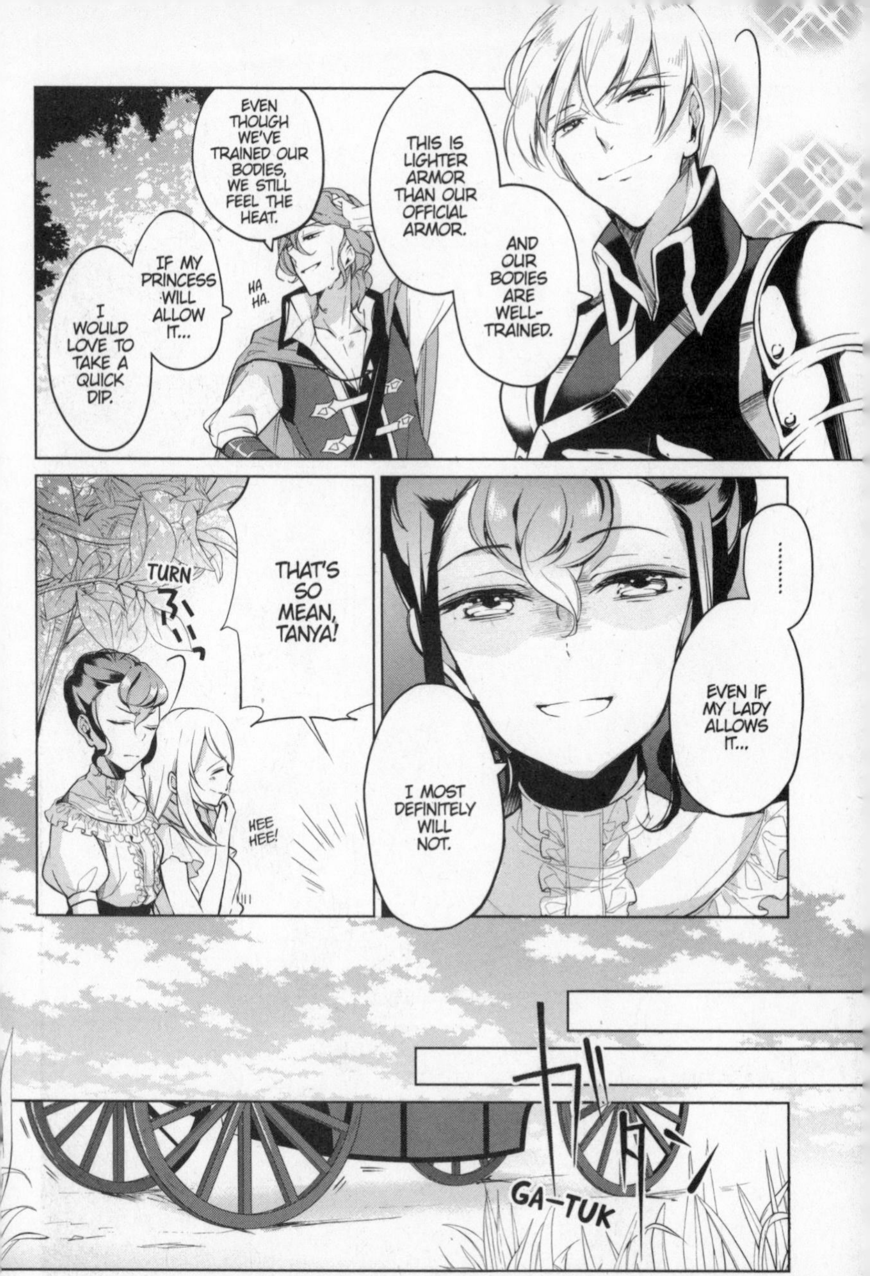
THIS IS LIGHTER ARMOR THAN OUR OFFICIAL ARMOR.
AND OUR BODIES ARE WELL-TRAINED.
EVEN THOUGH WE'VE TRAINED OUR BODIES, WE STILL FEEL THE HEAT.
HA HA.
IF MY PRINCESS WILL ALLOW IT...
I WOULD LOVE TO TAKE A QUICK DIP.
......
EVEN IF MY LADY ALLOWS IT...
I MOST DEFINITELY WILL NOT.
THAT'S SO MEAN, TANYA!
TURN
HEE HEE!
GA-TUK

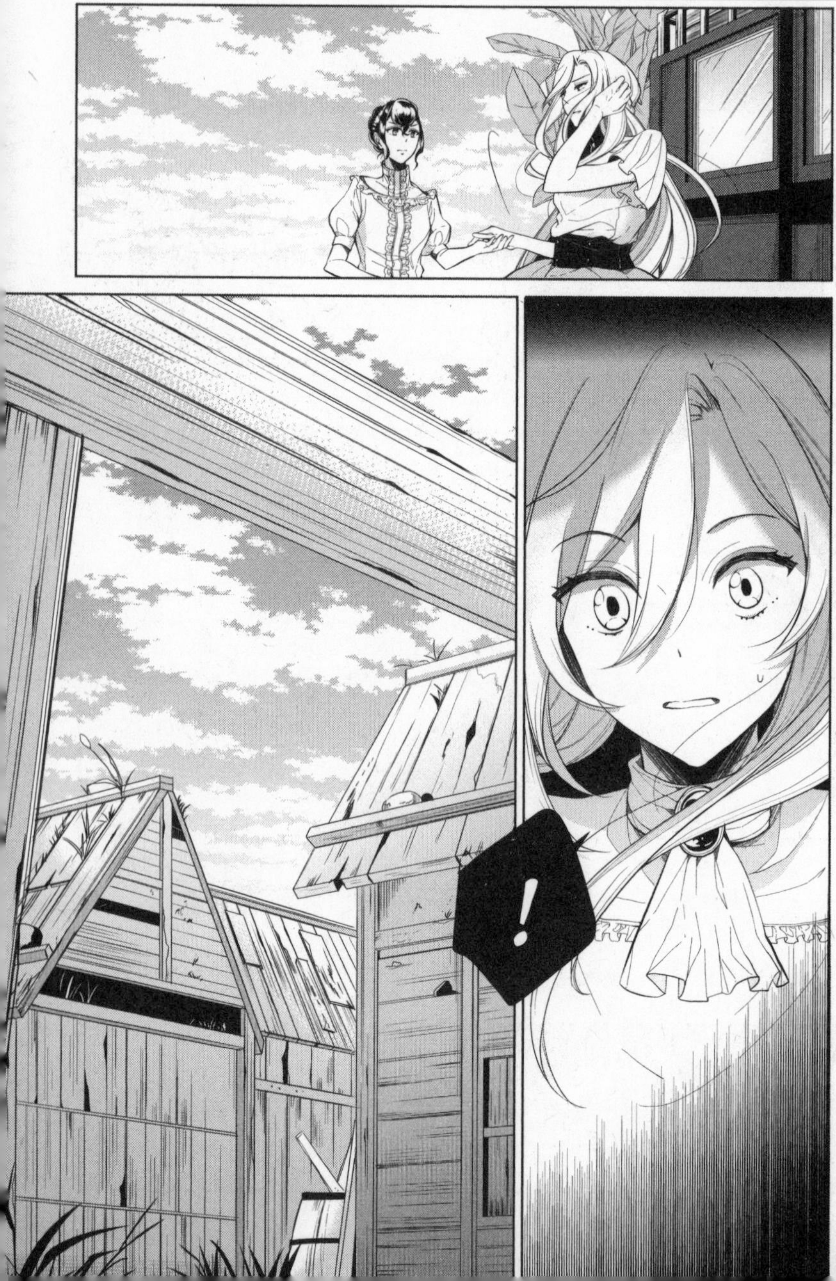
!

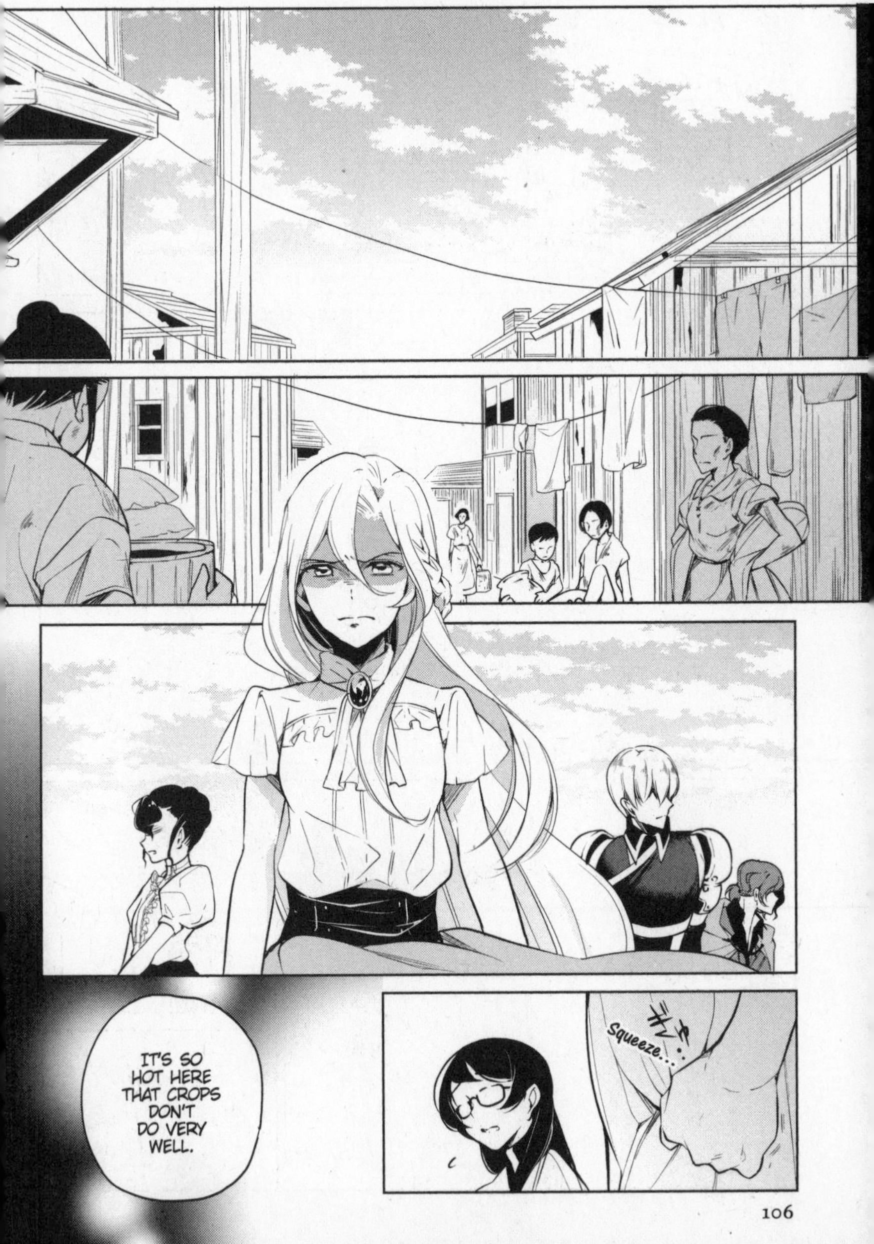
Squeeze...
IT'S SO HOT HERE THAT CROPS DON'T DO VERY WELL.

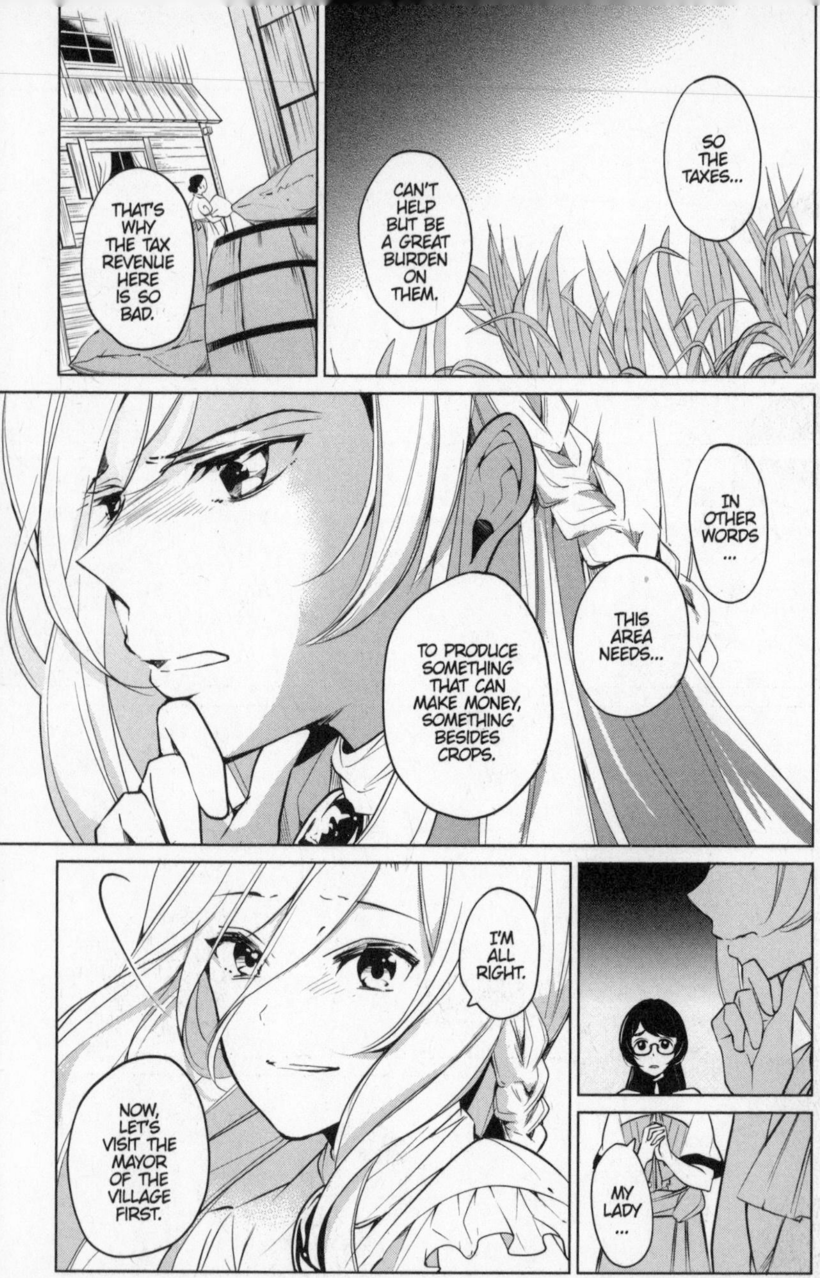
SO THE TAXES...
CAN'T HELP BUT BE A GREAT BURDEN ON THEM.
THAT'S WHY THE TAX REVENUE HERE IS SO BAD.
IN OTHER WORDS...
THIS AREA NEEDS...
TO PRODUCE SOMETHING THAT CAN MAKE MONEY, SOMETHING BESIDES CROPS.
MY LADY...
I'M ALL RIGHT.
NOW, LET'S VISIT THE MAYOR OF THE VILLAGE FIRST.

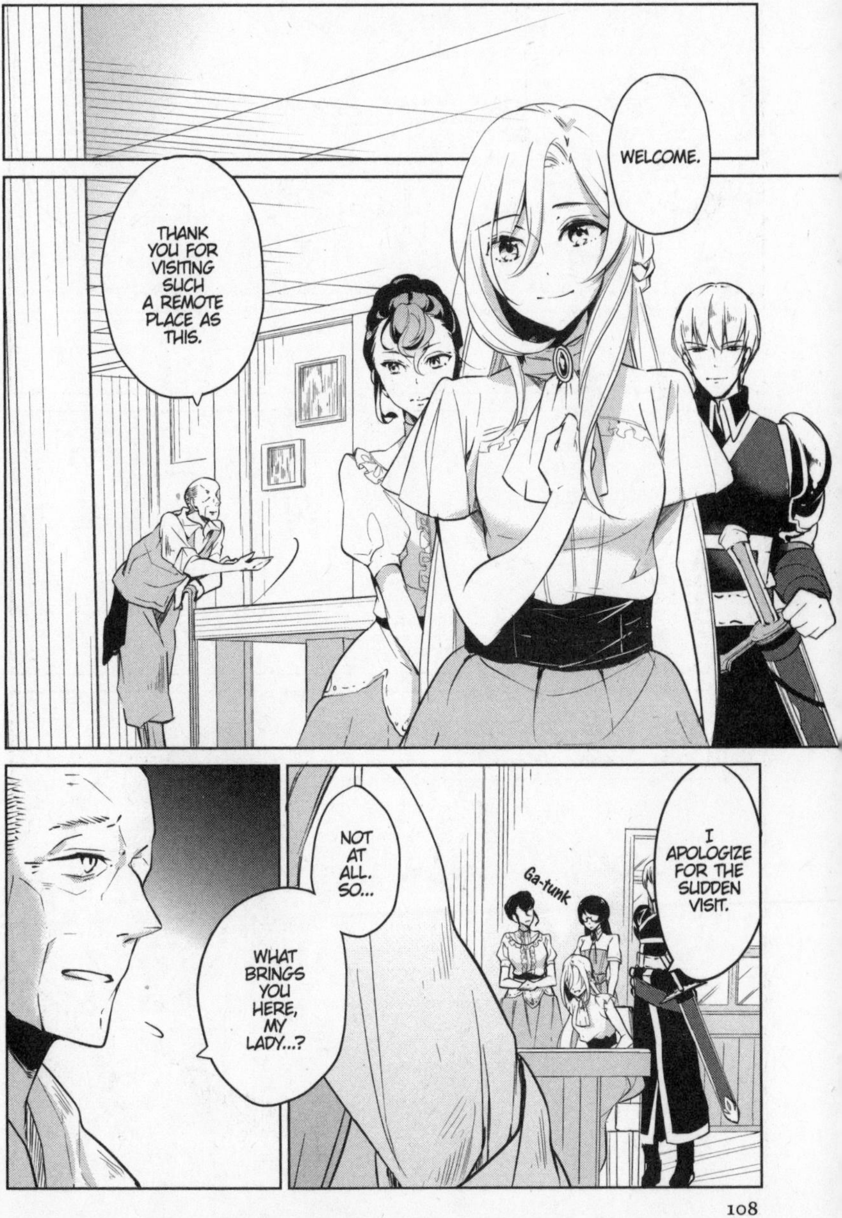
WELCOME.
THANK YOU FOR VISITING SUCH A REMOTE PLACE AS THIS.
I APOLOGIZE FOR THE SUDDEN VISIT.
Ga-tunk
NOT AT ALL. SO...
WHAT BRINGS YOU HERE, MY LADY...?

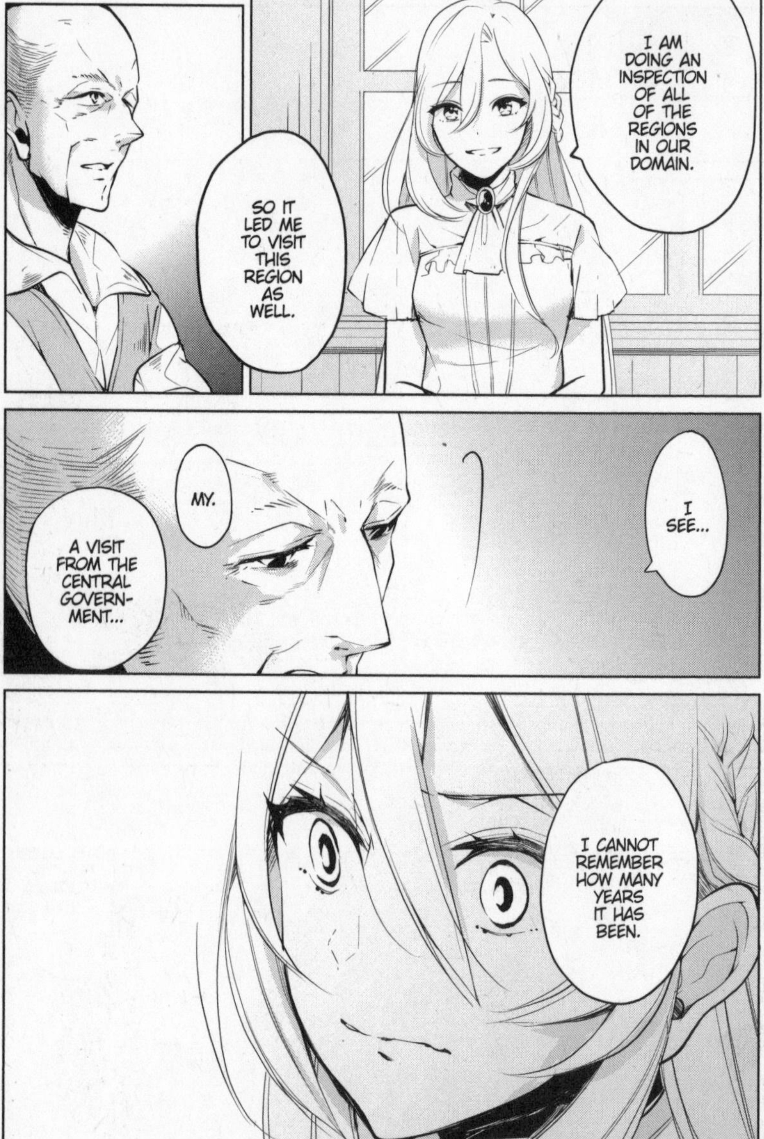
I AM DOING AN INSPECTION OF ALL OF THE REGIONS IN OUR DOMAIN.
SO IT LED ME TO VISIT THIS REGION AS WELL.
I SEE...
MY.
A VISIT FROM THE CENTRAL GOVERN-MENT...
I CANNOT REMEMBER HOW MANY YEARS IT HAS BEEN.

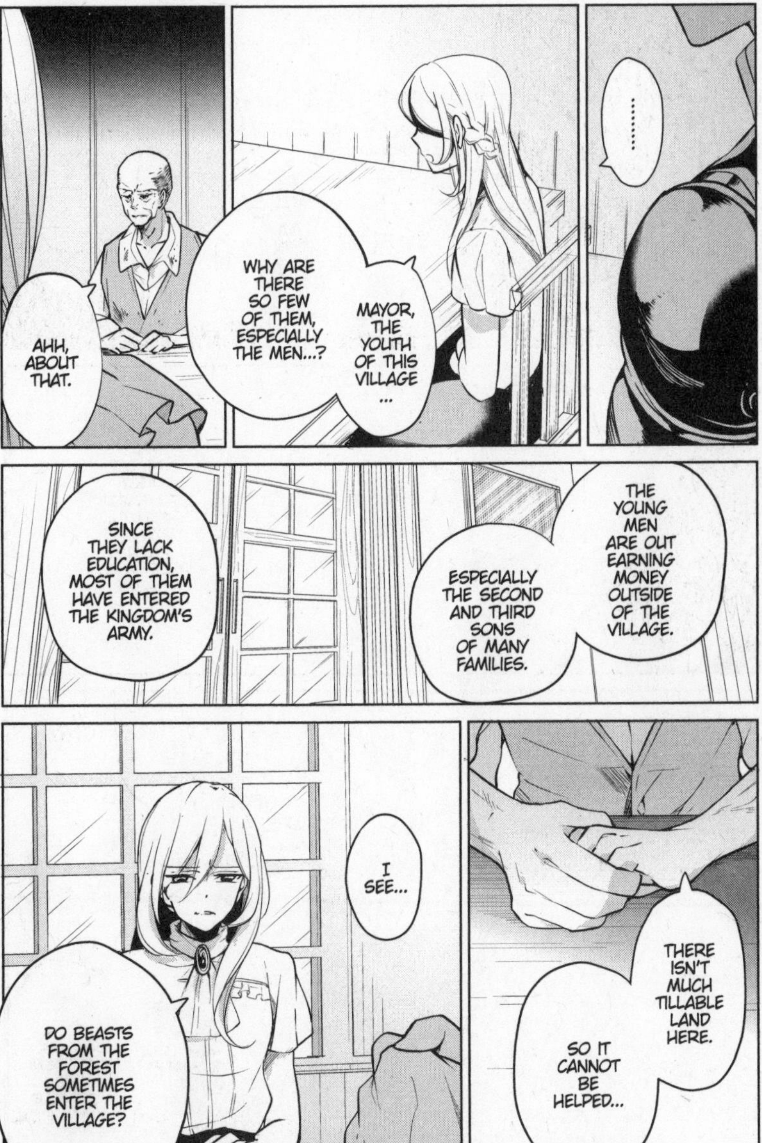
......
MAYOR, THE YOUTH OF THIS VILLAGE ...
WHY ARE THERE SO FEW OF THEM, ESPECIALLY THE MEN...?
AHH, ABOUT THAT.
THE YOUNG MEN ARE OUT EARNING MONEY OUTSIDE OF THE VILLAGE.
ESPECIALLY THE SECOND AND THIRD SONS OF MANY FAMILIES.
SINCE THEY LACK EDUCATION, MOST OF THEM HAVE ENTERED THE KINGDOM'S ARMY.
THERE ISN'T MUCH TILLABLE LAND HERE.
SO IT CANNOT BE HELPED...
I SEE...
DO BEASTS FROM THE FOREST SOMETIMES ENTER THE VILLAGE?

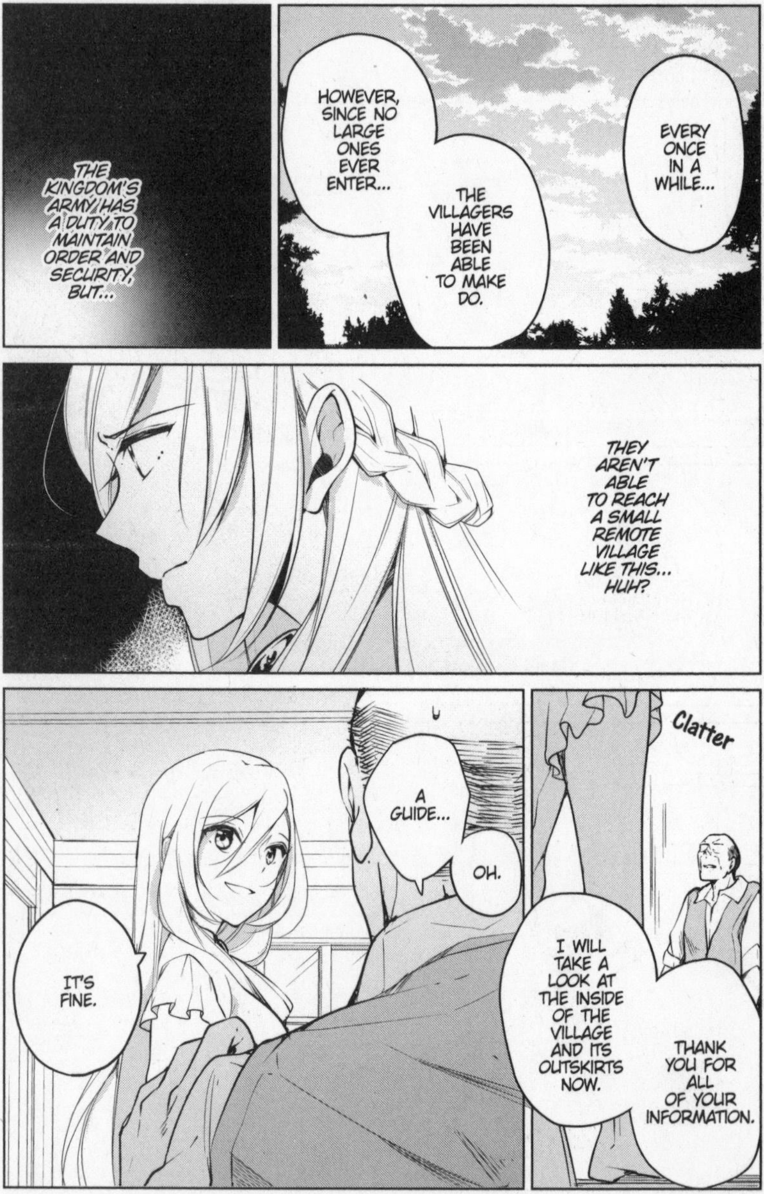
EVERY ONCE IN A WHILE...
HOWEVER, SINCE NO LARGE ONES EVER ENTER...
THE VILLAGERS HAVE BEEN ABLE TO MAKE DO.
THE KINGDOM'S ARMY HAS A DUTY TO MAINTAIN ORDER AND SECURITY, BUT...
THEY AREN'T ABLE TO REACH A SMALL REMOTE VILLAGE LIKE THIS... HUH?
Clatter
THANK YOU FOR ALL OF YOUR INFORMATION.
I WILL TAKE A LOOK AT THE INSIDE OF THE VILLAGE AND ITS OUTSKIRTS NOW.
A GUIDE...
OH.
IT'S FINE.

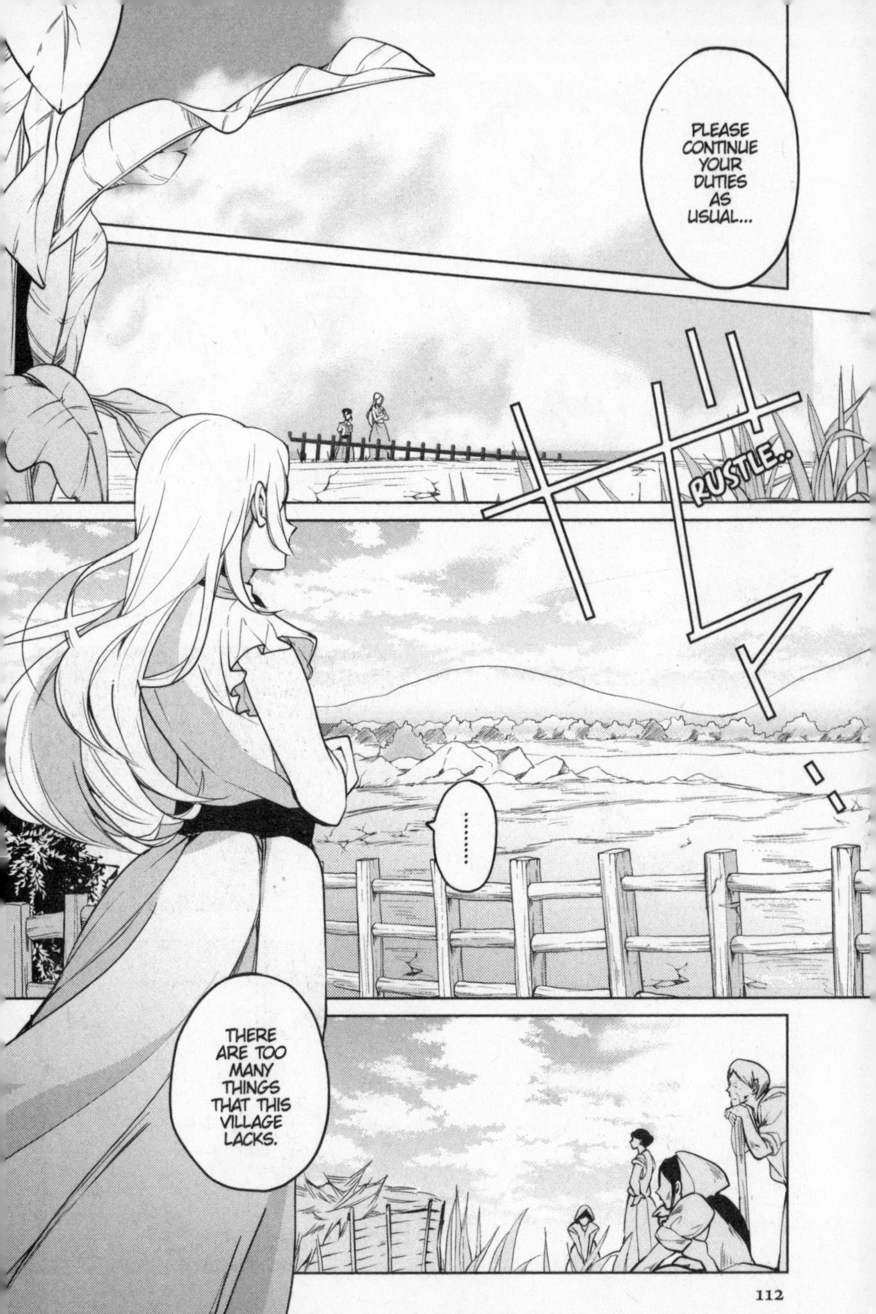
PLEASE CONTINUE YOUR DUTIES AS USUAL...
RUSTLE..
......
THERE ARE TOO MANY THINGS THAT THIS VILLAGE LACKS.

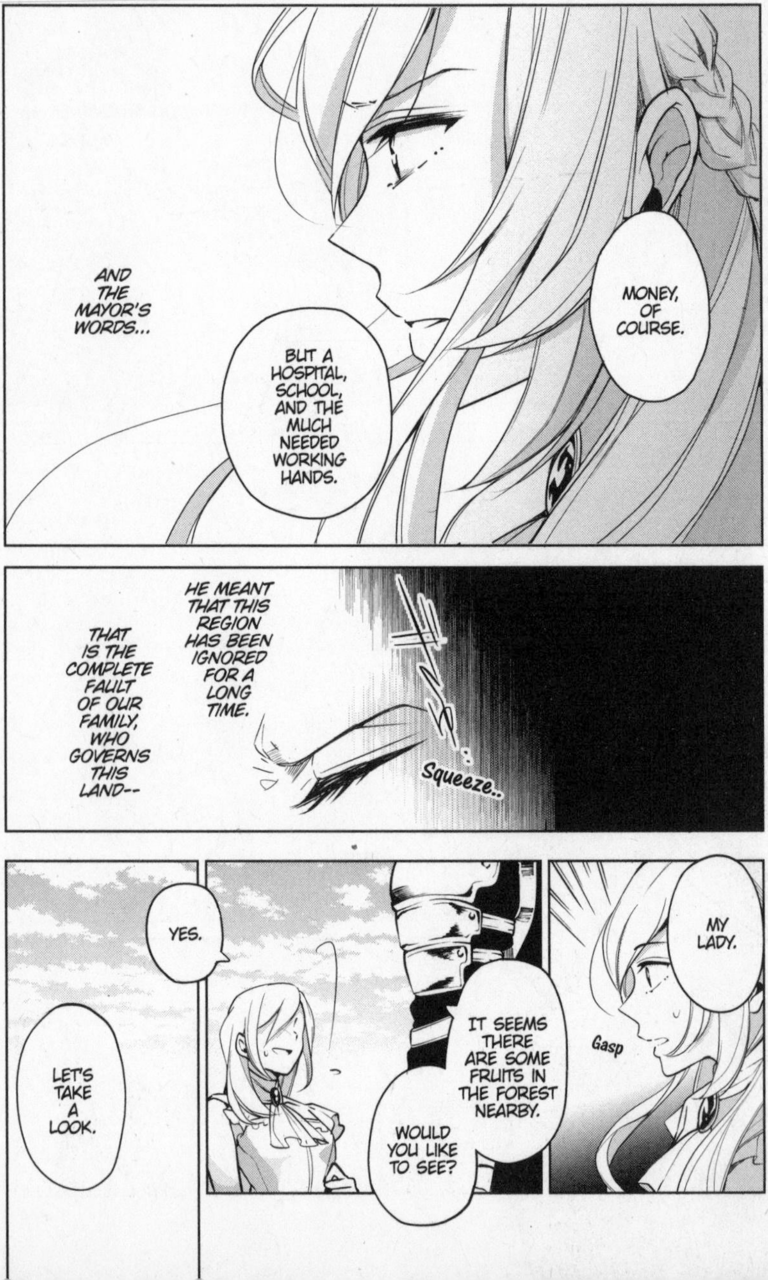
MONEY, OF COURSE.
BUT A HOSPITAL, SCHOOL, AND THE MUCH NEEDED WORKING HANDS.
AND THE MAYOR'S WORDS...
HE MEANT THAT THIS REGION HAS BEEN IGNORED FOR A LONG TIME.
THAT IS THE COMPLETE FAULT OF OUR FAMILY, WHO GOVERNS THIS LAND--
Squeeze..
MY LADY.
Gasp
IT SEEMS THERE ARE SOME FRUITS IN THE FOREST NEARBY.
WOULD YOU LIKE TO SEE?
YES.
LET'S TAKE A LOOK.

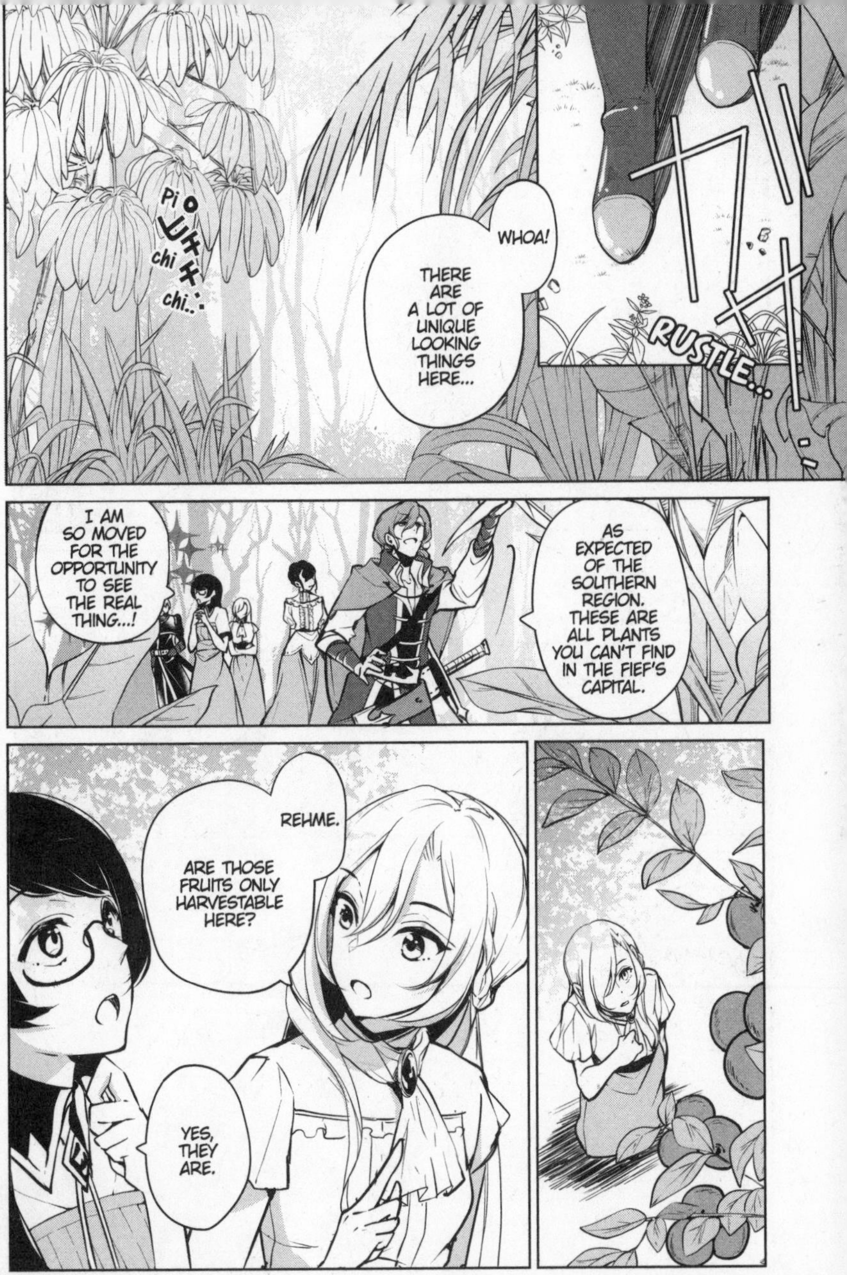
RUSTLE...
WHOA!
THERE ARE A LOT OF UNIQUE LOOKING THINGS HERE...
Pi chi chi...
AS EXPECTED OF THE SOUTHERN REGION. THESE ARE ALL PLANTS YOU CAN'T FIND IN THE FIEF'S CAPITAL.
I AM SO MOVED FOR THE OPPORTUNITY TO SEE THE REAL THING...!
REHME.
ARE THOSE FRUITS ONLY HARVESTABLE HERE?
YES, THEY ARE.

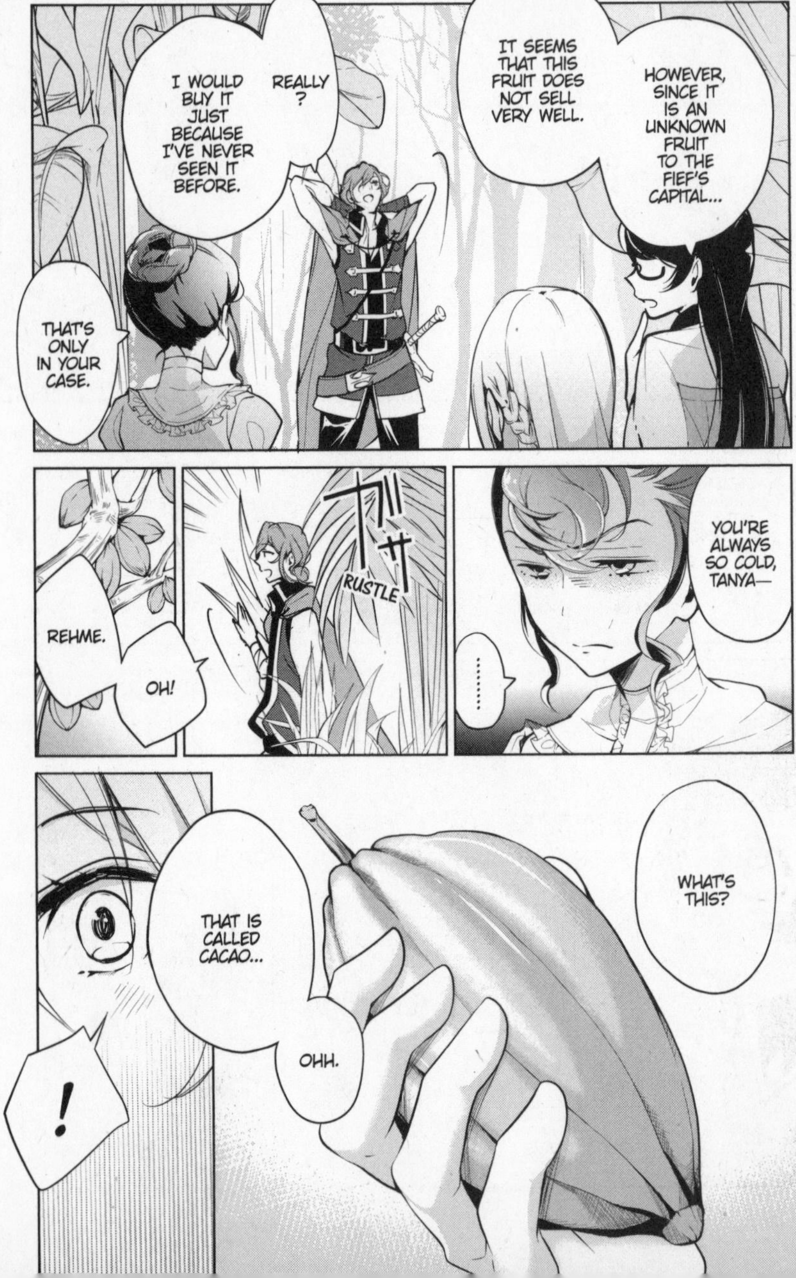
HOWEVER, SINCE IT IS AN UNKNOWN FRUIT TO THE FIEF'S CAPITAL...
IT SEEMS THAT THIS FRUIT DOES NOT SELL VERY WELL.
REALLY?
I WOULD BUY IT JUST BECAUSE I'VE NEVER SEEN IT BEFORE.
THAT'S ONLY IN YOUR CASE.
YOU'RE ALWAYS SO COLD, TANYA—
......
ガサ
RUSTLE
REHME.
OH!
WHAT'S THIS?
THAT IS CALLED CACAO...
OHH.
!

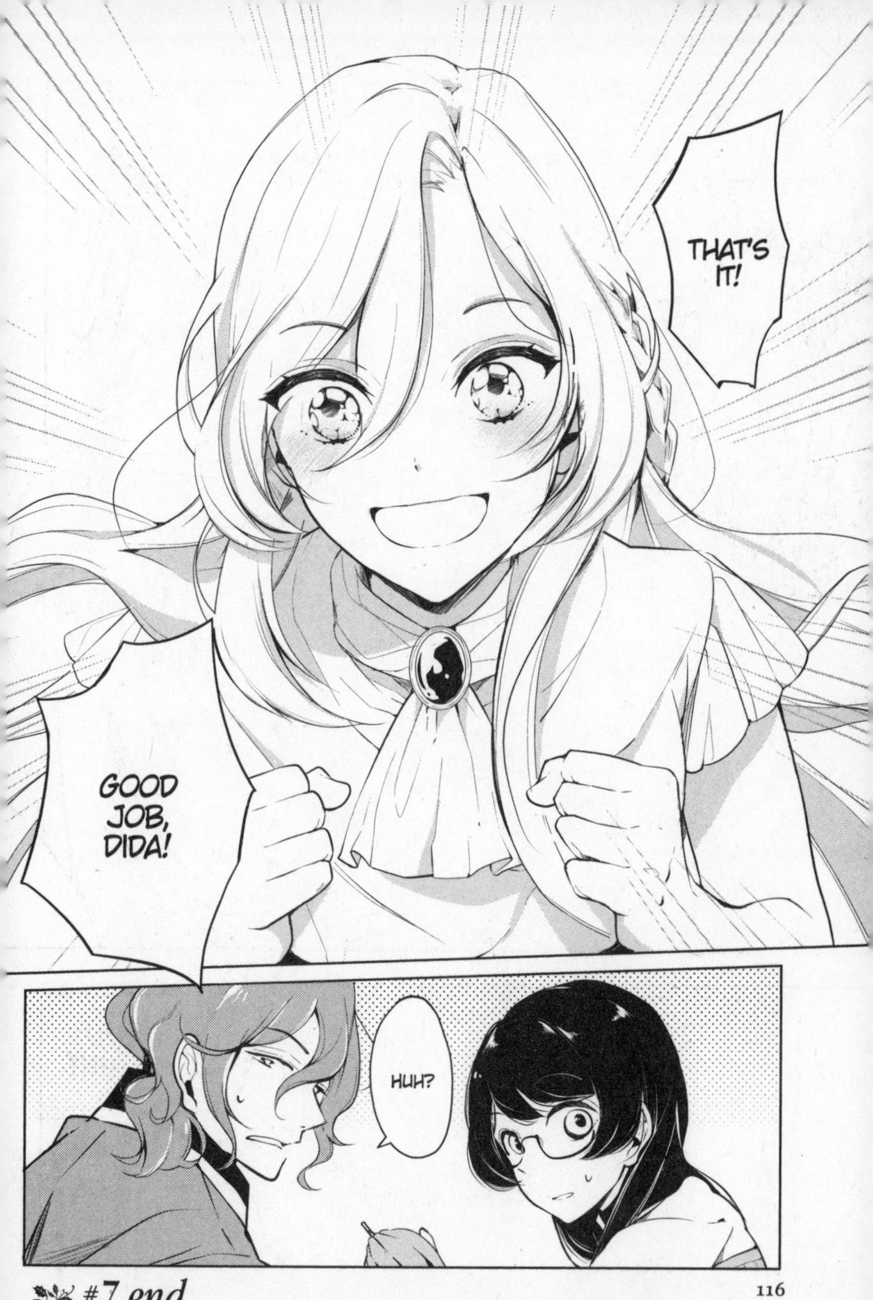
THAT'S IT!
GOOD JOB, DIDA!
HUH?

#7 end

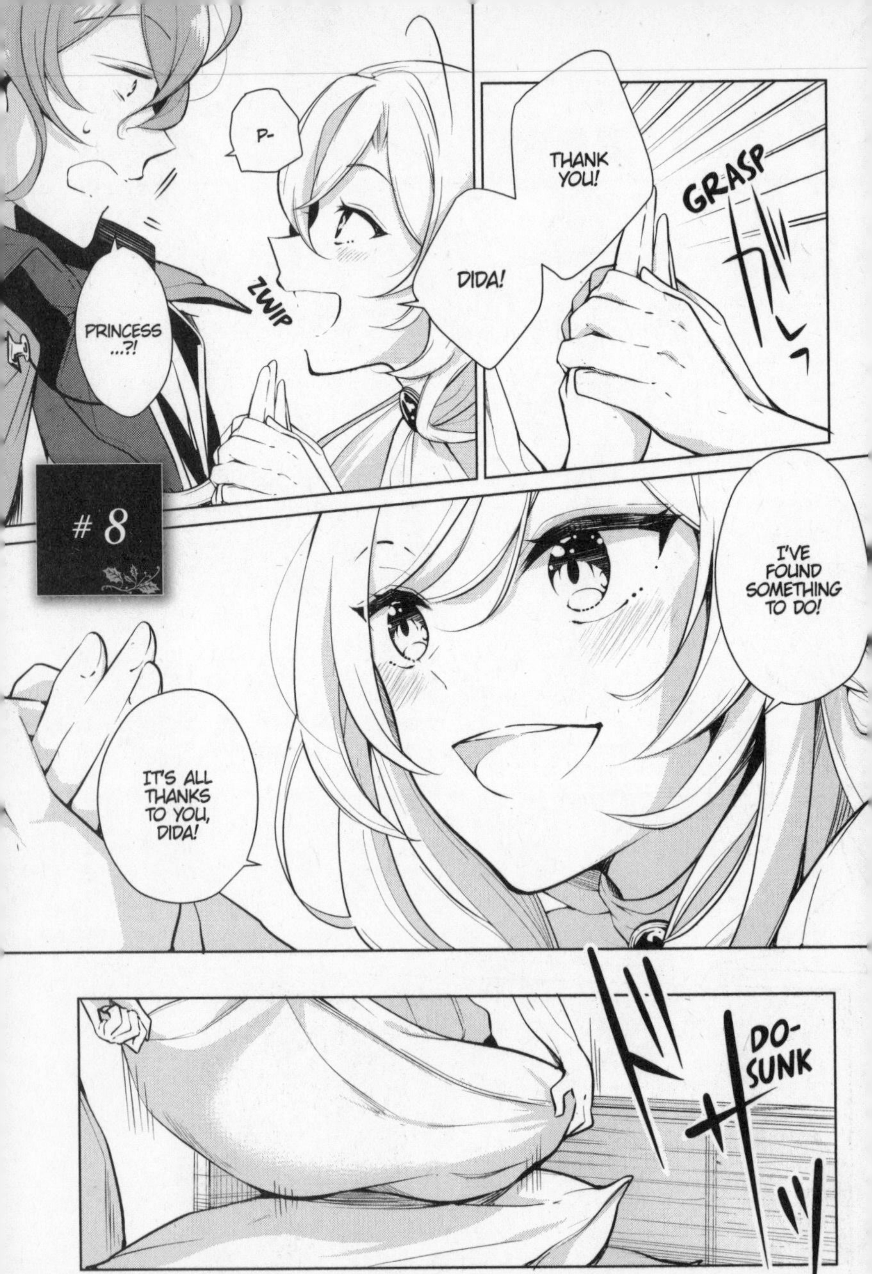

THANK YOU!
DIDA!
GRASP
P-
ZWIP
PRINCESS ...?!
8
I'VE FOUND SOMETHING TO DO!
IT'S ALL THANKS TO YOU, DIDA!
DO-SUNK

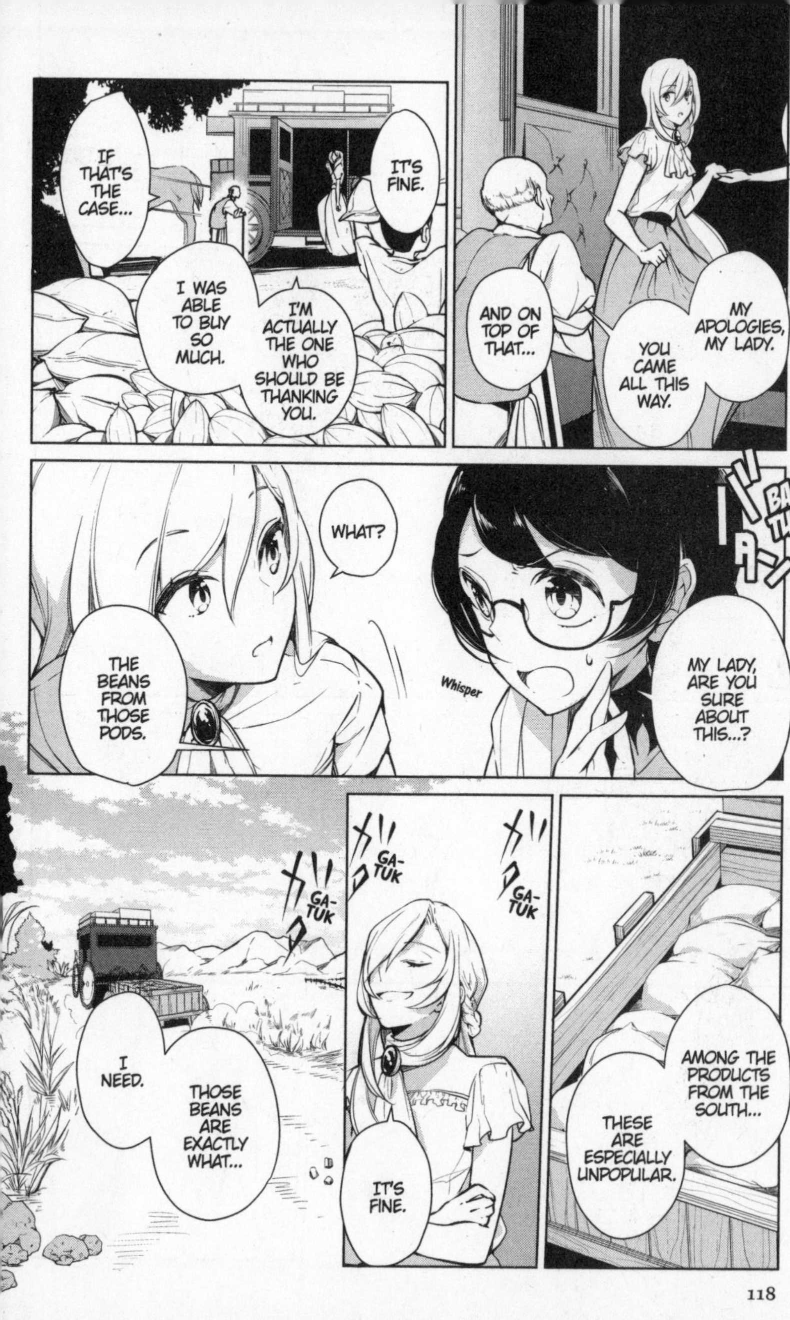
MY APOLOGIES, MY LADY.
YOU CAME ALL THIS WAY.
AND ON TOP OF THAT...
IT'S FINE.
I'M ACTUALLY THE ONE WHO SHOULD BE THANKING YOU.
I WAS ABLE TO BUY SO MUCH.
IF THAT'S THE CASE...
BA-TUNK
MY LADY, ARE YOU SURE ABOUT THIS...?
Whisper
WHAT?
THE BEANS FROM THOSE PODS.
AMONG THE PRODUCTS FROM THE SOUTH...
THESE ARE ESPECIALLY UNPOPULAR.
GA-TUK
IT'S FINE.
GA-TUK
GA-TUK
THOSE BEANS ARE EXACTLY WHAT...
I NEED.

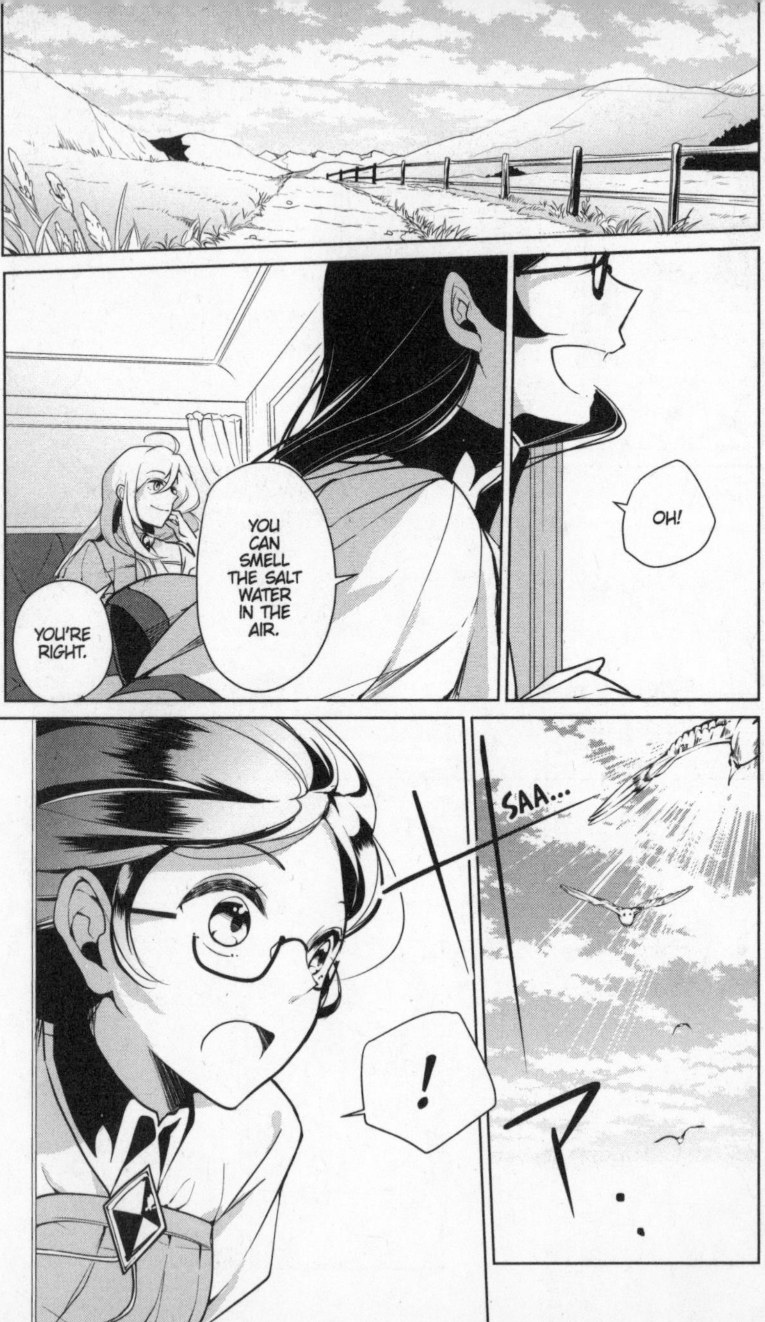
OH!
YOU CAN SMELL THE SALT WATER IN THE AIR.
YOU'RE RIGHT.
SAA...
!

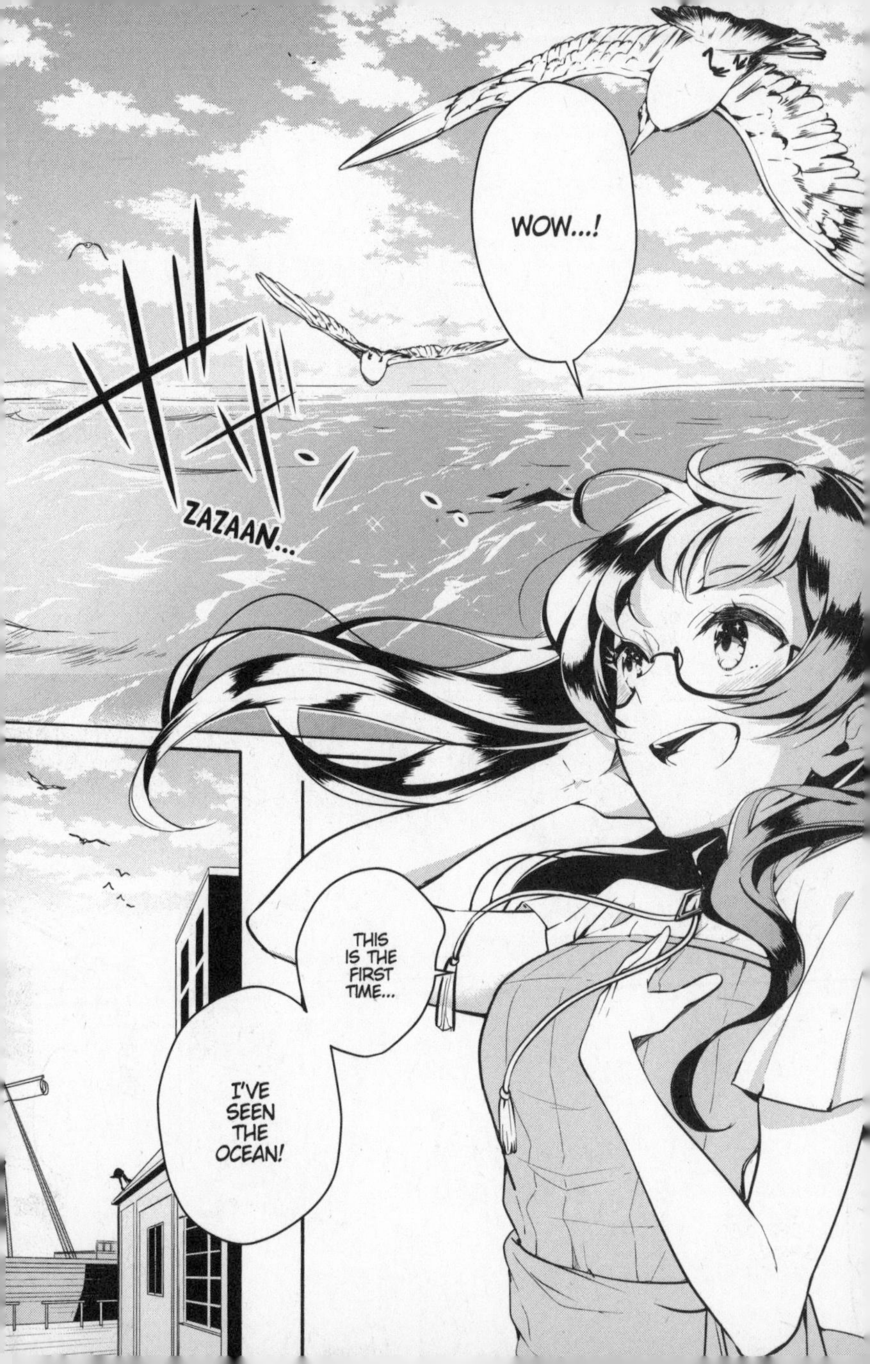
WOW...!
ZAZAAN...
THIS IS THE FIRST TIME...
I'VE SEEN THE OCEAN!

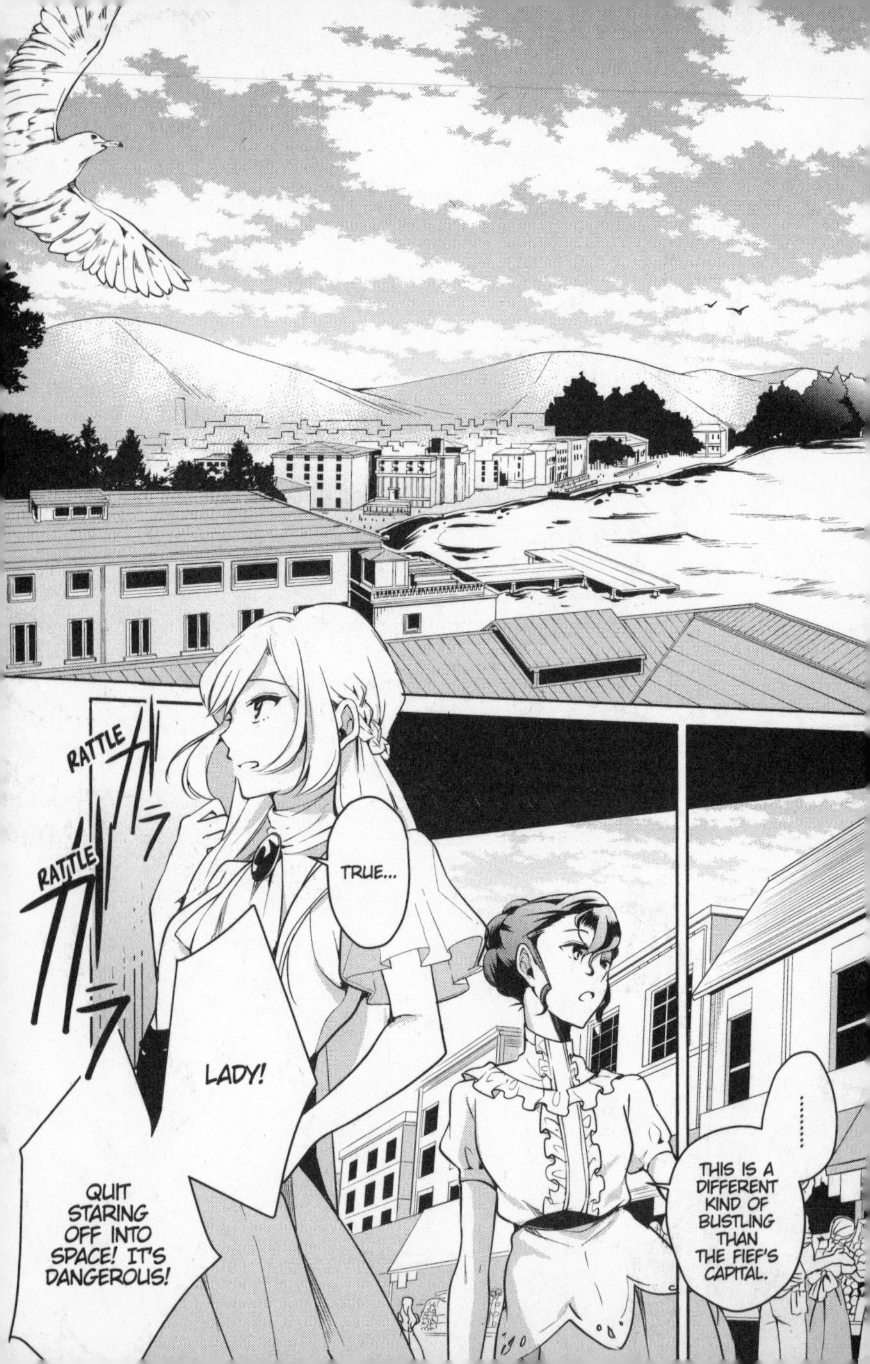
......
THIS IS A DIFFERENT KIND OF BUSTLING THAN THE FIEF'S CAPITAL.
TRUE...
RATTLE
RATTLE
LADY!
QUIT STARING OFF INTO SPACE! IT'S DANGEROUS!

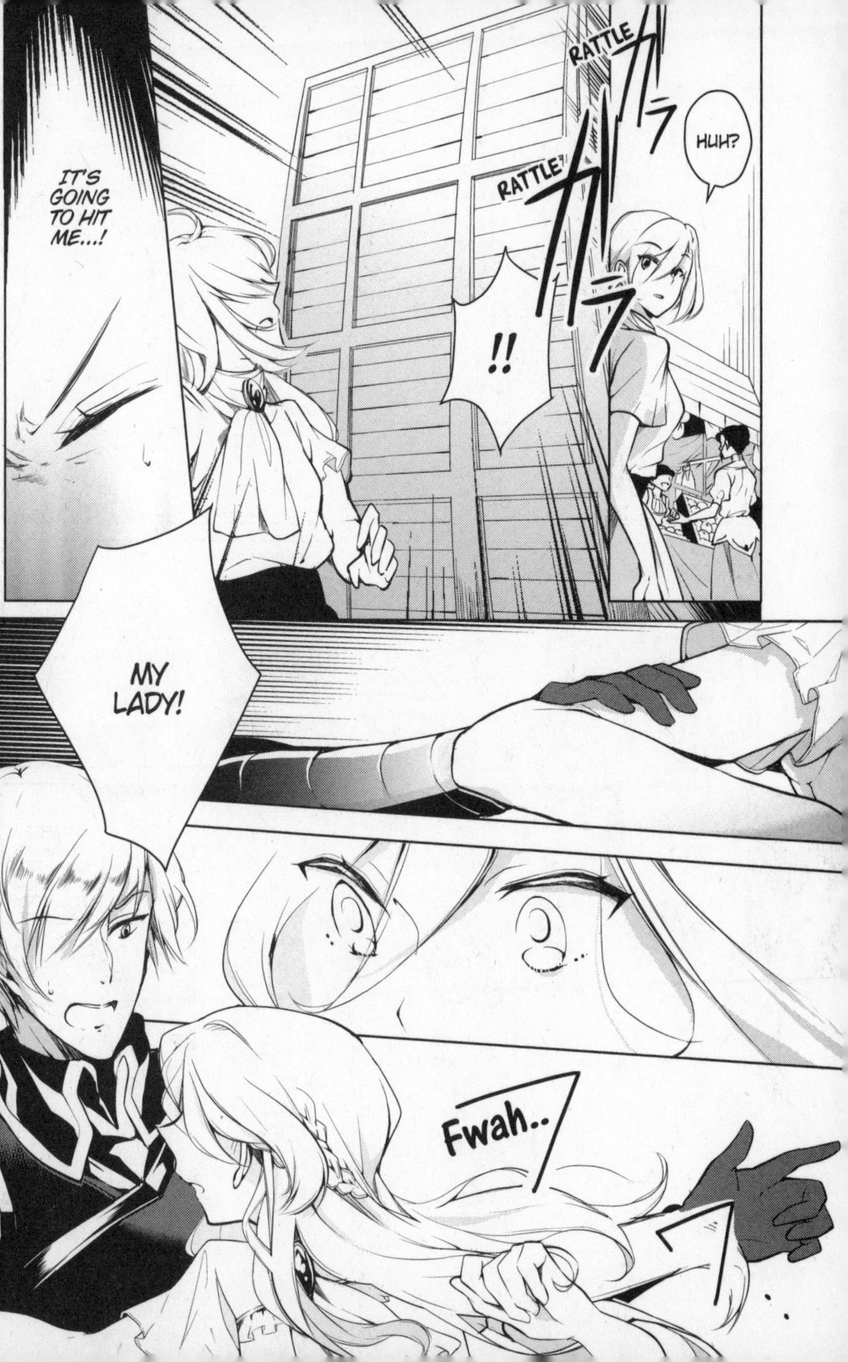

RATTLE
HUH?
RATTLE
!!
IT'S GOING TO HIT ME...!
MY LADY!
Fwah..

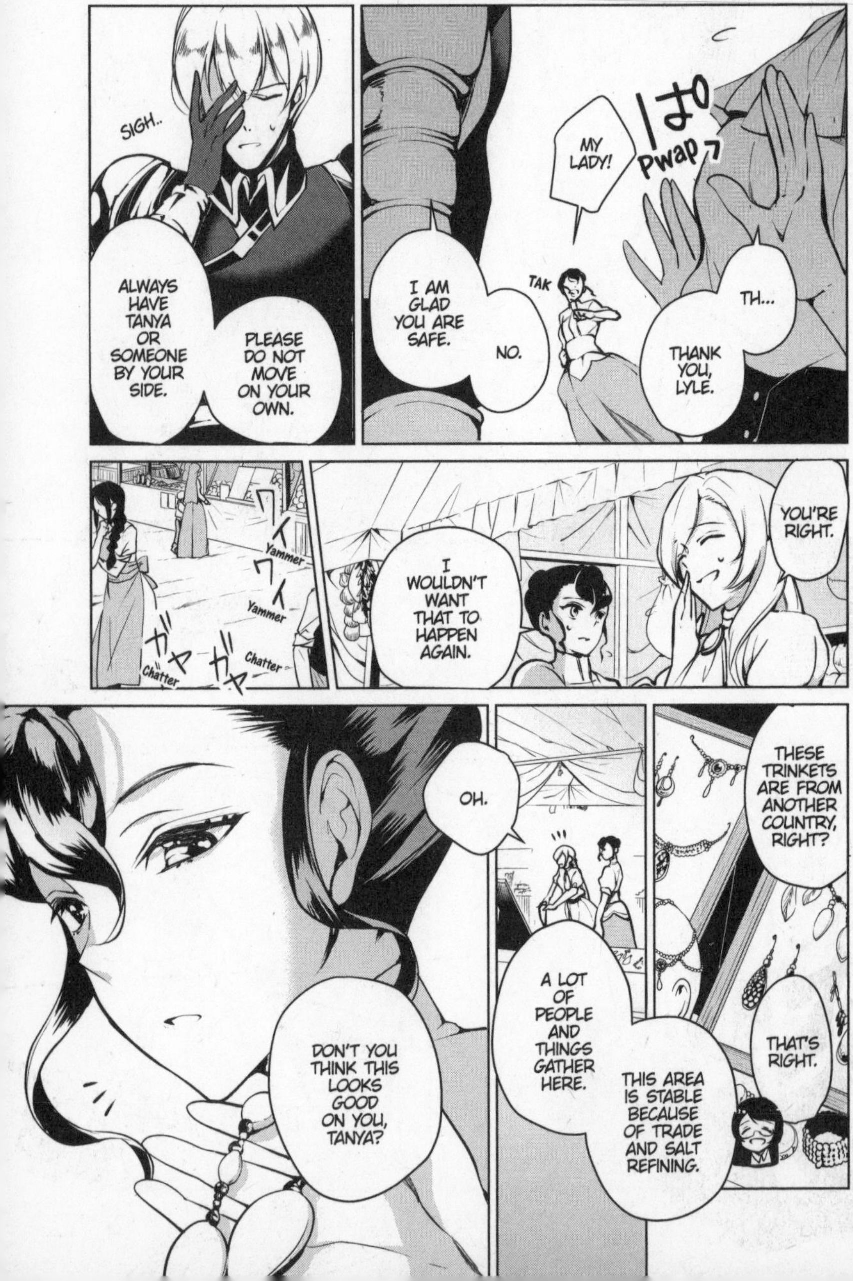
MY LADY!
Pwap
TH...
THANK YOU, LYLE.
NO.
TAK
I AM GLAD YOU ARE SAFE.
SIGH..
PLEASE DO NOT MOVE ON YOUR OWN.
ALWAYS HAVE TANYA OR SOMEONE BY YOUR SIDE.
YOU'RE RIGHT.
I WOULDN'T WANT THAT TO HAPPEN AGAIN.
Yammer
Yammer
Chatter
Chatter
THESE TRINKETS ARE FROM ANOTHER COUNTRY, RIGHT?
THAT'S RIGHT.
THIS AREA IS STABLE BECAUSE OF TRADE AND SALT REFINING.
A LOT OF PEOPLE AND THINGS GATHER HERE.
OH.
DON'T YOU THINK THIS LOOKS GOOD ON YOU, TANYA?

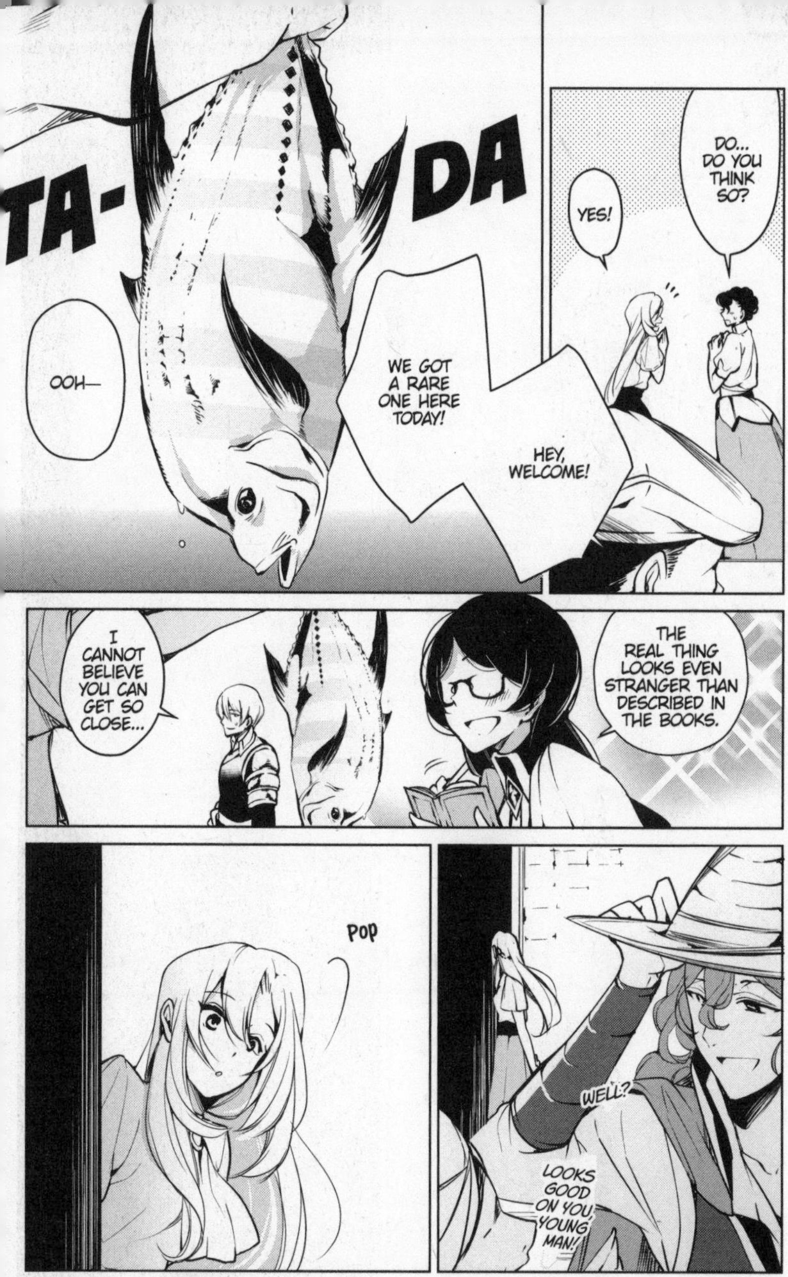
DO... DO YOU THINK SO?
YES!
TA-DA
HEY, WELCOME!
WE GOT A RARE ONE HERE TODAY!
OOH—
THE REAL THING LOOKS EVEN STRANGER THAN DESCRIBED IN THE BOOKS.
I CANNOT BELIEVE YOU CAN GET SO CLOSE...
WELL?
LOOKS GOOD ON YOU, YOUNG MAN!
POP

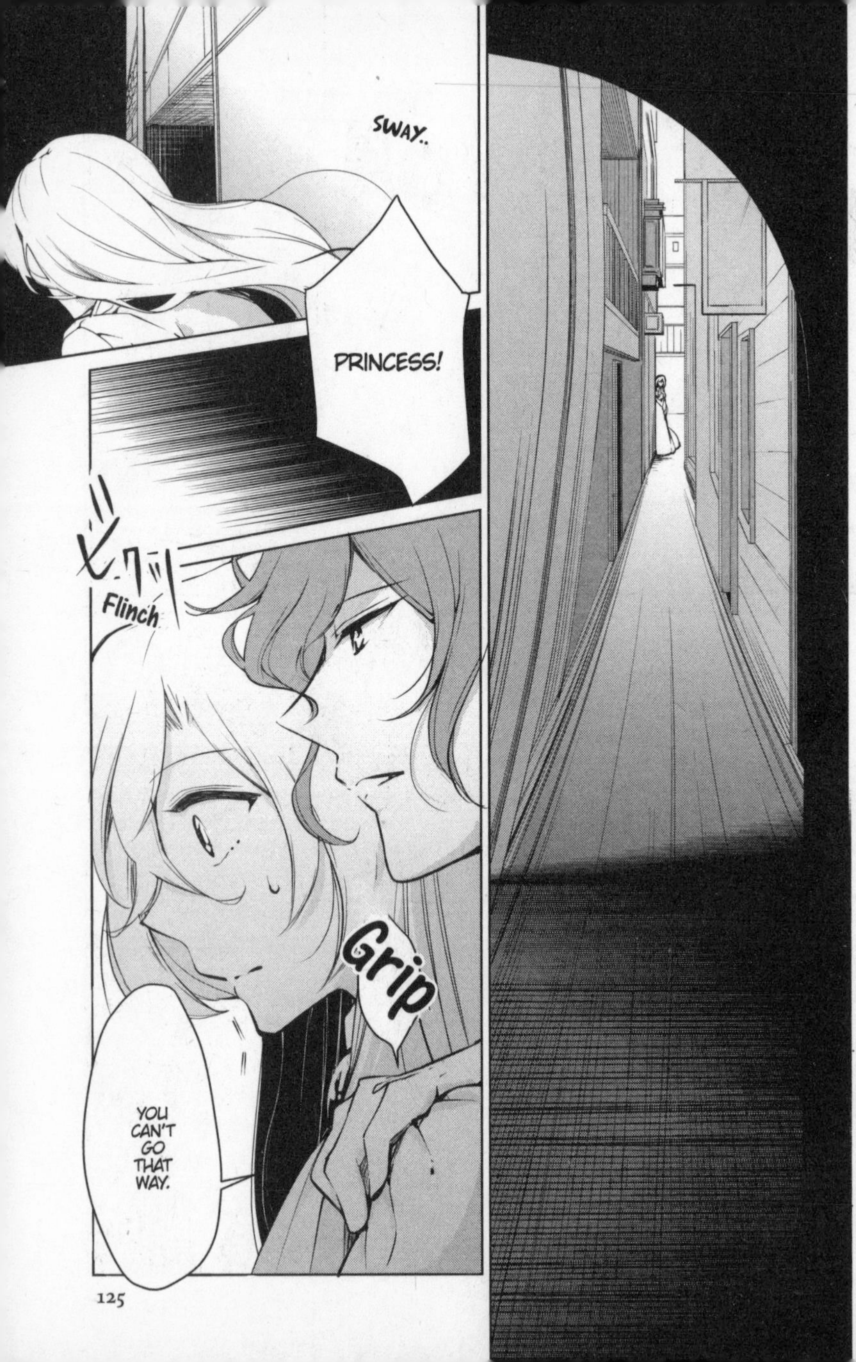
SWAY..
PRINCESS!
ビクッ
Flinch
Grip
YOU CAN'T GO THAT WAY.

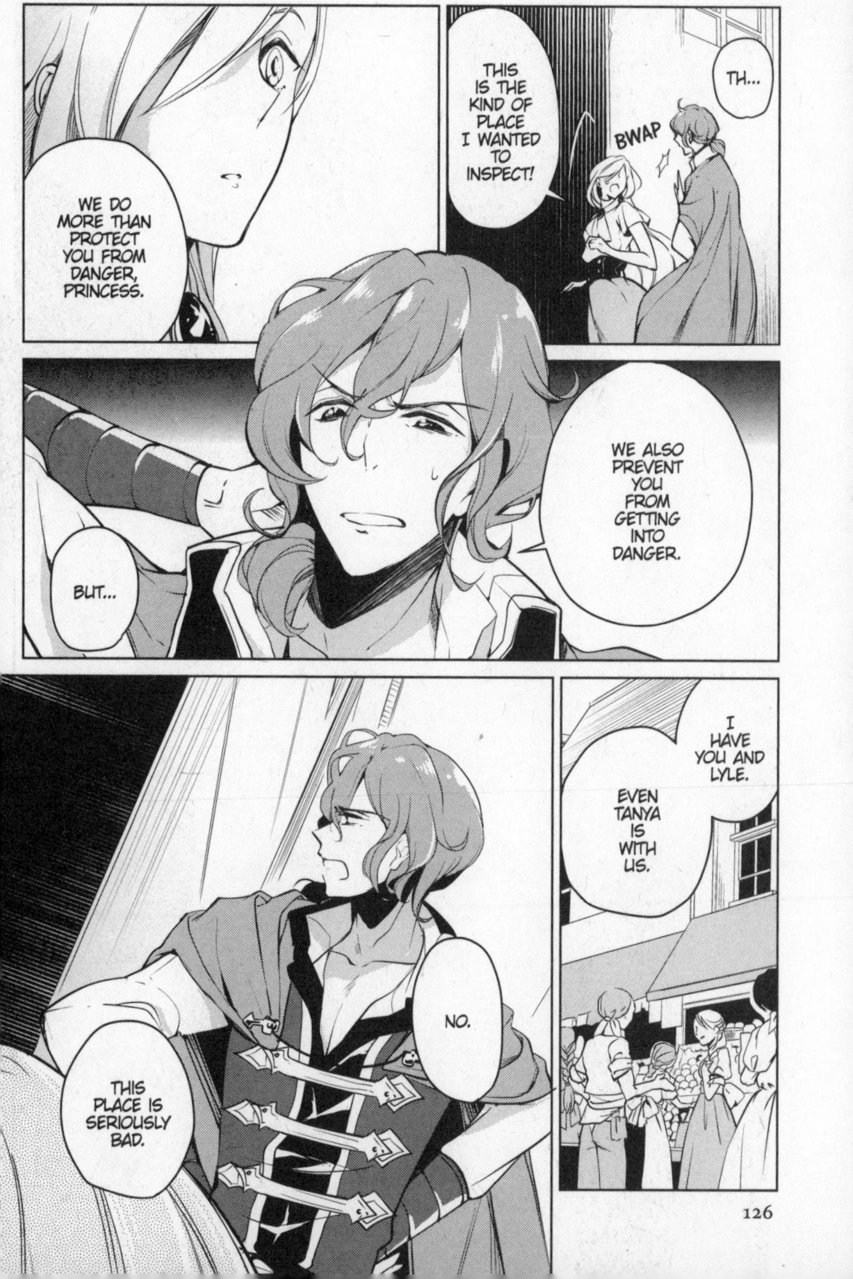
TH...
BWAP
THIS IS THE KIND OF PLACE I WANTED TO INSPECT!
WE DO MORE THAN PROTECT YOU FROM DANGER, PRINCESS.
WE ALSO PREVENT YOU FROM GETTING INTO DANGER.
BUT...
I HAVE YOU AND LYLE.
EVEN TANYA IS WITH US.
NO.
THIS PLACE IS SERIOUSLY BAD.

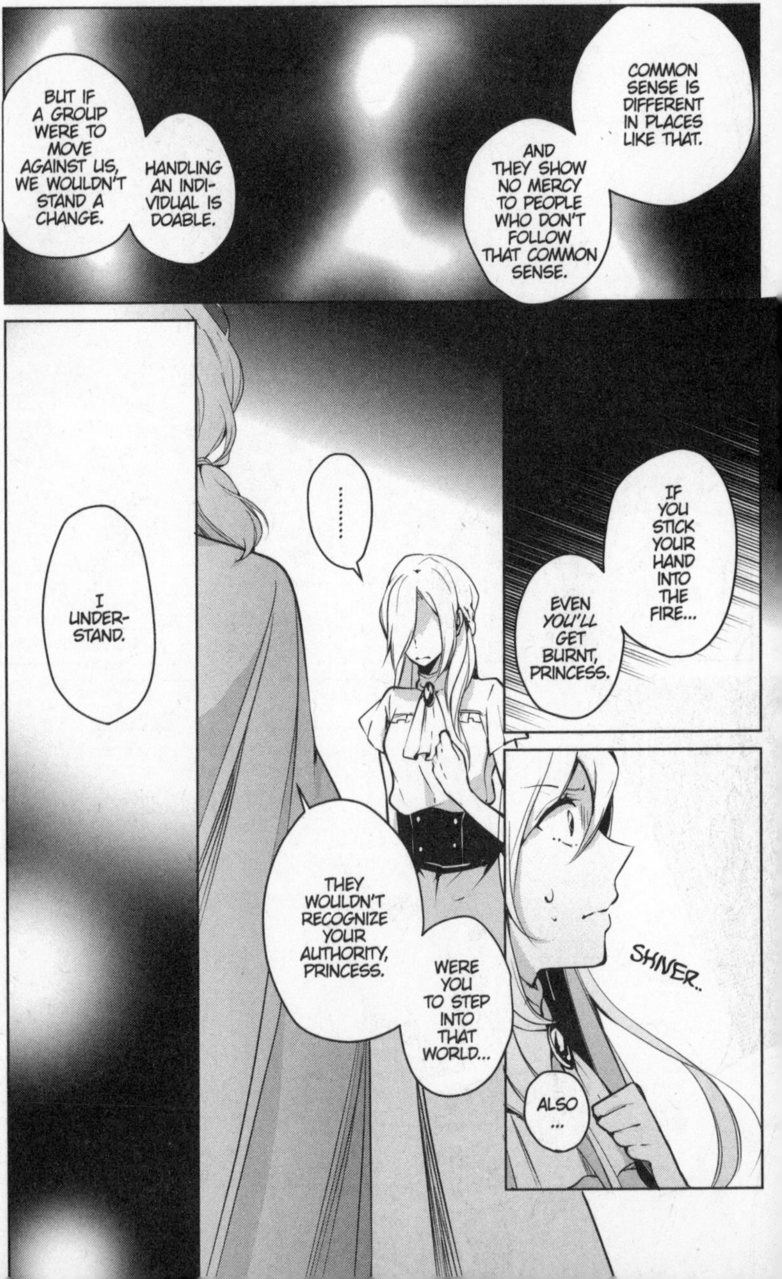
COMMON SENSE IS DIFFERENT IN PLACES LIKE THAT.
AND THEY SHOW NO MERCY TO PEOPLE WHO DON'T FOLLOW THAT COMMON SENSE.
HANDLING AN INDI-VIDUAL IS DOABLE.
BUT IF A GROUP WERE TO MOVE AGAINST US, WE WOULDN'T STAND A CHANGE.
IF YOU STICK YOUR HAND INTO THE FIRE...
EVEN YOU'LL GET BURNT, PRINCESS.
ALSO...
SHIVER..
WERE YOU TO STEP INTO THAT WORLD...
THEY WOULDN'T RECOGNIZE YOUR AUTHORITY, PRINCESS.
......
I UNDER-STAND.

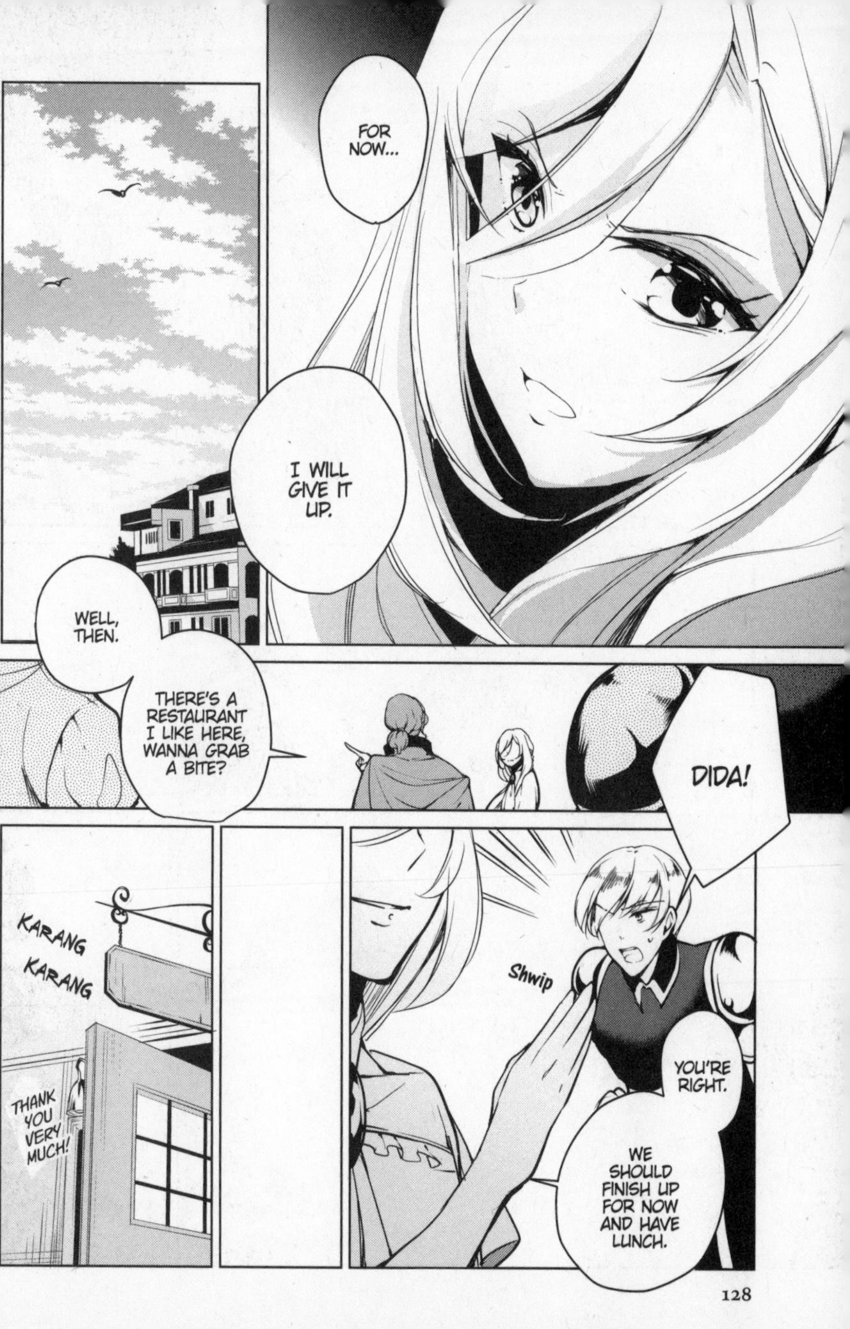
FOR NOW...
I WILL GIVE IT UP.
WELL, THEN.
DIDA!
THERE'S A RESTAURANT I LIKE HERE, WANNA GRAB A BITE?
Shwip
YOU'RE RIGHT.
WE SHOULD FINISH UP FOR NOW AND HAVE LUNCH.
KARANG
KARANG
THANK YOU VERY MUCH!

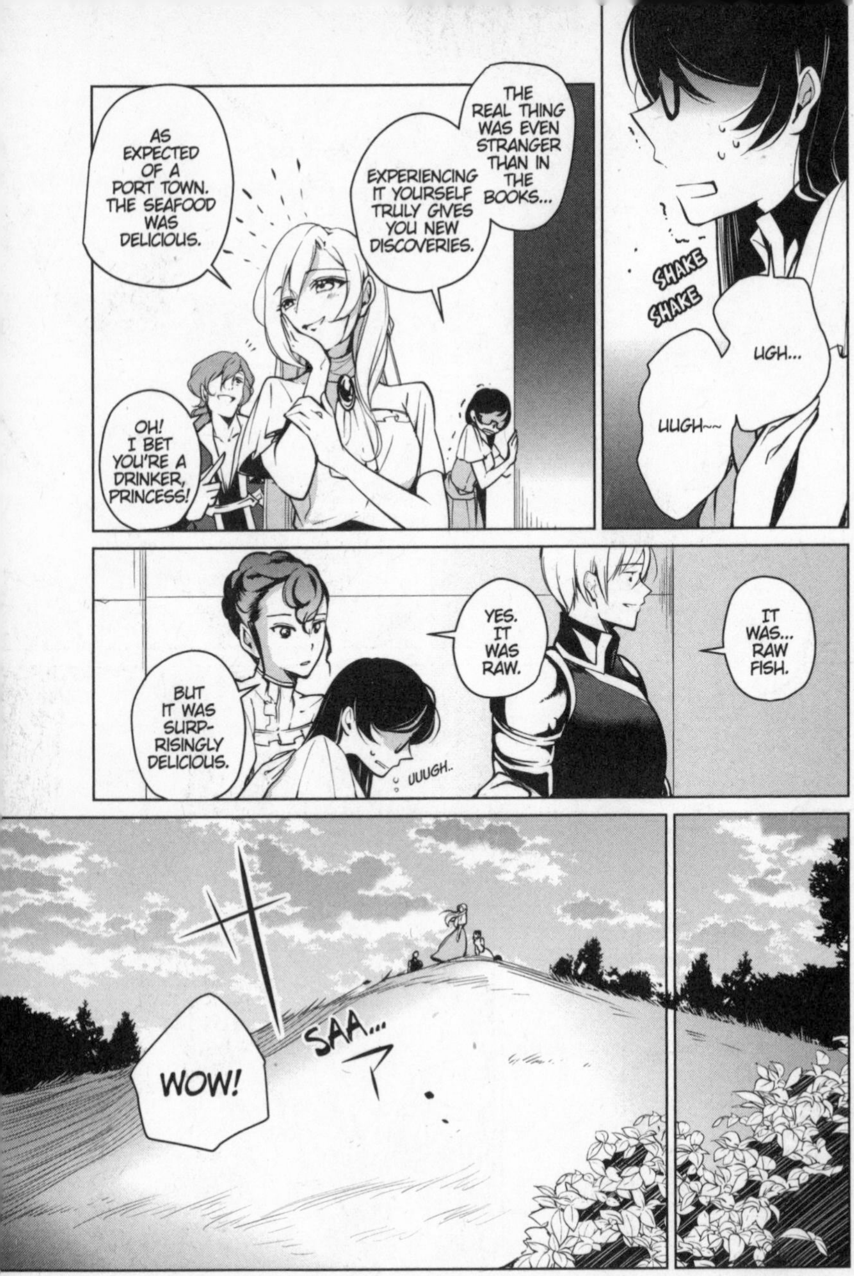
SHAKE
SHAKE
UGH...
UUGH~~
THE REAL THING WAS EVEN STRANGER THAN IN THE BOOKS...
EXPERIENCING IT YOURSELF TRULY GIVES YOU NEW DISCOVERIES.
AS EXPECTED OF A PORT TOWN. THE SEAFOOD WAS DELICIOUS.
OH! I BET YOU'RE A DRINKER, PRINCESS!
IT WAS... RAW FISH.
YES. IT WAS RAW.
BUT IT WAS SURP-RISINGLY DELICIOUS.
UUUGH..
SAA...
WOW!

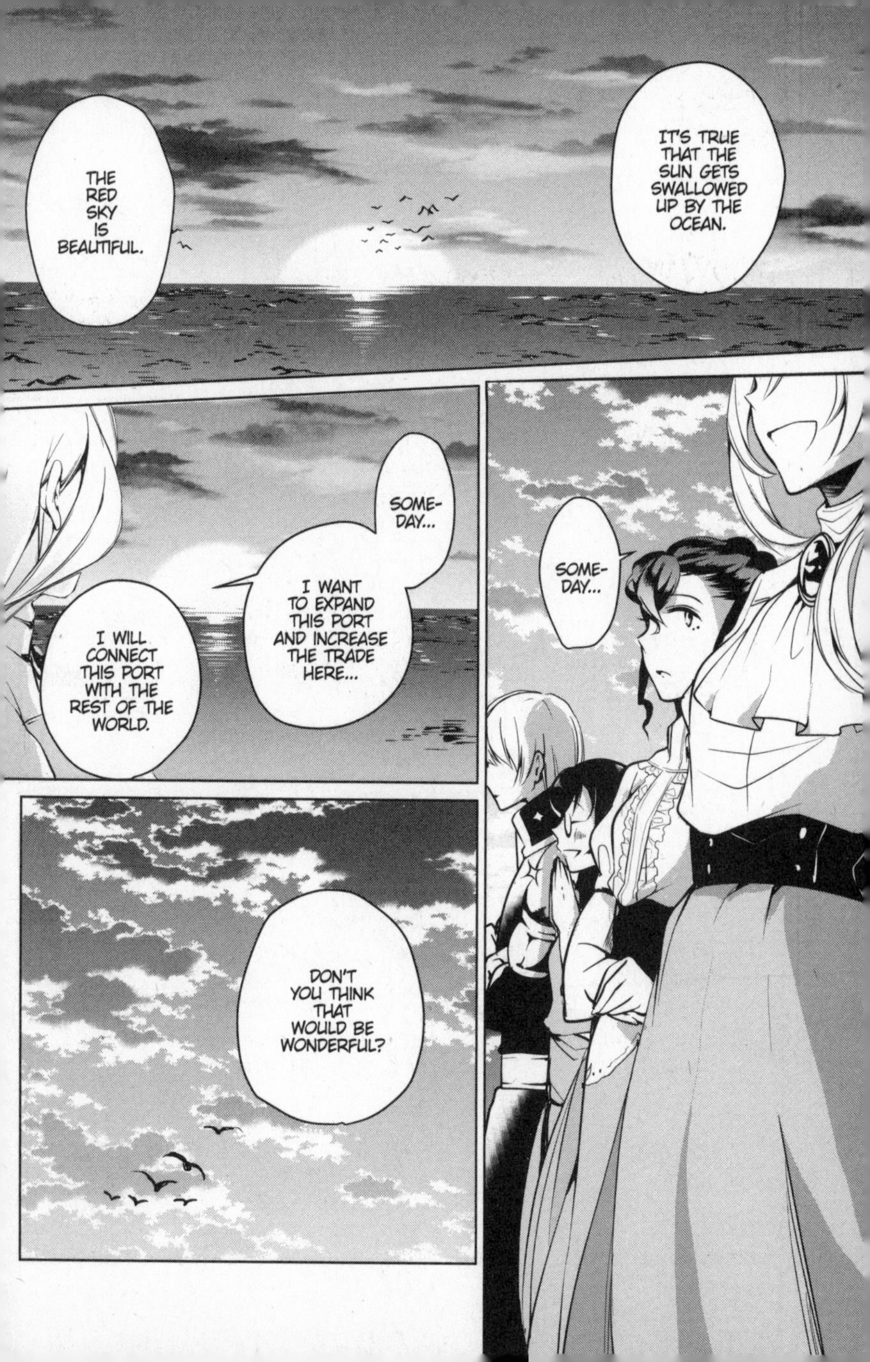
IT'S TRUE THAT THE SUN GETS SWALLOWED UP BY THE OCEAN.
THE RED SKY IS BEAUTIFUL.
SOME-DAY...
SOME-DAY...
I WANT TO EXPAND THIS PORT AND INCREASE THE TRADE HERE...
I WILL CONNECT THIS PORT WITH THE REST OF THE WORLD.
DON'T YOU THINK THAT WOULD BE WONDERFUL?

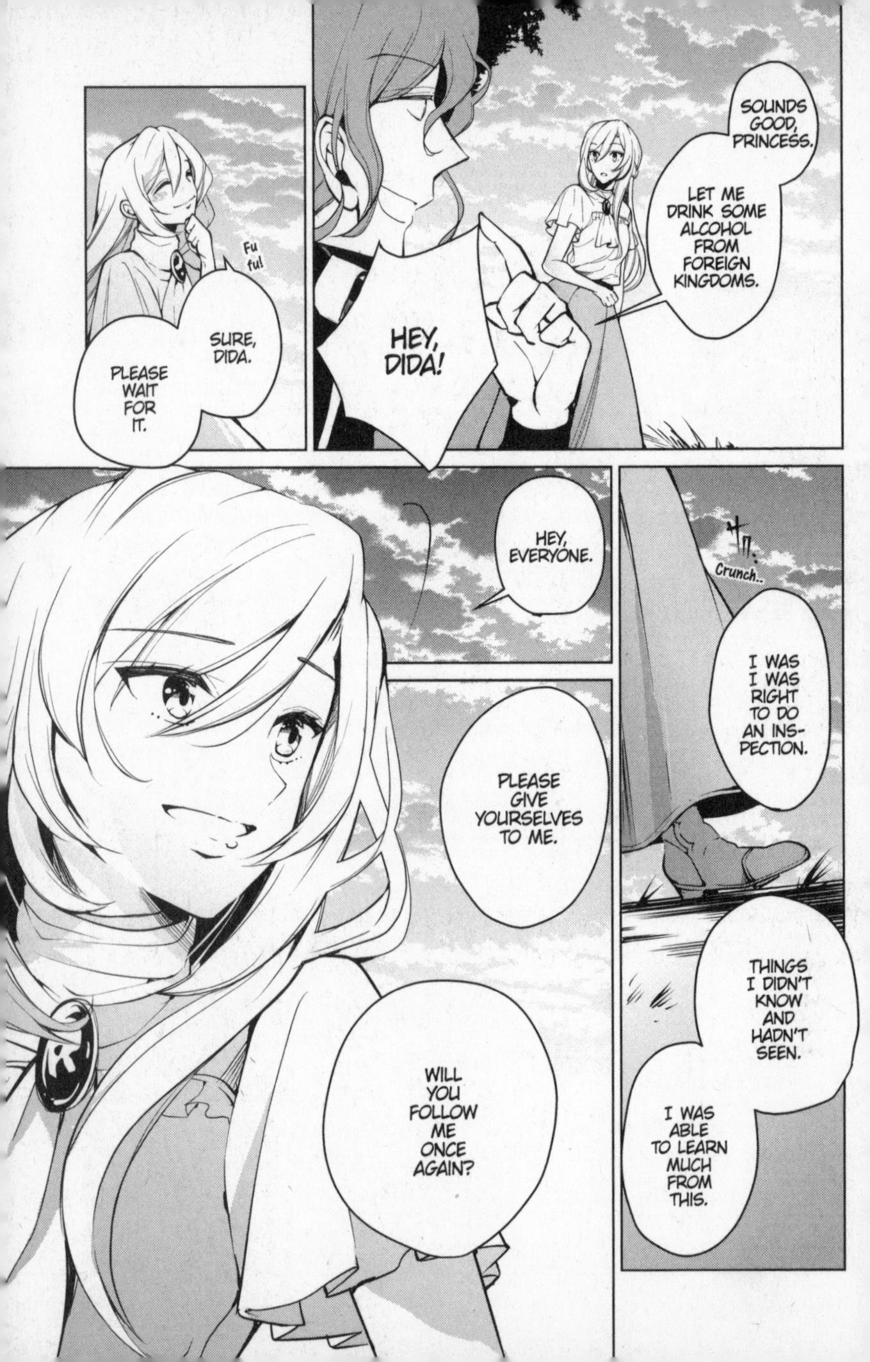
SOUNDS GOOD, PRINCESS.
LET ME DRINK SOME ALCOHOL FROM FOREIGN KINGDOMS.
HEY, DIDA!
Fu fu!
SURE, DIDA.
PLEASE WAIT FOR IT.
Crunch..
I WAS I WAS RIGHT TO DO AN INSPECTION.
THINGS I DIDN'T KNOW AND HADN'T SEEN.
I WAS ABLE TO LEARN MUCH FROM THIS.
HEY, EVERYONE.
PLEASE GIVE YOURSELVES TO ME.
WILL YOU FOLLOW ME ONCE AGAIN?

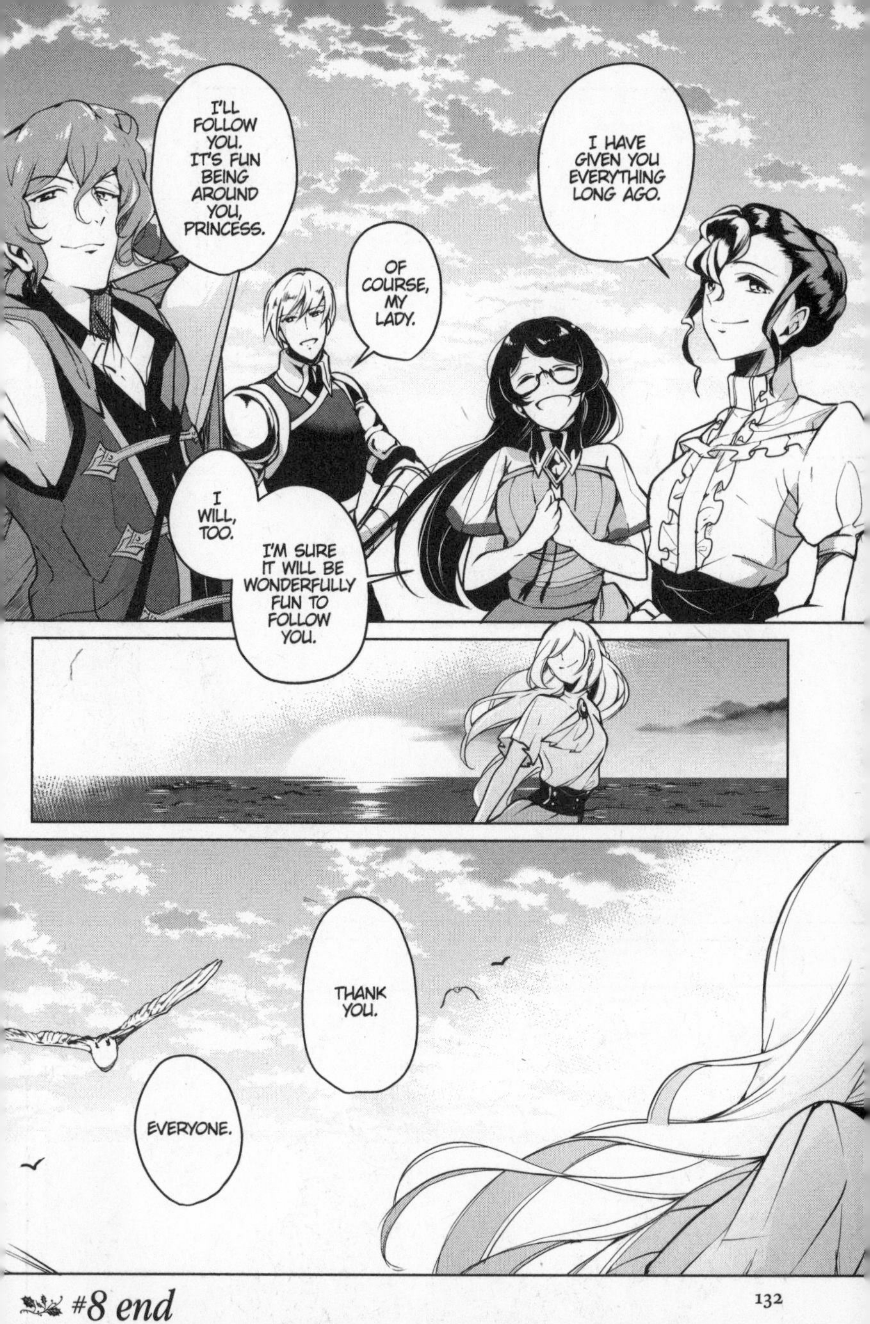
I HAVE GIVEN YOU EVERYTHING LONG AGO.
OF COURSE, MY LADY.
I'LL FOLLOW YOU. IT'S FUN BEING AROUND YOU, PRINCESS.
I WILL, TOO.
I'M SURE IT WILL BE WONDERFULLY FUN TO FOLLOW YOU.
THANK YOU.
EVERYONE.

#8 end

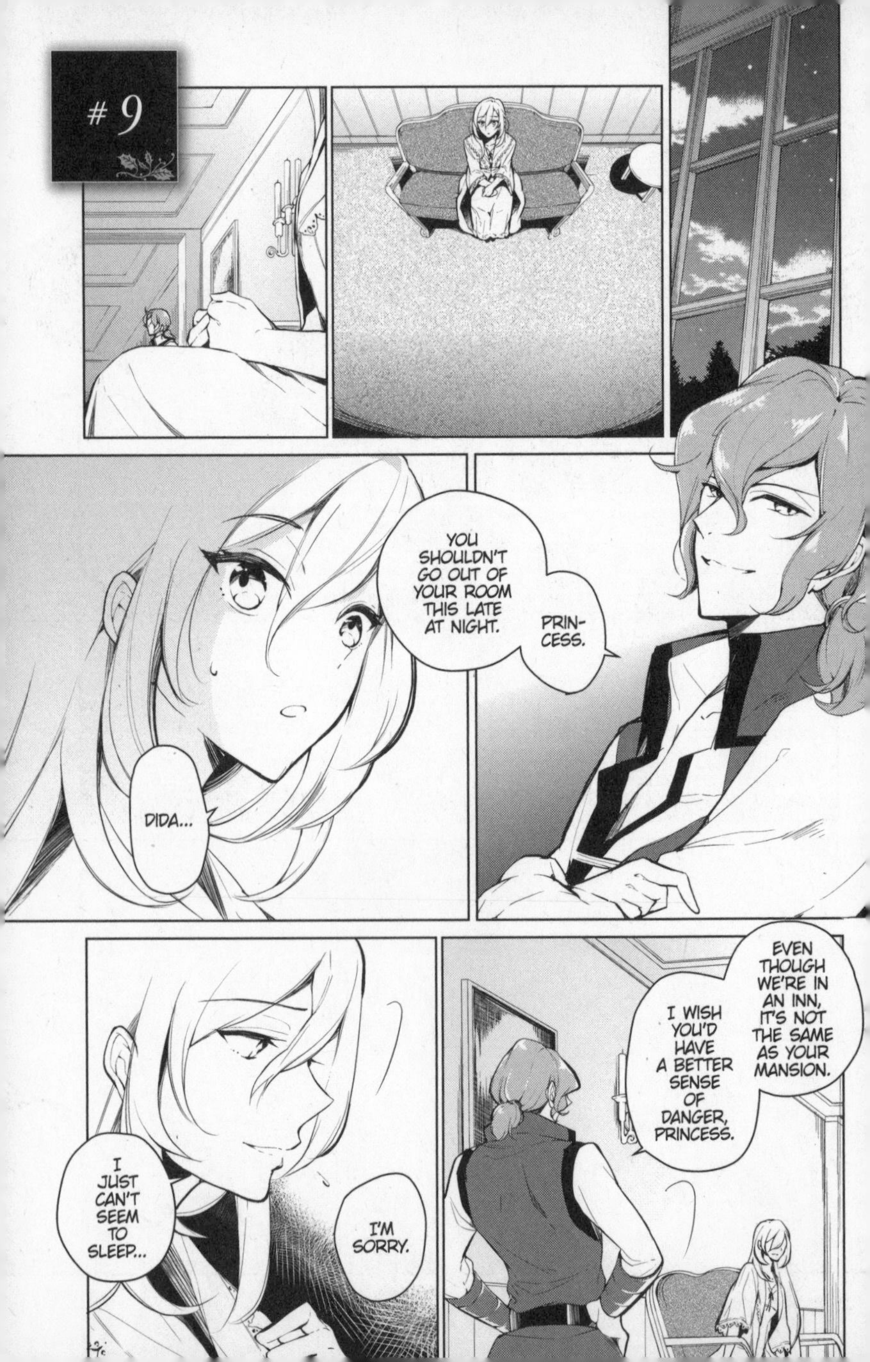

9
YOU SHOULDN'T GO OUT OF YOUR ROOM THIS LATE AT NIGHT.
PRIN-CESS.
DIDA...
EVEN THOUGH WE'RE IN AN INN, IT'S NOT THE SAME AS YOUR MANSION.
I WISH YOU'D HAVE A BETTER SENSE OF DANGER, PRINCESS.
I'M SORRY.
I JUST CAN'T SEEM TO SLEEP...

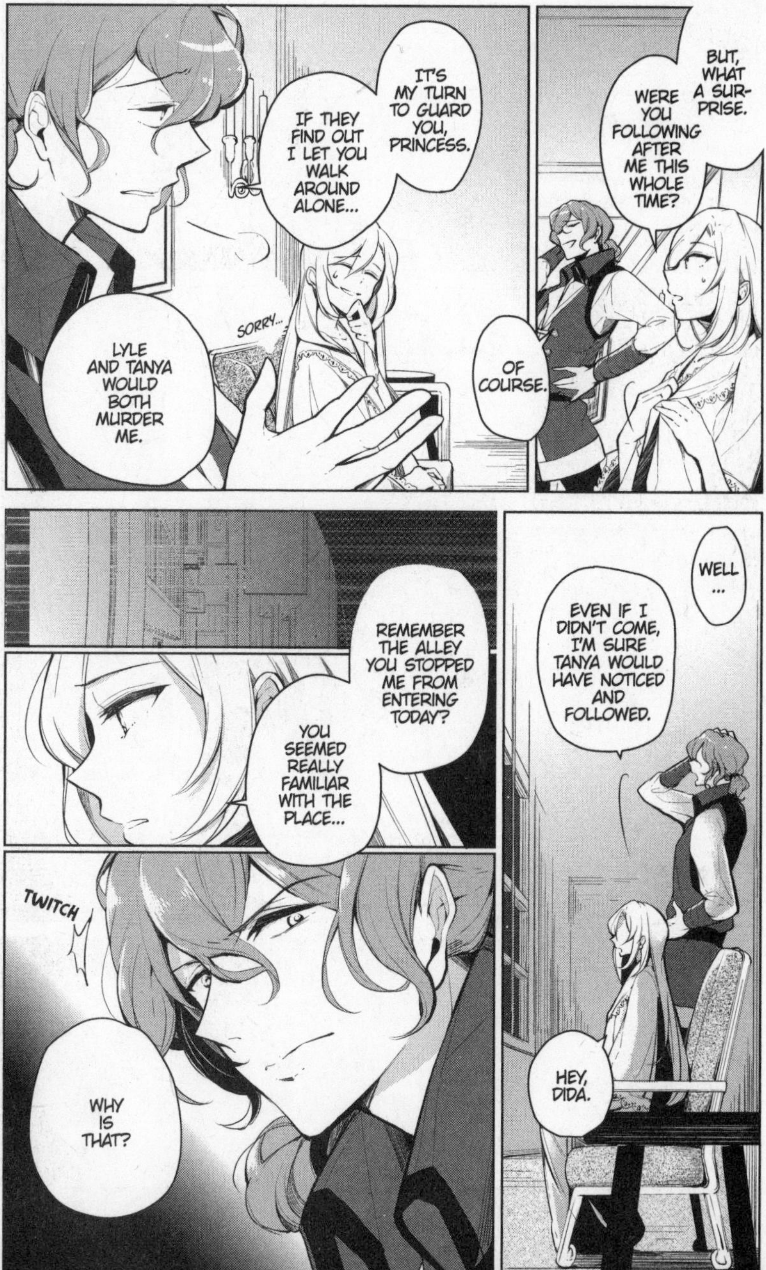
BUT, WHAT A SUR-PRISE.
WERE YOU FOLLOWING AFTER ME THIS WHOLE TIME?
OF COURSE.
IT'S MY TURN TO GUARD YOU, PRINCESS.
IF THEY FIND OUT I LET YOU WALK AROUND ALONE...
SORRY...
LYLE AND TANYA WOULD BOTH MURDER ME.
WELL...
EVEN IF I DIDN'T COME, I'M SURE TANYA WOULD HAVE NOTICED AND FOLLOWED.
HEY, DIDA.
REMEMBER THE ALLEY YOU STOPPED ME FROM ENTERING TODAY?
YOU SEEMED REALLY FAMILIAR WITH THE PLACE...
TWITCH
WHY IS THAT?

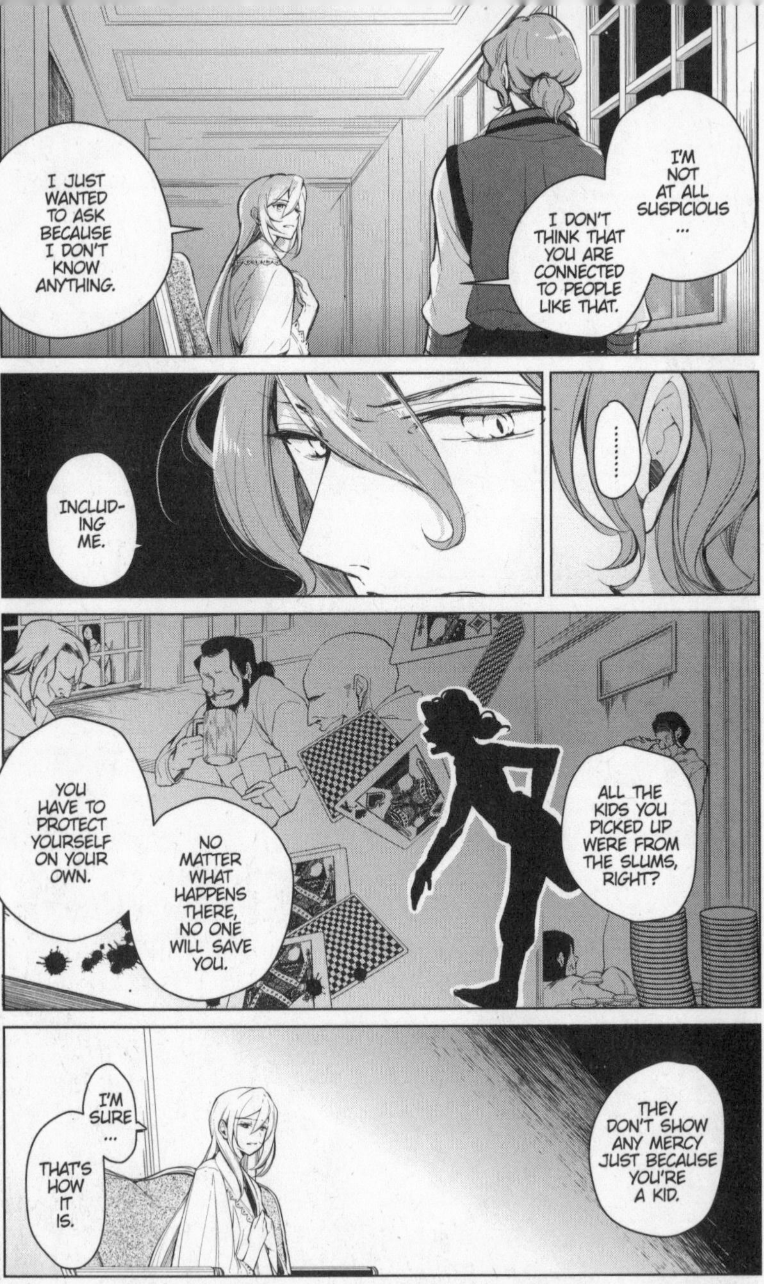
I'M NOT AT ALL SUSPICIOUS ...
I DON'T THINK THAT YOU ARE CONNECTED TO PEOPLE LIKE THAT.
I JUST WANTED TO ASK BECAUSE I DON'T KNOW ANYTHING.
......
INCLUDING ME.
ALL THE KIDS YOU PICKED UP WERE FROM THE SLUMS, RIGHT?
NO MATTER WHAT HAPPENS THERE, NO ONE WILL SAVE YOU.
YOU HAVE TO PROTECT YOURSELF ON YOUR OWN.
THEY DON'T SHOW ANY MERCY JUST BECAUSE YOU'RE A KID.
I'M SURE ...
THAT'S HOW IT IS.

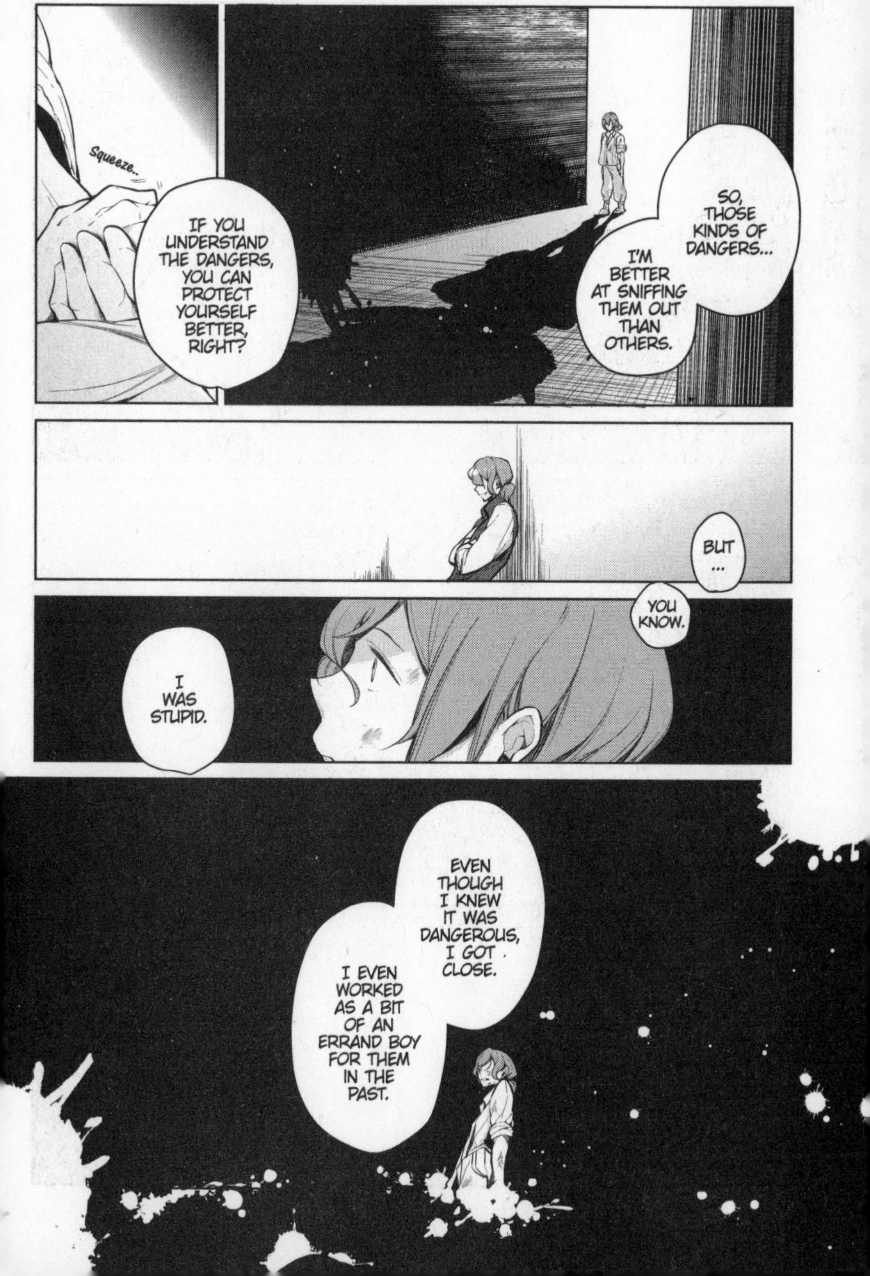
SO, THOSE KINDS OF DANGERS...
I'M BETTER AT SNIFFING THEM OUT THAN OTHERS.
Squeeze..
IF YOU UNDERSTAND THE DANGERS, YOU CAN PROTECT YOURSELF BETTER, RIGHT?
BUT ...
YOU KNOW.
I WAS STUPID.
EVEN THOUGH I KNEW IT WAS DANGEROUS, I GOT CLOSE.
I EVEN WORKED AS A BIT OF AN ERRAND BOY FOR THEM IN THE PAST.

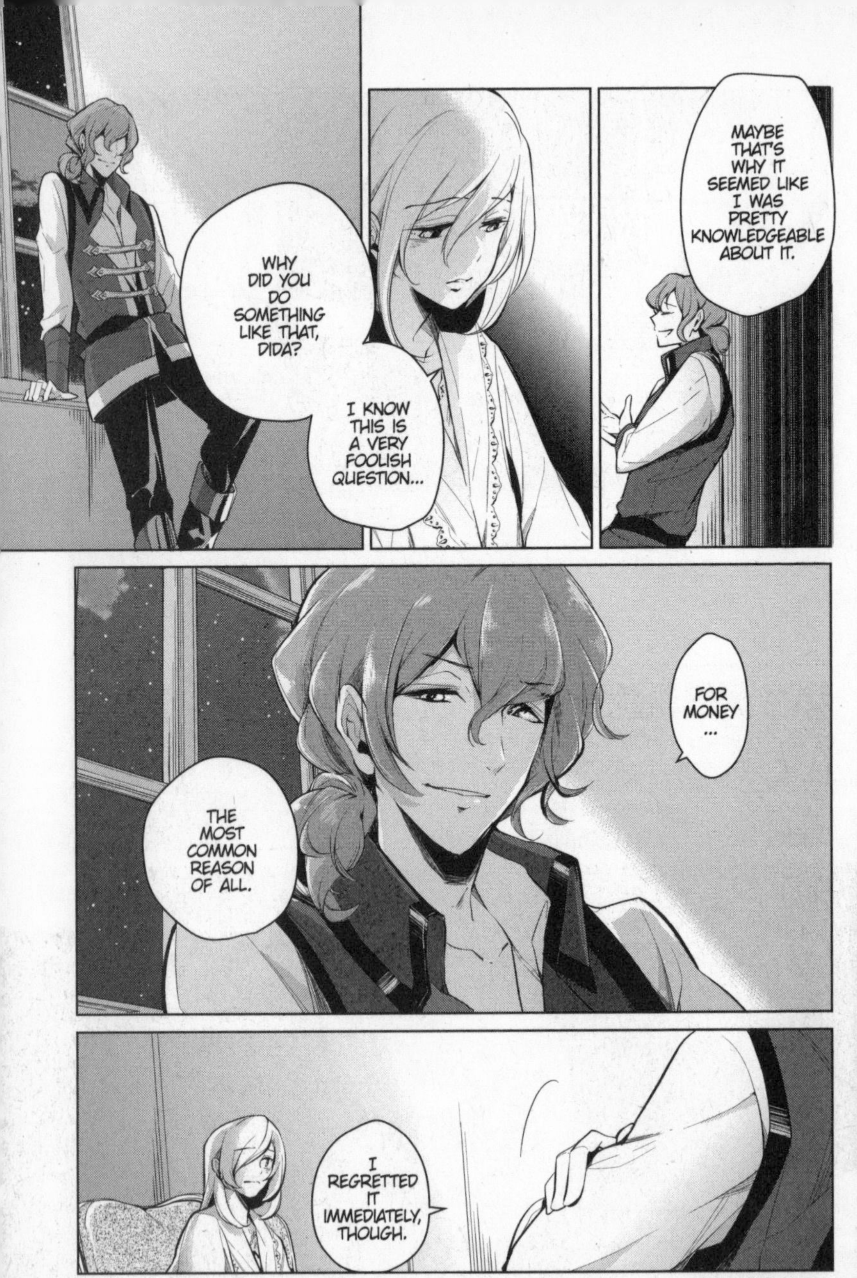
MAYBE THAT'S WHY IT SEEMED LIKE I WAS PRETTY KNOWLEDGEABLE ABOUT IT.
I KNOW THIS IS A VERY FOOLISH QUESTION...
WHY DID YOU DO SOMETHING LIKE THAT, DIDA?
FOR MONEY ...
THE MOST COMMON REASON OF ALL.
I REGRETTED IT IMMEDIATELY, THOUGH.

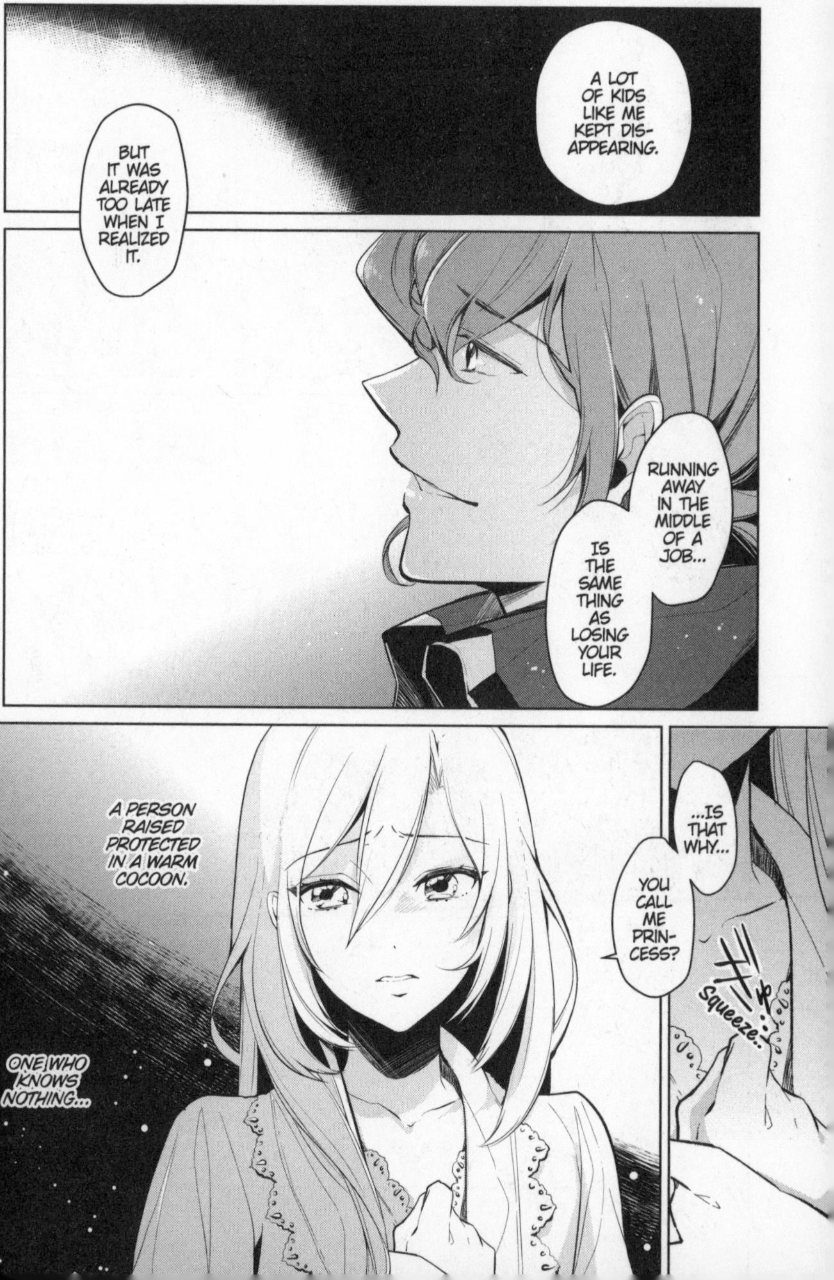
A LOT OF KIDS LIKE ME KEPT DIS-APPEARING.
BUT IT WAS ALREADY TOO LATE WHEN I REALIZED IT.
RUNNING AWAY IN THE MIDDLE OF A JOB...
IS THE SAME THING AS LOSING YOUR LIFE.
...IS THAT WHY...
YOU CALL ME PRIN-CESS?
Squeeze...
A PERSON RAISED PROTECTED IN A WARM COCOON.
ONE WHO KNOWS NOTHING...

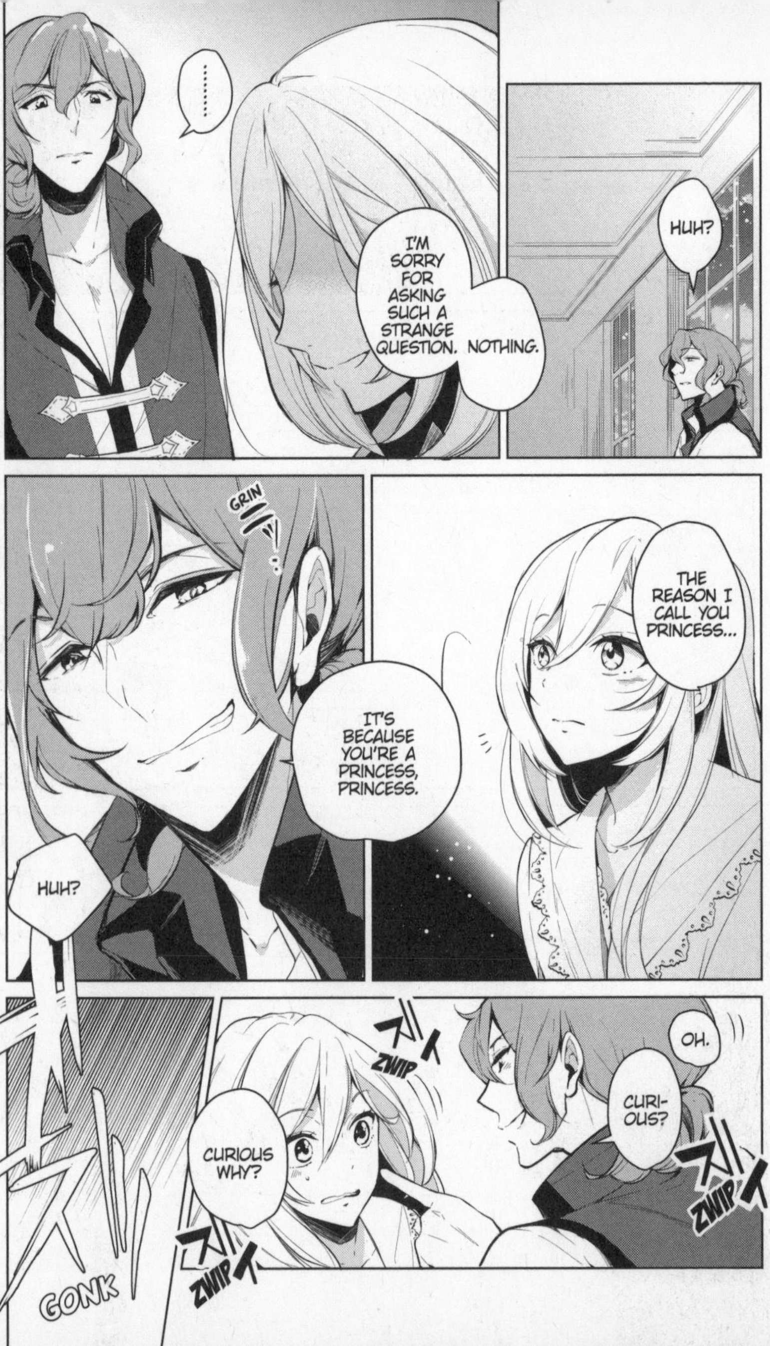
HUH?
NOTHING.
I'M SORRY FOR ASKING SUCH A STRANGE QUESTION.
......
THE REASON I CALL YOU PRINCESS...
GRIN
IT'S BECAUSE YOU'RE A PRINCESS, PRINCESS.
HUH?
OH.
CURI-OUS?
ZWIP
ZWIP
CURIOUS WHY?
ZWIP
GONK

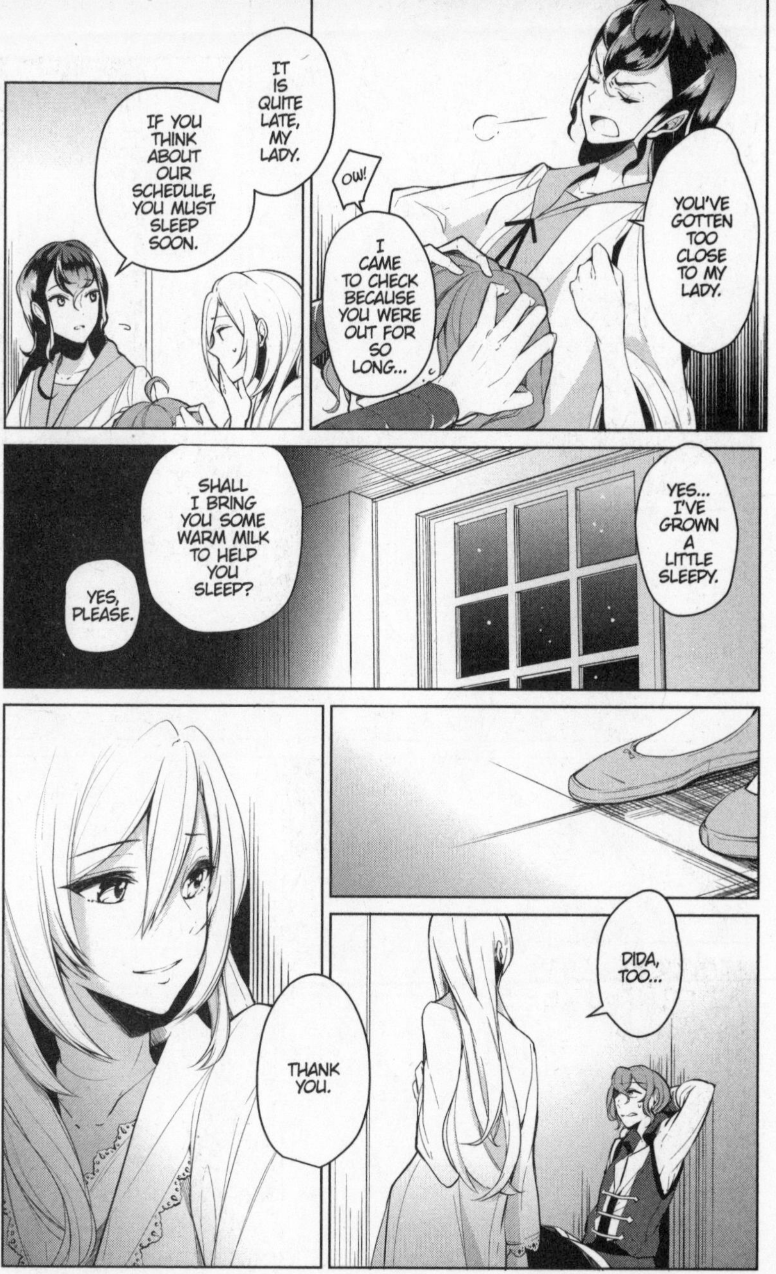
YOU'VE GOTTEN TOO CLOSE TO MY LADY.
OW!
I CAME TO CHECK BECAUSE YOU WERE OUT FOR SO LONG...
IT IS QUITE LATE, MY LADY.
IF YOU THINK ABOUT OUR SCHEDULE, YOU MUST SLEEP SOON.
YES... I'VE GROWN A LITTLE SLEEPY.
SHALL I BRING YOU SOME WARM MILK TO HELP YOU SLEEP?
YES, PLEASE.
DIDA, TOO...
THANK YOU.

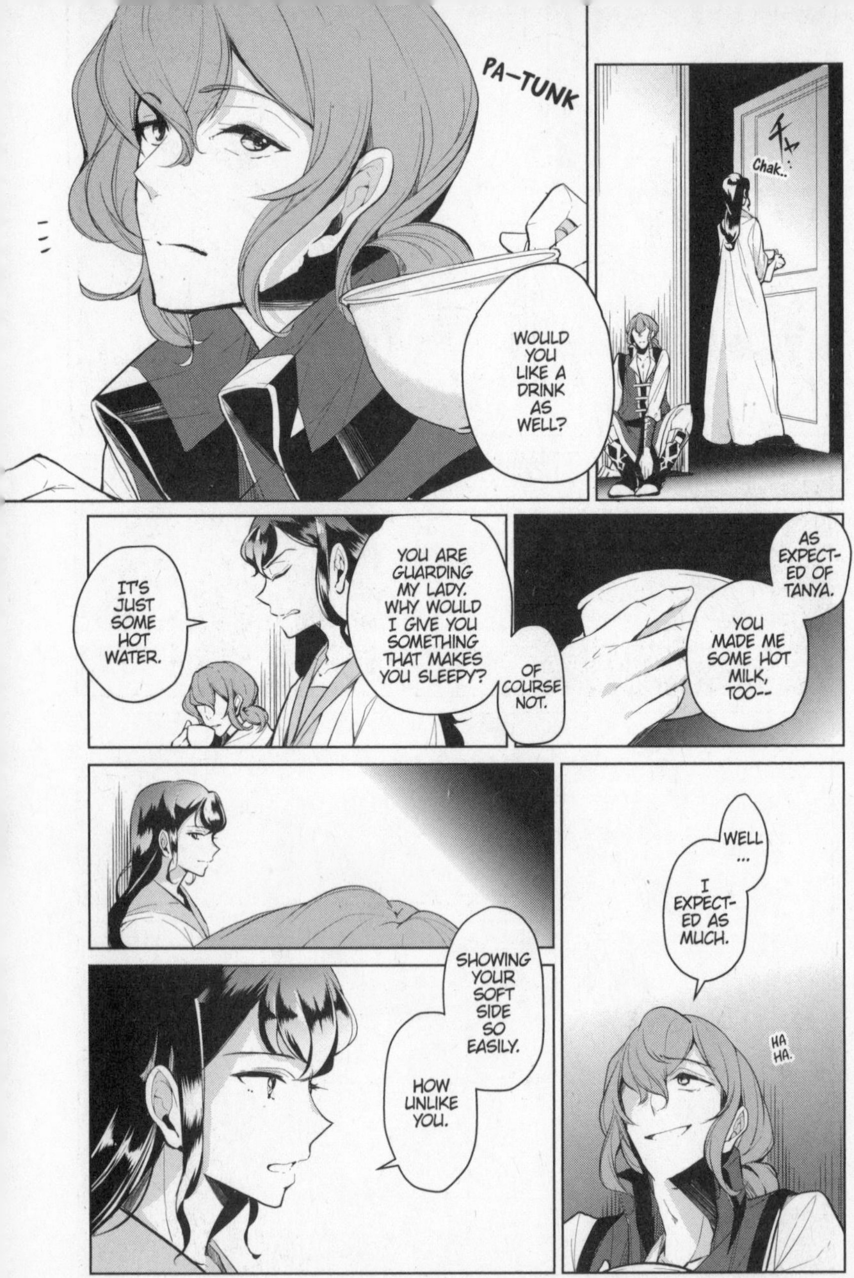
チャ
Chak..
PA-TUNK
...
WOULD YOU LIKE A DRINK AS WELL?
AS EXPECTED OF TANYA.
YOU MADE ME SOME HOT MILK, TOO--
OF COURSE NOT.
YOU ARE GUARDING MY LADY. WHY WOULD I GIVE YOU SOMETHING THAT MAKES YOU SLEEPY?
IT'S JUST SOME HOT WATER.
WELL...
I EXPECTED AS MUCH.
HA HA.
SHOWING YOUR SOFT SIDE SO EASILY.
HOW UNLIKE YOU.

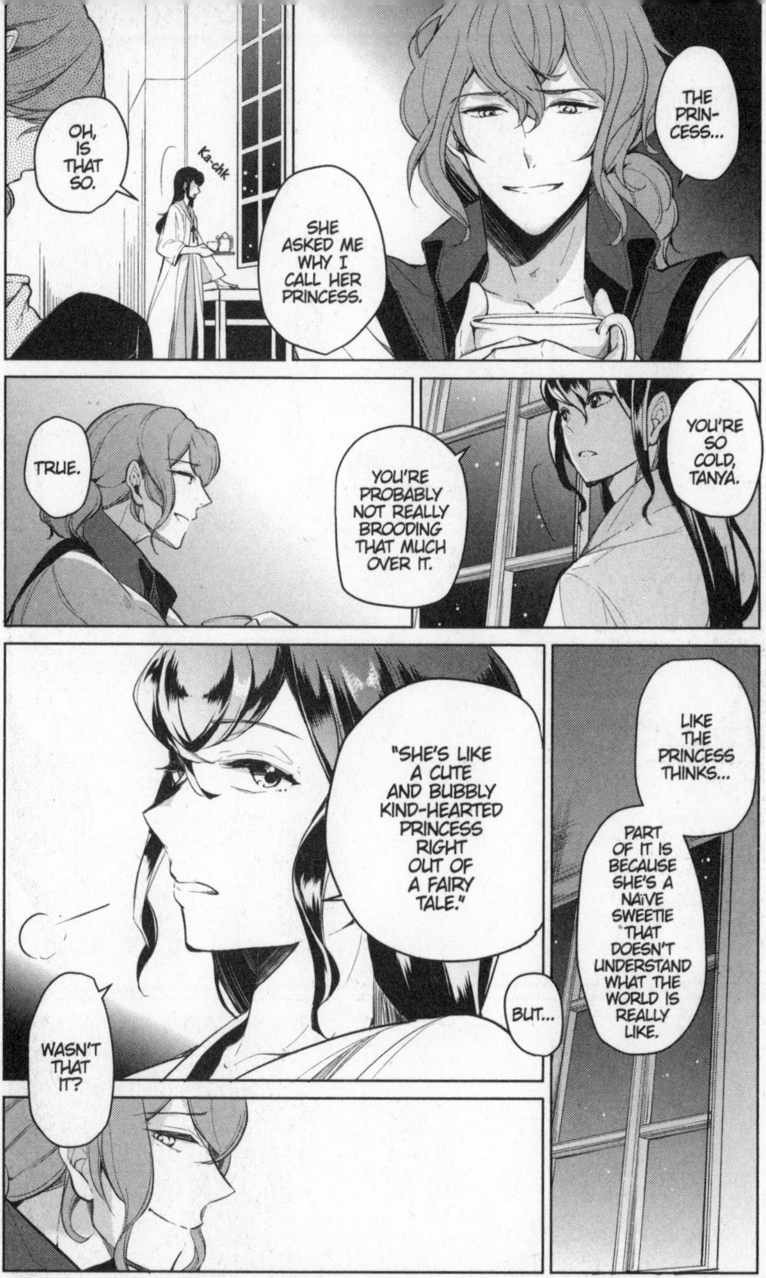
THE PRIN-CESS...
SHE ASKED ME WHY I CALL HER PRINCESS.
Ka-chk
OH, IS THAT SO.
YOU'RE SO COLD, TANYA.
YOU'RE PROBABLY NOT REALLY BROODING THAT MUCH OVER IT.
TRUE.
LIKE THE PRINCESS THINKS...
PART OF IT IS BECAUSE SHE'S A NAÏVE SWEETIE THAT DOESN'T UNDERSTAND WHAT THE WORLD IS REALLY LIKE.
BUT...
"SHE'S LIKE A CUTE AND BUBBLY KIND-HEARTED PRINCESS RIGHT OUT OF A FAIRY TALE."
WASN'T THAT IT?

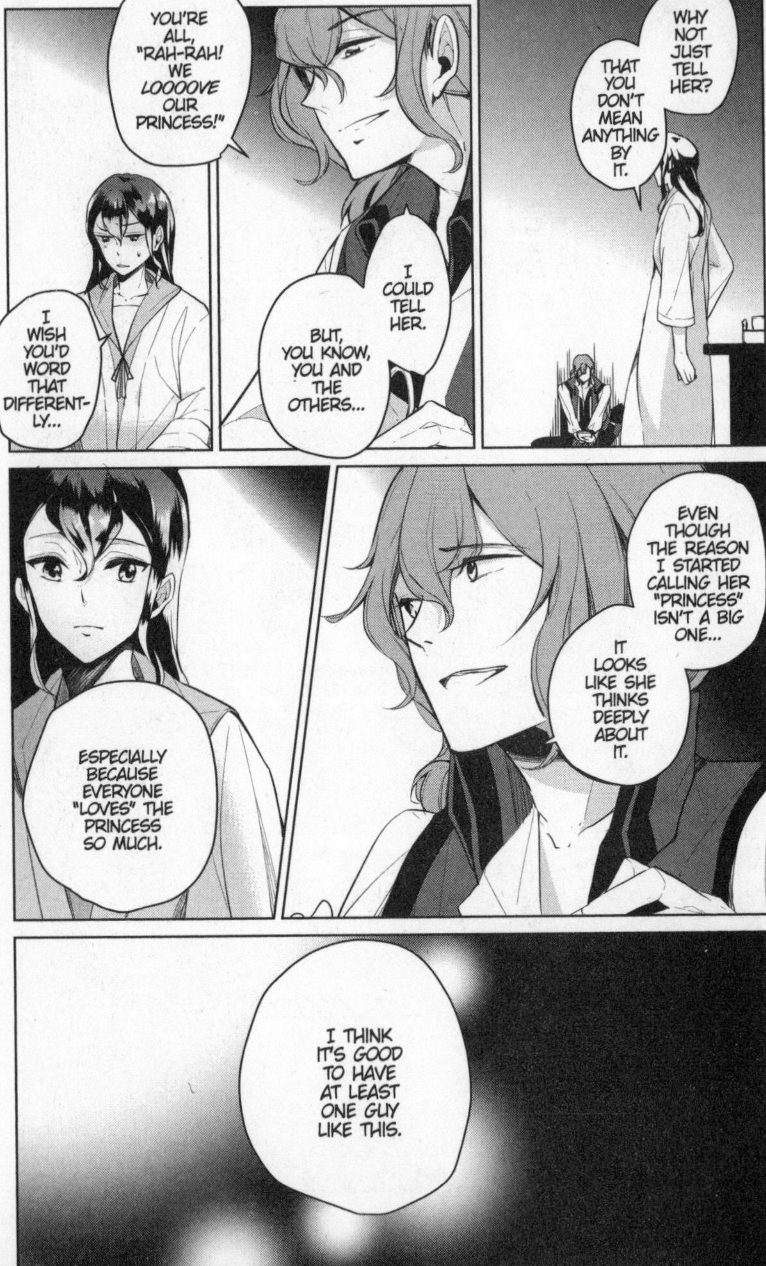
WHY NOT JUST TELL HER?
THAT YOU DON'T MEAN ANYTHING BY IT.
I COULD TELL HER.
BUT, YOU KNOW, YOU AND THE OTHERS...
YOU'RE ALL, "RAH-RAH! WE LOOOOVE OUR PRINCESS!"
I WISH YOU'D WORD THAT DIFFERENT-LY...
EVEN THOUGH THE REASON I STARTED CALLING HER "PRINCESS" ISN'T A BIG ONE...
IT LOOKS LIKE SHE THINKS DEEPLY ABOUT IT.
ESPECIALLY BECAUSE EVERYONE "LOVES" THE PRINCESS SO MUCH.
I THINK IT'S GOOD TO HAVE AT LEAST ONE GUY LIKE THIS.

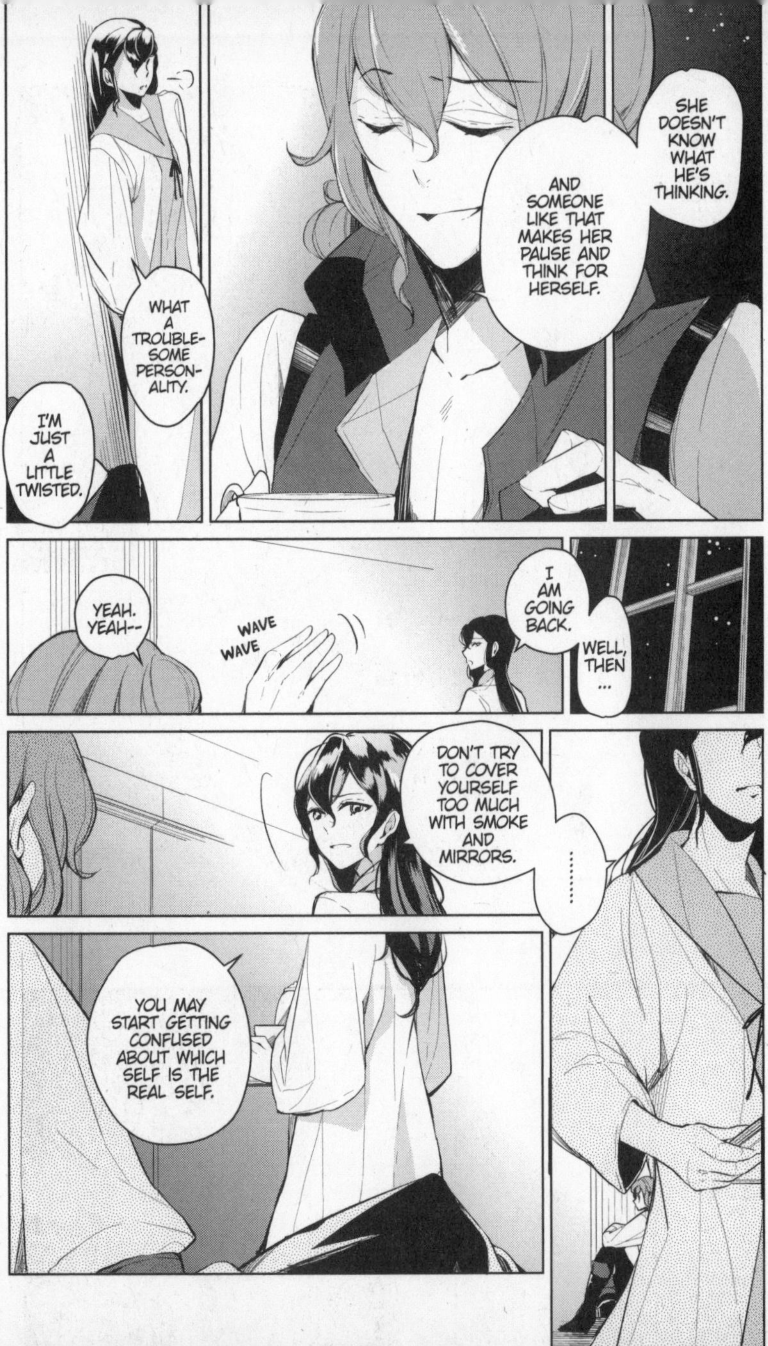
SHE DOESN'T KNOW WHAT HE'S THINKING.
AND SOMEONE LIKE THAT MAKES HER PAUSE AND THINK FOR HERSELF.
WHAT A TROUBLE-SOME PERSON-ALITY.
I'M JUST A LITTLE TWISTED.
WELL, THEN ...
I AM GOING BACK.
WAVE WAVE
YEAH. YEAH--
......
DON'T TRY TO COVER YOURSELF TOO MUCH WITH SMOKE AND MIRRORS.
YOU MAY START GETTING CONFUSED ABOUT WHICH SELF IS THE REAL SELF.

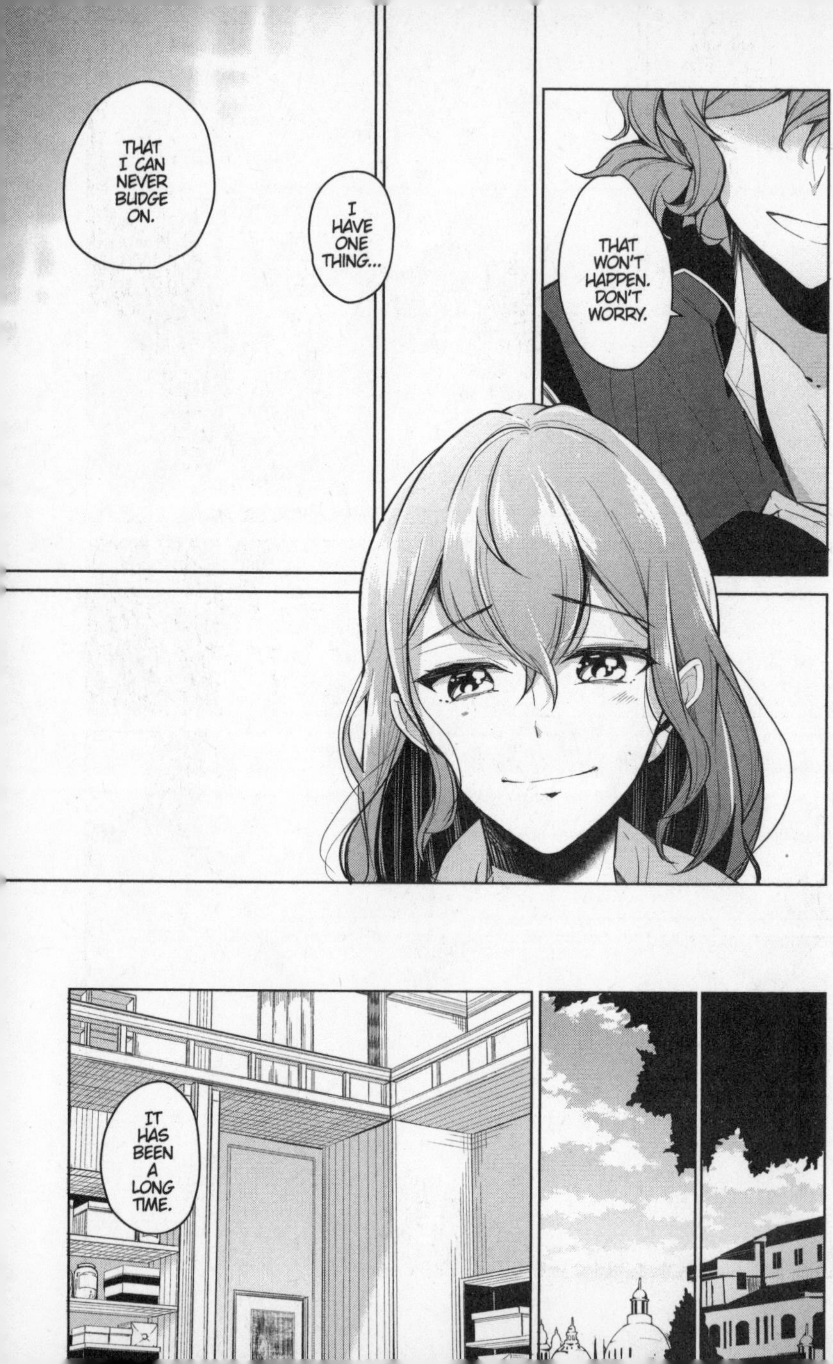
THAT WON'T HAPPEN. DON'T WORRY.
I HAVE ONE THING...
THAT I CAN NEVER BUDGE ON.
IT HAS BEEN A LONG TIME.

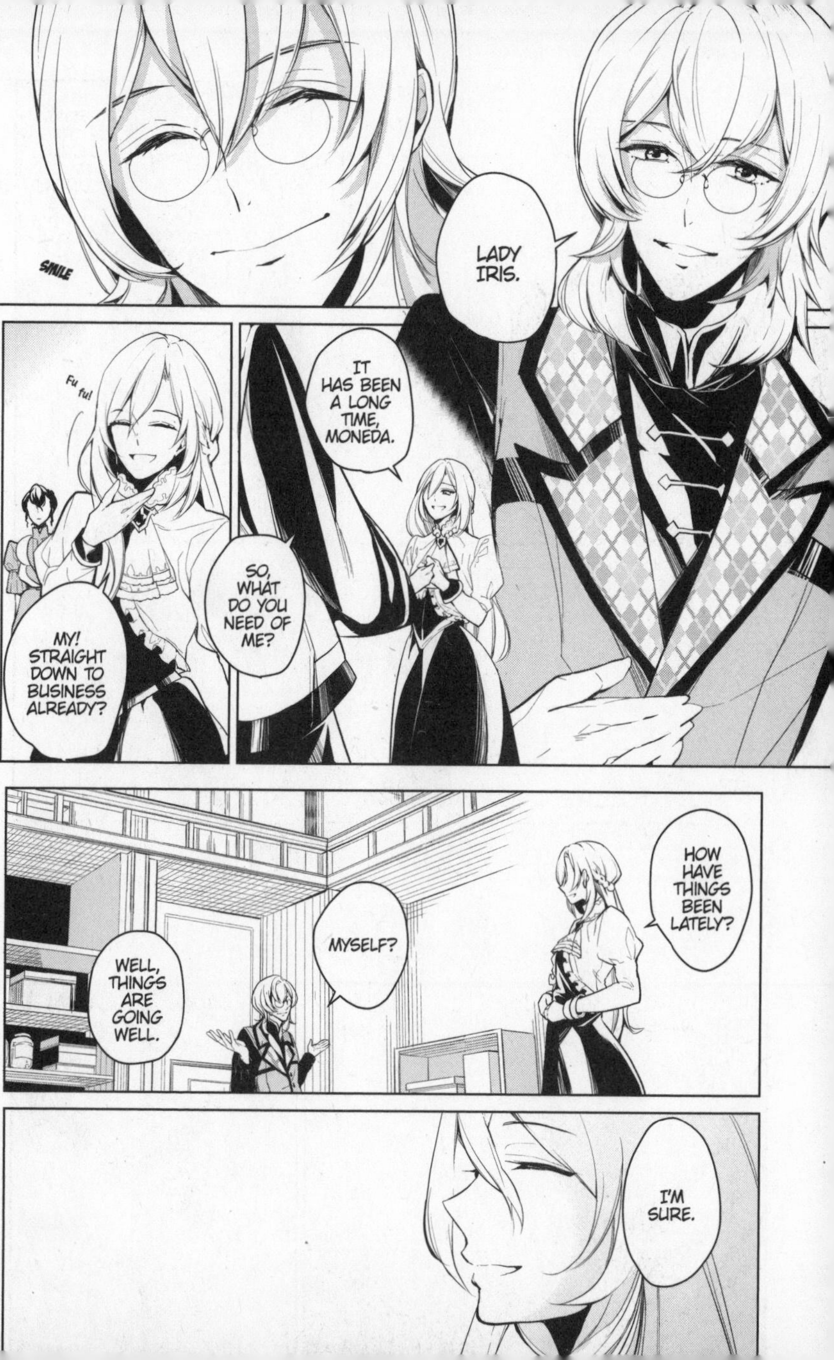
LADY IRIS.
SMILE
IT HAS BEEN A LONG TIME, MONEDA.
SO, WHAT DO YOU NEED OF ME?
Fu fu!
MY! STRAIGHT DOWN TO BUSINESS ALREADY?
HOW HAVE THINGS BEEN LATELY?
MYSELF?
WELL, THINGS ARE GOING WELL.
I'M SURE.

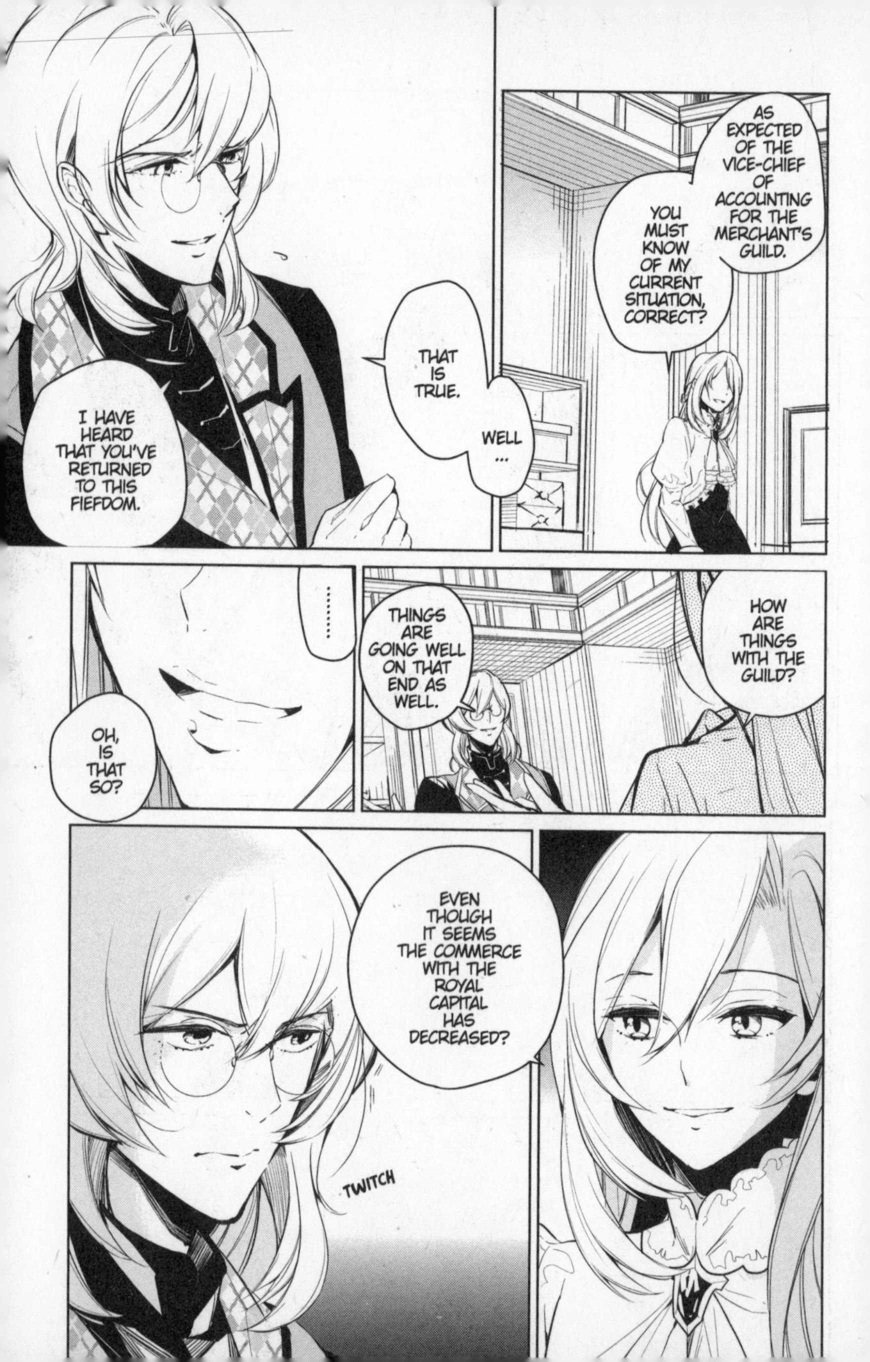
AS EXPECTED OF THE VICE-CHIEF OF ACCOUNTING FOR THE MERCHANT'S GUILD.
YOU MUST KNOW OF MY CURRENT SITUATION, CORRECT?
THAT IS TRUE.
WELL ...
I HAVE HEARD THAT YOU'VE RETURNED TO THIS FIEFDOM.
HOW ARE THINGS WITH THE GUILD?
THINGS ARE GOING WELL ON THAT END AS WELL.
......
OH, IS THAT SO?
EVEN THOUGH IT SEEMS THE COMMERCE WITH THE ROYAL CAPITAL HAS DECREASED?
TWITCH

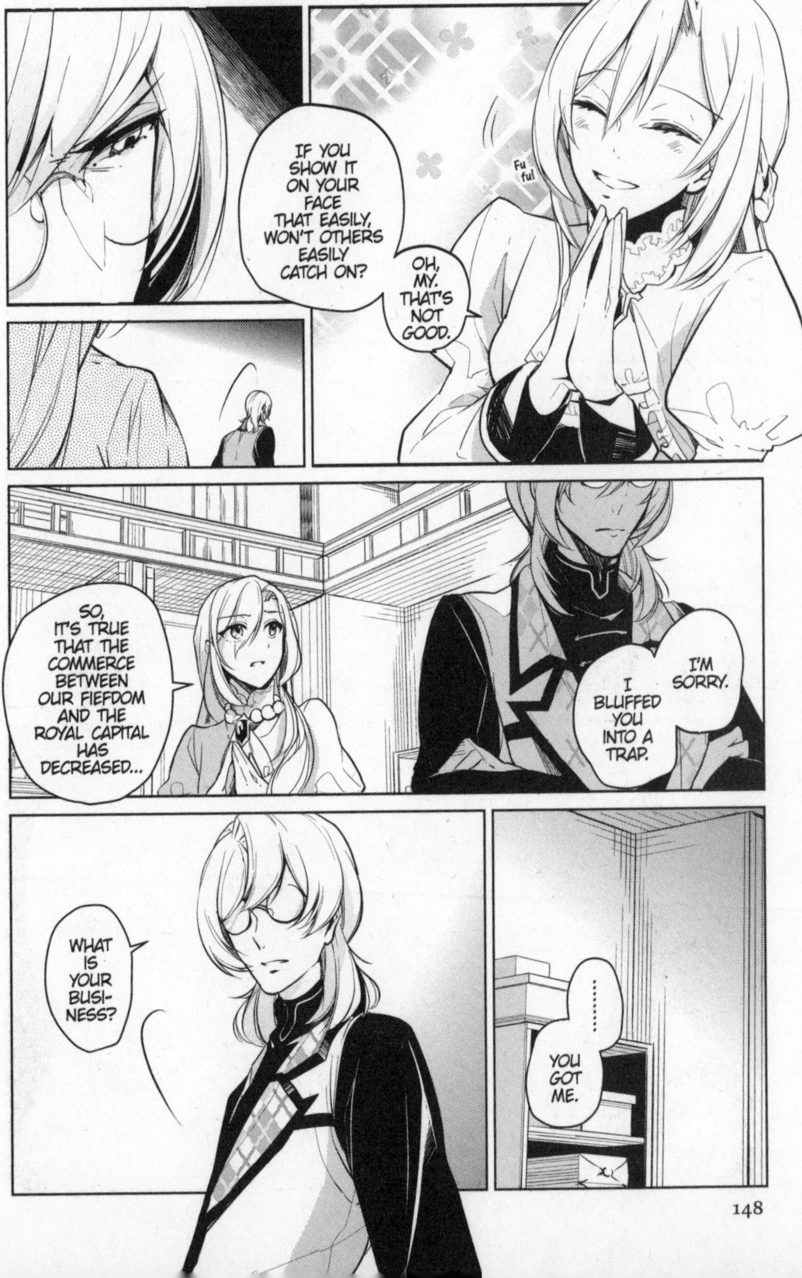
IF YOU SHOW IT ON YOUR FACE THAT EASILY, WON'T OTHERS EASILY CATCH ON?
Fu fu!
OH, MY. THAT'S NOT GOOD.
I'M SORRY.
I BLUFFED YOU INTO A TRAP.
SO, IT'S TRUE THAT THE COMMERCE BETWEEN OUR FIEFDOM AND THE ROYAL CAPITAL HAS DECREASED...
......
YOU GOT ME.
WHAT IS YOUR BUSI-NESS?

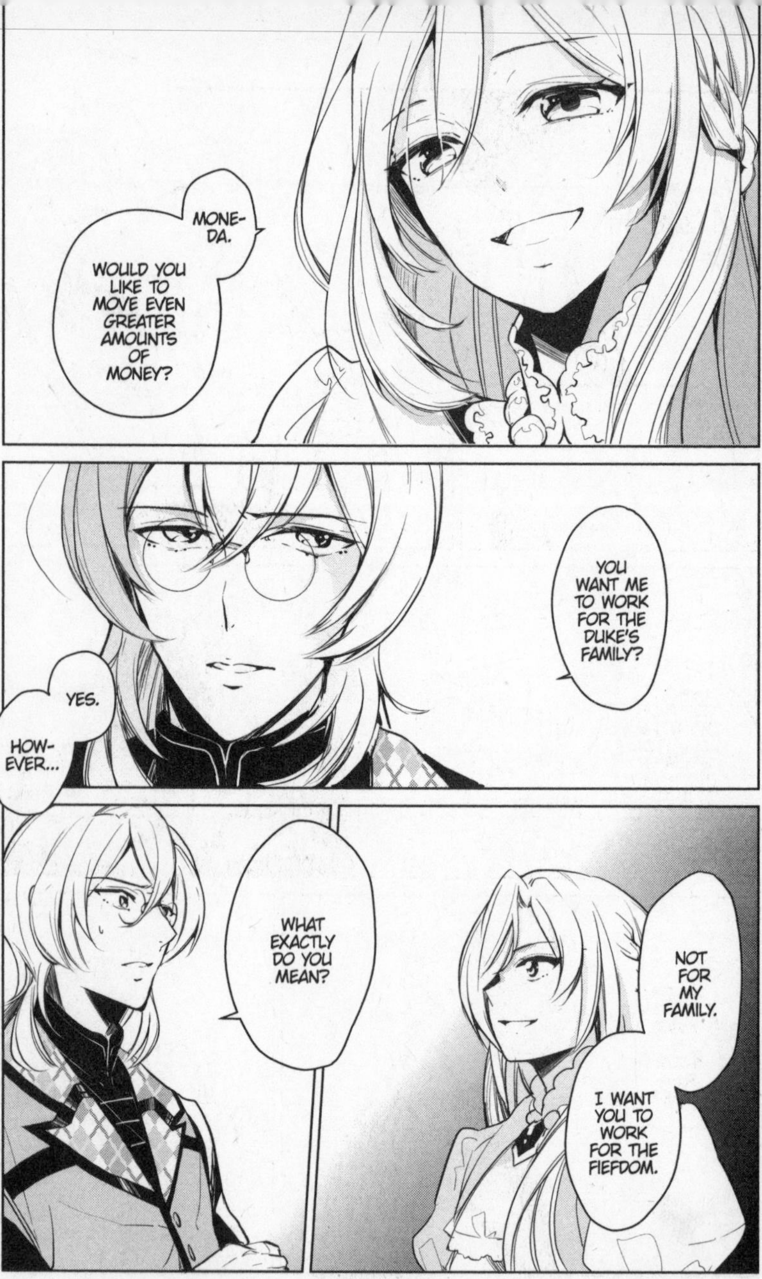
MONE-DA.
WOULD YOU LIKE TO MOVE EVEN GREATER AMOUNTS OF MONEY?
YOU WANT ME TO WORK FOR THE DUKE'S FAMILY?
YES.
HOW-EVER...
NOT FOR MY FAMILY.
I WANT YOU TO WORK FOR THE FIEFDOM.
WHAT EXACTLY DO YOU MEAN?

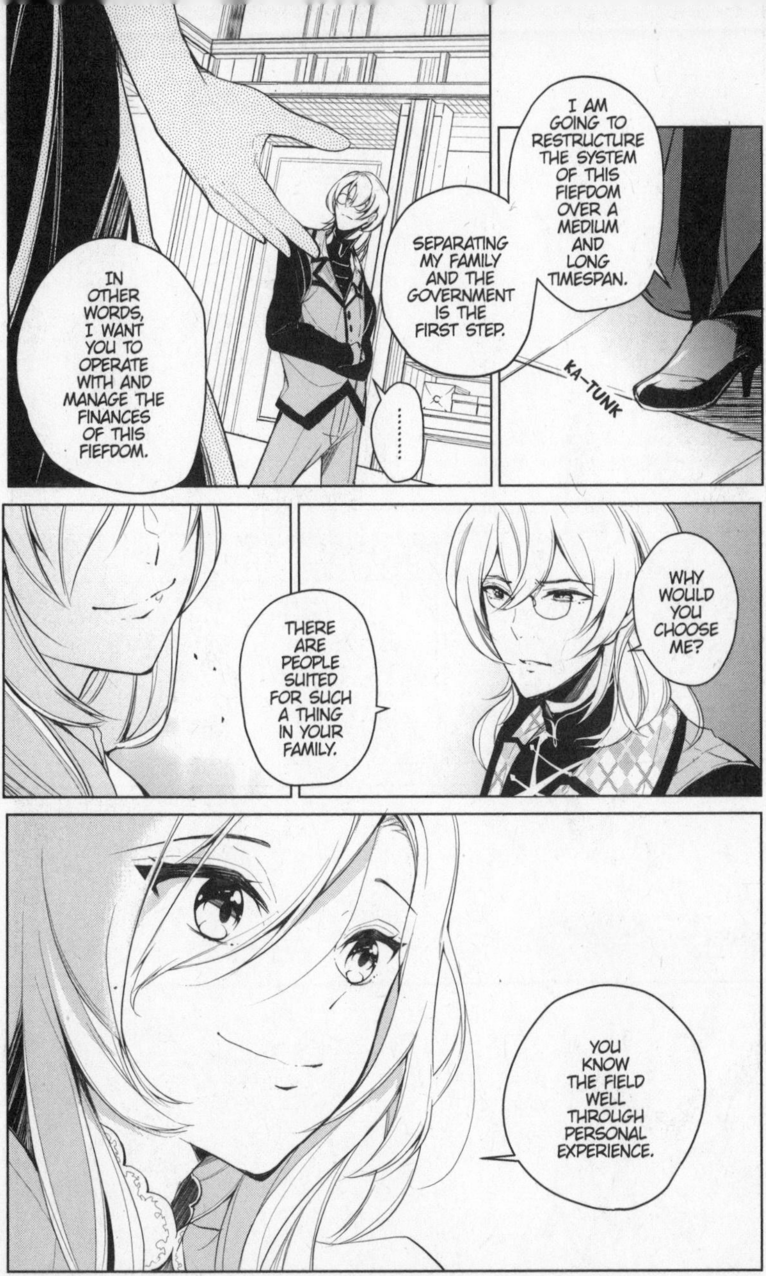
I AM GOING TO RESTRUCTURE THE SYSTEM OF THIS FIEFDOM OVER A MEDIUM AND LONG TIMESPAN.
SEPARATING MY FAMILY AND THE GOVERNMENT IS THE FIRST STEP.
KA-TUNK
IN OTHER WORDS, I WANT YOU TO OPERATE WITH AND MANAGE THE FINANCES OF THIS FIEFDOM.
....
WHY WOULD YOU CHOOSE ME?
THERE ARE PEOPLE SUITED FOR SUCH A THING IN YOUR FAMILY.
YOU KNOW THE FIELD WELL THROUGH PERSONAL EXPERIENCE.

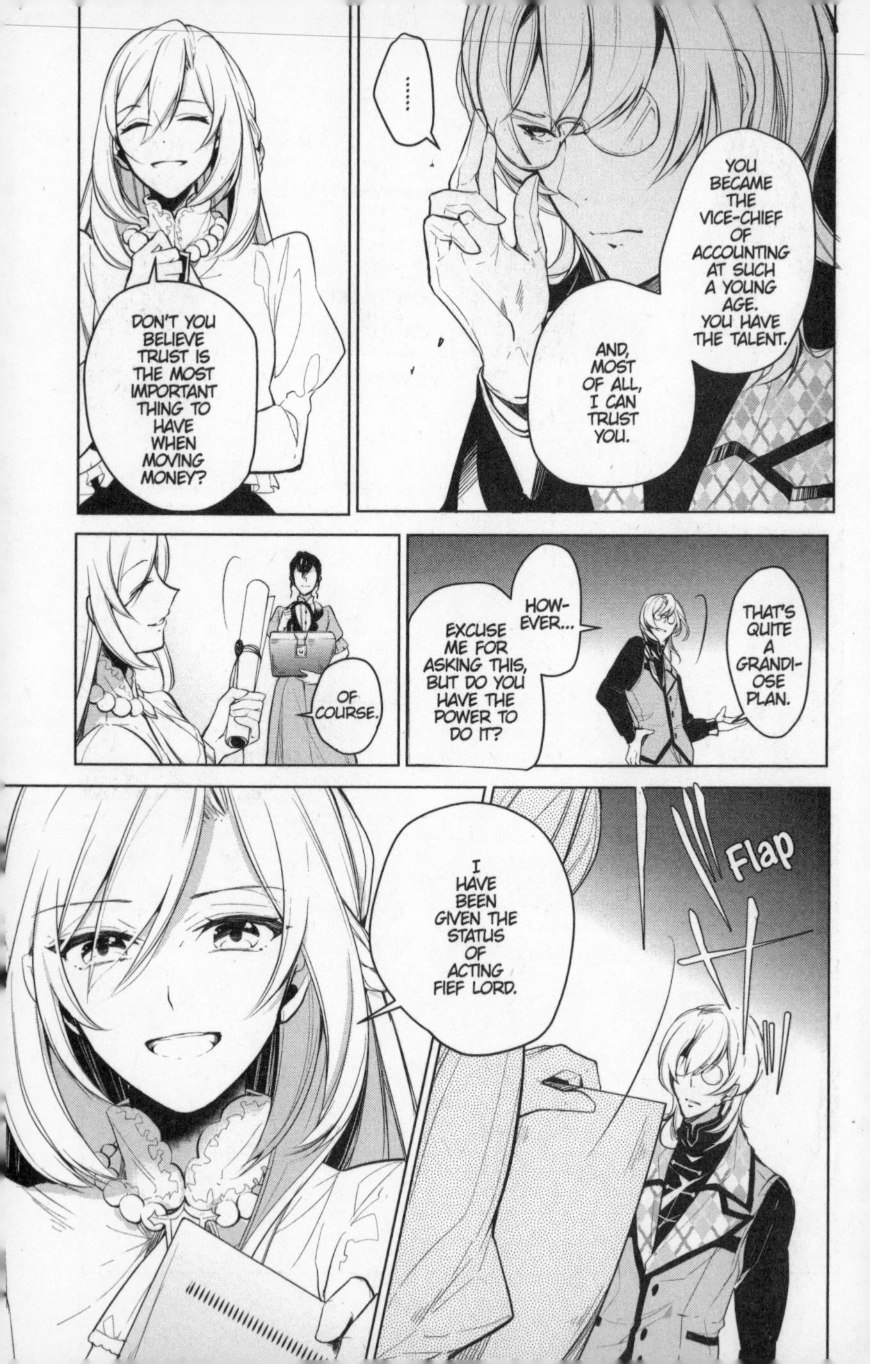
YOU BECAME THE VICE-CHIEF OF ACCOUNTING AT SUCH A YOUNG AGE. YOU HAVE THE TALENT.
AND, MOST OF ALL, I CAN TRUST YOU.
......
DON'T YOU BELIEVE TRUST IS THE MOST IMPORTANT THING TO HAVE WHEN MOVING MONEY?
THAT'S QUITE A GRANDI-OSE PLAN.
HOW-EVER...
EXCUSE ME FOR ASKING THIS, BUT DO YOU HAVE THE POWER TO DO IT?
OF COURSE.
Flap
I HAVE BEEN GIVEN THE STATUS OF ACTING FIEF LORD.

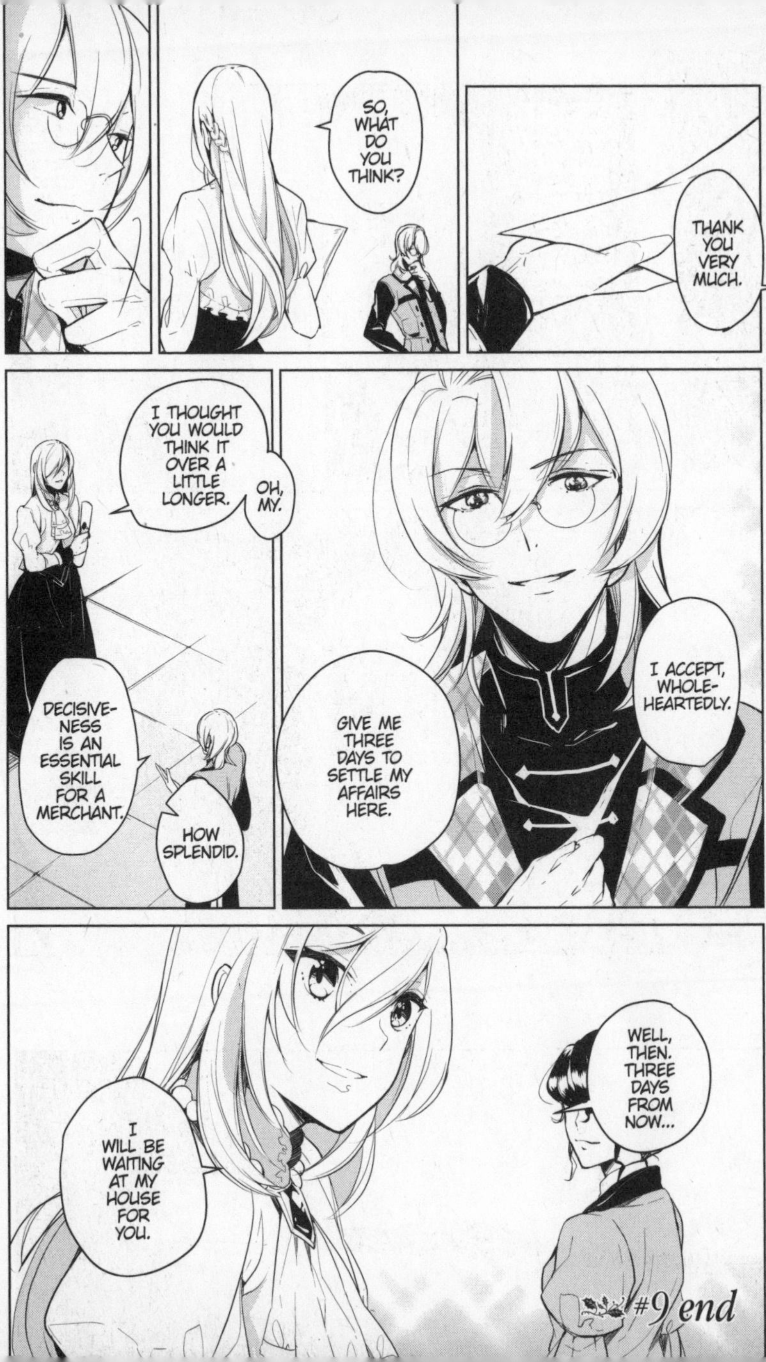
THANK YOU VERY MUCH.
SO, WHAT DO YOU THINK?
I ACCEPT, WHOLE-HEARTEDLY.
GIVE ME THREE DAYS TO SETTLE MY AFFAIRS HERE.
OH, MY.
I THOUGHT YOU WOULD THINK IT OVER A LITTLE LONGER.
DECISIVE-NESS IS AN ESSENTIAL SKILL FOR A MERCHANT.
HOW SPLENDID.
WELL, THEN. THREE DAYS FROM NOW...
I WILL BE WAITING AT MY HOUSE FOR YOU.
#9 end

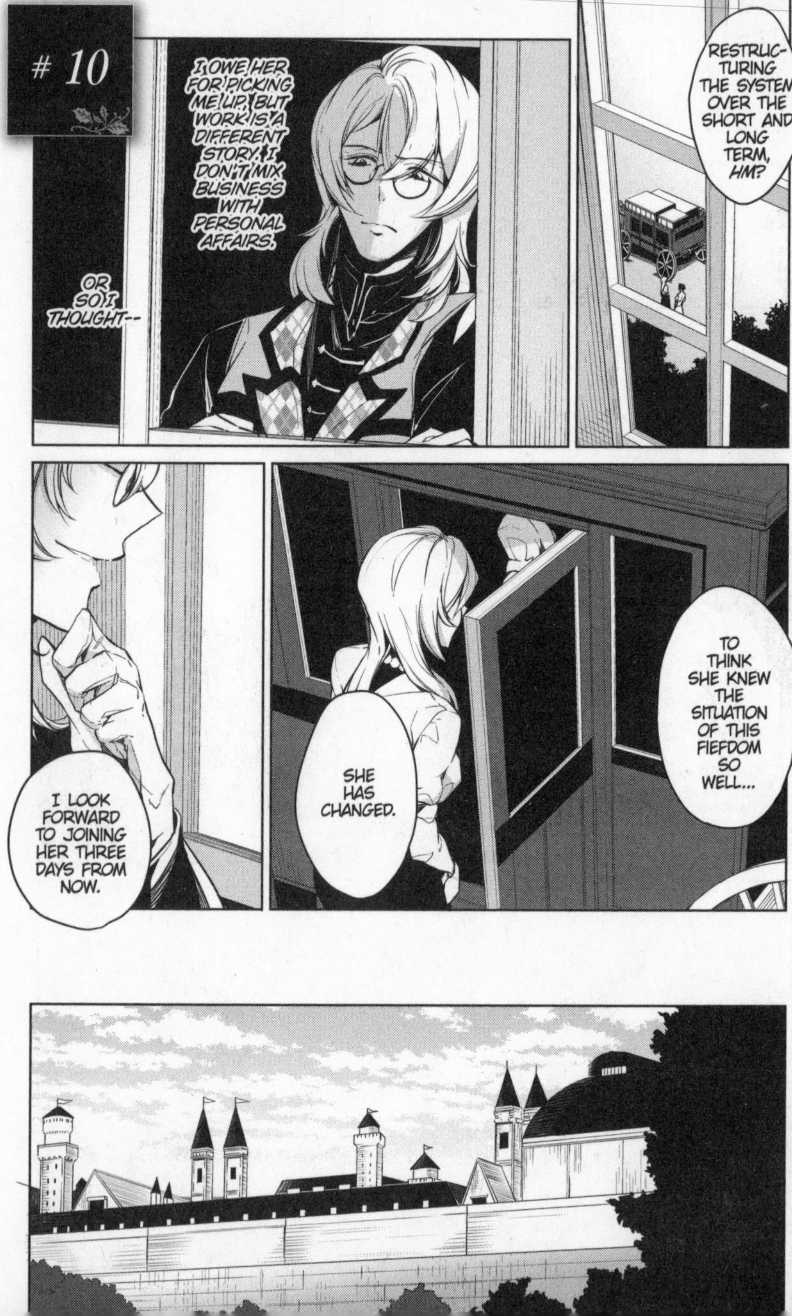

10
RESTRUCTURING THE SYSTEM OVER THE SHORT AND LONG TERM, HM?
I OWE HER FOR PICKING ME UP, BUT WORK IS A DIFFERENT STORY. I DON'T MIX BUSINESS WITH PERSONAL AFFAIRS.
OR SO I THOUGHT--
TO THINK SHE KNEW THE SITUATION OF THIS FIEFDOM SO WELL...
SHE HAS CHANGED.
I LOOK FORWARD TO JOINING HER THREE DAYS FROM NOW.

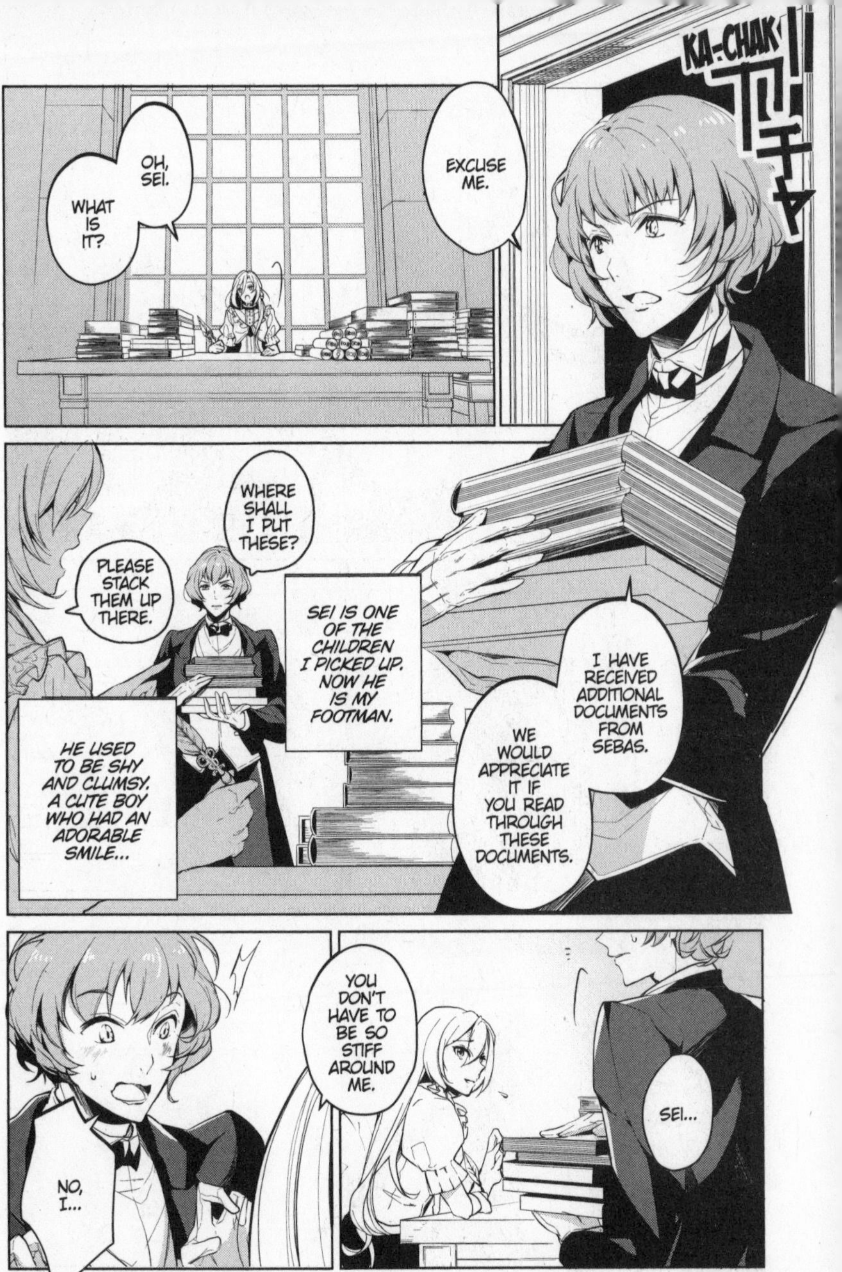
KA-CHAK
EXCUSE ME.
OH, SEI.
WHAT IS IT?
I HAVE RECEIVED ADDITIONAL DOCUMENTS FROM SEBAS.
WE WOULD APPRECIATE IT IF YOU READ THROUGH THESE DOCUMENTS.
WHERE SHALL I PUT THESE?
PLEASE STACK THEM UP THERE.
SEI IS ONE OF THE CHILDREN I PICKED UP. NOW HE IS MY FOOTMAN.
HE USED TO BE SHY AND CLUMSY. A CUTE BOY WHO HAD AN ADORABLE SMILE...
SEI...
YOU DON'T HAVE TO BE SO STIFF AROUND ME.
NO, I...

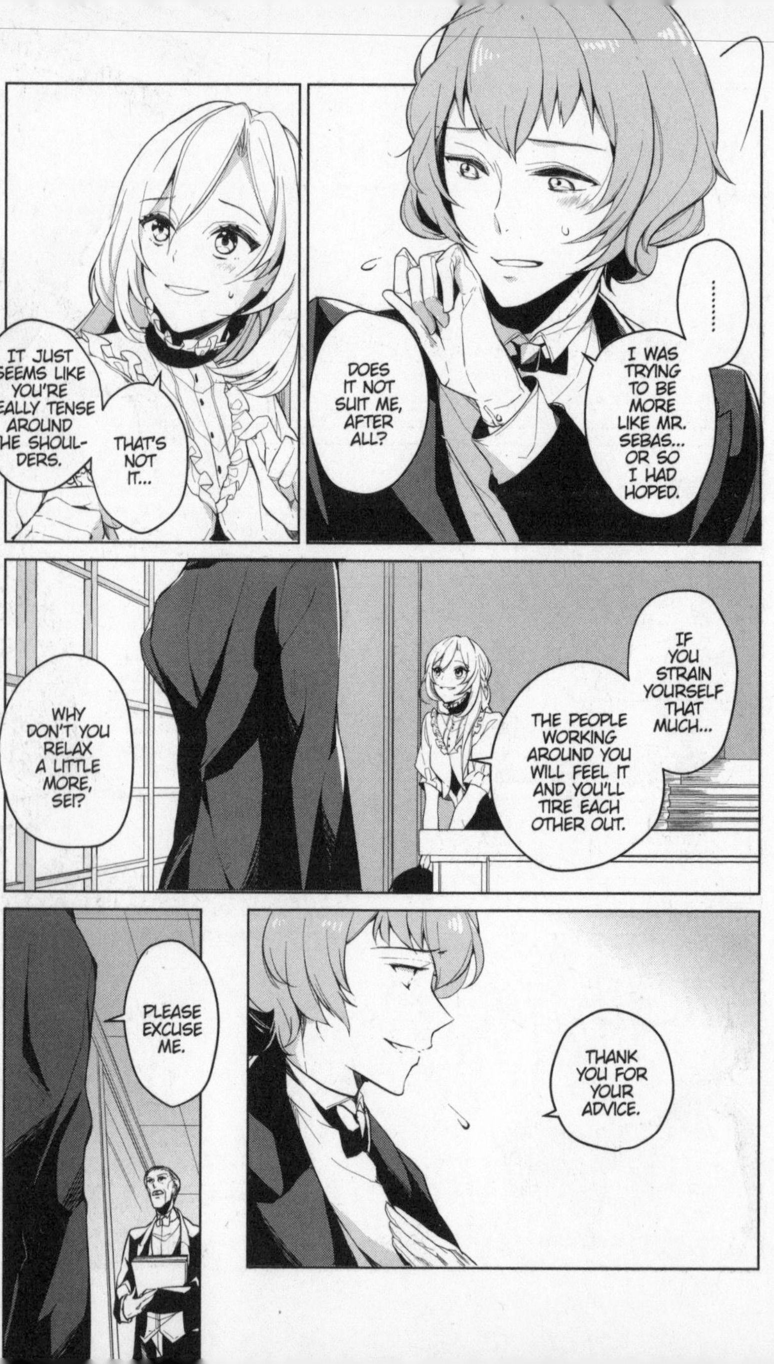
......
I WAS TRYING TO BE MORE LIKE MR. SEBAS... OR SO I HAD HOPED.
DOES IT NOT SUIT ME, AFTER ALL?
THAT'S NOT IT...
IT JUST SEEMS LIKE YOU'RE REALLY TENSE AROUND THE SHOULDERS.
IF YOU STRAIN YOURSELF THAT MUCH...
THE PEOPLE WORKING AROUND YOU WILL FEEL IT AND YOU'LL TIRE EACH OTHER OUT.
WHY DON'T YOU RELAX A LITTLE MORE, SEI?
THANK YOU FOR YOUR ADVICE.
PLEASE EXCUSE ME.

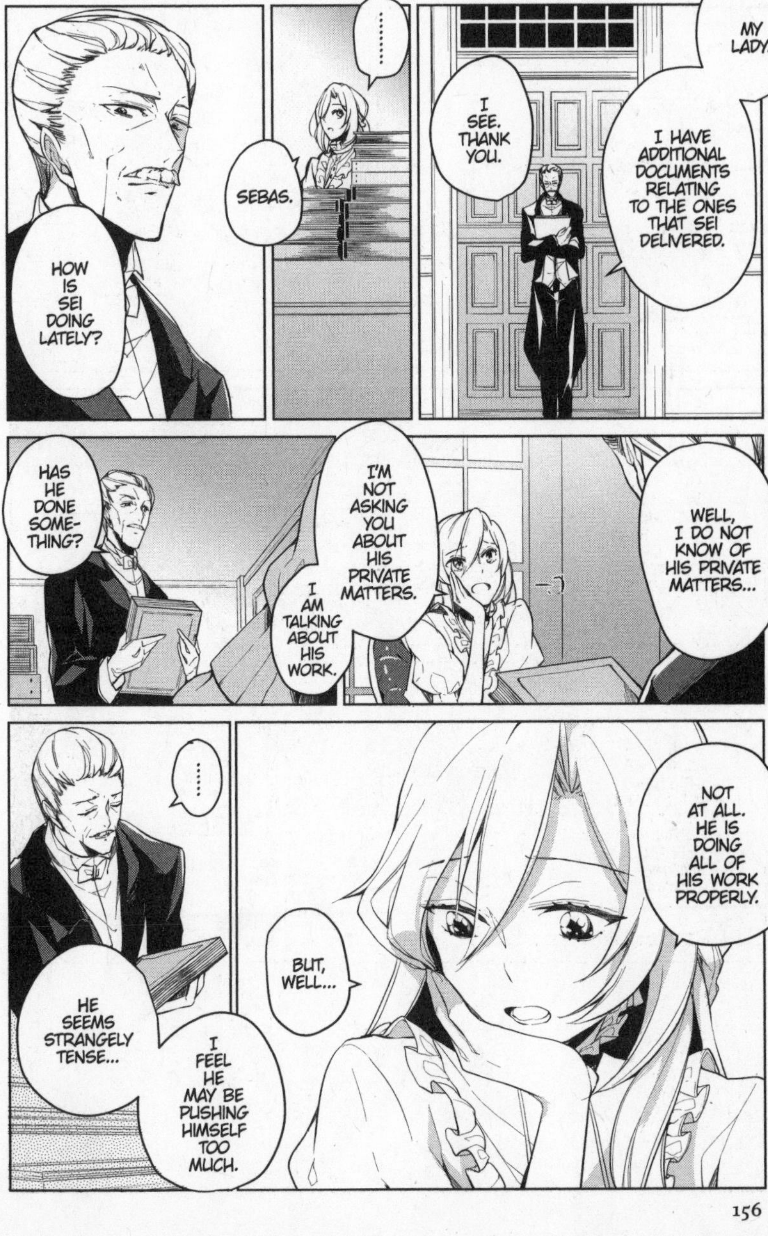
MY LADY.
I HAVE ADDITIONAL DOCUMENTS RELATING TO THE ONES THAT SEI DELIVERED.
I SEE. THANK YOU.
......
SEBAS.
HOW IS SEI DOING LATELY?
WELL, I DO NOT KNOW OF HIS PRIVATE MATTERS...
I'M NOT ASKING YOU ABOUT HIS PRIVATE MATTERS.
I AM TALKING ABOUT HIS WORK.
HAS HE DONE SOME-THING?
NOT AT ALL. HE IS DOING ALL OF HIS WORK PROPERLY.
BUT, WELL...
......
HE SEEMS STRANGELY TENSE...
I FEEL HE MAY BE PUSHING HIMSELF TOO MUCH.

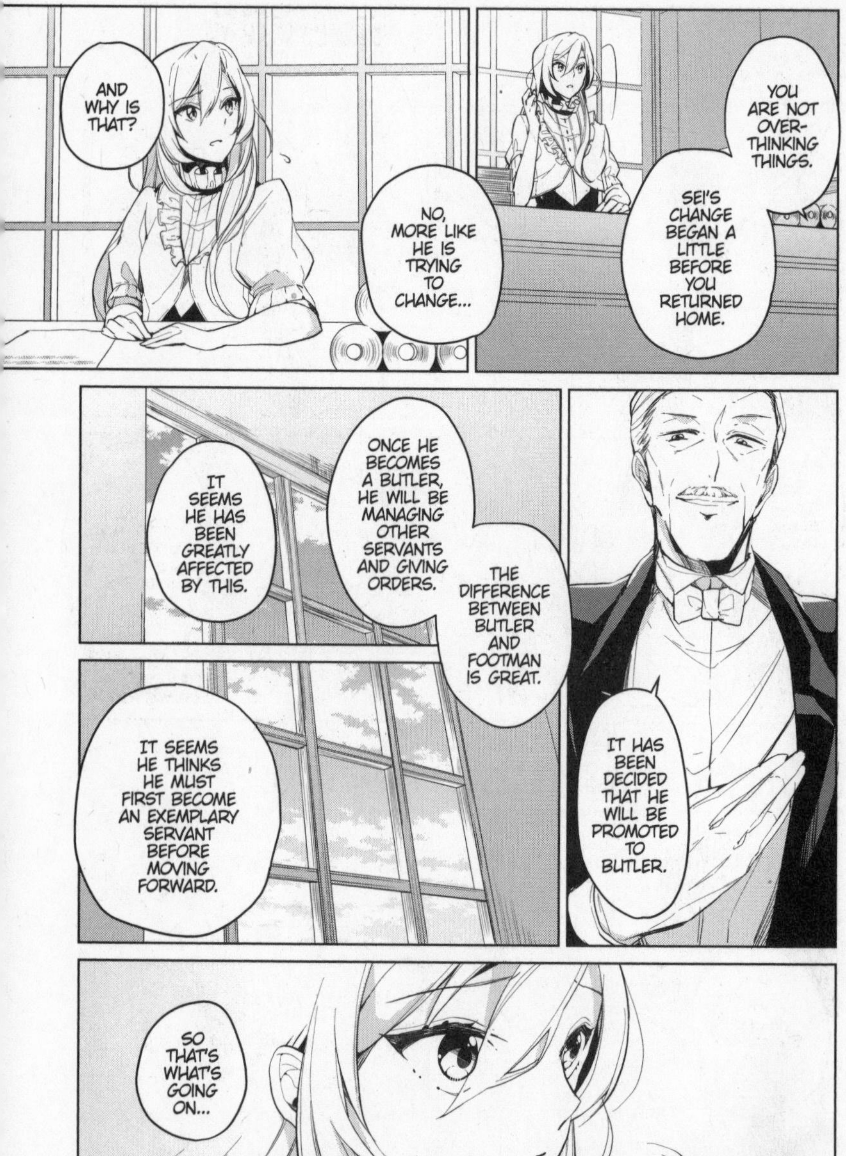
YOU ARE NOT OVER-THINKING THINGS.
SEI'S CHANGE BEGAN A LITTLE BEFORE YOU RETURNED HOME.
AND WHY IS THAT?
NO, MORE LIKE HE IS TRYING TO CHANGE...
IT HAS BEEN DECIDED THAT HE WILL BE PROMOTED TO BUTLER.
THE DIFFERENCE BETWEEN BUTLER AND FOOTMAN IS GREAT.
ONCE HE BECOMES A BUTLER, HE WILL BE MANAGING OTHER SERVANTS AND GIVING ORDERS.
IT SEEMS HE HAS BEEN GREATLY AFFECTED BY THIS.
IT SEEMS HE THINKS HE MUST FIRST BECOME AN EXEMPLARY SERVANT BEFORE MOVING FORWARD.
SO THAT'S WHAT'S GOING ON...

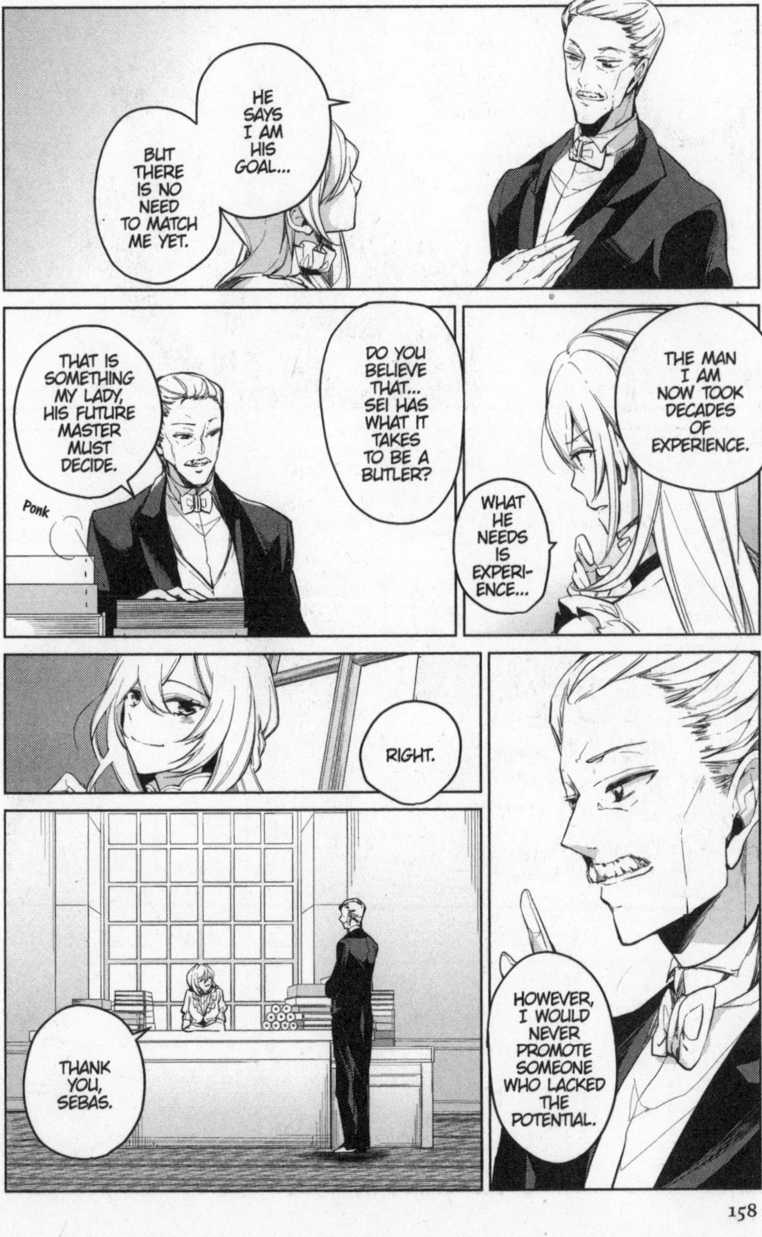
HE SAYS I AM HIS GOAL...
BUT THERE IS NO NEED TO MATCH ME YET.
THE MAN I AM NOW TOOK DECADES OF EXPERIENCE.
WHAT HE NEEDS IS EXPERIENCE...
DO YOU BELIEVE THAT... SEI HAS WHAT IT TAKES TO BE A BUTLER?
THAT IS SOMETHING MY LADY, HIS FUTURE MASTER MUST DECIDE.
Ponk
HOWEVER, I WOULD NEVER PROMOTE SOMEONE WHO LACKED THE POTENTIAL.
RIGHT.
THANK YOU, SEBAS.

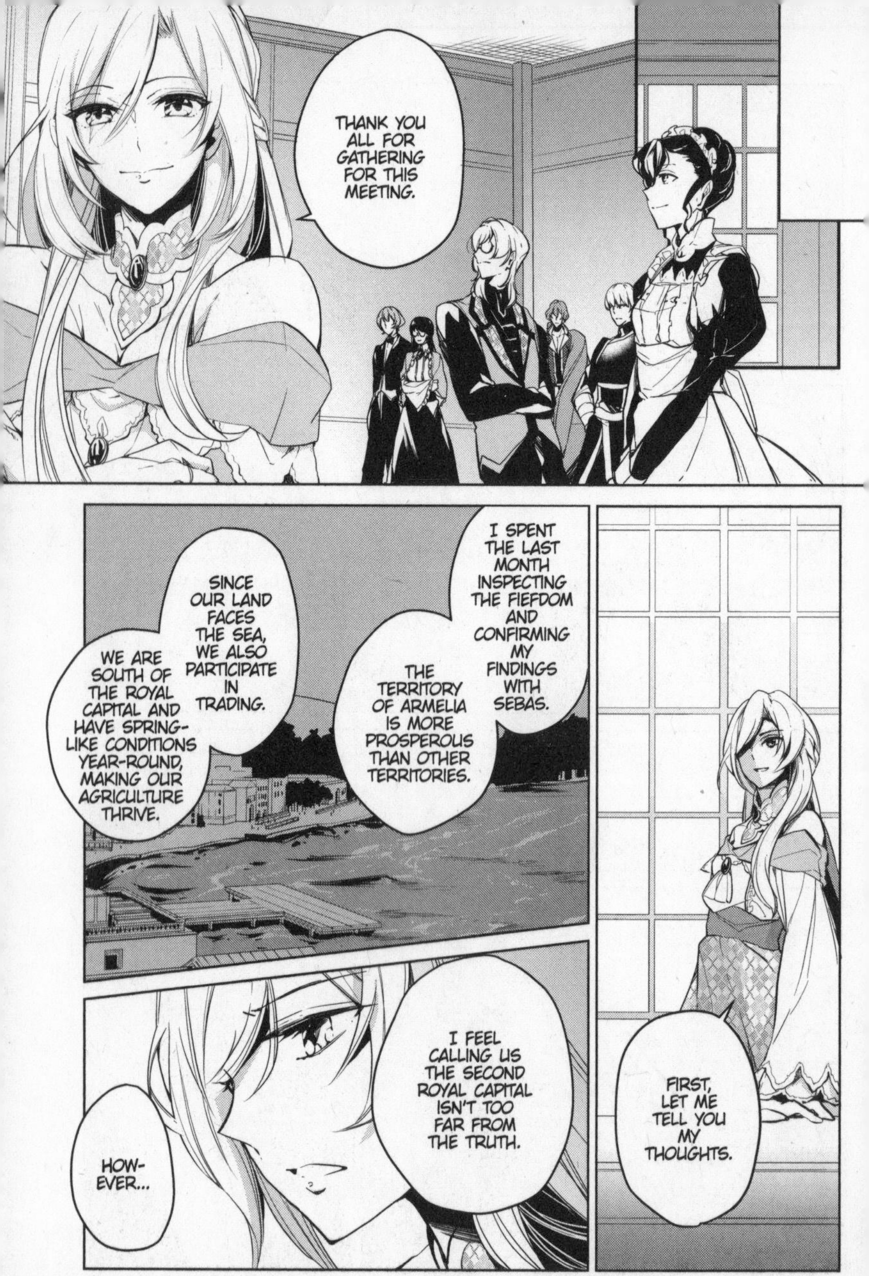
THANK YOU ALL FOR GATHERING FOR THIS MEETING.
FIRST, LET ME TELL YOU MY THOUGHTS.
I SPENT THE LAST MONTH INSPECTING THE FIEFDOM AND CONFIRMING MY FINDINGS WITH SEBAS.
THE TERRITORY OF ARMELIA IS MORE PROSPEROUS THAN OTHER TERRITORIES.
SINCE OUR LAND FACES THE SEA, WE ALSO PARTICIPATE IN TRADING.
WE ARE SOUTH OF THE ROYAL CAPITAL AND HAVE SPRING-LIKE CONDITIONS YEAR-ROUND, MAKING OUR AGRICULTURE THRIVE.
I FEEL CALLING US THE SECOND ROYAL CAPITAL ISN'T TOO FAR FROM THE TRUTH.
HOW-EVER...

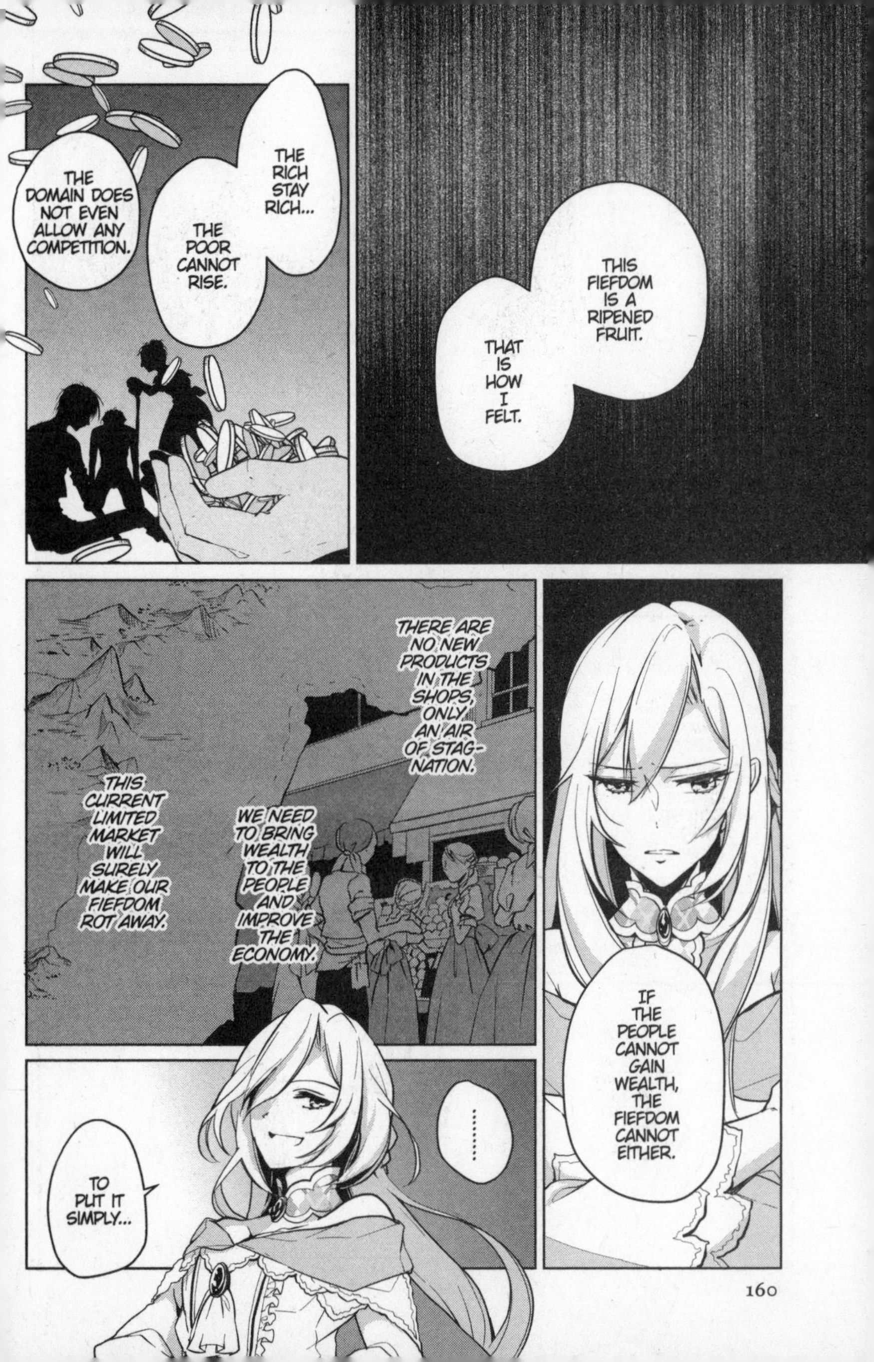

THIS FIEFDOM IS A RIPENED FRUIT.
THAT IS HOW I FELT.
THE RICH STAY RICH...
THE POOR CANNOT RISE.
THE DOMAIN DOES NOT EVEN ALLOW ANY COMPETITION.
IF THE PEOPLE CANNOT GAIN WEALTH, THE FIEFDOM CANNOT EITHER.
THERE ARE NO NEW PRODUCTS IN THE SHOPS, ONLY AN AIR OF STAG-NATION.
WE NEED TO BRING WEALTH TO THE PEOPLE AND IMPROVE THE ECONOMY.
THIS CURRENT LIMITED MARKET WILL SURELY MAKE OUR FIEFDOM ROT AWAY.
......
TO PUT IT SIMPLY...

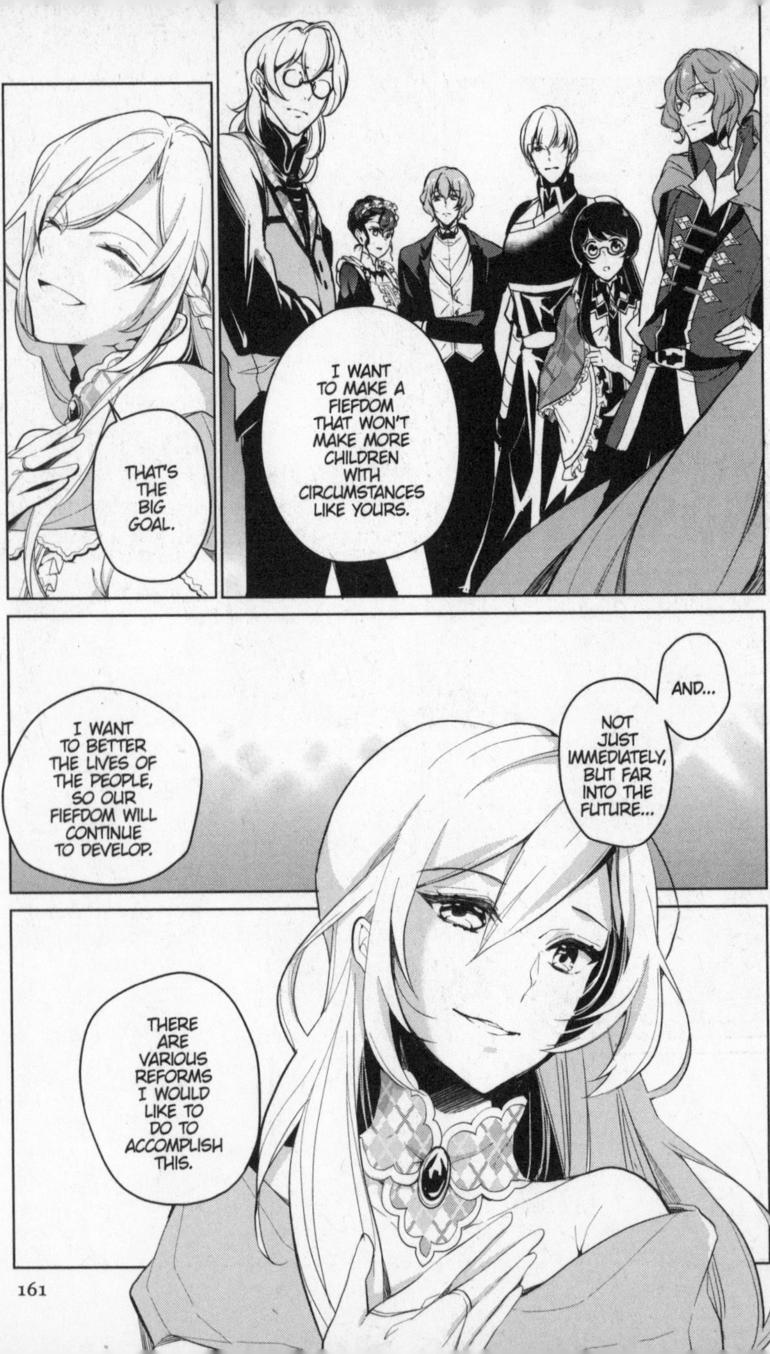
I WANT TO MAKE A FIEFDOM THAT WON'T MAKE MORE CHILDREN WITH CIRCUMSTANCES LIKE YOURS.
THAT'S THE BIG GOAL.
AND...
NOT JUST IMMEDIATELY, BUT FAR INTO THE FUTURE...
I WANT TO BETTER THE LIVES OF THE PEOPLE, SO OUR FIEFDOM WILL CONTINUE TO DEVELOP.
THERE ARE VARIOUS REFORMS I WOULD LIKE TO DO TO ACCOMPLISH THIS.

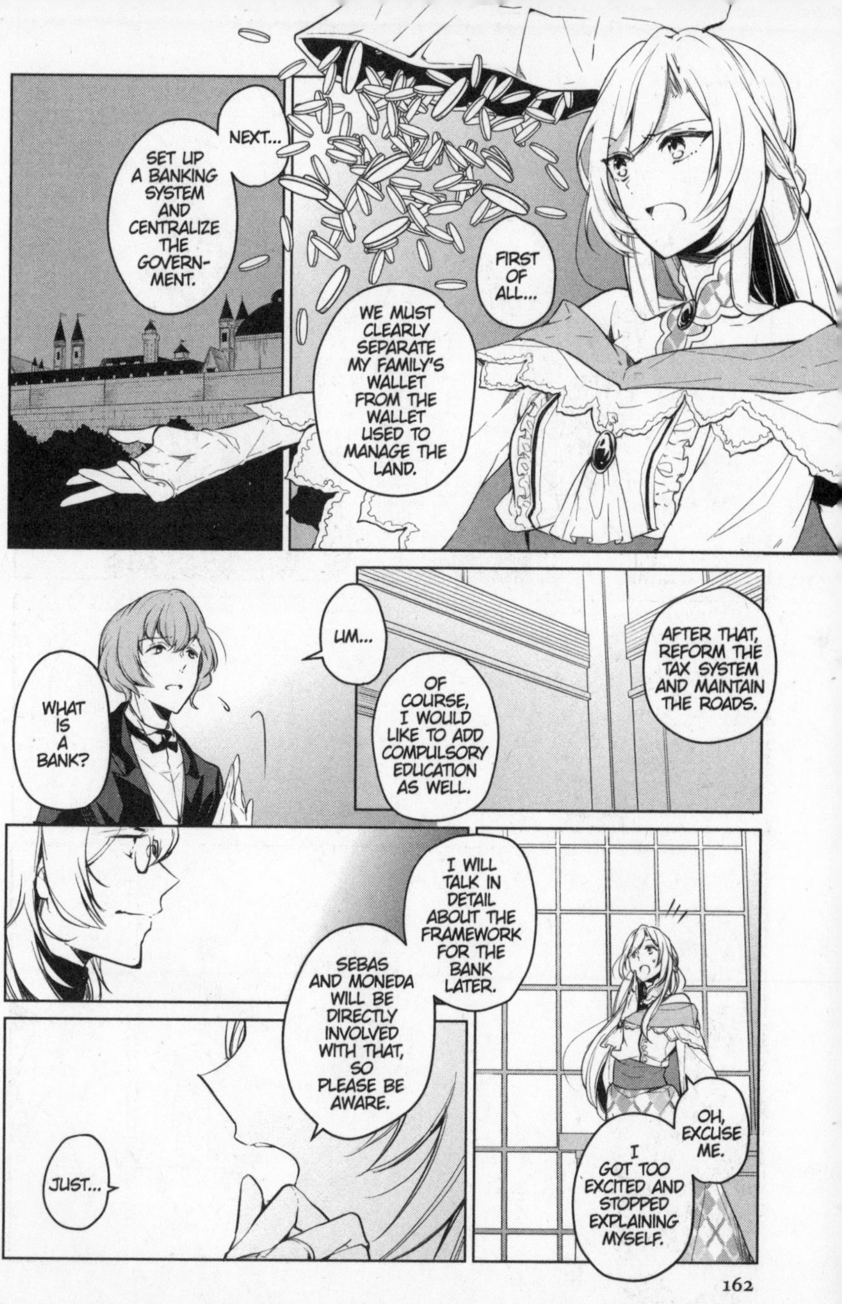

FIRST OF ALL...
WE MUST CLEARLY SEPARATE MY FAMILY'S WALLET FROM THE WALLET USED TO MANAGE THE LAND.
NEXT...
SET UP A BANKING SYSTEM AND CENTRALIZE THE GOVERN-MENT.
AFTER THAT, REFORM THE TAX SYSTEM AND MAINTAIN THE ROADS.
OF COURSE, I WOULD LIKE TO ADD COMPULSORY EDUCATION AS WELL.
UM...
WHAT IS A BANK?
OH, EXCUSE ME.
I GOT TOO EXCITED AND STOPPED EXPLAINING MYSELF.
I WILL TALK IN DETAIL ABOUT THE FRAMEWORK FOR THE BANK LATER.
SEBAS AND MONEDA WILL BE DIRECTLY INVOLVED WITH THAT, SO PLEASE BE AWARE.
JUST...

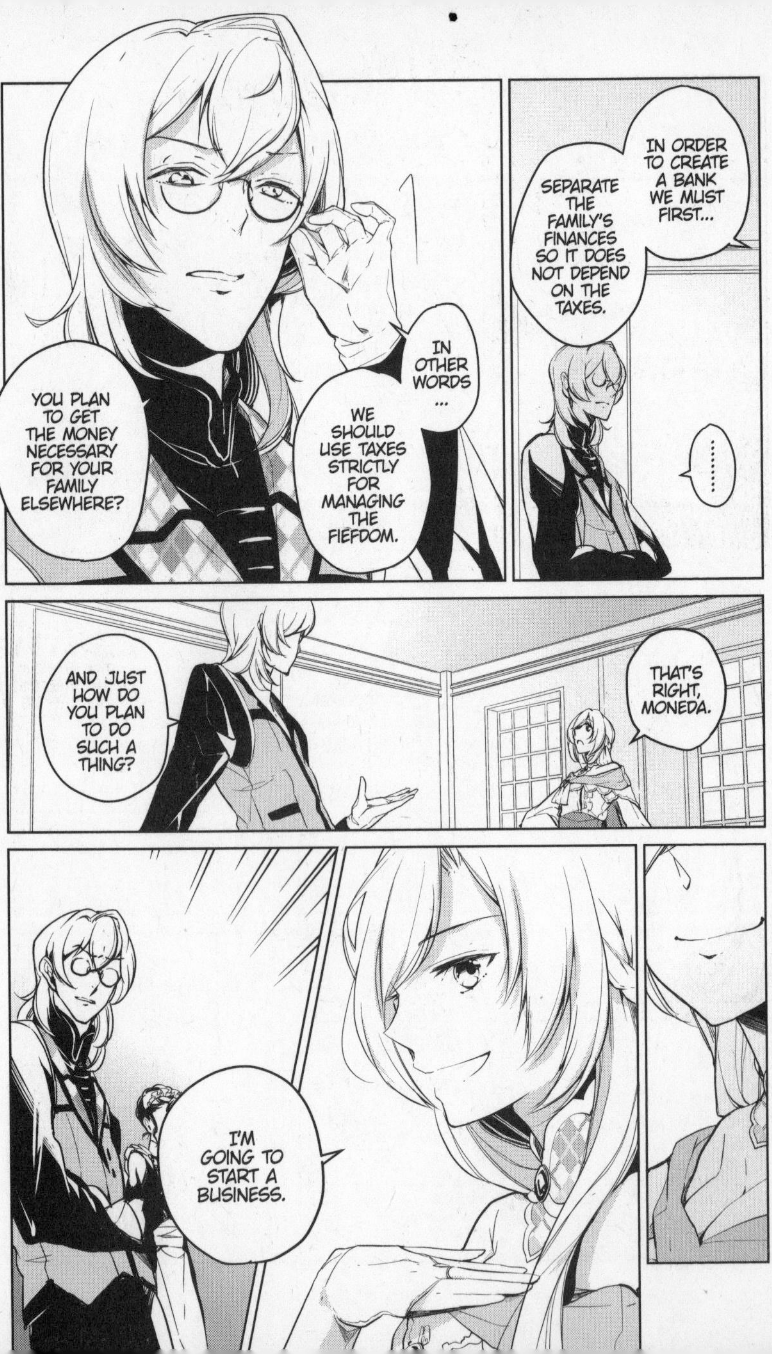
IN ORDER TO CREATE A BANK WE MUST FIRST...
SEPARATE THE FAMILY'S FINANCES SO IT DOES NOT DEPEND ON THE TAXES.
......
IN OTHER WORDS ...
WE SHOULD USE TAXES STRICTLY FOR MANAGING THE FIEFDOM.
YOU PLAN TO GET THE MONEY NECESSARY FOR YOUR FAMILY ELSEWHERE?
THAT'S RIGHT, MONEDA.
AND JUST HOW DO YOU PLAN TO DO SUCH A THING?
I'M GOING TO START A BUSINESS.

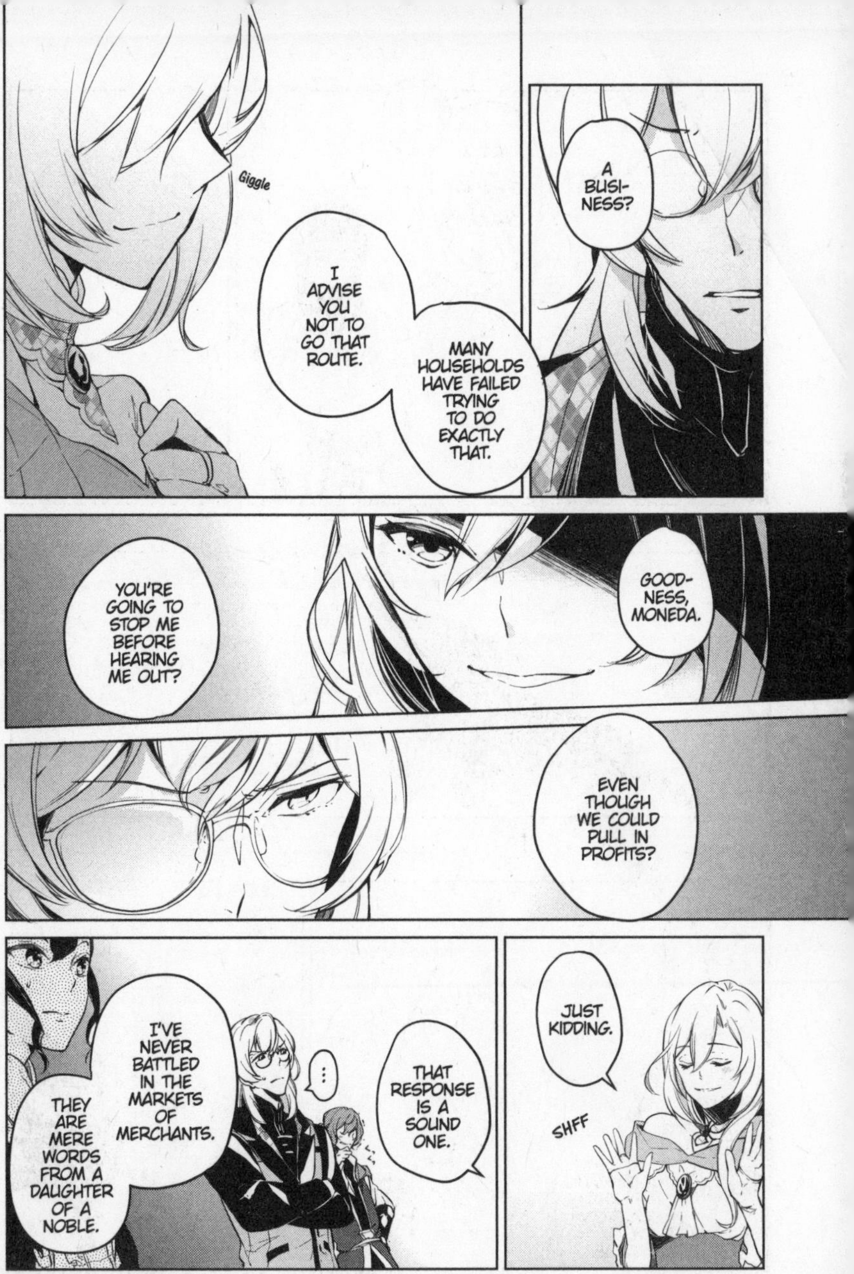
A BUSI-NESS?
Giggle
I ADVISE YOU NOT TO GO THAT ROUTE.
MANY HOUSEHOLDS HAVE FAILED TRYING TO DO EXACTLY THAT.
GOOD-NESS, MONEDA.
YOU'RE GOING TO STOP ME BEFORE HEARING ME OUT?
EVEN THOUGH WE COULD PULL IN PROFITS?
JUST KIDDING.
SHFF
THAT RESPONSE IS A SOUND ONE.
...
I'VE NEVER BATTLED IN THE MARKETS OF MERCHANTS.
THEY ARE MERE WORDS FROM A DAUGHTER OF A NOBLE.

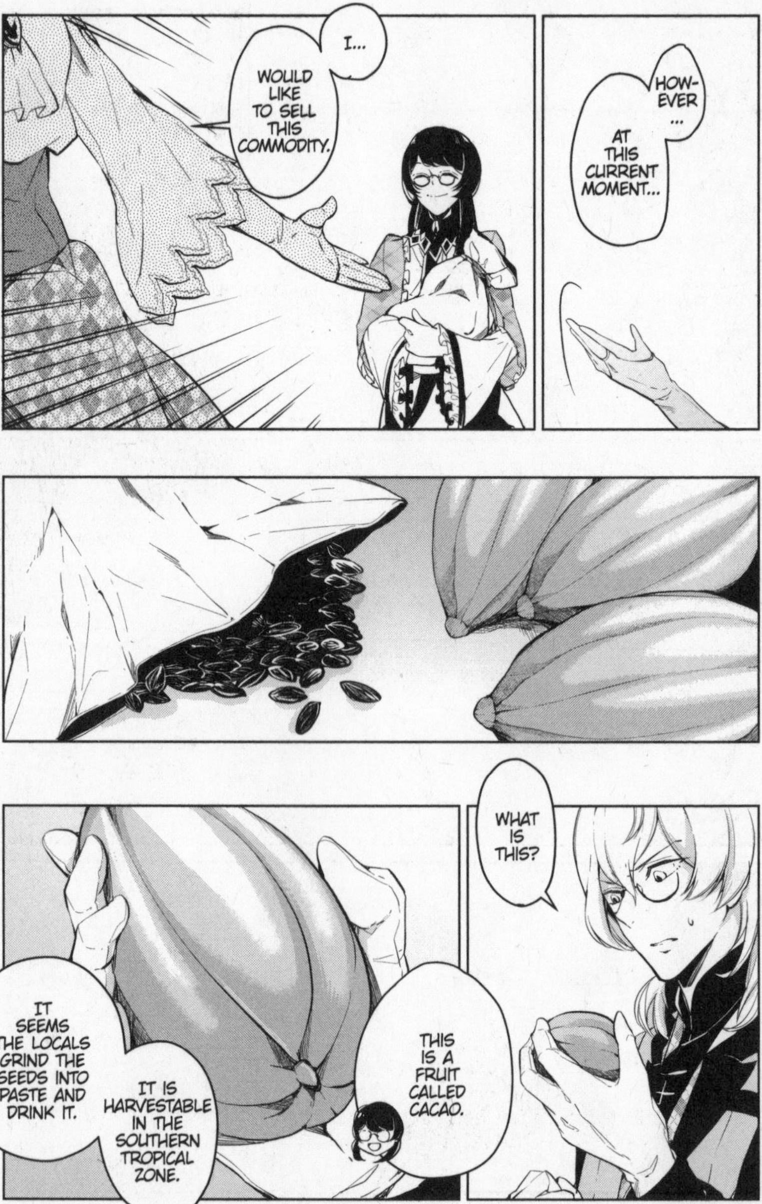
HOW-EVER...
AT THIS CURRENT MOMENT...
I...
WOULD LIKE TO SELL THIS COMMODITY.
WHAT IS THIS?
THIS IS A FRUIT CALLED CACAO.
IT IS HARVESTABLE IN THE SOUTHERN TROPICAL ZONE.
IT SEEMS THE LOCALS GRIND THE SEEDS INTO PASTE AND DRINK IT.

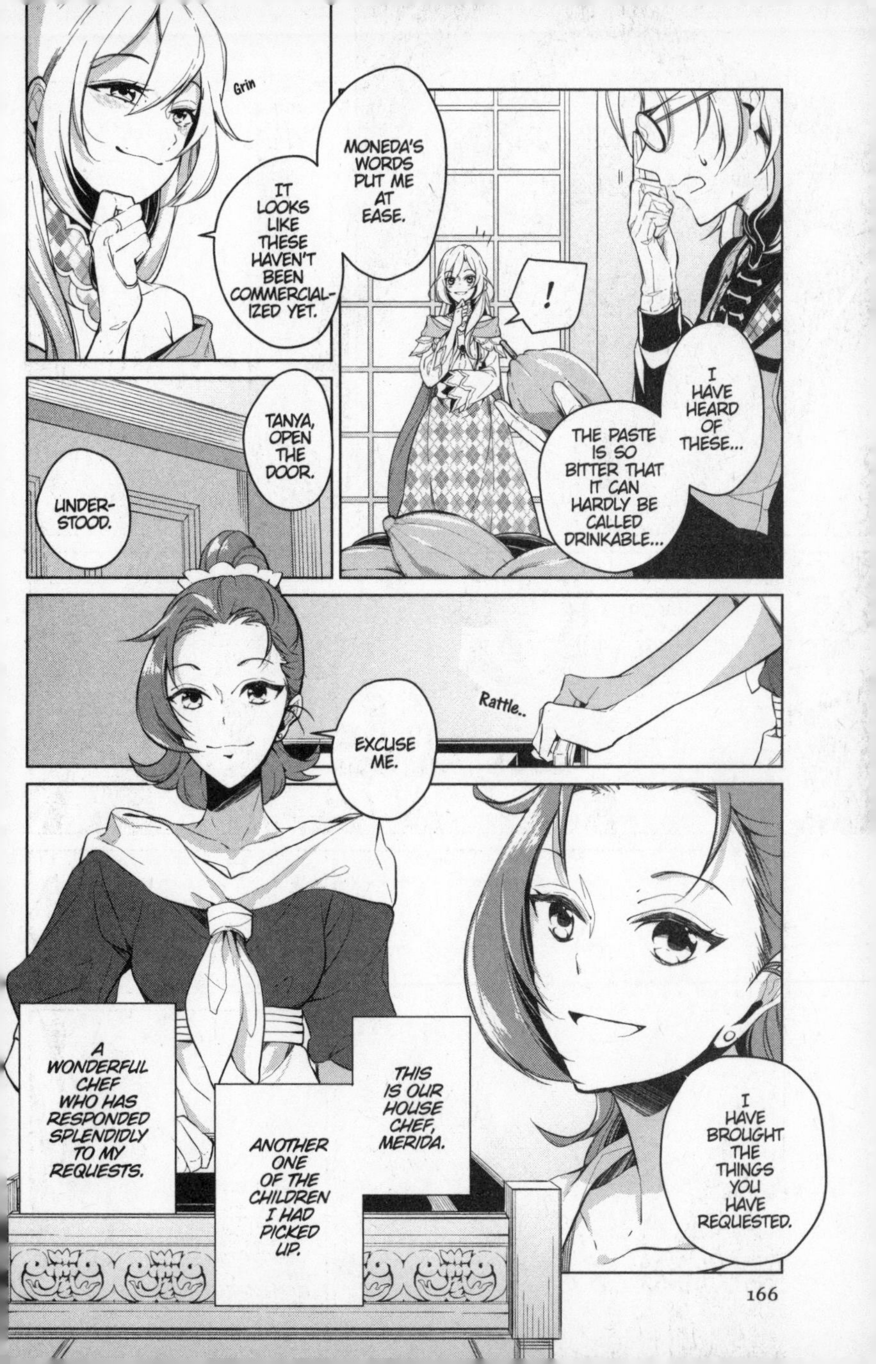
!
I HAVE HEARD OF THESE...
THE PASTE IS SO BITTER THAT IT CAN HARDLY BE CALLED DRINKABLE...
Grin
MONEDA'S WORDS PUT ME AT EASE.
IT LOOKS LIKE THESE HAVEN'T BEEN COMMERCIAL-IZED YET.
TANYA, OPEN THE DOOR.
UNDER-STOOD.
Rattle..
EXCUSE ME.
I HAVE BROUGHT THE THINGS YOU HAVE REQUESTED.
THIS IS OUR HOUSE CHEF, MERIDA.
ANOTHER ONE OF THE CHILDREN I HAD PICKED UP.
A WONDERFUL CHEF WHO HAS RESPONDED SPLENDIDLY TO MY REQUESTS.

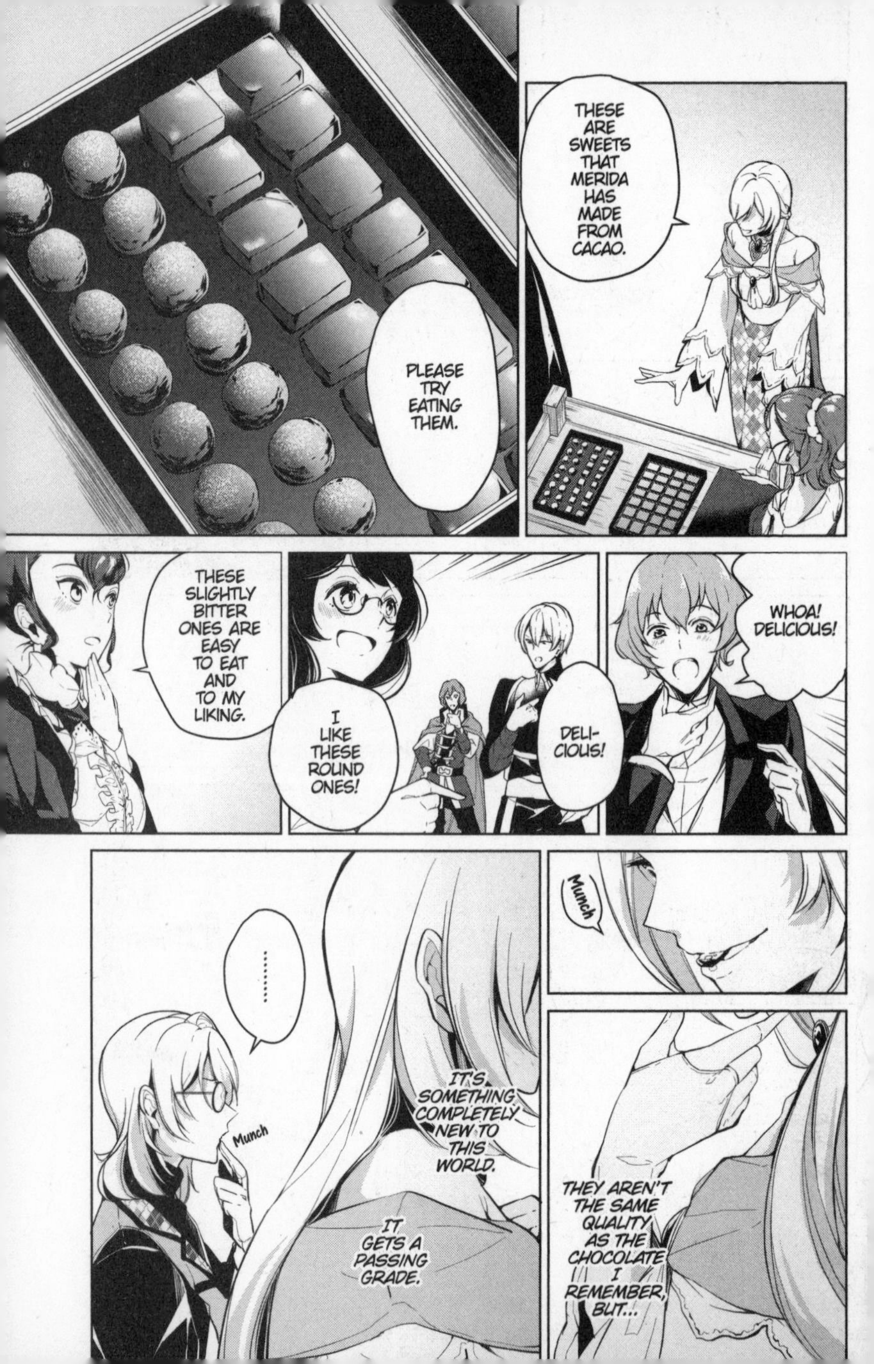
THESE ARE SWEETS THAT MERIDA HAS MADE FROM CACAO.
PLEASE TRY EATING THEM.
WHOA! DELICIOUS!
DELI-CIOUS!
I LIKE THESE ROUND ONES!
THESE SLIGHTLY BITTER ONES ARE EASY TO EAT AND TO MY LIKING.
Munch
THEY AREN'T THE SAME QUALITY AS THE CHOCOLATE I REMEMBER, BUT...
......
IT'S SOMETHING COMPLETELY NEW TO THIS WORLD.
Munch
IT GETS A PASSING GRADE.

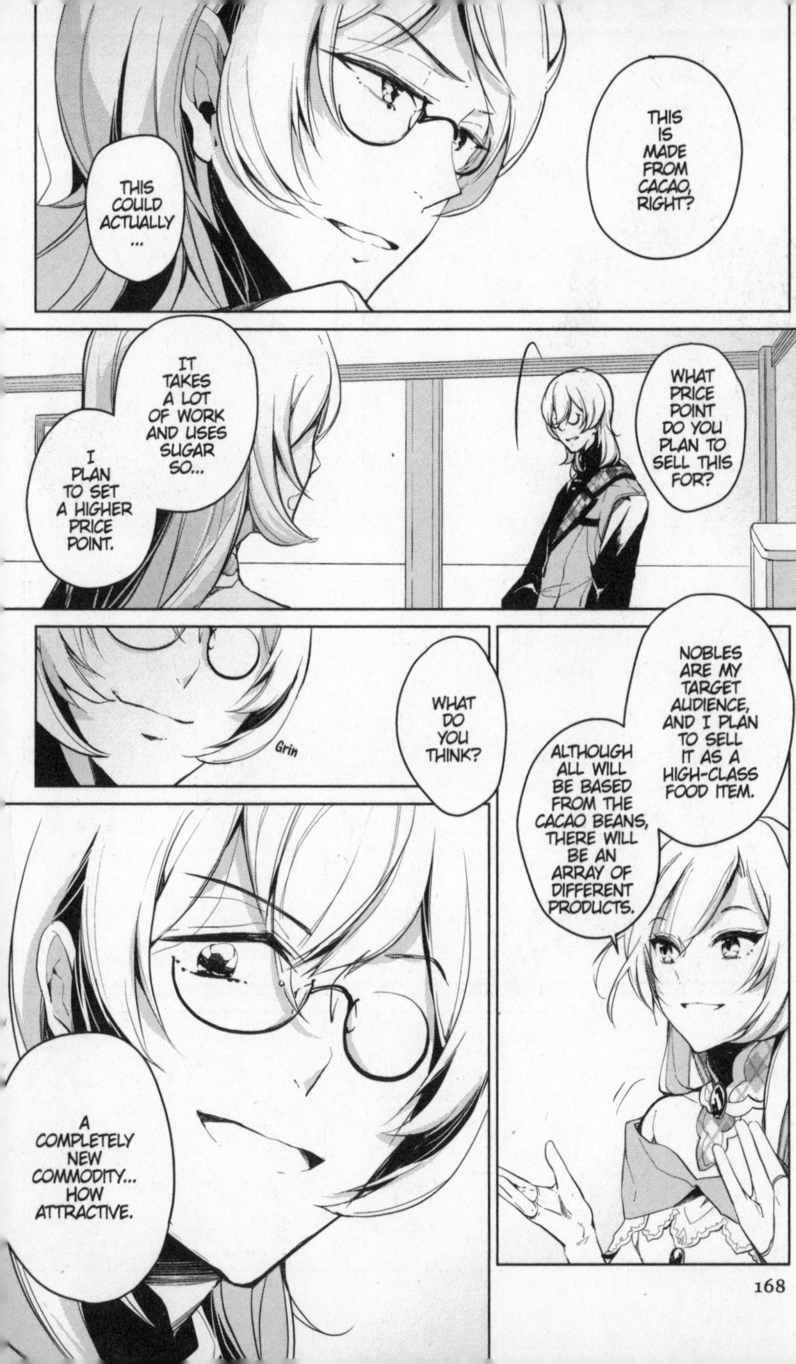
THIS IS MADE FROM CACAO, RIGHT?
THIS COULD ACTUALLY ...
WHAT PRICE POINT DO YOU PLAN TO SELL THIS FOR?
IT TAKES A LOT OF WORK AND USES SUGAR SO...
I PLAN TO SET A HIGHER PRICE POINT.
NOBLES ARE MY TARGET AUDIENCE, AND I PLAN TO SELL IT AS A HIGH-CLASS FOOD ITEM.
ALTHOUGH ALL WILL BE BASED FROM THE CACAO BEANS, THERE WILL BE AN ARRAY OF DIFFERENT PRODUCTS.
WHAT DO YOU THINK?
Grin
A COMPLETELY NEW COMMODITY... HOW ATTRACTIVE.

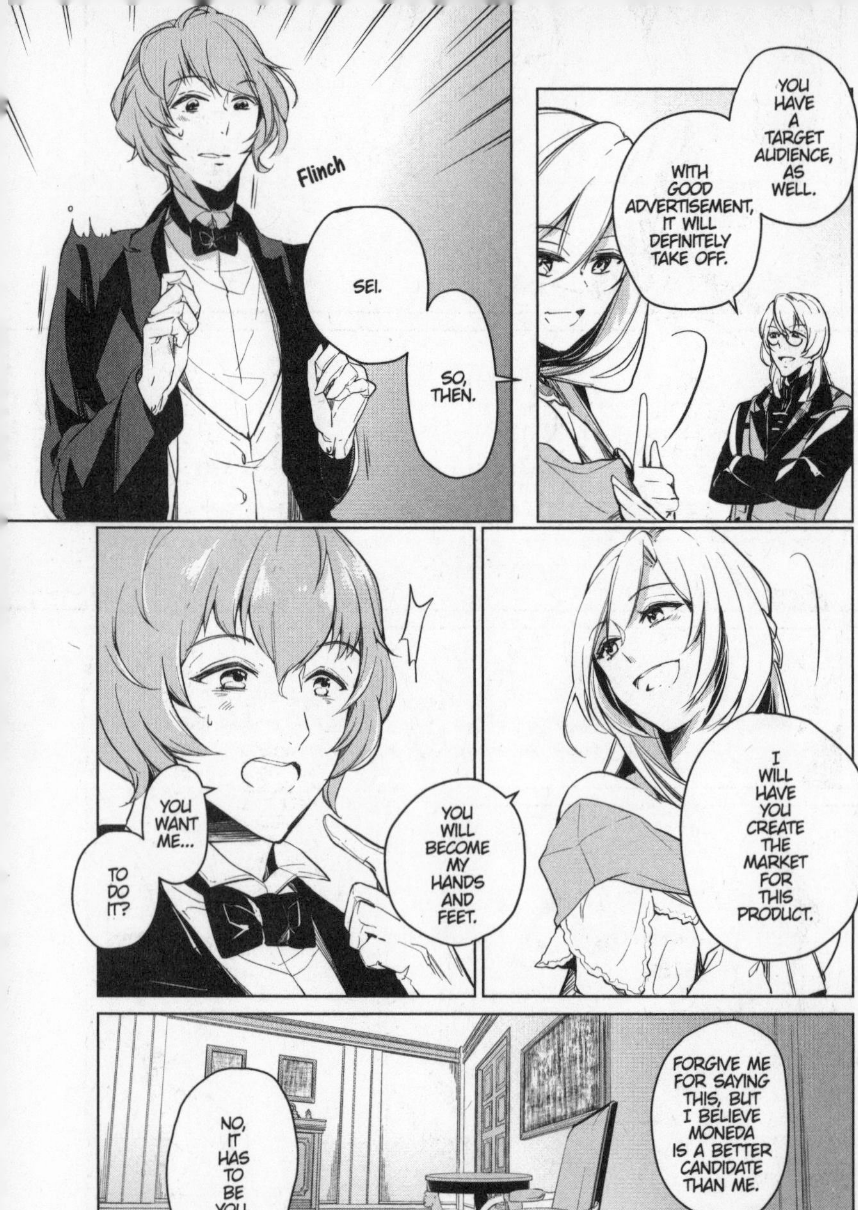
YOU HAVE A TARGET AUDIENCE, AS WELL.
WITH GOOD ADVERTISEMENT, IT WILL DEFINITELY TAKE OFF.
Flinch
SEI.
SO, THEN.
I WILL HAVE YOU CREATE THE MARKET FOR THIS PRODUCT.
YOU WILL BECOME MY HANDS AND FEET.
YOU WANT ME...
TO DO IT?
FORGIVE ME FOR SAYING THIS, BUT I BELIEVE MONEDA IS A BETTER CANDIDATE THAN ME.
NO, IT HAS TO BE YOU.

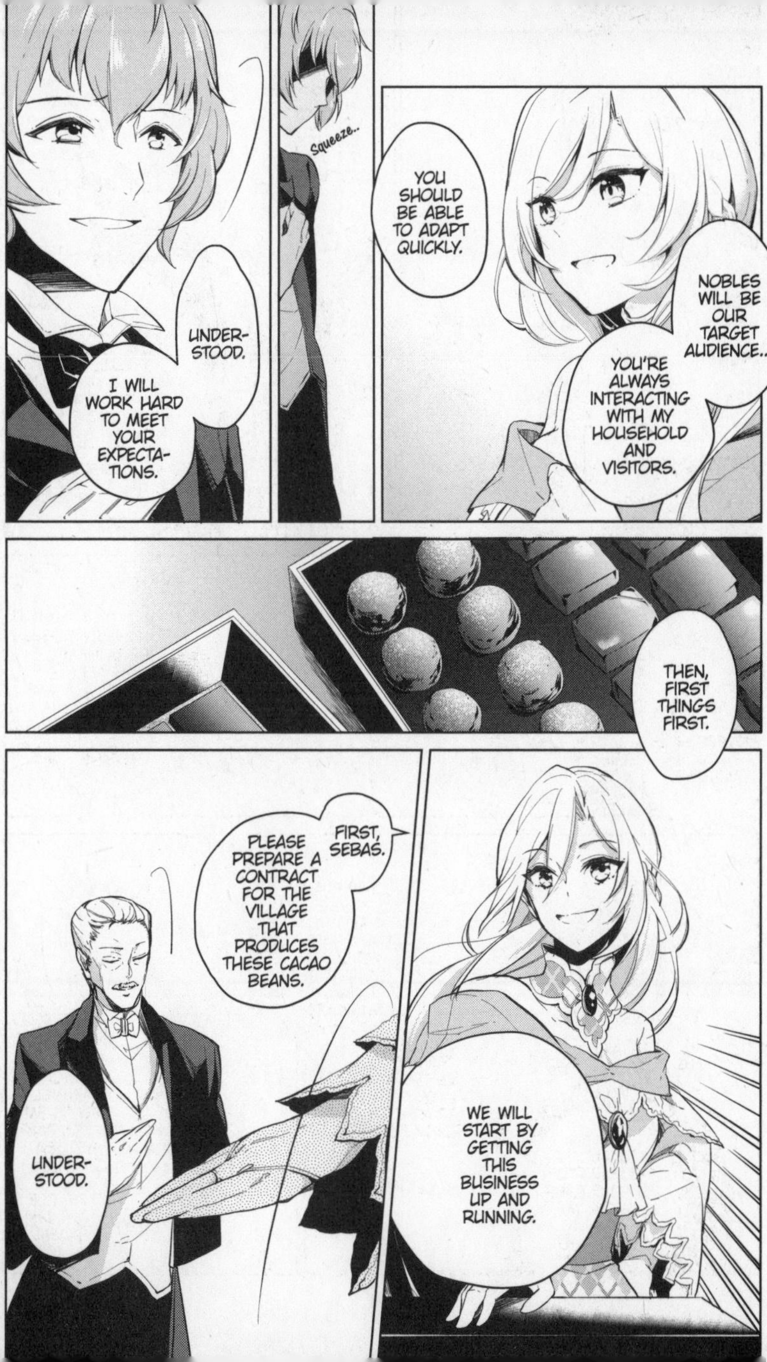
NOBLES WILL BE OUR TARGET AUDIENCE...
YOU'RE ALWAYS INTERACTING WITH MY HOUSEHOLD AND VISITORS.
YOU SHOULD BE ABLE TO ADAPT QUICKLY.
Squeeze...
UNDER-STOOD.
I WILL WORK HARD TO MEET YOUR EXPECTA-TIONS.
THEN, FIRST THINGS FIRST.
WE WILL START BY GETTING THIS BUSINESS UP AND RUNNING.
FIRST, SEBAS.
PLEASE PREPARE A CONTRACT FOR THE VILLAGE THAT PRODUCES THESE CACAO BEANS.
UNDER-STOOD.

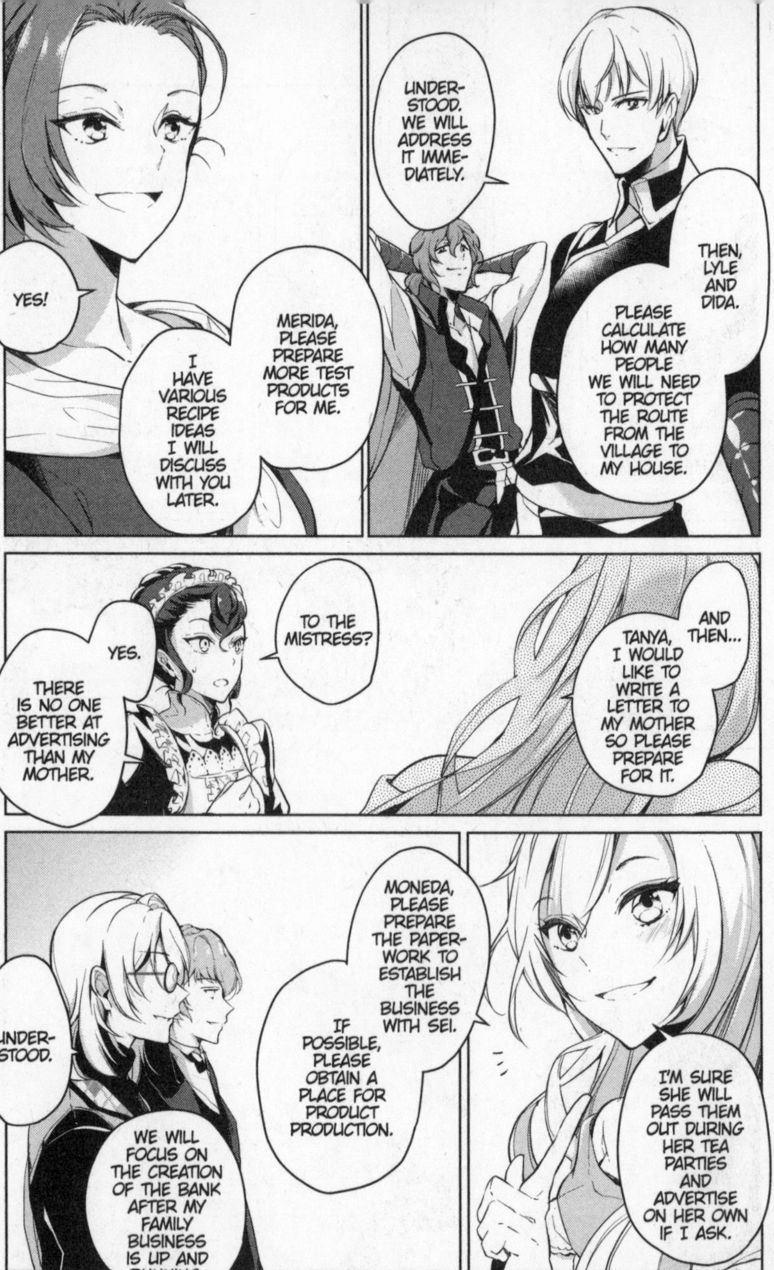
THEN, LYLE AND DIDA.
PLEASE CALCULATE HOW MANY PEOPLE WE WILL NEED TO PROTECT THE ROUTE FROM THE VILLAGE TO MY HOUSE.
UNDERSTOOD. WE WILL ADDRESS IT IMMEDIATELY.
MERIDA, PLEASE PREPARE MORE TEST PRODUCTS FOR ME.
I HAVE VARIOUS RECIPE IDEAS I WILL DISCUSS WITH YOU LATER.
YES!
AND THEN...
TANYA, I WOULD LIKE TO WRITE A LETTER TO MY MOTHER SO PLEASE PREPARE FOR IT.
TO THE MISTRESS?
YES.
THERE IS NO ONE BETTER AT ADVERTISING THAN MY MOTHER.
I'M SURE SHE WILL PASS THEM OUT DURING HER TEA PARTIES AND ADVERTISE ON HER OWN IF I ASK.
MONEDA, PLEASE PREPARE THE PAPERWORK TO ESTABLISH THE BUSINESS WITH SEI.
IF POSSIBLE, PLEASE OBTAIN A PLACE FOR PRODUCT PRODUCTION.
UNDERSTOOD.
WE WILL FOCUS ON THE CREATION OF THE BANK AFTER MY FAMILY BUSINESS IS UP AND RUNNING.

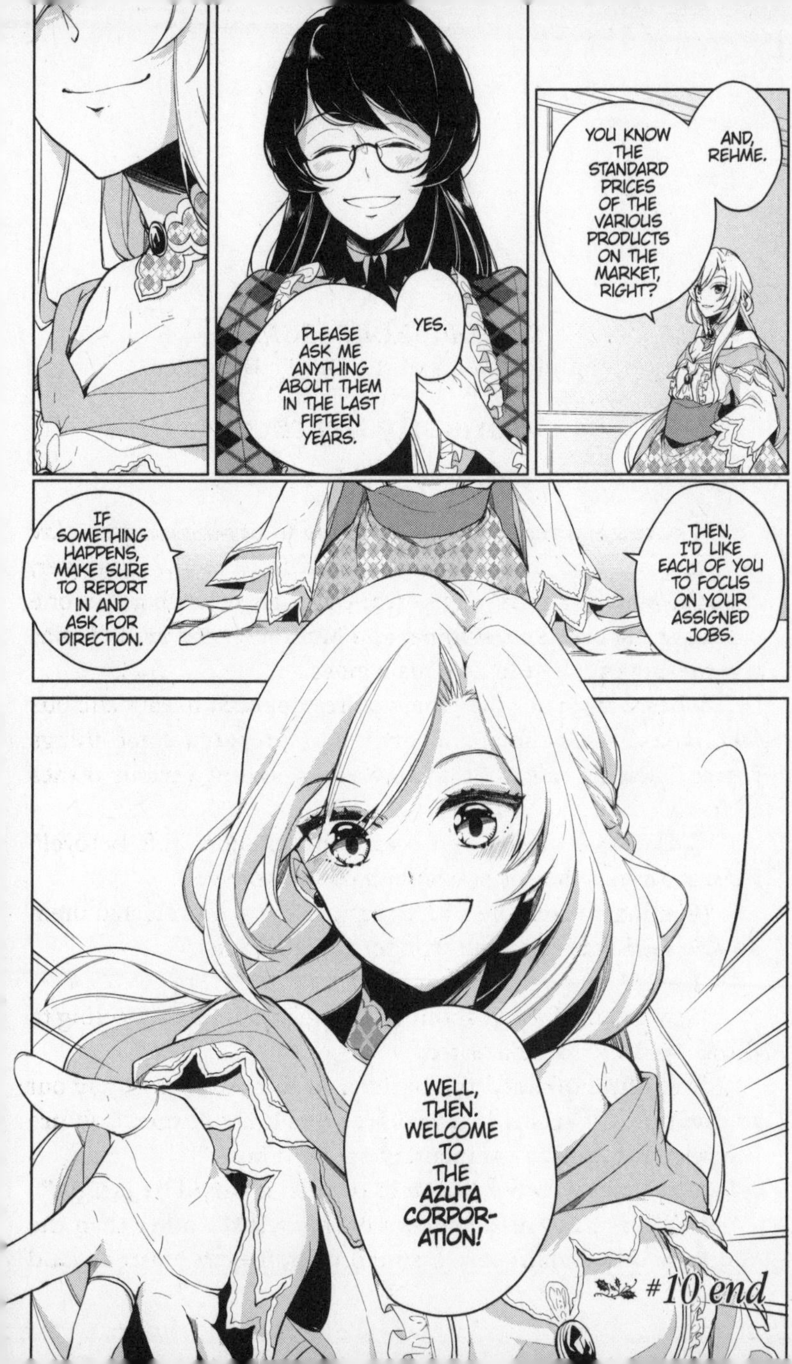
AND, REHME.
YOU KNOW THE STANDARD PRICES OF THE VARIOUS PRODUCTS ON THE MARKET, RIGHT?
YES.
PLEASE ASK ME ANYTHING ABOUT THEM IN THE LAST FIFTEEN YEARS.
THEN, I'D LIKE EACH OF YOU TO FOCUS ON YOUR ASSIGNED JOBS.
IF SOMETHING HAPPENS, MAKE SURE TO REPORT IN AND ASK FOR DIRECTION.
WELL, THEN. WELCOME TO THE AZUTA CORPOR-ATION!
#10 end

SPECIAL SHORT STORY
Accomplishments of the Duke's Daughter

Womanly Secrets

By Reia

"I have been requested by our lady to organize a girls' day out, and so, I have gathered you both here today. I wonder, though, what *is* a girls' day out?" Tanya tilted her head to one side as she spoke. She, Rehme, and Merida sat at a table. It was a gathering of Iris's closet female aides.

"I heard from our lady that you're supposed to eat delicious food and drink delicious alcohol, so I prepared some things for us," Merida said. The table was covered in various dishes of food.

"Wow! I've never even seen some of this stuff before!" Rehme's eyes shone as she looked the dishes over.

"Our lady taught me a lot of recipes for today. I tasted them all and I think they are all wonderfully delicious."

"I see..."

"So what do we talk about while we eat? Is this a meeting to discuss work?" Merida asked.

"No. She explained the basic procedure of a girls' day out to me, but... it seems it is a place to talk about men you are interested in, and to complain about your boss."

"Oh, that's why our lady told me that it would be just us."

"Well, I'm not dissatisfied with my work... other than the rudeness of a certain careless man who likes to hover around

my lady," said Tanya. Though she did not mention who that was, Rehme and Merida immediately thought of Dida and gave wry smiles.

"I have no issues either. Until a little while ago, as a woman in the kitchen... well, there was a lot of criticism, but they've accepted me now," said Merida.

"Come to think of it, Miss Merida, why did you want to become a chef? I mean, the kitchen is a man's world, after all." Tanya took a bite of food as she spoke.

"Well, our lady picked me up when I was lying on the side of the road, dying of hunger. At this house, I got to eat things I had never eaten before. To put it simply, I was moved. I wanted to make something like this myself."

Tanya smiled. "I see. So you're the same as me."

"The same?"

"Yes. Our lady read a book to me once. She told me that the world was big, and books brought that great world closer to us. I wanted to know more about the world. I wanted to know more about it and be of use to our lady."

"I see. So, everyone does the things they do because of our lady." Merida laughed heartily. The other two women joined in.

"If you think about it, the fact that we can feel nostalgic about the past is pretty amazing," Merida said. Tanya and Rehme both smiled at her words. All the people here, or at least all of Iris's closest aides, carried scars of some kind. Scars from earlier in their lives, often from things better off forgotten. Still, they could reminisce and feel nostalgic because even those pasts had led them to Iris.

"I can only say words of thanks about our lady." The other two nodded seriously at Tanya's words. Silence fell.

"So much for the girls' day out." Merida smiled apologetically. "But there really isn't anything to complain about work-wise."

Rehme sighed. "Actually, I wish we could have Lady Iris

join us." The other two nodded in agreement to Rehme's great idea. "But, I wonder if that would be too rude of us."

"Our lady would not be angry with us for such a thing," said Tanya.

"Then we'll leave it to you to go ask her!" Rehme said.

"No, Merida would be better at it than me," Tanya replied.

Merida pondered how she could convince their lady to join them.

2. In the Study of Lady Iris.

"Taste-testing of new products?" I said. Merida was standing in front of my desk with a big smile.

"Yes. I tried making a lot of new things. I would love it if my lady would try them and give me an opinion."

"*Hmm...*" I would love to go, but I had so much work to do.

"Mr. Sebas and Tanya have already adjusted your schedule, my lady."

Her level of preparation made me smile. If she had done that much, I would have to go.

"Then I will join you as soon as I finish this document."

"Fantastic! We shall meet in the garden. I'll inform Tanya and she will escort you."

"I understand."

And so, I finished my work and Tanya guided me to the garden. There sat Merida and Rehme.

"This is..." I couldn't believe what I was seeing. The table was laid out with amazing-looking foods.

"We tried having a girls' day out, but everyone said they'd rather have our lady here. Since you're so busy, I took this chance to get some taste-testing done as well." Merida was beaming.

"H-huh? I'm happy to be invited, but won't that make it hard to talk about certain things?"

"Nothing we have to say needs to be hidden from our lady." The other two nodded emphatically at Tanya's words.

"Is it really all right?" I hoped it was, though I didn't want to appear too eager.

"Yes, my lady. We would love to talk to you as well."

"I understand. I would love to join you all."

And so, the four of us clinked our glasses together and began a girls' day out.

"Come to think of it, how is that rude man?" Merida asked.

"How...?" Tanya blushed.

"I saw the two of you out drinking the other day after work."

"What! Really?!" I couldn't help leaning forward after hearing Merida's testimony. Rehme also looked quite curious.

"Our training master gave us some alcohol, so we decided to share it. That's all," Tanya stammered.

"Well, when a man and a woman drink together, romance often follows," said Merida with a smile.

"S-so adult..." Rehme's face flushed while listening to Merida.

"To begin with, I do not really understand love and romance. Oh, but I worship my lady, so *that* kind of love I do understand." Everyone laughed at Tanya's very Tanya-like response.

"That makes me happy." I said. "But Tanya, I want you to find your own happiness, too."

"I see... What about you, Merida? How are things with you? I see you going out with Sei quite often lately."

Even Merida was surprised by how much Tanya knew. "H-how do you know about that?"

"My information network is large."

"You don't need to use it for something like that!" Merida blushed as she spoke. However, she looked more embarrassed than angry. "W-we're doing inspections for the Azuta Corporation... We travel together to test sweets." The way she

fidgeted as she spoke was adorable. "E-enough about me... Rehme! What about you, Rehme?" She desperately changed the subject and turned to Rehme, who was bright red.

"W-well... Um..." Everyone looked at her at this unexpected response.

"Don't tell me...you have someone, too?!"

"Um...W-well..."

"Oh! Sorry! We went too far."

"N-no... Um, there is someone I like..." As she stammered out her words, my heart raced.

"U-um... He works so hard and is always so serious. I think he's wonderful..."

"O-oooh!" All the girls' eyes shone as she uttered these lines straight out of a romance novel. "You're so cute, Rehme!"

The women were speaking all at once, so excitedly that no one noticed Dida, Lyle, and Sei off to one side, behind a tree.

"Oh, is this that girls' day out thing? So that's what's going on." Dida gave a wry grin as he spoke.

"I-It's not good to eavesdrop. If they find out we're here..." Sei said, flustered.

"We will surely receive some kind of punishment if we are caught," Lyle said with a serious expression.

"Come on! It's a garden of women! Don't you want to know what they normally talk about?!" All the men, save Moneda, had gathered as well. They stayed and listened.

A few days later, Tanya discovered that they had eavesdropped, and as Lyle had surmised, the men all received proper punishment. They found out it's very hard to eavesdrop when the sound of sweeping fills the air!

~END~

SEVEN SEAS ENTERTAINMENT PRESENTS

Accomplishments of the Duke's Daughter

VOLUME 1

story by REIA

character design by [...]

W9-AND-720

TRANSLATION
Angela Liu

ADAPTATION
Tracy Barnett

LETTERING AND RETOUCH
Alexandra Gunawan

COVER DESIGN
KC Fabellon

PROOFREADER
B. Lana Guggenheim
Janet Houck

EDITOR
Shannon Fay

PRODUCTION ASSISTANT
CK Russell

PRODUCTION MANAGER
Lissa Pattillo

EDITOR-IN-CHIEF
Adam Arnold

PUBLISHER
Jason DeAngelis

KOUSHAKU REIJOU NO TASHINAMI VOL. 1
© Reia, Haduki Futaba 2016
© Suki UMEMIYA 2016
First published in Japan in 2016 by KADOKAWA CORPORATION, Tokyo.
English translation rights arranged with KADOKAWA CORPORATION, Tokyo,
through TOHAN CORPORATION, Tokyo.

Seven Seas books may be purchased in bulk for promotional, educational, or
business use. Please contact your local bookseller or the Macmillan Corporate
and Premium Sales Department at 1-800-221-7945, extension 5442, or by
e-mail at MacmillanSpecialMarkets@macmillan.com.

Seven Seas and the Seven Seas logo are trademarks of
Seven Seas Entertainment, LLC. All rights reserved.

ISBN: 978-1-626928-66-4

Printed in Canada

First Printing: August 2018

10 9 8 7 6 5 4 3 2 1

FOLLOW US ONLINE: *www.sevenseasentertainment.com*

READING DIRECTIONS

This book reads from *right to left*, Japanese style.
If this is your first time reading manga, you start
reading from the top right panel on each page and
take it from there. If you get lost, just follow the
numbered diagram here. It may seem backwards at
first, but you'll get the hang of it! Have fun!!

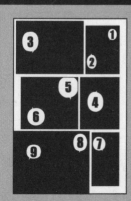